T0313550

THE
hip-hop
MBA

Also by Nels Abbey

Think Like a White Man

THE
hip-hop
MBA

Lessons in Cut-Throat
Capitalism from
Rap's Moguls

NELS ABBEY

CANONGATE

First published in Great Britain in 2024
by Canongate Books Ltd, 14 High Street, Edinburgh EH1 1TE

canongate.co.uk

1

British Library Cataloguing-in-Publication Data
A catalogue record for this book is available on
request from the British Library

ISBN 978 1 83885 640 3

Typeset in Garamond 3 LT Std by
Palimpsest Book Production Ltd, Falkirk, Stirlingshire

Printed and bound by CPI Group (UK) Ltd, Croydon CR0 4YY

For the struggle. For the culture.
For the sheer ingenuity of the wretched of the earth.

CONTENTS

SECTION 4: STAYING UP

SECTION 5: SPREADING OUT

'In all of the programmes that I attended, all of the education that I had – college, public and otherwise – nobody ever told me that America is business and without business you will have nothing and be nothing. And nobody ever told me how to organise business so that I would be able to develop institutions in my own community.'

Sister Souljah on *Donahue* in 1992

'If I was born black, I would not have had the opportunities I have had.'

The never knowingly underquoted Warren Buffett

Introduction

THE RISE OF THE NOBODIES

I've been blessed and highly favoured (i.e. privileged) enough to study economics and business at university and then work in some of the world's most successful corporations – both in finance and media. Throughout my journey as a professional, I kept count of the number of times someone who looked, sounded or struggled like me – Black and from a working-class background – was cited as an example of business genius, financial wisdom or groundbreaking thinking: zero. It never happened. Not once. Far too often, people who shared my phenotype and socio-economic standing were viewed dismissively rather than with admiration.

The people who were upheld as being exemplarily brilliant business minds looked and sounded like the people with the power to do the upholding. The ways these minds thought about and approached business became 'the norm', and those who offered alternative ways of thinking came from the exact same background as those who'd established 'the norm'. To highlight a name outside the designated usual suspects was to risk your own credibility. Understandably, perhaps the most cited person was the billionaire investor, Warren Buffett.

Buffett is never knowingly underquoted for very good reason. He is unimaginably successful, unbelievably wealthy and he is admired by those with authority, those who determine who is to

1

be adored and who is to be ignored. As a result, his name is almost as synonymous with capitalism as Christ's is with Christianity. His words are the gospel of commerce.

Nevertheless, a key constant in capitalism is that the crowd will eventually be proved wrong (a large drop in the price of assets is called a 'correction' for good reason). So, what if the crowd is wrong on Buffett, Branson, Gates, Musk and their ilk? What if they are not the brightest lights in a dark room? Or what if they are too blindingly bright (i.e. uniquely successful) to look at and attain any form of learnable and applicable information? Or what if they are not the self-made business icons they are portrayed as? Are they role models or outliers?

If a person really wishes to attain an understanding of how to 'win' in modern capitalism and modern business, are Buffett et al really the best case studies?

Crazy as it may sound, I found a more thorough and ingenious understanding of winning in the world of modern capitalism by listening to and studying people a little more entertaining, enlightening, edgy and self-made. Someone like, say . . . Shawn Corey Carter, popularly known to the world as 'Jay-Z'.

THE STOCK PICKER VS THE BEAT PICKER

Although they operate in entirely different areas, the stock picker (i.e. the professional investor) and the beat picker (i.e. the rapper) fundamentally do the same thing. They are both trying to work their way through noise and distractions to pick a lucrative hit (a stock or a song) which they can accrue long-term value from. The mind of the successful stock picker gravitates towards companies they believe will serve a long-term lucrative purpose (i.e. that will yield a return). The mind of the successful beat picker gravitates towards music and ventures they believe offer the same long-term benefit.

Both Warren Buffet and Jay-Z are captains of industry; both

are gravity-defying successes; both are businessmen of wit and wisdom. But whereas professional investors are seen as being at the pinnacle of the professional elite, rappers are often not viewed as professionals at all. Yet when we remove all biases, who do we actually stand to learn more from about business?

Let's see how they stack up against each other:

	Warren Buffett (b. 1930) Stock Picker	Shawn 'Jay-Z' Carter (b. 1969) Beat Picker
Parent's profession (main breadwinner)	Father: businessman, investor, and elected politician	Mother: office clerk
Tertiary education	Attended the University of Pennsylvania, the University of Nebraska, Columbia and the New York Institute of Finance	'I got my MBA from Marcy Projects.'[1]
Criminal record?	No	Yes
Inherited wealth?	Yes	No
Early ventures	Sold chewing gum, Coca-Cola bottles, and weekly magazines door to door	Sold crack cocaine
Early setbacks	Rejected by Harvard despite being unbelievably talented	Rejected by every major record label despite being unbelievably talented Lost 92 bricks of cocaine
Impact of early setbacks	Had to settle for attending Columbia (instead of Harvard) and got to learn from investment guru Benjamin Graham	Started his own independent record label Somehow survived losing 92 bricks of cocaine

	Warren Buffett (b. 1930) Stock Picker	Shawn 'Jay-Z' Carter (b. 1969) Beat Picker
Family lineage in core business?	Yes	No
Estimated net worth	$100bn	$1.4bn

Table 1: The Stock Picker vs The Beat Picker

Success in business and risk-taking are like alcohol and intoxication (or money and hangers-on): where there is one the other is often not far away. And in the same way that jumping out of a window is easier when you know you have a safety net and a parachute to soften your landing and a paramedic waiting, if need be, to save your life, it is easier to take a risk when you come from the sort of background Buffett does.

Buffett is exactly the sort of person who wins in the world of business. He is highly educated in the conventional sense of the term, very well connected, comes from generations of money as well as professional expertise, and, in investment management, he went into an established 600-year-old industry – one in which people like him have always been embraced to the point that they are synonymous with 'normal'. Plus, he was lucky. It was arguably more difficult for him to fail in life than to succeed. Buffett himself admits that by his early twenties he knew he was going to be very wealthy. Critically, in his own words: 'If I was born black, I would not have had the opportunities I have had.'[2]

Jay-Z is the exact sort of person who loses in society. And loses badly. Even worse, in the realm of cut-throat capitalism, Jay-Z is the sort of person who normally finds his throat being cut. Black, little formal education, from an economically challenged single-parent household with no real connections to the professional domain. With such a dearth of opportunity, it should come as no surprise that he too took risks, only his were more extreme and came without a safety net. Selling crack cocaine, for example, came with all the danger of the street drug trade as well as prison terms 100 times more severe than those for selling powdered cocaine.[3] By 1991, the odds were massively in favour of Jay-Z being dead, destitute or indefinitely detained by the end of the decade. Yet by 1999 he was a self-made, meritocratic and legitimate multi-millionaire. Today he is a billionaire, one who has helped make many others rich along the way.

Jay-Z's success is not due to accident, inheritance, proceeds of crime or a chance lottery-ticket purchase. It is the sweet fruit of consistent, bitter hard work, risk-taking and hardnosed business savvy. And, yes, a little bit of luck too.

Of course, the argument that the $100bn man has more to teach us than the $1.4bn man is an understandably seductive one. But seduction often entails a healthy dosage of deception, and when the fog of deceptive statistics is cleared, an indisputable fact emerges: Jay-Z went from rags to riches, Buffett went from riches to more riches. On this basis alone, Jay-Z can teach the world much more than Warren Buffett can about truly 'making it' in the world of business. For he, unlike Buffett, has the lived experience of making something out of absolutely nothing.

CAPITALISM'S FOUNDING VICTIMS

The backstory of Jay-Z (and others like him) growing up as a nobody on the high road to fantastic failure, and his vehicle for escaping that story – Hip-Hop itself – are related by-products of the social and economic order that emerged from events that started centuries earlier. Indeed, they emerged from what can be described as capitalism's big bang.

In the middle of the sixteenth century, European empires began the inhumanely brutal yet highly lucrative process of kidnapping Africans and transporting them around the world, mainly to the Americas, to be mercilessly exploited and, in some cases, bred, for profit – on an intergenerational basis. Over the centuries of its existence, the 'transatlantic slave trade' became the settled name of the most rewarding and vast organised criminal enterprise humanity has ever known.

In pursuit of profit for Europeans, these stolen Africans were robbed of absolutely everything a human can possess – name, rights, religion, culture, identity, dignity, consent, their bodies, their reproductive capacity, their children (and their children's children), their families, their inventions, their history, their stories, the ability or freedom to learn how to read or write – absolutely everything. The Africans were regarded and treated only marginally better than animals – in many cases, worse. In the truest, most authoritative use of the term, they were reduced to absolute nobodies.

Unique in human history in their scale and scope, these acts would change the world for ever and shape the world as we know it today. Critically, the slave trade helped create an economic system that made participating European states and empires eye-wateringly rich and Africans (wherever they were) dirt poor, destitute, disregarded and depopulated.

The intergenerational blood, sweat and tears of the African became the intergenerational profit, power and privilege of the European.

This robber and robbed, slaver and enslaved 'exchange' became the basis of what we today know as international free-market capitalism, otherwise known as 'the economic order'. At the top of this 'order' were white Europeans (i.e. the somebodies) and nations dominated by those descended from them. At the bottom were the Africans (i.e. the nobodies).

In addition to their humanity and creative ingenuity, one of the few things that the somebodies could not snatch away from the nobodies was their souls. Their souls became a critical base on which the nobodies were able to survive, build and eventually thrive. They gave them a voice, strength, a sense of perseverance, determination and defiance, a method of transferring information, and globally admired soft power. Critically, they offered the nobodies something on which they could build empires of their own.

Fastforward five centuries, and in possibly one of the most beautiful of ugly ironies, some of the (still uncompensated and unhealed) descendants of the original and foremost victims of international free market capitalism – enslaved Africans, the nobodies – have somehow become its most influential, important and famous crusaders, marketers and, in a few situations, beneficiaries. And they have 'risen' to this feat through a profound and powerful cultural, social, political and economic miracle rooted in the souls of the nobodies: it is known to the world as Hip-Hop.

Hip-Hop (often loosely synonymised with rap music and other similar genres in this book) was born of the creative and innovative genius rooted in the sound and culture of the intergenerational pain of the poorest of the poor, the nobodies. Black people – African Americans and other descendants of enslaved Africans – who could only dream of affording musical instruments, let alone regular music lessons or studio sessions, and so found other ways to make and share their music.

Perhaps it should come as no shock that Hip-Hop emerged as a cohesive and aggressively innovative artform and lifestyle in the most impoverished of the New York boroughs, the Bronx, during the 1973–75 recession.

The music itself was dismissed by some as 'not music', but noise, negro-clatter, the howling of the hoodlums, the diatribe of the drive-by. Many who could see, hear or feel the appeal still dismissed it as a fad that would quickly fizzle away. The unconventional, brilliant and at times controversial business ideas, practices and philosophies permeating from and underpinning Hip-Hop were taken even less seriously than the art.

The doubters now have over half a century of egg on their faces. Hip-Hop is the most popular, commercially lucrative and most politically and socially powerful artform in the world.[4] Both the art and the business that facilitates it are a concoction of innovation, risk-taking (within and outside the confines of the law), creative genius and commercial excellence. As a result, its sphere of influence is still growing daily.

Hip-Hop has gone a lot further than rock 'n' roll, pop or any other music genre you can name. It is now America's foremost cultural export and a fundamental part of American soft power and commercial prowess.[5]

It was not always like this. It was not always influential, powerful or lucrative. And its rise didn't happen by accident or through osmosis. It took risk-takers and entrepreneurs to make Hip-Hop what it is today. Like Jay-Z, many of these risk-takers and entrepreneurs were themselves designated to be society's nobodies, and thus were often taking risks that were likely to end in legal or financial disaster.

Some of these 'nobodies' have now used Hip-Hop – the sound, culture, business and even politics – to become comfortable middle-class professionals, millionaires and even billionaires. Many of them were school dropouts, people with criminal records, products of 'broken homes', poorly funded education systems and despair. This is a truly monumental achievement and, as you might expect, the stories and details of how they did it make for an often thrilling, and sometimes chilling, ride.

The descendants of Africans enslaved in America turned the sound, pain and culture permeating from economic destitution into economic empowerment and aspiration. Along the way, they have developed, refined and remixed various ways of doing and seeing business, of navigating the business environment and all the challenges that come with it. As a result, they, Hip-Hop's businesspeople, have something to say, something to show and something to teach us about the business world.

The Hip-Hop MBA will take you into this unconventional and sometimes crazy world of Hip-Hop entrepreneurship, shedding light on the business practices and personalities within it, and charting its ascendancy from a once underground and often beleaguered hustle into an empire that is shaping and influencing both America's and the world's commercial, social, cultural and political landscapes.

In addition to profound business case studies and what we can learn from them, *The Hip-Hop MBA* will also tell you many inspirational and sometimes cautionary tales of have-nots and nobodies who have used Hip-Hop to maximum advantage, to truly make something out of absolutely nothing, and ultimately become somebodies and have-it-alls. Even though much of the business world seldom bothers to understand them properly, these alternative moguls have so much to teach us: for, in real time, they are reshaping the business world in their own image.

HIP-HOP: A MODERN VALUE DRIVER

Value drivers are 'factors that increase the worth of a product, service, asset or business'.[6] For example, value drivers are the things that can help you turn a two-cent container of sugar-rammed fizzy water with a drop of lemon and lime concentrate into a '*$2 can of Sprite – OBEY YOUR THIRST!*'

Hip-Hop has become a value driver for many business areas and products, not least because of its immense popularity amongst the young. It is a well-known truism that there are fortunes to be made out of young people – they are more excitable, more trigger-happy with spending and, in many cases, likely to be spending their parents' money (rarely is anyone truly a fiscal conservative when they're spending someone else's money). And a lot of the products and services that appeal to young people gain or lose favour in their eyes based on how they are viewed, promoted and demoted in Hip-Hop. But to understand how Hip-Hop drives demand in products and services, we first need to look at elasticity of demand.

HIP-HOP ELASTICITY OF DEMAND

Elasticity of demand is an economic concept which seeks to calculate the responsiveness in demand to changes in an economic factor.

In other words: elasticity of demand observes how much you, the happy-clappy consumer, keeps on buying shit when shit changes either for you (whether you're now broke or rich) or the item you consume or use (such as if its price goes up or down). When the demand for a product is responsive to a change in an economic factor it is said to be 'elastic'. When it is not responsive it is 'inelastic'.

Traditional academia (which I also like to call 'white people said so' academia) argues that there are four main types of elasticity of demand:

- **Price elasticity of demand (PED)** – how much more or less of a product you consume when the price changes. Example: *If the price of a Birkin bag falls, does it make you more or less likely to purchase it?*
- **Income elasticity of demand (IED)*** – how much more or less of a product you consume when your fortunes change. Example: *If your salary increases and your rent falls, does that make you more or less likely to purchase a Birkin bag?*
- **Cross elasticity of demand (XED)** – how much more or less of a product you consume when an alternative to that product becomes available. Example: *How likely are you to buy a Birkin bag if Louis Vuitton releases a new bag?*
- **Advertising elasticity of demand (AED)** – how much more or less of a product you consume when it is advertised more or less. Example: *If there is an advertising blitz for Birkin bags, how much more likely are you to buy one?*

---

* Not to be mistaken for an Improvised Explosive Device.

Owing to its clear economic influence, enduring popularity and, therefore, power, Hip-Hop has created a new kind of elasticity of demand:

- **Hip-Hop elasticity of demand (HHED)** – the responsiveness of a product, service or campaign to being mentioned, championed, embraced or disregarded within Hip-Hop, most notably within rap songs and videos. Example: *How much more likely are you to buy a Birkin bag if Drake mentions it in a record, or Megan Thee Stallion is pictured carrying one onto her private jet?*

In the current age, for many products, goods, services and campaigns, Hip-Hop elasticity of demand supersedes advertising elasticity of demand. Even conventional advertising itself often relies heavily on Hip-Hop to effectively get its message across.

Some examples of Hip-Hop Elasticity of Demand in action:

Hollywood

Hollywood is very aware that it has a high HHED. Ever pitched an idea to a Hollywood executive? If not, know this: senior Hollywood executives will fall in love with you and your (credible) idea if you have a popular rapper associated with your project. *'Do you know Fofty* [sic] *Cent or Snoop Dogg or Jay-Z? Can you get them to back this project?'*

It is no coincidence that a rapper's ceremonial executive producer role is often announced before the stars or directors of a film, TV show or play. Why? Because it significantly enhances its chances of becoming a hit, it increases exposure, excitement and ultimately demand – because it has a high Hip-Hop elasticity of demand. Modern examples of this include Will Smith and Drake saving TV shows *Cobra Kai* and *Top Boy*, respectively, from the cancellation trash can by executive producing them. Both are now international hits for Netflix. Russell Simmons' *Def Comedy Jam* was a pre-*Sopranos*, *The Wire* and *Sex & The City* hit for HBO, helping to boost the network's subscribers and credibility, and also helped a slew of Black comedians reach the mainstream. 50 Cent has done similar for the Starz network with projects such as *Power* and *BMF*.

Fast Food

Hip-Hop and fast food have a long and dubious history. In 1992, on the less-than-well-thought-through side, MC Hammer danced for fried chicken in a successful KFC ad campaign (the money shot was Hammer shuffling as a piece of chicken was thrown into his mouth). Uniquely, the tail end of the adverts contained an advert for MC Hammer's upcoming shows, reflecting a savvy or bargaining power on his part not seen in modern times. In 2012, Mary J. Blige, the Queen of Hip-Hop Soul, passionately sang about fried chicken in a Burger King advert – the widely mocked commercial was condemned by Mary J. Blige herself as racist and quietly pulled.

On the more positive side: following the success of Snoop Dogg and Martha Stewart's* cookery show, *Martha & Snoop's Potluck Dinner Party*, as well as Snoop's cookbook *From Crook to Cook*, the Anglo-Danish food delivery company Just Eat sensed a brand synergy opportunity. They paid Snoop Dogg $7m (£5.3m) for a 2020 advertising campaign. Alongside the global pandemic making eating out a non-starter, the positive association and brand awareness this generated helped push Just Eat's year-on-year revenue up by 44 per cent to £900m. Their orders went up by 32 per cent to 257 million, and their number of active users went up from 44 million to 54 million. The ad helped to establish Just Eat as a brand that will be in the minds of consumers for years to come.

---

* One of this unlikely duo has spent a solid amount of time in prison. And it is not the one you're thinking.

Fashion

The influence of Hip-Hop in fashion is often the difference between being a failing fashion brand and being worth billions. Tommy Hilfiger, Timberland (whom the rapper and producer Timbaland named himself after), Adidas, Nike, Moschino, Versace, Guess, Filth Mart, Chloe, Ralph Lauren, Gucci, Prada, Nautica, Christian Dior, DKNY – all owe much of their modern popularity and profitability to rappers. Luciano Pavarotti, by comparison, didn't help sell a single silk sock in his time on this planet.

Technology

In the old days, the intersection between media, electronics and the advancement in popularity of technology was spurred on by the pornography industry – the VHS is a perfect example of this. Despite being the first entrant, Sony's Betamax was ultimately driven out of the market by JVC's VHS. Sony's defeat is often attributed to the fact that they would not permit pornographic content to be released on Betamax, whereas JVC turned a blind eye.[7]

Now, if you want to break an app, get a rapper to use it – Instagram publicly credits Snoop Dogg with helping them take off by being the first celebrity on the platform.[8] If you want to sell hardware, slap a rapper's name on it or get a rapper to be the face of it – the first thirty seconds of 50 Cent's 'P.I.M.P.' video feature him exploring what was then a new device (complete with then unheard of white headphones) known as the iPod.

From memes to movements to digital currencies – Hip-Hop is the driving sound of social media (and often its seed investment too). In 2016, Microsoft even tapped up Lonnie 'Common' Lynn to front their campaign explaining the possibilities of artificial intelligence.

Tourism

Hip-Hop has helped transform tourism no-go areas into places visitors want to be photographed in. Compton, South Central LA, the Marcy Projects, Queensbridge Housing Projects, Dade County Miami, the Southside of Chicago and many other low-income hotbeds of deprivation where lots of rappers grew up have now become tourism hotspots. Companies such as LA Hood Tours have sprung up to feed this demand.

Whether or not the idea of a gold-toothed former drug dealer with a penchant for fast-paced poetry teaching the masses about business disgusts a business-school scholar, financial journalist, oligarch or industrialist is entirely immaterial, because in the real world this is already happening. Hip-Hop is rewriting the rules of business, and *The Hip-Hop MBA* takes you on a guided tour of just how and what we can all learn from it.

AIMS AND LEARNING OUTCOMES
OF THE HIP-HOP MBA

The aim of *The Hip-Hop MBA* is to provide a conceptual framework for business thinking which draws insights from Hip-Hop's ingenious, insanely unconventional and criminally underrated (and sometimes just criminal) world.

'Students' who successfully complete the Hip-Hop MBA will:

- Have an understanding of how Hip-Hop and its moguls navigated the political, economic, social, technological and legal hurdles they faced as individual businesses and as an industry
- Learn about the business of Hip-Hop and its role in shaping the modern business world
- Understand why Hip-Hop did not become the fad many predicted it would be
- Be equipped to apply creative thinking and innovative leadership to the creation and management of wealth, industry, services, assets and enterprise on a global basis. Or to at least recognise when you are crashing and burning
- Have a champion's mindset that makes you ready for the world as it really is
- Enhance your effectiveness as business leaders and go-getters
- Certainly not learn how to rap

The Hip-Hop MBA is broken down into five sections, mirroring the concept of the product life cycle, covering the universal themes faced by all professionals and businesspeople. In Section 1, titled Breaking In (not to be mistaken with 'breaking and entering'), we will cover market research, business development, raising capital and market entry. Section 2, Breaking Out (not to be mistaken for 'escaping from jail'), covers reputation and brand, risk and reward, negotiation, promotion, and vision and mission.

Section 3 is Moving Up, and is broken down into leadership, people management, diversity, innovation and competition. In Section 4, Staying Up, we'll look at evolution, undervalued assets and customers, and finance and legal affairs. Finally, Section 5 – Spreading Out (or falling off) – explores diversification.

By the time you end this 'course', you should have attained a thorough understanding of 'getting that gwop', 'securing the bag' and 'stunting on these hoes', meaning you will properly grasp the true nature of modern capitalism and how to win within it. Or at least lose memorably.

SECTION 1

BREAKING IN

Money, Cash, Cream

YOU
ARE
HERE

Broke as
a joke

Section 1
Breaking In

1.

MARKET RESEARCH

O nce upon a time, Sean 'Puff Daddy' Combs was just like you: a no-frills nobody with bad skin and a dream. Marion 'Suge' Knight, once upon a time a $50-a-day bodyguard, was also just like you (without the dermatology struggles): a nobody with a big dream of becoming somebody and something. It is a scenario everyone who dreams of success has had to face: how do you go about realising your dreams? How or where do you start? The answer is: you need to find a way to understand how everything around your dream works. You need to conduct some market research.

Market research has been defined as 'the process of evaluating the viability of a new service or product through research conducted directly with potential customers. Market research allows a company to define its target market and get opinions and other feedback from potential consumers about their interest in a product or service.'[1]

In short: market research is the equivalent of dipping your toe into the water to see if it is right for you, or even dipping the tip of your pinky finger into the white powder you've stumbled across to see if it's icing sugar, cocaine or anthrax. Market research provides you with an opportunity to properly comprehend the market, business or industry you wish to break into, in order to see how best you can penetrate it and how, or if, your product or service will prove popular.

If success can be thought of as a metaphoric (and deliciously calorific) cheesecake, then market research would be the base. It may not be the main thrill, but mess it up and you'll ruin the rest of the cake.

Everyone has to learn about the market they wish to enter. On an individual professional basis, a conventional approach is through an internship (i.e. legalised indentured servitude). For the average person, an internship is defined as 'the position of a student or trainee who works in an organization, sometimes without pay, in order to gain work experience or satisfy requirements for a qualification' (or perhaps being let out on probation).[2] For Hip-Hop's aspiring moguls, an internship was a way to research their intended market in order to find a route to break into the business – and then to dominate it. There is perhaps no greater intern success story than Sean 'Puff Daddy' Combs. You could say he remixed the internship.

The first 'law' of Robert Greene's *The 48 Laws of Power* – perhaps the most read book amongst Hip-Hop's moguls; 50 Cent even co-wrote a follow-up called *The 50th Law* – is that one must 'never outshine the master'. But laws, like jaws, are made to be broken. And if there is one person who spits champagne in the face of the *48 Laws of Power* (and, from time to time, a few other laws too), especially this first one, it is Puff Daddy.

His opportunity to research his market came in the early 1990s. After dropping out of Howard University, Puff Daddy was hired as an intern at the record label Uptown Records, home to future R'n'B stars such as Al B. Sure!, Christopher Williams, Guy, Heavy D & The Boyz, Father MC, Jodeci, Mary J. Blige and Soul for Real. Uptown was founded and run by Andre Harrell, who had found fame a decade earlier as one half of the shiny-business-suit-wearing rap group Dr. Jeckyll & Mr. Hyde, and was now a super-charming, slickly dressed, ultra-smooth music executive.

As an intern, Puff Daddy hit the ground running. Sprinting

even. He quickly developed a reputation for excellence in production, creation, image moulding, audience building, marketing, innovation, promotion . . . pretty much everything. The twenty-year-old intern was a bottomless pool of creativity and commercially lucrative ideas. He made the music sound bigger, louder, more cinematic, yet still authentic to the core audience. He transformed the remix of a song from a condiment to the main course, regularly overshadowing the original. He often made it an entirely different song to the original – not just a different beat. He crafted memorable images for artists – turning conventional good-looking people into global sex symbols. The albums and artists he worked on became some of the most successful on Uptown's roster, indeed of the era – perhaps most notably Mary J. Blige, whose sound and image Puff Daddy helped craft, leading to her being labelled the 'Queen of Hip-Hop Soul' and helping propel her to become a generational talent with an extensive and fruitful career to match.

It was clear Puff was going places, and he didn't hide it. He certainly didn't hide it from his boss, Harrell. Far from not outshining the master, Puff Daddy swiftly eclipsed him, and in a moment of bad decision-making that is up there with Blockbuster passing on buying Netflix, Harrell gave Puff Daddy his marching orders. 'Fired his Black ass' is the more Hip-Hop-friendly term. In a 2014 interview with the *Wall Street Journal*, Harrell revealed that he fired Puff in order to help him better understand how corporate mechanisms worked and to facilitate his growth as a businessman.[3] A claim supported by the fact that even after firing him, Harrell kept Puff on the payroll until he had found his feet.

Ever a man with a plan, Puff Daddy (then twenty-three years old) went on to found Bad Boy Records – a company which would enjoy era-defining success. Uptown Records crumbled and, years later, Harrell swallowed his pride and eventually went to work for the intern-turned-emperor he had famously fired.

A Puff Daddy-Inspired Career Management Lesson

For most, a major setback such as getting fired means go home, cry, drink something, smoke something, get your CV together and hawk yourself to the highest bidder. For Puff Daddy, it meant go home, draw up a business plan and eventually hire the person who fired you. Puff Daddy's career management methods also teach us that:

1. Career path frameworks – the designated steps you follow on an organisational chart to excel in your career – happen to be one of the bigger illusions in business.

2. Career paths are for suckers, fools and schmucks – otherwise known as 'good employees'. For potential high flyers, they're to be ignored.

3. The career path framework is essentially corporate opium for the masses, a mechanism for controlling and exerting effort, and for getting employees to be patient and keep on working. Once upon a time, 'The Man' would have struck you with a whip, now he tells you you're only six grades away on your SMART objectives from being elevated to the next level on the career path framework.

4. The career path framework should be viewed with similar suspicion to the free office breakfast you once thought was so amazing and now consider to be part of a dystopian masterplan to encourage you to spend more of your leisure time at work.

5. It's helpful to think of most careers as you would an enterprise, a business in which you are the CEO. With the right ideas and right moves, you can go from pawn to king in a few steps. And of course, with a few mistakes, right back down to pawn again.

Finding or stumbling on an opportunity to research the marketplace before penetrating it may lead you into rather unconventional and bizarre places. Cases in point:

- Cardi B found her opportunity while dancing on the pole in a strip club (as well as drugging and robbing men – i.e. her clients)[4] and then in reality TV
- Tupac was a dancer (without a pole) for Hip-Hop group Digital Underground
- Snoop Dogg sold weed at a party to his future mentor and partner in rhyme, Dr. Dre
- For Bryan Turner, founder and CEO of Priority Records, market research was going to a club in 1981 and noticing how people would get up and dance when rap records came on, but then sit down when the DJ played disco. It told him all he needed to know about the future of music.

Opportunities to research a market can present themselves in many guises – formal, informal, conventional or unconventional. A programme or a mere conversation, ad hoc or a mixture of all the above. The key thing is to recognise the opportunity to learn about how a business area works and then figure out how you can service it. For a unique method of market research, we turn to a bodyguard who became a mogul.

THE BODYGUARD WHO RESEARCHED THE MARKET

Size matters. And massively so. Thiam Tidjane, the seniormost Black banker in the history of the City of London, is living proof of this maxim.

As a young banker, Tidjane – the future CEO of Prudential and then Credit Suisse – was contacted by a headhunter trying to lure him to a new job. After carefully listening to his pitch, Tidjane calmly asked the recruiter to let the prospective employer know that he was:

'Black, African, Francophone and 6 foot 4.'[5]

It is fair to assume that speaking French didn't damage his prospects, but the rest of the attributes he highlighted – especially when combined – clearly could have done.

What Tidjane said to the headhunter is the opposite of 'ordinary' banker talk. Banking is a traditionally very conservative industry. One in which you do all you can to 'blend into the wallpaper', to appear to be 'normal', and be 'one of us'.

The fact that he was explicit about his size, ethnicity, nationality and colour illustrates Tidjane's awareness of himself, of how he appeared in comparison to his peers and of the fact that he stood out like a professional basketballer at a jockey convention. But rather than playing down these characteristics, he embraced them and used them to his advantage. Ballsy move.

He might not know it, but in this regard, if no other, Tidjane has something in common with one of Hip-Hop's most fascinating, controversial and (once upon a time) powerful figures: Marion 'Suge' Knight.

Knight is the once deeply feared founder and former CEO of the iconic label Death Row Records. A man whose name was once synonymous with success, record sales, super-assertiveness, and scandal.

There are of course differences between the two men. Where Tidjane is slender, Suge – also 6 foot four – weighed in at 150kg of (mostly) muscle in his heyday. Where Tidjane is the son of an Ivorian journalist and politician and descended from royalty, Suge is the definitive Compton baby and the descendant of enslaved Africans.

But both men were fully aware of the impact their size and ethnicity would have on their prospects – and they decided to embrace that impact: to own it, rather than be owned by it. They also both happened to be brilliant businessmen.

For Suge, the dream of becoming a powerful executive could not have been more intense. In the late 1980s heyday of rap group

NWA, Jerry Heller, a veteran executive of the rock 'n' roll era turned NWA's manager, walked into his office and found Suge (then still a bodyguard) staring at his executive chair. It was clear to Heller that right here, in a position similar to his own, was where Suge wanted to be. And within a quick couple of years, that is where he was. But how did he overcome the vicious cocktail of negativity associated with the compound of his ethnicity, class and size? A mix that means men like Suge struggle to break into the professional realm? Rarely does a recruiter look at a large Black man and think: *This guy would make a smooth salesman for our funds* or *He will fit in perfectly as our new dental assistant.*

Proving that one person's trash is another's treasure (or more aptly: one person's bust is another's buck), the very attributes that hold men like Suge back in the professional realm make them very appealing in two areas: sports and security.

Suge gravitated to the sport of choice for aggressive men with a high body mass index, American football, and got an athletic scholarship to attend the University of Las Vegas. Trouncing expectations, he excelled academically (he was on the dean's list)[6] but it was on the football field that he became a star, with dreams of becoming a professional National Football League (NFL) player.

But Suge was not drafted by the NFL, and his dream of becoming a professional footballer did not materialise . . . until the regular NFL players went on strike.

In early signs of his determined, ruthless and savvy nature, Suge leapt at the opportunity of crossing the picket line and became a replacement player (or 'scab') for the Los Angeles Rams. He played a grand total of two games before the regular players returned.* When they did, for Suge, the game was over. So was his football career.

His next move was to gravitate towards another career where his size, class and ethnicity would not be held against him:

---

* Not for long in name, not for long in nature.

bodyguarding. It was here that Suge Knight found a unique opportunity to research the market he was really going to excel in: the music business.

As a bodyguard, he took advantage of the unparalleled access granted him by just shutting up, listening and watching while stood at the door or behind his client. In Mr Knight's own words:

> I was out there looking and learning. And I seen different people complain. I seen artists, I seen people trying to be an artist, I hear people talk about songs . . . I'm just listening. I'm hearing it all.[7]

Suge's method of research here is known as 'observational market research'. Suge didn't pioneer observational market research, he just perfected it and leveraged it better than most would. He tailored it to suit his own needs and opportunities, and was being paid while actively researching and creating connections in a market he wished to penetrate. Market research is normally the other way round: you pay – in time, cash or labour, or some other coin of exchange – to research the market. In the process, he got the opportunity to learn the technical details of how the business really works – from marketing and ownership of masters right down to industry marauding. Ultimately, he used observational market research to go from one of the lowest positions in the business to the absolute pinnacle.

Suge's research revealed some dark industry truths in critical detail:

- The record business is a viper's nest and artists are regularly mercilessly exploited
- The business, especially on the executive side, is full of 'paper and pen gangsters' (i.e. people who are neither brave nor tough, but are lawyered-up to the back teeth)
- Successful artists, especially in the Hip-Hop and R'n'B realm, often have three types of compounded problems: personal; business and legal; and street.[8]

What Suge's research allowed him to do was to position himself in the right place in the right business at the perfect time. The truths he identified (listed above) became his areas of expertise.

As fate would have it, one of his main clients as a bodyguard was Bobby Brown, then a smoking hot R'n'B star, indeed the 'B in R'n'B' according to Whitney Houston, his ex-wife. He was also a Molotov cocktail of personal, business & legal and street problems.

In a 2018 phone interview with BET (from San Diego's Richard J. Donovan Correctional Facility, where he was two years into a twenty-eight-year sentence for voluntary manslaughter), Suge claimed:

> Bobby Brown wanted to go on tour, on the My Prerogative Tour, but he owed some guys [drug dealers] some money and they had a contract on Bobby. They were out to kill Bobby. So, we were not able to tour because Bobby was scared of these guys trying to kill him. So, I confronted the guys, I dealt with the guys and I was aggressive. And I made that guy apologise to Bobby. So, the word travelled round that I was a stand-up guy.

And just like that, by robustly solving a street problem (a contract killing) linked to a personal problem (cocaine use) which permitted Bobby Brown to resolve a business problem (the inability to go on tour due to fear of being assassinated) Suge Knight proved his value. Or that's how he claimed it happened.

This was the end of Suge Knight the bodyguard and the birth of Suge Knight the problem-solving, street-savvy record executive. This approach to market research would be replicated in many of his endeavours – sometimes with great success, sometimes with disastrous results.

It is not clear how Suge found out about the drug dealer threatening Brown, how he found him, how he leaned on him or how much of the story is even true, but one can only assume that somewhere along the way he carried out some unique and highly successful observational market research.

Suge Knight-Inspired Lessons in Market Research

1. Market research is at its most effective when done by stealth. It works best when the people who constitute the market you're attempting to gain insight into are not aware that they are being researched. If they are aware, there is a good chance that their behaviour patterns may change in a bid to maintain competitive advantage, social cache or political perception.

2. Every conversation, meeting, interaction and guarding of a door (or body) is an opportunity to learn about the true nature of a market and any potential gaping holes within it.

3. Physical expressions of dissatisfaction (e.g. not going on a money-spinning tour out of fear of being murdered over a drug debt) speak louder than anything anyone will ever say in an interview (on or off record), survey or focus group.

4. Market research is best applied to services that you can feasibly offer. Suge, for example, might have known Bobby Brown needed a addiction counsellor, but that was not a service he could provide. Muscle was.

5. You don't have to pay for market research – on the contrary, you can get paid at the same time as researching a market.

A critical aspect of Suge Knight and Puff Daddy's market research strategies is that they put their research into action, for market research without eventual action is akin to onanism: you're screwing yourself. Hence, having researched your market, the next step is to develop your approach to business.

2.

BUSINESS DEVELOPMENT

B usiness development is 'the creation of long-term value for an organization from customers, markets, and relationships'.[1] Adapted and adjusted for a Hip-Hop audience, business development simply means: *making shit happen*. Putting your ideas into action, using whatever means you have at your disposal to create cash-money-moolah (revenue) out of an existing or potential customer base, existing or potential relationships and an existing or potential market.

Business development is where you begin the process of moving from *speaking* about something to *being* about something. Like the birth of humanity, this heavy lifting at the birth of the business of rap music was, of course, performed by a Black woman.

HIP-HOP'S PIONEERING BUSINESS DEVELOPER

Time for a quick two-step task:

1. Grab a sheet of paper. Set a timer for one minute. Write down the names of all of the executive and creative leaders you can name in Hip-Hop.
2. Treat yourself to something special for every female leader you named.

You're probably not treating yourself at all.

Today, Hip-Hop is, for the most part, dominated by men.

Especially on the executive and creative leadership side of things. The sad irony here is that the first executive and creative leader to make and break a Hip-Hop song in the commercial realm was a woman – her work lifted an emerging musical genre into a commercial force and a tool for social change.

Sylvia Robinson (then known by her maiden name, Sylvia Vanderpool) got her break in the music business in 1950 at the preciously tender age of fourteen. A blues singer with skill, depth and soul way beyond her years, Sylvia made her debut alongside the famed jazz trumpeter, blues singer and band leader Hot Lips Page, one of the founding fathers of rhythm and blues. The duo gifted the world heart-melting classics such as 'Chocolate Candy Blues', 'Sharp Little Sister' and 'I Was Under The Impression'.

Hot Lips Page died in 1954 at the age of forty-six. Sylvia, meanwhile, was still only eighteen. Two years later, already with over half a decade's experience in the music business, Sylvia joined forces with the guitarist and session musician Mickey Baker to form the rhythm and blues duo Mickey & Sylvia. The same year, they released their classic single 'Love Is Strange' – it was a number-one hit at the time, but is perhaps best known in modern times for featuring in the 1987 movie *Dirty Dancing*). In 1973, she had a huge hit with the self-penned prototypical disco track 'Pillow Talk'.[2] The sound, vibe and overtly sexual nature of 'Pillow Talk' would go on to be emulated far and wide, perhaps most notably on Donna Summer's classic disco hit 'Love To Love You Baby'.

Over the course of her career, she had hits in multiple genres as a singer, writer and producer. However, it was behind the scenes in Hip-Hop that Sylvia Robinson would establish herself as a great and entirely unorthodox business developer.

In 1979, Sylvia was forty-three and down on her luck, despite being a three-decade veteran of the music business. Her best days seemed far behind her. But that same year, Sylvia and her husband Joe (funded by famously mafia-backed record executives Tony

Riviera and Morris Levy)[3] founded Sugar Hill Records. The label was named after the Sugar Hill area of Manhattan, an area Black artists and the then growing Black middle classes flocked to during the Harlem Renaissance of the 1920s and 1930s.

In the late 1970s, Hip-Hop was still in its infancy and remained a live performance genre, based predominantly in parks, at parties and in clubs. There had hardly been any Hip-Hop vinyl pressings or cassette recordings. As a result, there had not been a hit.

On a chance visit to a club with her son, Sylvia heard someone rapping over the disco music being played. She immediately saw and heard the future. In her own words:

> As I was sitting there, the dee jay was playing music and talking over the music, and the kids were going crazy. All of a sudden, something said to me, 'Put something like that on a record, and it will be the biggest thing.' I didn't even know you called it rap.[4]

Success in business is so often about seeing what others don't, seeing opportunity where most see obstacles.

The role of the business developer is to see a jungle or a desert and figure out exactly where and how a city might be built there. That is what Benjamin 'Bugsy' Siegel and Meyer Lansky did with Las Vegas. And that is what Sylvia did with Hip-Hop. Where many saw young Black people shouting gibberish over classic disco records, Sylvia Robinson saw commercial and artistic opportunity, and set in motion the wheels of what Hip-Hop is today.

It was not the most auspicious of beginnings.

Sylvia did not know any rappers. There was no such thing as a Hip-Hop producer at the time. There was no radio programming format to follow. There was no network of people to reach out to. There were no established rules whatsoever. Undeterred, Sylvia's first step was to find her artists.

Legend has it that her son came across a rapper who was working at the local pizza parlour. Together they went to meet

Big Bank Hank (real name Henry Lee Jackson), 'the rapping pizza guy'.

There was just one issue: unbeknownst to Sylvia and her son, Big Bank Hank, an overweight yet handsome and effortlessly charming man with real star aura, was not really a rapper. He was managing a highly respected rapper called Grandmaster Caz. The tape he would play in the pizza parlour and rap along to was Grandmaster Caz's music.

Sylvia and her son asked Hank to audition. Here was the genesis of much unscrupulous behaviour in Hip-Hop, for Big Bank Hank recited Grandmaster Caz's rap verses, not even bothering to change the part where Grandmaster Caz spelt out his other moniker (Casanova Fly) in the rap. He was recruited on the spot, and within the twenty-four hours would become a pioneering part of Hip-Hop history, without having written as much as a single bar.

Another two rappers were swiftly found by trial and error on the street. According to Grandmaster Caz,[*] Sylvia and her son would see someone pass by and yell: 'HEY, YOU! CAN YOU RAP? COME OVER HERE!'

Their next recruits were Wonder Mike (real name: Michael Anthony Wright) and Master Gee (real name: Guy O'Brien). On that very same day, Big Bank Hank, Wonder Mike and Master Gee found themselves in Sylvia's mansion, where she moulded them into a group. She called them the Sugarhill Gang.

Their task was clear and simple: Sylvia wanted them to do exactly what she had seen being done in the club but on a record: rap over disco tracks. As this was pre-sampling, she hired session musicians (for peanuts) and got them to recreate the music to the Chic hit 'Good Times' (without Chic's permission).

The newly formed Sugarhill Gang rapped for fifteen minutes

---

[*] His is one version, but it has been told so many times it could be chalked up to legend.

straight and 'Rapper's Delight' – the first hit Hip-Hop single – was created . . . in one take. That one take also signalled the birth of Hip-Hop's first business developer.

We can now return to the definition of business development as 'the creation of long-term value for an organization from customers, markets, and relationships' and assess how Sylvia Robinson fared on each point.

Customers

The customer base was clear: Sylvia had already seen the reaction the music was getting in the clubs. That was all she needed to know. Also, 'Good Times' was a huge hit record. The music for 'Rapper's Delight' was a straightforward interpolation (i.e. rip-off, in this instance) of 'Good Times'. People who enjoyed grooving to 'Good Times' would probably love 'Rapper's Delight'. So, converting the disco crowd to Hip-Hop was already proving to be an uncomplicated affair.

Market

The customer is always right. And therefore, the customer creates the market. Where there is demand, there is supply (or lunacy-driven negligence, or the government).

When a customer hears a song they love, they go and find it. Any retailer that doesn't have it will be losing money and market share to rivals. The more 'Rapper's Delight' was heard in clubs, the more addictive it became to clubbers, and the more it was in demand in stores. And they would all want the next big single too.

Value

The determination that drove Sylvia Robinson's business development endeavour resulted in:

• A manufactured, mismatched rap group

- A copycat with limited musical ability becoming the first internationally recognisable rapper
- A manager who stole his only client's intellectual property to create his own career
- A ripped-off disco record (which resulted in Hip-Hop's first lawsuit)
- Eventually, a bitter dispute over royalties, who owned the name 'Sugarhill Gang' and who was even in the group

It would, however, be wrong to focus on these relatively minor negatives, for Sylvia's business development crusade also created:

- Hip-Hop's first hit record
- Hip-Hop's first producer and executive (who went on to produce Hip-Hop's second iconic single, 'The Message' by Grandmaster Flash and the Furious Five, as well as other groups)
- The first steps towards the billions and billions generated by Hip-Hop today, its enduring social and political influence and global cultural impact
- Arguably a better and much more fun world

Two Sylvia Robinson-inspired Business Development Tips

1. Business development principally creates three things: mechanisms, money and madness.

2. The business development process is messy and may require a high degree of work ethic and determination but a low degree of ethics to work.

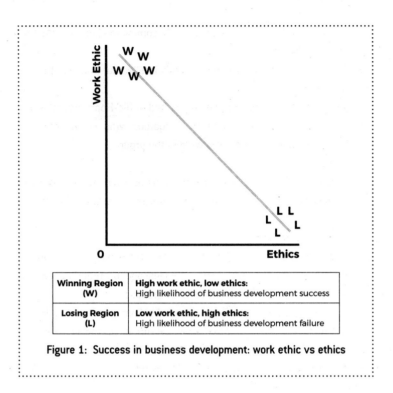

Winning Region (W)	**High work ethic, low ethics:** High likelihood of business development success
Losing Region (L)	**Low work ethic, high ethics:** High likelihood of business development failure

Figure 1: Success in business development: work ethic vs ethics

As the old saying goes: over-analysis leads to paralysis. So, as opposed to doing what the average business development executive would do – i.e. write a report, write a plan, seek feedback, doubt the report and plan, shelve it and then come back to it six months later to repeat the cycle – Sylvia developed her business in the most effective way possible: hitting the streets to get it done, by hook, crook or cruelty.

Sylvia Robinson took expired eggs, sour milk, off butter, rotten syrup – and baked up the most amazing cake. Depending on who you ask, to date, 'Rapper's Delight' has sold either half a million copies or tens of millions. What is not disputable is that it proved the early artistic and commercial case for the genre that has now influenced hundreds of millions of people and generated immense wealth.

3.

RAISING CAPITAL

S tarting any capitalist venture without capital is about as ambitious yet delusional as planning to make fried chicken without chicken and oil. A lack of start-up capital is why many ideas remain just that – ideas.

Given the environment they often come from, for many rappers starting out, the local drug dealer is likely to be their first financier. Case in point: in 1986, Eric 'Eazy-E' Wright, a diminutive 'local pharmaceutical entrepreneur' from Compton, Los Angeles, was persuaded to invest in setting up a record company by a local Hip-Hop and electro DJ, Andre 'Dr. Dre' Young.

Wright established Ruthless Records and invested an estimate $5,000 into making NWA's debut album *Straight Outta Compton*, an investment that has directly generated well over $25,000,000, marking a return of 439,900 per cent. Many would consider that a sound investment. What's more, Eazy-E's $5,000 investment in Ruthless Records was, arguably, the acorn from which the mighty oak tree that is the modern music business has grown.

By 1987 (pre-NWA), the commercial case for rap music had been made. Successes were popping all over America and internationally, as were native Hip-Hop recording companies. As detailed in Chapter 2, Sugar Hill Records had found success with the Sugar Hill Gang and Grandmaster Flash and the Furious Five. New York remained the centre of the Hip-Hop world:

Tommy Boy records had launched the career of Afrika Bambaataa and Soulsonic Force; Russell Simmons and Rick Rubin's Def Jam Recordings was home to LL Cool J and the Beastie Boys; and Profile Records had Run DMC and Dr. Jeckyll & Mr. Hyde on their roster.

Despite this proven track record, it remained easier to fit a camel through a needle's eye than to attain 'conventional' start-up funding to launch a rap music-focused record label (or, for Black populations, to launch pretty much any other form of business – which remains the case to this day).

The good people at American Express[1] offer eight ways of raising capital for a venture – but how realistic were they in the pursuit of putting good and potentially lucrative Hip-Hop ideas into action?

AMERICAN EXPRESS FUNDRAISING IDEAS VS HIP-HOP REALITY

Bootstrapping

Definition: Self-funding an enterprise by reining in all excesses and making the most of your resources. Also known as 'pulling yourself up by the boot straps'.

Viability in Hip-Hop: As the clichéd response to the cliché goes: you have to have boots in order to pull yourself up by the bootstraps.

Family donations

Definition: Asking your family to donate to your business ambitions

Viability in Hip-Hop: Persuading your mother to invest in 'I Wanna Kill My Mum Entertainment' may be a hard sell, nevertheless, some successful Hip-Hop labels were founded by family loans or donations.

Government grants

Definition: Turning to the state for investment in your company.

Viability in Hip-Hop: In the 1980s and into the 1990s, governments were actively trying to ban Hip-Hop.

Business loans

Definition: Approach a bank or another type of financial institution for a loan.

Viability in Hip-Hop: Banks in Hip-Hop's early days were reluctant to loan Black people money to buy their own houses, let alone set up a Hip-Hop-related business.

Crowdfunding

Definition: Pooled money raised through a website or company. May or may not be in exchange for equity in the venture.

Viability in Hip-Hop: Possible in today's world – certainly on an individual project basis, but seeking funding to set up a record label may prove hard.

Venture capitalists

Definition: Venture capital generally comes from well-off investors, investment banks and any other financial institutions.

Viability in Hip-Hop: See 'business loans' above.

Angel investors

Definition: According to Investopedia, angel investors 'are high-wealth individuals who provide start-up capital to entrepreneurs in exchange for a percentage of equity in the company.'[2]

Viability in Hip-Hop: Angel investors in Hip-Hop were often more closely aligned with the devil – but this was definitely a possibility. We'll come back to this below.

Get creative

Definition: Find unorthodox ways to fund your venture.

Viability in Hip-Hop: This is where Hip-Hop moguls excelled. Again, see below.

As is clear, raising capital to get a Hip-Hop-related endeavour off the ground was not straightforward. But the last two of American Express's suggestions proved to be more fertile ground for Hip-Hop's moguls-in-waiting.

HIP-HOP'S ANGEL INVESTORS

With access to 'formal' routes to capital out of the question, Hip-Hop's budding entrepreneurs had to develop creative ways to raise funds, which usually meant turning to less than angelic 'angel investors'. Let's take a look at how the major players got Hip-Hop funded in its early days.

Major labels

Major labels are the pharaohs and dictators of popular music. Given their cartel-like share of the market, they're more than likely to be responsible for that song stuck in your cranium right now. They are the establishment of the music business.

The first rapper to sign a record deal with a major label was twenty-year-old Kurtis Blow in 1979 (Sugarhill Gang was on an indie). It is no coincidence that he was also the first rapper to achieve (certifiable) major commercial success on a sustained basis.

Blow signed to Mercury Records through their London offices. His first record, 'Christmas Rappin'', was a domestic UK release. As he explained in a 2017 VladTV interview: 'John Stainze was a guy from England – London.* Mercury Records loved the song. He said, "Oh, let's sign him up. We can recoup this record in

---

* John Stainze, a white English A&R man working at Phonogram's London office.

six months." So, they signed me up. I was actually an English artist, from the UK, and my record came back to America on an import.'

He goes on to explain the economics of his deal: 'I had this strange deal. I had to sell 30,000 records on the first single – and then I'd get to make another single. If the next single sold 50,000 copies, I could make an album.'[3]

He exceeded both sales requirements – comfortably.

When adjusted for inflation, 'Christmas Rappin'' and his second single 'The Breaks' collectively generated in excess of $8m. A nice pay day for Mercury, but what about Kurtis Blow?

Raising capital through a major label can seem like an obviously appealing idea, because it increases the likelihood of success. However, a record advance, as rap supremo Steve Stoute regularly warns, may be one of the most expensive and exploitative 'loans' known to man – one in which you may not actually own the asset once you have paid off the loan. It is also a 'loan' you're forced to pay tax on.

The 'interest' on the advance could not be more exploitative. When an artist receives a 10 per cent royalty rate it effectively means that they pay $10 for every $1 advanced; on a 15 per cent royalty rate it drops to $6.66 for every dollar advanced.[*]

The finer details of Kurtis Blow's deal are not publicly available, but by all indications he probably would have made the bulk of his money from live performances, just as many major acts still do today.

Case Study: Roc-A-Fella Records

Despite being highly respected by his peers and spending nearly a decade proving himself again and again, Jay-Z was turned down by every major record label. Paradoxically, this might have been the single best thing that could have happened to him. In 1994,

---

[*] It could be worse – they could have the figures of a book publishing deal.

he partnered with Damon 'Dame' Dash, an extra-extroverted, flamboyant and well-connected music business brain and Kareem 'Biggs' Burke, an introverted money guy. Out of necessity and rejection, they created Roc-A-Fella Records, an independent record label. They signed a press and distribution deal with Priority Records and released Jay-Z's first album, *Reasonable Doubt*. As Jay-Z tells it:

> We were forced, in the beginning. I wish I could say we were geniuses and were going to start our own company . . . that is not what happened. From the beginning we went to every single label. And every single label shut their door on us. The genius thing that we did was that we didn't give up. We used that 'what do they know?' approach. We didn't give up at that point. I think that is the genius thing we did: we started selling our own CDs and we built up our own buzz and the record company came back to us. So now we had a different negotiation. It wasn't the same artist–label relationship. We retained ownership of our own company. It was the best thing for us.[4]

So, not getting a record contract (and crucially not giving up) was a blessing cloaked as a curse to Jay-Z; it forced him to become his own boss, which paved the way for him to become a mogul. Roc-A-Fella was living proof that:

- The word of gatekeepers is not to be mistaken for the gospel – they are frequently wrong
- Numbers hold more weight than opinions. Hence working and succeeding independently will eventually render the perspective of the gatekeeper entirely irrelevant. Most of the people who rejected Jay-Z once upon a time would jump in front of a moving train to wash his feet today
- Rejection should be seen as a gift, a learning opportunity cloaked as a curse – provided you don't give up

Advantages and Disadvantages of Establishment Funding

Advantages

- **Access to 'the club'.** The larger establishment companies should be able to automatically open doors that would otherwise be triple-bolted shut.

- **Legitimacy in the business.** You will cease to come across as a chancer or an amateur and be taken seriously as a player in an industry.

- **Reliability.** Establishment corporations actually tend to pay. So, struggling to extract the agreed funding from them may be less tasking.

- **Star power.** As the marketing department jumps into action, there's no greater rush than seeing your name in a newspaper as having gone into business with a major company.

- **Comfort and peace of mind.** At least in the short term – until you have to pay the money back.

Disadvantages

- **They'll want their pound of flesh.** It's probably the single highest-interest loan you'll ever take out.

- **No certainty.** Though the debt is guaranteed, there's still no guarantee of success.

- **Tie-ins.** Contractual lock-ins may limit your ability to move when a deal fails.

- **Abandonment.** High likelihood of being dropped if things go south.

Family donations

Several successful early Hip-Hop native record labels were established with loans and/or donations from family members. A few notable examples are detailed below.

Profile Records: In 1980, Cory Robbins, then a fresh-faced twenty-three-year-old record executive, and the songwriter Steve Plotnicki (who also happens to be the owner of the cult British TV show, *Robot Wars*), both borrowed $17,000 from their parents ($63,000 in 2023, when adjusted for inflation). They used this loan from the bank of Mum and Dad to establish Profile Records.

After burning through the first $34,000 with no success or return to show for it, they found a company-saving triumph in a rap cover of Tom Tom Club's 1981 hit 'Genius Of Love',[5] creatively titled 'Genius Rap'. The song was made by business suit-rap pioneers Dr. Jeckyll & Mr. Hyde (Alonzo Brown and future Hip-Hop visionary, Andre Harrell). 'Genius Rap' (also released in 1981) sold 150,000 copies, generating hundreds of thousands of dollars for Profile.

From their $700-a-month office in New York City,[6] Robbins and Plotnicki signed and struck gold with Run DMC (the first rap group to sell over a million copies of an album), Rob Base and DJ E-Z Rock, Poor Righteous Teachers, DJ Quik and others. Thanks to the $34,000 acorn investment, the American duo of Robbins and Plotnicki helped turbo-charge rap music as a commercial force.

Tommy Boy Records: In 1981, a year after Profile was founded, Tom Silverman, a slender, highly innovative American businessman with a classic old-school New York no-bullshitting demeanour (complete with the accent to back it up), borrowed $5,000 ($18,500 in 2023) from his parents to set up Tommy Boy from his New York City apartment. He signed Afrika

Bambaataa and Soulsonic Force, Stetsasonic, Queen Latifah, De La Soul, Naughty by Nature, Coolio, Capone and Noreaga and more . . . and made millions. In June 2021, it was announced that Silverman had sold Tommy Boy for $100m.[7]

Delicious Vinyl: In 1987, Michael Ross, a UCLA student, met Matt Dike, a local DJ with an 'encyclopaedic knowledge of rock, soul and funk'[8] in a nightclub in Los Angeles. Funded with a $5,000 loan from Ross's father, they founded Delicious Vinyl . . . and found success in signing Tone Loc, a charismatic and hand-some Los Angeles crip. The Robert Palmer-inspired $500 video for his debut single, 'Wild Thing', became a mainstay on MTV and the record sold 2.5 million copies in its first year (1989), generating more than $5,000,000 for Delicious Vinyl in their second year of operations. Delicious Vinyl went on to sign the Pharcyde, Young MC, Masta Ace, J Dilla, Brand New Heavies and more.[9]

Advantages and Disadvantages of Attaining Funding from Family

Advantages:

- **Rapid decisions.** By merely glancing in their eyes, you should be able to tell immediately if your family member is going to hand over the cash or not.

- **Less red tape.** They may not require that you offer them a detailed business plan, credit score, invoice pipeline, etc.

- **Low cost and highly adaptable.** Assuming they are not loan sharks, family funding is likely to be the cheapest funding you'll ever gain access to.

- **Familiarity.** Family members know you're a dreamer and therefore probably suspect you won't pay the money back.

- **Less risk**. Defaulting will not impact your credit rating, your kneecaps, your mental health or your presence on this planet. Additionally, you should be able to run the 'Parable of the Unforgiving Debtor' hustle (Matthew 18:21–35) on your nearest and dearest.

Disadvantages:

- **It has its limits.** Family funding is likely to only ever be a micro-loan, therefore you may need more financing to scale up.

- **Impact on family relations**. Defaulting may mean that you'll have to skip Christmas, Kwanza, Easter, Thanksgiving, Eid, Hanukkah, Purim, Christenings and other family gatherings for a few years.

- **Expectation of further involvement/a kickback**. If the business succeeds, the family member may attempt to 'remix' the loan into an equity stake. 'I owe you 15,000 dollars,' says successful businessperson. 'No, you do not. You owe me 15 per cent of that company I bought shares in,' responds Uncle Andrew.

- **Risk of emotional blackmail.** 'If you don't pay me back, your nephew will miss out on school trips, never be able to go to college, starve to death', etc.

The reverse is true of everything listed here if you're approached to invest in a family business or loan a family member start-up cash.

It is no coincidence that the people who were able to attain loans or family donations to establish the early Hip-Hop-focused record labels were, in the main, white men. The fruits of intergenerational wealth, whiteness and masculinity granted some white entrepreneurs a head start in Hip-Hop. Head starts that would prove both pivotal and highly lucrative – for the early entrepreneurs as well as the culture in general. Hip-Hop entrepreneurs who looked like and came from the type of places the originators of the music came from often had to take on much more risk than a family loan.

Urban pharmacists

Miami. American hegemony in the Middle East and South America. Private prisons. The Sackler family. Johnson & Johnson. Bitcoin. Many an empire has been built or maintained on drugs or the proceeds of the sale of drugs. Some companies and success stories in Hip-Hop are no different.

Hip-Hop is flooded with records paying homage to the ultimate risk-taker and angel investor: the narcotic retailer. 'A Bird in the Hand' ('better known as a kilo'– Ice Cube), 'Rubber Band Man', 'Brown Paper Bag', 'Dope Man', 'Birdman', 'Gone Till November', 'Drug Dealers Anonymous', 'I'm Your Pusher', '10 Crack Commandments', 'Hustlin'', 'Pocket Full Of Stones', 'Love's Gonna Get'cha', 'Blowing Money Fast', 'Crack It Up' (a satirical anti-crack cocaine record, but sadly the satire went over many people's heads and therefore it sounded like a pro-crack record) . . . The list is truly endless.

In fact, beyond records, almost from Hip-Hop's inception DJs and rappers have included references to taking drugs, selling drugs or drug dealers in their names – Coke La Rock, Eddie Cheeba, Kurtis Blow, Love Bug Star Ski, Busy Bee Starski, Rick Ross,[*] Freeway, Griselda Records, Nas Escobar, Noreaga, Scarface, French Montana . . .

---

[*] Whom the actual drug baron Rick Ross would go on to sue for using his name.

There is a good reason for all of the above: the drug dealer, as vilified and criminalised a vocation as it may be, is perhaps the most successful and financially liquid person in many an economically challenged environment. On the first song on his first album, Kanye West conceded to looking up to the local drug dealer, as he was the only grown-up he knew who wasn't broke. Freeway Rick Ross (not to be mistaken for the bearded rappers Rick Ross or Freeway), a stark, illiterate tennis prodigy (trained by Richard Williams, father of Serena and Venus) turned 1980s cocaine kingpin, made a similar observation in a 2021 interview with VladTV: 'The first successful entrepreneur most Black men ever meet is the local drug dealer.'[10]

People placed in boxes often become skilled at cutting corners. Without the drug dealer, Hip-Hop would not exist as the commercial and creative force we know today. Hip-Hop has a reciprocal relationship with the dope man that fluctuates between symbiotic and parasitic.

The Symbiotic (and Sometimes Parasitic) Relationship Between Rappers and Drug Dealers

What rappers gain from drug dealers:

- **Swag.** Oversized white T-shirts, sneakers (especially Nike Air Jordans), shiny suits, jehri curls, heavy sunglasses, furs – drug dealers have long provided the style template for successive generations of rappers.

- **Identity.** Rappers often take the names of notorious drug dealers (as well as gangsters, pimps and the occasional dictator) – and then build their public personas around them.

- **Drugs.** Creative genius and drugs are often not far apart – and, therefore, the narcotic supplier is never far away.

- **Stories.** Hip-Hop is flooded with glorious stories of drug sales. Many of these are lifted wholesale from lived experience . . . of other people who sold drugs.

- **Legitimacy (aka street credibility).** A star drug dealer endorsing a rapper's authenticity can elevate a rapper's career. Having an established drug dealer in a crew is akin to having an established businessperson on the board of any company. It signifies seriousness, potential and legitimacy.

- **Work experience.** From 50 Cent to Jay-Z to Russell Simmons, many rap moguls cut their capitalist teeth in the drug business. It is fertile ground to learn about risk and reward, demand and supply, the consequences of failure and building a customer base.

- **Start-up capital.** Though many would consider them far from godly, drug dealers have served as Hip-Hop's angel investors on many occasions.

What drug dealers gain from rappers:

- **Fame.** Big Meech, Alpo, Azie Faison, Rich Porter, Kenneth 'Supreme' McGriff, Rayful Edmund, the real Freeway Rick Ross – Hip-Hop has made many a drug dealer famous by paying homage to them. Although . . .

- **Jail time.** A famous (active) drug dealer is never far away from prison. In making these very people famous, rappers are effectively dry-snitching.[11] Which may not be a bad idea if you have no intention of repaying any investment a drug dealer has made in your company, or paying them for 'legitimacy' or street credibility services rendered. (See Michael 'Harry-O' Harris and Black Mafia Family below.)

- **A way out.** Hip-Hop has served as a way out for ex-drug dealers looking to make a living with significantly less associated risk. It is a culture they know and helped develop so transitioning to working within it often proves viable and profitable.

- **Investment opportunities.** Drug dealers are always on the hunt for investment opportunities for their 'excess' cash. The high-risk and high-glamour music business has often been an attractive destination for 'fast money'.

- **Money-cleansing opportunities.** See above. Charities, strippers, arms dealers, the London property market, shops, car dealerships, crypto currencies, religious institutions – nowhere is sacred when it comes to laundering money. Hip-Hop, too, has served as a great location to place, layer and integrate money from the wrong side of the tracks. More on which to follow.

- **Return on investment.** A drug dealer who invests in a company should surely get something back in return, right? It's complicated.

It is virtually impossible to chronicle fundraising in rap without covering the involvement of the narcotics trade. In this realm, two entities in particular stick out: Death Row Records and the Black Mafia Family.

DEATH ROW RECORDS

After successfully and, it is widely alleged, violently extracting Dr. Dre from his contract with Eazy-E's Ruthless Records (a contract music industry veteran Dick Griffey described as the worst he'd ever seen) and all but ending NWA, in 1991, Suge

Knight and Dr. Dre (both men were twenty-six at the time), rapper the DOC (then twenty-four) and Dick Griffey (the fifty-four-year-old CEO of SOLAR Records)[12] founded Death Row Records. Dre and DOC brought the musical talent to the table; Suge and Dick brought everything else. Unbeknownst to Griffey, who claimed to have been swiftly double-crossed out of the picture, in the shadows was the money man: Michael 'Harry-O' Harris, an incarcerated Los Angeles drug baron and entertainment mogul.

Harry-O was the Costco of the 1980s cocaine distribution business, a true wholesaler working directly with the pinnacle of the Colombian cartels. After finding 'financial freedom' in the narcotics business, Harry-O set his eyes on legitimacy in the entertainment business – despite being behind bars. One of his early investments was a Broadway play called *Checkers*, which gifted a young Denzel Washington a career break.

Then there was Suge Knight, who allegedly attained $1.5m in seed funding (and the services of David Kenner, Harris's badass lawyer). In exchange for what is the equivalent of $3m in 2022, Harry-O became a silent partner with a 50 per cent stake in Death Row Records.

Demonstrating the extent of Harry-O's importance, Suge Knight maintained a phoneline dedicated to him at Death Row's offices. In order to ensure Harry-O could call in (from prison) and check on his investments at any given time, it was strictly forbidden for anyone to use the phone. When some artists did just that, Suge made an example of them: he made them strip off all their clothes and shot at them – purposefully missing.

With seed investment in the bank, Dr. Dre and the newly minted Death Row Records crew (which included a newly discovered Snoop Dogg) got to work creating Dre's era-defining rap album, *The Chronic*. Despite the undeniably excellent nature of the music, it was widely turned down for distribution deals due to the prevailing Tipper Gore-led anti-gangsta rap hysteria of the time. That was until Interscope, a small arm of Warner Music founded in 1990 by record executive Jimmy Iovine and the movie mogul Ted Field, an heir to the Field-Marshall dynasty, caught a whiff of what Dr. Dre and Suge Knight were cooking. In *The Chronic* (which would go on to sell over five million copies), Interscope heard their future; in Suge Knight and Dr. Dre, Interscope saw their future.

Suge, it is alleged (including in court documents),[13] took Harry-O's $1.5m and the professional expertise of his legal brain (David Kenner) and, despite Death Row proving a runaway success, never paid him as much as a copper penny in return.

In response, Harry-O calmly listed his legal grievances on a prison typewriter and informed Interscope of his intention to sue. In full knowledge of the cash cow that Death Row had become, and suspicious that Death Row had been founded on the proceeds of crime (potentially putting their investment in peril), Interscope settled with Harry-O's wife, Lydia Harris, to the sum of $300,000.

To put this into perspective: Death Row was the saviour of Interscope (according to Dick Griffey, they were about to close doors), which is today the main cash cow of the Universal Music Group, which itself has the largest market share of the record business by revenue. Ground down, this means that it can be argued much of the modern music business is built on the proceeds of the risk-taking of two drug dealers – Michael 'Harry-O' Harris & Eric 'Eazy-E' Wright. The deeper the pockets, the deeper the secrets.

THE BLACK MAFIA FAMILY

There are two types of drug dealers:

1. Those who know to keep their mouths shut, keep their circle small and fly under the radar.

2. Those who take out billboards, invite the press and make documentaries on their still-active [let alone within the statute of limitations] illegal sales and attempts to invest those proceeds into legitimate enterprises that are fairly obvious fronts.

Michael 'Harry-O' Harris fell into the first category. The Black Mafia Family defined the latter.

BMF. Blowing Money Fast. 'Big Meech' Flenory. Founded in 1989 by Detroit brothers Demetrius 'Big Meech' Flenory (who was inspired by the movie *Scarface*) and Terry 'Southwest T' Flenory, the Black Mafia Family was probably the most blatant drug-trafficking and money-laundering organisation this side of *Scarface*'s Montana Management Co. At their noughties height, BMF had hundreds of members across the nation and reportedly controlled close to 75 per cent of the American wholesale cocaine market.

In the early noughties, Big Meech founded BMF Entertainment, a Hip-Hop label. The intention was obvious: launder the proceeds of their cocaine distribution and, perhaps, earn a legitimate income. In a bid to promote the label, BMF (the narcotics empire) did a slew of straight-to-DVD (or straight-to-Bittorrent or MegaUpload) 'hood' documentaries and a range of interviews and threw hugely lavish parties.

In one of the documentaries, Big Meech effectively told on himself (and, by extension, his hundreds of associates) by looking directly into the camera and declaring that BMF was awash with unexplainable income, all while giving a socialist/capitalist leadership sermon that would somehow be simultaneously satisfying to Tony Robbins, Hugo Chávez and Donald Trump.[14]

Perhaps the cherry on top of BMF's 'WE ARE BLATANTLY AN INTERNATIONAL DRUG-TRAFFICKING RING' cake was when they took out a huge billboard in downtown Atlanta with words everyone who has seen *Scarface*[15] recognises too well: 'BMF: THE WORLD IS BMF'S'.

When you literally announce and flaunt yourself as a criminal enterprise (a 'mafia'), there is a risk the state may believe you. And the state did believe BMF.

The Drug Enforcement Agency (DEA) conducted a massive investigation into BMF, which culminated in the seizure of nearly a ton of cocaine and tens of millions in cash. Hundreds of members of BMF were arrested, charged and incarcerated. Included in the list of those locked up were, bewilderingly, the Hip-Hop jeweller Jacob Arabo, professionally known as Jacob the Jeweller (founder of Jacob & Company – which boasted Cristiano Ronaldo as a brand ambassador, and Jay-Z, Kanye West, David Beckham and many others as regular customers). Despite being arrested under suspicion of conspiring to launder $270m for BMF, following a plea agreement he was convicted of falsifying records and giving false statements to investigators. He received a two-and-a-half-year federal prison sentence and a $50,000 fine and was ordered to make a $2 million forfeiture payment to the government. In an added twist of irony, the $2 million forfeiture was paid to the IRS via a cashier's cheque (a financial instrument which is often used to conceal the source of illicit proceeds).[16]

Big Meech and his brother Southwest T, the leaders of BMF, were both charged and sentenced to thirty years apiece.

In a more just world, there can be no doubt they would have been leaders of Fortune 500 companies. Big Meech and Southwest T demonstrably had the business talent and tenacity. What they lacked was education, access, experience and exposure in the legitimate world. Of course, ethnicity and class certainly played a role in their life chances.

Over the course of their operations, BMF was estimated to have made nearly $300m. Despite having start-up money Death Row could only have dreamt of, in Hip-Hop BMF made little more than a fascinating spectacle. They didn't produce anything that could be remotely confused for a hit, though they did provide the backdrop and credibility vouch for the rise of Young Jeezy.

Capital-raising Lessons from
Urban Pharmacists in Hip-Hop

1. The 'underground economy' does indeed present vast yet extremely high-risk empire-building opportunities. Taking advantage of those opportunities may land you in a palace, but, perhaps more likely, a prison.

2. Hyperlocal opportunities may be less sexy than national or international opportunities but can prove just as lucrative.

3. In unorthodox business areas, you're more likely to attain investment from people (with money) who understand you and the unorthodox nature of the business. Dr. Dre could have gone chasing waterfalls looking for investors, but by approaching someone who understood him, the value of the product he could create and the nature of opportunities associated with it, he found investment . . . from the neighbourhood crack peddler.

4. If you are representing a company or shopping for a deal on their behalf, ensure you have a watertight legal agreement in place with them. If you don't, like Dick Griffey, it could not be easier to cut you out of the deal – and potentially millions.

5. Beware of investors who are enthralled to needless publicity.

6. Money does not guarantee greatness or success and is no substitute for talent. With micro-fractions of the money BMF Entertainment had access to, Death Row and Ruthless Records were light years more successful.

7. Most entities built on the proceeds of crime tend to attain legitimacy by pretending the crime never happened. Think: Britain and slavery.

8. Double crossing your business partners and mentors is likely to come back to haunt you.

9. Where there is success, skeletons cease to matter . . . until someone feels they can make money out of those skeletons.

10. Watching *Scarface* too many times is far from a business blueprint. It will cloud your judgement and, eventually, force you to self-destruct.

RUPERT MURDOCH

'Hip-hop has done more damage to young African Americans than racism in the last 10 years.' – Geraldo Rivera, Fox News correspondent and one of Rupert Murdoch's long-term henchmen

Yes, you read that heading correctly. We'll end this chapter with one of Hip-Hop's most unlikely financial backers. Modern outrage in conservative circles as we know it (love it or hate it) is shaped principally by the business model of one man: the Australian media magnate Rupert Murdoch. His mindset, his media empire, his lieutenants, his determination, drive and ruthlessness have undisputedly shaped thinking and policy on the right-wing for well over half a century.

Murdoch is to right-wing conservative movements what the Pope is to the Catholic Church. And to right-wing conservatives, Hip-Hop and other forms of Black culture are the work of Satan itself and the source of many of society's woes. As a result, conservatives, from David Cameron[17] in the UK to Dan Quayle[18] in the US, especially those trying to woo favour from Rupert Murdoch, have long used opposition to Black culture – especially rap music – as stepping stones to power (liberals are often not much better – just more polite and lovely about it).

Whether in print media like the *Sun* and *The Times*, or broadcast media like Fox News in the US and Sky News Australia (which was once banned from YouTube for misinformation),[19] a running constant across Murdoch-owned news outlets is for-profit or for-principle (a distinction without difference) hostility to Black culture. Especially rap music.

Fox News stalwart and America's grumpy grandfather figure Bill O'Reilly spent a good slice of the noughties building an audience by, in part, taking on rappers on morality grounds. One of his key small wins was against Christopher 'Ludacris' Bridges, a rapper who, musically at least, was very much in touch with his sexual side. His hits 'Area Codes' (hook: 'I've got hoes in different area codes'), 'Pussy Poppin'', 'Pimpin' All Over The World', and many more classics, all dripped with libido.

Pepsi, a company with a high Hip-Hop elasticity of demand, saw profit in Ludacris: he was risqué, photogenic, super-talented, smoking hot on the charts and, above all, respected and popular in Hip-Hop. Ludacris was the perfect youth ambassador, so they built an advertising campaign around him.

In the union between Pepsi and Ludacris, O'Reilly saw outrage, obscenity and therefore opportunity. And, of course, like Pepsi, he saw profit. O'Reilly immediately took to the airwaves and objected in the strongest terms during one of his frequent moral-panic segments:

> I'm calling for all responsible Americans to fight back and punish Pepsi for using a man who degrades women, who encourages substance abuse, and does all the things that hurt particularly the poor in our society. I'm calling for all Americans to say, 'Hey, Pepsi, I'm not drinking your stuff. You want to hang around with Ludacris, you do that, I'm not hanging around with you.'[20]

O'Reilly mobilised his already radicalised audience (median age: seventy-two),[21] who registered their disdain with Pepsi directly. Pepsi crumbled. They dropped Ludacris and shelved his advert (also featuring the singer Shakira)* just days later.[22]

Demonstrating that hypocrisy and moral panic go arm in arm, fifteen years after O'Reilly mobilised a digital-age mob to force Pepsi to cancel Ludacris for 'degrading women', it emerged that O'Reilly himself had settled a string of sexual harassment cases. In one case alone, he paid a former Fox News legal analyst $32m to settle a case.[23] Ludacris's star continues to shine bright.

Ironically, moral outrage-driven conservative backlash and demands for censorship have helped legitimise many a Black cultural phenomenon and driven profits within it – rendering it a greater source of investment.

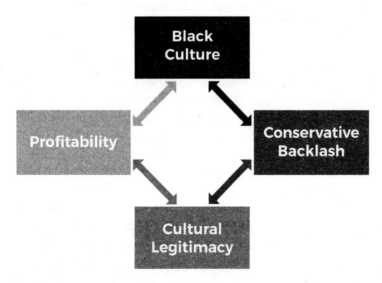

Figure 2: The conservative anti-black cloutrage model

---

* Ludacris was the focus of the campaign, not Shakira, whose lyrics and videos are also sexualised, just in a different way. What did O'Reilly see in Ludacris specifically, one wonders . . .

Given the role of profitability in the cycle shown in Figure 2, perhaps it shouldn't be too much of a surprise that conservative Murdoch money has found its way into the Hip-Hop industry. I'd love to be able to reveal that this investment came about after Rupert himself went to a Miami nightclub, saw 2 Live Crew perform 'Me So Horny' and decided he wanted to pour his billions into this 'rapping stuff' – but he didn't directly invest in Hip-Hop. His money found its way into the culture through his offspring.

In 1995, Rawkus Records was established by gently spoken schoolmates and Hip-Hop fans Brian Brater and Jarret Myer, along with a wealthy Harvard dropout named James Murdoch (son of the media billionaire). Brian and Jarret handled the culture, music and corporate side of things; James was the money man.

Given that Rawkus indirectly obtained its funding from Hip-Hop's equivalent of Darth Vader, it's surprising that the music the label released was quite alternative. At a time when Hip-Hop more broadly was celebrating the excesses of free-market capitalism, cut-throat competition (which led to actual murders) and empire building, a time when diamonds were a rapper's best friend – the 'bling' era – Rawkus released socially thoughtful, soulful and progressive Hip-Hop. They championed intellectual prowess over gangsta credentials.

Rawkus's signature artists, such as Talib Kweli, Mos Def (now known as Yassin Bey) and Pharoahe Monch, made music that spoke to the polar opposite of everything the Rupert Murdoch brand usually stands for: Black liberation, female equality (though the label never signed a female rapper), opposition to cultural appropriation and much more.

Perplexingly, it would be no exaggeration to say that the Murdoch-funded Rawkus was a Black nationalist rap label, one that served as the lead antidote to the 'money, hoes and clothes' regime that had been embraced in the mainstream and personified by the likes of Puff Daddy and Jay-Z.

In a MySpace profile of the company, beloved Brooklyn party DJ and one third of the Rub, DJ Eleven (who worked in Rawkus's production department), remembered a company flush with cash. '[Rawkus] had really deep pockets, so they were able to make things happen and they had a tremendous amount of goodwill and everybody loved the label and everybody loved what they put out.'[24]

As is common, this absence of funding worries perhaps dulled the label's commercial incision. Case in point: although he did some of his early work with them, Rawkus passed on signing Eminem in order to appease Mos Def who, according to Rawkus boss Brian Brater, 'didn't like what he [Eminem] represents'.[25] Mos Def was an 'inflexible' (Brater's word), seriously minded and highly thoughtful political rapper with true star quality; Eminem was an emphatically talented slap-stick shock rapper . . . who happened to be white. Rawkus stuck with Mos Def, who would go on to become the lynchpin of their brand. In hindsight, the decision is hard to justify on a commercial basis: Mos Def's highest-selling album, *Black On Both Sides*, has sold over 500,000 copies at time of writing. Impressive, but Eminem's biggest success, *The Marshall Mathers LP*, has sold over 20 million.

The label also passed on Kanye West and Pitbull, and lost out on signing Common and superstar producer Dr Luke (Rawkus released his first records). Rawkus took on the 'Cristal, caviar, clothes, cash and ho's' era and lost. For all of its funding (the company was acquired by Rupert Murdoch's News Corp. in 1996), righteousness and cultural credibility, Rawkus didn't become a money-printing machine.

Capital-raising Lessons from Rawkus

1. If you are friends or associates with the child of a billionaire (or at least a very rich person) and they are showing hints of a rebellious streak, invite them to invest in a project that is the polar opposite of everything their wealthy parents stand for.

2. Rebellious streaks don't last for ever. Eventually, every rich child realises they are in direct competition with, say, the cat refuge for their inheritance. Make hay while the sun (or son) shines.

3. Assuming you're not a deeply despised and evil class clown, the more elite the schools you go to, the more likely you are to be able to raise capital from your old classmates. Despair not if you went to a 'normal' school, as was aforementioned: drug dealers are also great sources of investment.

4. It is critical not to write off potential investors or funding sources due to the seeming absolute lunacy or hostility of their (or their family's) politics. Treasure is usually buried in the least obvious of places.

5. A strong, steady and reliable pipeline of capital can cloud judgement. Rawkus was very comfortable with investing in 'underground' acts to the point where that became their brand. Perhaps as a result, they missed out on opportunities to scale up and hit the big time.

6. The pursuit of profit and prosperity often means principles and politics are abandoned.

Brian Brater and Jarret Myer went on to launch other ventures in Hip-Hop (they currently own the Hip-Hop website Hip-Hop DX); James Murdoch went full throttle into the family business and quickly emerged as one of News Corp.'s foremost executives (in 2021 he walked away from the family business, a billionaire in his own right, expressing disgust at some of the content on Fox News).

Rupert Murdoch remained Rupert Murdoch: the world's most powerful conservative media mogul and one-time funder of a Black nationalist rap label.

4.

MARKET ENTRY

Recap time:

- Similarly to Suge Knight the bodyguard, you've meticulously researched your market and identified a gap or at least a place where you can prove viable and competitive
- Just like Sylvia Robinson, you've developed your business approach or are at least able to leverage the work of someone else
- And, like Eazy-E, Big Meech, James Murdoch and Tom Silverman, you've secured some funding through either nefarious or non-nefarious means, or a bit of both

Now is the time to make your move, your giant step into the fairly well-researched unknown. With all of the knowledge in place, now is your moment to really break into the market.

Cometh the moment, cometh the market entry and introduction strategy. And cometh the madness.

Market entry is a series of processes that includes all the activities involved in bringing a product or service to a new market – whether that market is a new country, demographic or customer segment.[1] Market introduction is the process of making consumers aware of the product and its benefits. This often includes spending large sums of money on advertising and marketing.[2] In short, market entry is the equivalent of walking into a room; market introduction is making your presence in the room known. Given the overlap, for simplicity, market entry and market introduction are at times used interchangeably.

Market entry and market introduction refer to a cocktail of strategies and processes that ensure you effectively penetrate the market by:

1. Creating an awareness of your presence in the market.
2. Beginning to establish your customer base.
3. Networking to build alliances, partnerships, joint ventures or co-operative agreements.
4. Establishing a competitive advantage.
5. Potentially disrupting the prevailing order of the market.

As endearing as it is to think there is enough pie for all of us or enough room for everyone, the reality is that no established business environment appreciates the threat of new entrants and the innovation, competition and frustration they may bring with them. For example, when Master P was setting up shop in Los Angeles, he got a threatening call from an incarcerated Suge Knight, warning him that California 'wasn't big enough' for Suge, Master P and Puff Daddy. Master P responded: 'So when are you leaving?'[3]

One person's entrance or disruption often spells another's exit. As a result, penetrating, disrupting or establishing a presence of any kind in any market is testing. It costs time, money, emotion and, from time to time, even murder. Some examples of great moments in disruptive market entry include the launch of the iPhone, which decimated the market dominance of Nokia and other traditional mobile phone providers; the emergence of WhatsApp, which decimated the multi-billion-dollar text message industry; and the emergence of 50 Cent, which led to the decimation of anyone or anything that stood in his path.

STANDING OUT FROM THE CROWD

Despite being affiliated with Jam Master Jay's JMJ Records since 1996 and appearing in an Onyx video in 1998, Curtis '50 Cent' Jackson properly announced his professional presence in Hip-Hop in 1999. And he did it in a profound way: by publicly and satirically fantasising about violently robbing many of the leading artists and executives of the day on his debut single, 'How To Rob'.[4]

He went in and he went in *hard*. A full roll call of everyone he insulted: Lil' Kim, Puff Daddy, Bobby Brown and his then wife Whitney Houston, Brian McKnight, Keith Sweat, Cardan, Harlem World, Mase, Ol' Dirty Bastard, Foxy Brown and her then boyfriend Kurupt, Jay-Z, Case, Trackmasters (who actually produced the song), Slick Rick, Stevie J, Big Pun, Master P, Silkk The Shocker, Will Smith and Jada Pinkett Smith, Timbaland and Missy Elliott, Joe, Jermaine Dupri and Da Brat, DMX, Treach, DJ Clue, TQ, Raekwon, Ghostface Killah and RZA, Sticky Fingaz, Fredro Starr, Canibus, Heavy D, Juvenile, Blackstreet, Boyz II Men and Michael Bivins, Mike Tyson and Robin Givens, Mister Cee, Busta Rhymes and his crew, the Flipmode Squad and the gospel singer Kirk Franklin.

The song was catchy, controversial, funny and mildly risky. Most importantly, it did its job perfectly: everyone knew 50 Cent had arrived. It created an awareness of him and his burgeoning brand, a buzz that would generate sales and an appetite for more of his music. Not bad for something that took him minutes to write in the back of a taxi while on his way to a studio.

It also helped him create numerous enemies and rivalries, some quite lucrative.

Perhaps the most potent and profitable of all of the 'enemies' he created was Jay-Z.

Jay-Z, then at the top of his game (where, more than two decades later, he remains), was one of the first to respond to 50

Cent. And he did so with his usual class, grace, elegance and piercingly effective wordplay – in the presence of a live concert audience of 30,000 people. A simple one-line subliminal diss:

I'm about a dollar, what the fuck is 50 Cent?

50 Cent would later express gratitude to Jay-Z for responding to him – speaking in an interview for the documentary *Beef* (2003), he revealed that he didn't think 30,000 people knew who he was at the time.

Ghostface Killah, Raekwon, Kurupt and Missy Elliot all responded in seemingly good-natured enough fashion. This further legitimised 50 Cent and made it clear that, whoever the hell he was, he was a man of potential. Simultaneously, as 50 Cent's star was gradually rising, Jeffrey 'Ja Rule' Atkins, another rapper from Queens, was flourishing. The two of them began to collide. The root cause of the collision was, in 50 Cent's eyes, a matter of coincidence and company.

In his 2006 autobiography, *From Pieces to Weight,* 50 Cent claims that the issues started when Ja Rule saw him in a club with a man who had robbed him (Ja Rule) at gunpoint while he was shooting a video in the Jamaica neighbourhood of Queens, where 50 Cent is from. The man who robbed Ja Rule happened to be a friend of 50 Cent.

It is not hard to see why Ja Rule would be annoyed or at least suspicious if he saw the person who robbed him merrily associating with Mr How to Rob. For his part, Ja Rule claims their issues stem from 50 Cent feeling shunned by Murder Inc., the crew and company Ja Rule was signed to (and aligned with).

Either way, it was clear they were not fans of each other. Their mutual disdain manifested itself in fights, stabbings,[5] diss tracks, memes, pranks and sabotage which still persist over twenty years later.

50 Cent's more serious problems, however, came after he

recorded a song called 'Ghetto Quran' – a song in which he touched on the stories of a good number of New York's most dedicated and feared criminals, many of whom he grew up admiring. Emulating the name-dropping formula of 'How To Rob', on 'Ghetto Quran' 50 Cent paid heartfelt homage to a slew of 1980s drug barons and gangsters, including Lorenzo 'Fat Cat' Nichols, Howard 'Pappy' Mason, Gus Rivera, James 'Bimmy' Antney, Ernesto 'Puerto Rican Righteous' Piniella, Chaz 'Slim' Williams (who at the time was 50 Cent's manager), Tyran 'Tah-Tah' Moore, James 'Wall' Corley, Thomas 'Tony Montana' Mickens, Alpo Martinez, Donald 'Duckie' Corley and Ronnie 'Bumps' Bassett. Notably, most of the people he paid homage to were from his native Queens and members of 1980s crack cocaine enterprise the Supreme Team. Included in 'Ghetto Quran's name drops were the leaders of the Supreme Team – Kenneth 'Supreme' McGriff and his nephew Gerald Prince Miller, a professional killer who is currently incarcerated without the possibility of parole.

Some of these drug barons had found their way into Hip-Hop and were affiliated with various rap crews. McGriff was himself affiliated with the aforementioned Murder Inc., home to Ja Rule.

With 'How To Rob', 50 Cent's market-entry strategy had proven effective. As he put it: 'There's a hundred artists on that label, you gotta separate yourself from that group and make yourself relevant.' And relevant he became. Though not a single, 'Ghetto Quran' and some of the diss tracks aimed at Ja Rule helped further heighten the buzz around 50 Cent in Hip-Hop circles, but they also had a more serious outcome.

On 24 May 2000, days before he was scheduled to shoot the video for his upcoming single 'Thug Love', a track featuring Destiny's Child aimed at making him a mainstream contender, he was gunned down. His attempt to penetrate the market had been interrupted by bullets penetrating his hand, arm, hip, both legs, chest and left cheek. He is very lucky he survived.

Rumour has it that 'Ghetto Quran' was part of the root cause of his shooting. 50 Cent's alleged shooter, Darryl 'Hommo' Baum, a close friend and occasional bodyguard of Mike Tyson, was then killed three weeks later.

As 50 Cent lay recovering from his near-death experience, Columbia, his record label, dropped him, literally and figuratively leaving him for dead. He was also blackballed from the record business.

Through the physiotherapy needed for his recovery, 50 Cent lost weight and developed a muscular physique. After recovering – and while still blackballed – he moved to Canada and got back in the studio.

Time to enter and introduce himself to the market for a second time. This time, leveraging the then underestimated promotional power of mixtapes, 50 Cent re-recorded lots of popular radio singles by other rappers and singers and made them in his own image, sound and brand. These mixtapes, often produced cheaply, burnt to CD and sold via street vendors, began to create a buzz around him all over again.

Mixtapes had long been a staple in Hip-Hop, but 50 Cent used them in a new way to make a comeback and rebuild an international audience from scratch, attain a competitive advantage over his rivals and secure a $1m record deal – while supposedly still blackballed.

The Mixtape: Pre-50 Cent	The Mixtape: Post-50 Cent
Principally a post-deal profile builder	Principally a pre-deal leverage builder
Builds a fanbase and customer base mostly for the hosting DJ	Builds a fanbase and customer base for the rapper
Compilation of artists	Single-artist focused
Distinctly different from an album – all songs are mixed into each other	Often an album in anything but name – songs tend to stand alone as per a conventional album

The Mixtape: Pre-50 Cent	The Mixtape: Post-50 Cent
Leaked copyrighted material	Remakes of copyrighted material
Frowned on by record labels	Worshipped by record labels
Contains material unlikely to be played on the radio	Contains material that is both likely and unlikely to be played on the radio
Poor production values	High production values
Usually free	Usually for sale
Flooded with shoutouts and insults to drug dealers, gangsters and other rappers	Flooded with shoutouts and insults to drug dealers, gangsters and other rappers

Table 2: The mixtape pre- and post-50 Cent

At this point, 50 Cent's main enemies, Murder Inc., were the toast of the music business – hit after hit after hit. With songs like 'Always On Time', 'Living It Up', 'Mesmerise', 'Down Ass Bitch' and 'Put It On Me', they were making the soundtracks to young people's lives across the world. But the hits also presented a weakness: despite their name, Murder Inc. had essentially become a pop music crew. As a result, they were very vulnerable to someone with indisputable street credibility, complete with the marketing dynamite of surviving an attempted murder – aka 50 Cent.

Still, even with all of the new buzz, 50 Cent was still black-balled, so the establishment New York labels remained closed doors.

However, the buzz he'd created on the mixtape circuit was deafening. He could no longer be ignored. In the latter days of 2002, Dr. Dre and Eminem (from Los Angeles and Detroit respectively) ignored the blackball and signed him jointly to Dre's Aftermath label and Eminem's Shady Records (both distributed by Interscope). Months later, 50 Cent released his first major-label single, 'In Da Club', and before you knew it, he was a global superstar. As you would expect, 50 Cent – an aggressive and highly competitive man – did everything in his power to destroy Ja Rule and Murder Inc., which further solidified his brand and presence in the market.[6]

As with all elements of business, there was a degree of luck involved in 50 Cent's entrance into the marketplace that is Hip-Hop. But by refusing to give up and refusing to accept defeat, or even death, he created his own luck. He turned tragedy into triumph and, in the process, circumvented the usual requirement to spend a fortune in order to create an awareness for a product or service. Instead, he did it by demanding everyone's attention in a quirky and then a very nearly deadly way.

Business Lessons from 50 Cent's Market Entry

1. **Awareness.** Before the phrases 'clout' and 'attention economy' proliferated in the business world, 50 Cent was a master of the attention economy and clout-seeking. He developed and maintained a clear strategy to cut through all of the noise. In doing so, he made it clear who he was, what he had to offer, what his unique selling points were and what to expect from him going forward.

2. **Customer base.** In an era before the internet was as integral to daily life as it is today and the traditional routes to building a customer base were also cut off, innovation was 50 Cent's salvation. Reinventing and upgrading the mixtape was a stroke of strategic genius. It meant that he didn't have to over-worry about copyright issues (it was still promotional), formal retail or the industry collusion against him, and it made him more popular with taste-making DJs. He successfully built his audience and the leverage that would all but guarantee that he was eventually offered a lucrative deal.

3. **Networking, partnerships and alliances.** The leverage 50 Cent built on the mixtape circuit should have granted him the opportunity to pick and choose whichever partners he wanted. As he was still curtailed by the blacklist, his options were limited. This forced him to:

  - **View global as local.** With New York doors shut, 50 Cent ended up building an alliance with significantly stronger partners further afield in Eminem and Dr. Dre, and became part of a dream team.[7] Steel sharpens steel. And sharpened steel facilitates the steal.

  - **Make the publicists' and journalists' job easy.** No one goes into journalism or PR to work hard. Any market-entry strategy must be siesta-lover friendly. The nature of the partners 50 Cent picked and the dream team they formed made every journalist in the know salivate. Attracting publicity could not have been easier.

4. **Competitive advantage**. With one signature, 50 Cent went from blackballed victim of attempted murder to global superstar in the making. His competitors didn't stand a chance. He knew it, and they (Murder Inc. and others) more than likely knew it too. As the saying goes, it ain't no fun when the rabbit's got the gun. When you have the upper hand, it is smart business to ensure you futureproof your advantage by conclusively taking out the competition. Doing so restricts them from regrouping, relocking and reloading (hopefully not literally).

5. **Adversity during market entry.** In the middle of introducing a product into a market or establishing a presence in a new field, disaster may strike. 50 Cent also exemplified how to perfectly turn adversity and disaster during the market-entry process into an enhanced market entry. He did this by:

- Staying true to the vision and sticking to a clearly defined strategy – even when he lay in a hospital bed riddled with bullets and abandoned by his partners. It should be noted that in dropping 50 Cent, Columbia Records panic-abandoned a lucrative asset at the first sight of a distress and when their asset needed them the most.

- Swiftly adapting and adjusting to new realities. For example, moving to Canada to focus, get healthy, stay safe and beat the blackball.

- Accepting that even near-fatal publicity can be trans-formed into 'good' publicity and therefore fuel market entry.

- Innovating in the face of adversity. 50 Cent's use of mixtapes to beat the blackball and rebuild a buzz was a stroke of genius.

- Quite literally embracing the notion that what doesn't kill you makes you stronger.

- Embracing the disgrace and cuddling the controversy. 50 Cent didn't allow his adversaries and adversities to define him negatively; he used them as lessons (for himself and others) and as a stepping stone to get where he needed to be.

DRAKE: STARTING FROM THE BOTTOM

Former child stars often struggle to break out of the time capsule they're in and get taken seriously as adults. New York street rapper Jim Jones, for example, turned down the chance to sign Drake as he didn't know what to do with a former child actor best known for playing a wheelchair-bound character 'on, like, uh, what is it, Disney Channel?' (*Degrassi*, the show Drake starred in, was not broadcast on the Disney Channel].[8] Drake didn't just beat the odds of being a former child actor who made it in Hip-Hop, he has enjoyed one of the longest runs at the boundary-pushing pinnacle of the culture. Below, we explore his market-entry strategy.

Creating an awareness of your presence in the market

In 2006, Drake took his first steps along the path 50 Cent had laid by releasing appetite-whetting mixtapes. His first, *Room For Improvement*, sold 6,000 copies, netting him life-changing royalties of $300.

Outcome: In this step, Drake established himself as a blip on Hip-Hop's radar.

The beginning of the establishment of a customer base

His second mixtape, *Comeback Season*, featured songs with the highly respected rap group Little Brother and R'n'B superstar-in-the-making Trey Songz. Intentionally or not, this helped signal that he was serious about his craft. The buzz was building.

Outcome: Drake developed grassroots credibility and built up leverage, a customer base and a reputation. He also shed any limitations permeating from previous brand and career associations.

Building alliances, partnerships, joint ventures or co-operative agreements

Comeback Season helped Drake grab the attention of Jas Prince, second-generation Hip-Hop royalty (he is the son of Houston Hip-Hop mogul J Prince, a man whose name is synonymous with respect). Jas Prince convinced Lil Wayne, then a smoking-hot superstar in the middle of his own resurgence, that Drake was worth the time of day. Lil Wayne eventually saw the light, took Drake on his 2008–09 I Am Music Tour (otherwise known as Tha Carter III Tour), mentored him and made music with him.

Outcome: Drake developed the partnerships necessary to help him explode.

Establishing a competitive advantage

Alliances beget alliances. Money attracts money. With everything in place, Drake robustly penetrated the market with his third mixtape, *So Far Gone* (2009).

So Far Gone was the most immaculately produced mixtape of the era and boasted features from Lil Wayne, Bun B, Omarion, Lloyd and Trey Songz. It was universally well received and helped establish Drake as an international superstar, propelling him to the pinnacle of Hip-Hop's elite.

Outcome: Drake robustly entered the market and immediately established himself as a serious contender.

Potentially disrupting the prevailing order of the market?

In a 2020 SelectCon conversation between the Hip-Hop and advertising supremo Steve Stoute (a man who has successfully navigated every side of the business of Hip-Hop) and the popular independent rapper Russ, both argued that Drake becoming an independent artist would pose an existential threat to the record business as it stands. Their reasoning is part hundredth-monkey effect, part raw accounting and commerce.

'If Drake posts a picture on the 'Gram [Instagram] of his new album, link in bio – fuck a link in bio, "new album out" – and he was fully independent, Drake will make $10 million a week for fucking sixty weeks,' opined Russ.

To wit, Stoute responded: 'I said this before, Drake is about to come out in the next six months, Drake is about to get the biggest bag in the history of the music business by far. Both A and B [the record labels], they don't want that to happen. Because the day that happens, they might as well close the business down.'

In 2022, Drake re-signed with Universal for a reported half a billion dollars.[9]

Strategic insight: The true extent of Drake's powers is yet to be revealed.

AN UNORTHODOX MARKET ENTRY

We'll end Section 1 where we began it – with Suge Knight. The exploitation of Black artists is a staple ingredient in the success of the music industry. From cultural appropriation through to stolen credits to outright legalised robbery, as far back as anyone can remember in the music business (including Hip-Hop), Black artists have been mercilessly pillaged. Robert 'Vanilla Ice' Van Winkle, a white pop rapper, allegedly attempted to carry on this tradition, and Suge Knight made his entry into the market by bringing this tradition to a pause.

The allegation was that Vanilla Ice's 1990 hit record 'Ice Ice Baby' (the first rap single to go number one on the *Billboard* Hot 100) was written by a rapper called Mario 'Chocolate' Johnson. Vanilla Ice, then at the top of the world, didn't credit or pay Johnson and didn't return his calls. Johnson turned to an up-and-coming music industry 'problem solver' who needed to make his presence in the market known: Suge Knight. Some form of representation arrangement was made between the two men.

In 1990, Vanilla Ice was the opposite of ice cold – he was as hot as Cecil Rhodes' corner of hell. 'Ice Ice Baby' was a money gun and had blown him up into one of the biggest stars in the world, complete with a huge security entourage.

This did not deter Suge in the slightest. He recruited several members of the feared Piru Blood gang from his native Compton,*

---

* Gang warfare trivia: the Pirus are a sub-set of the Bloods; their rivals are the Crips. Piru is actually the word 'Crip' spelt backwards with the C on its back.

and worked to persistently secure information on Vanilla Ice's location whenever he was in Los Angeles. According to Vanilla Ice, whenever he was in LA, Suge would show up, overpower his security detail, sit directly face to face with him and simply ask: 'How are you doing?'

Urban folklore has it that Vanilla Ice returned to his hotel room one evening and found Suge Knight waiting for him. Suge took the already petrified Vanilla Ice to the balcony and, according to the various stories told by Vanilla Ice himself, either:

- Dangled him over the balcony by his ankles
- Told him to look over the balcony
- Severely intimidated him
- Spoke to him in a manner that was firm on the message and menacingly friendly in delivery

When asked about the incident in an interview, Suge simply smirked and said: 'Yeah, I hung out with Vanilla Ice.'

Whatever happened, Vanilla Ice said he 'had to wear a diaper that day' and agreed to settle 'out of balcony'. He paid Mario 'Chocolate' Johnson the best part of $4m. He would later sarcastically recall that he was an 'investor in Death Row Records who never got a return on his money'.[10] In the process, he became the reverse of many a Black artist in relation to many a white record label.

With a satisfied customer under his belt, Suge Knight was now in the business as a guy who knew how to solve problems. And he was on the hunt for other clients.

Market Entry & Introduction Lessons from Suge Knight

1. **Creating an awareness of your presence in the market.** As seen earlier, through his work with Bobby Brown, Suge had created an awareness of his presence in the market. He created a very literal awareness of his presence by showing up whenever Vanilla Ice was in town.

2. **The beginning of the establishment of a customer base.** Mario 'Chocolate' Johnson was Suge Knight's first real customer. And successfully delivering a multi-million-dollar settlement for someone as little known as Chocolate proved Suge's worth.

3. **Building alliances, partnerships, joint ventures or co-operative agreements.** What Suge had was brains and connections; what he needed was muscle men who could scare and intimidate. By recruiting Piru gang members, Suge aligned himself with the perfect people to establish his brand of firm and conclusive problem-solving.

4. **Establishing a competitive advantage.** Following his work with Mario 'Chocolate' Johnson, Suge became the go-to man for disgruntled, undervalued or unpaid artists. He would go on to land an absolute whale in Dr. Dre. From there, he built an unrivalled empire of his own.

SECTION 2

BREAKING OUT

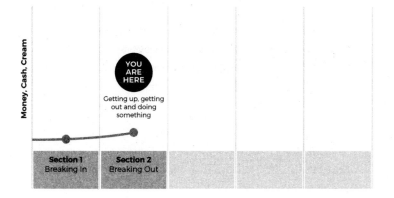

Money, Cash, Cream

YOU ARE HERE

Getting up, getting out and doing something

Section 1
Breaking In

Section 2
Breaking Out

5.

REPUTATION AND BRAND

In Section 1, we looked at how Hip-Hop's moguls broke into the business and established a name for themselves. The logical next step is to parlay that name into a reputation and ultimately a brand, both of which can be commodified or at least monetised in the long term.

It goes without saying, reputations can be good or bad. 'A good name,' says the good book (Proverbs 22:1), 'is more desirable than great riches; to be esteemed is better than silver or gold.' And that is what a reputation is.

Reputation, by its formal definition, is 'a widely held opinion of a social entity (a person, a social group, an organisation, or a place) that is typically a result of social evaluation on a set of criteria, such as behaviour or performance'.[1] The Notorious BIG explained in 'What's Beef?' that his sullied reputation made his name 'taste like ass'; he is not believed to have meant that in a nice way. And, as Benjamin Franklin explained, 'it takes many good deeds to build a good reputation, and only one bad one to lose it'.

On 'Name Of The Game', a record by the respected Hip-Hop duo Hi Tek and Talib Kweli (collectively known as Reflection Eternal), Kweli laid down how good reputations are built: 'Persistence, dedication / Consistent, motivation, resistance to stagnation'.

The key thing that Hip-Hop's top-tier moguls have in common

is that they all followed Kweli's formula. For the most part, Hip-Hop's moguls all fall into one of the following categories:

- They made and performed music people loved
- They managed the musicians who made music people loved
- They marketed and promoted music people loved
- They protected (or extorted), solved (or created) problems for any of the above

The reputations of these musicians, managers, marketeers and muscle manoeuvrers were not built on thin air. They all had to make solid and substantial contributions to the commercial and cultural realm of the music. Below, we explore how a series of key figures in Hip-Hop built their reputations.

PHARRELL WILLIAMS: BEATS, RHYMES AND ETERNAL YOUTH

Pharrell Williams – a softly spoken, thoughtful man with a seeming inability to age – made his name through persistence and dedication, leveraging the musical talents he had developed as a child. While in the seventh grade, Pharrell met Chad Hugo in a music class at Princess Anne High School, one of the very best schools in the Virginia Beach area of Virginia. Pharrell and Chad cultivated their partnership, making music and writing songs at Chad's parents' house. In 1992, consistency, dedication and persistence met opportunity for the duo: they were spotted at a local talent show by a man with the Midas touch and the music industry at his feet: the iconic new jack swing and R'n'B producer, Teddy Riley.

Teddy Riley was one of the primary architects of popular music from the late 1980s through to the early noughties. He produced monster classics such as 'I Want Her' for Keith Sweat, 'My Prerogative' by Bobby Brown, 'Remember The Time' by Michael Jackson, 'No Diggity' by Blackstreet (a group he was one fourth of as well as the producer) and all of Guy's music (including the TikTok favourite 'I Like'). Pharrell and Chad had struck gold – getting to learn from Teddy Riley at such a young age was the equivalent of trying to break into car engineering and then getting Henry Ford I, Elon Musk or, hopefully, someone great with cars who doesn't have alarmingly unsavory views, to bring you under their tutelage. Musk to bring you under his tutelage. They named their duo the Neptunes and never looked back.

The duo hit the ground running by writing and producing songs for artists closely associated with Riley, under his supervision. While still in high school, Pharrell and Chad wrote Riley's verse on the 1992 saxophone- and sex-drenched new jack swing anthem 'Rump Shaker' by Wreckx-N-Effects (a Riley-affiliated duo). The first time anyone heard Pharrell's voice on a song was on SWV's Riley-produced debut single 'Right Here', where he performed the punchy 'S . . . Double . . . U . . . V!' chant.

In the heyday of Puff Daddy's Bad Boy Records, the Neptunes helped extend that label's period of dominance by producing the third and final single of Mase's five-times platinum debut album *Harlem World* (1997) – the rather alternative 'Looking At Me'.

But it was the Neptunes' next major production that really solidified them as star producers in the business with their own distinct sound. Performing under the name Noreaga, Victor 'N.O.R.E.' Santiago Jr.'s 'Superthug' (1998) put the Neptunes firmly on the map. The sound was refreshingly original; the energy it created combined an adrenaline rush with mellow harmonising by Pharrell and Tammy Lucas – marking a potent mixture of rugged and smooth that became the Neptunes' signature sound. The chorus for 'Superthug' may be one of the most deliciously simple yet violent pieces of music ever made: the word 'what' repeated seven times with defiance, rhythm and violence.*

---

* I personally witnessed someone get accidentally knocked out by a woman throwing air punches in time to the song's opening.

Following their success with N.O.R.E., other rappers soon came knocking. Their good reputation was paying off. They produced hits for Mystikal, Wu Tang's Ol' Dirty Bastard and the Jamaican dancehall legend Beenie Man. They also introduced Kelis to the world – by writing and producing her entire debut album.

And then came Mr Jay-Z, a man who always makes everything bigger and greater. The Neptunes and Jay-Z's first collaboration birthed 'I Just Wanna Love U (Give It 2 Me)'. From there the hits just kept rolling in. The sound of the Neptunes was infectious and quickly spread across genres, the charts and the world. They broke other new artists, such as The Clipse; they helped rebirth Justin Timberlake from a teenybopper to a grown and sexy R'n'B star; and they delivered hits for many others – Nelly, N*SYNC, Babyface, Ludacris, Ray J, Foxy Brown, Britney Spears, Janet Jackson, Busta Rhymes, Fabolous, Usher, 702, Beyoncé, Toni Braxton, Common, Snoop Dogg, LL Cool J, Lupe Fiasco, Gwen Stefani, Twista, Monica and more. They ended 2009 with a *Billboard* recognition as the top producers of the decade.

Just when it felt like things were about to dry up for the Neptunes, Pharrell, who was always at the forefront of the duo, went solo and became bigger than ever. He collaborated with the French electronic duo Daft Punk to deliver the summer 2013 anthems 'Get Lucky' and 'Lose Yourself To Dance'. His next solo single, 'Happy', an up-tempo, feel-good record proved universally appealing, and is arguably the crowning achievement of his career to date.

On the foundation of great, versatile and shape-shifting music (including N*E*R*D, a Hip-Hop and alternative rock side group consisting of Pharell, Chad and Shay Haley), Pharrell was able to build his reputation as a business, a mogul and a legend. His rise might look meteoric, but he'd been building his reputation for well over a decade before he and Chad Hugo emerged from 'nowhere'.

STEVE STOUTE: THE BRIDGE

What sort of mind conceives of and then convinces a blue-chip multinational corporation (McDonald's) to bet their name, brand and market value on a rapper (Pusha T) who raps almost exclusively about selling crack cocaine to pen their new advertising campaign? What sort of mind conceives of and then convinces a major sports clothing company (Reebok) to do a shoe deal with a non-athlete (Jay-Z)? The answer is simple: the sort of mind Steve Stoute possesses.

Steve Stoute is probably best described as the bridge between corporate America and Hip-Hop. He is seen in Hip-Hop as corporate America's man and seen in corporate America as the guy who really understands Hip-Hop and how to leverage it to create value. In reality, he effortlessly straddles both and helps connect the two worlds. Or perhaps he could be better described as a translator.

After flirting with the idea of becoming a mortgage broker, Stoute's career in Hip-Hop started through a friendship with Mark 'DJ Wiz' Eastmond, DJ for the legendary 1980s rapping, dancing and acting duo, Kid 'n' Play. Stoute's initial role in the industry was the humblest possible: carrying records for DJs. A task so simple it has now been fully digitised and largely automated.[*]

Stoute recalled in his book *The Tanning of America* how he was a young Hip-Hop fan eager to learn more about how the business worked, but Wiz saw more than that in him.[2] Wiz saw creative and executive leadership potential in Stoute that Stoute couldn't at that point see in himself. He proved himself and became a trusted source of advice, insight and instincts. He quickly moved

---

[*] For the benefit of the young: in the days before iPods, iPads and iPhones, DJs had to carry actual physical records to shows and performances. And they were heavy.

up from Kid 'n' Play's roadie to road manager to manager. Stoute ended up with an immense understanding of the inner workings of music, TV and film production.

Stoute may not have known what DJ Wiz saw in him, but Chris 'Kid' Reid of Kid 'n' Play saw it too:

'[Stoute] is built for this industry, this cut-throat type industry. He is perfect for that. He is a shark. And I am not a shark . . . I'm a tuna. And that is not how you win; you win by being Steve Stoute-ish'.[3]

This shark-like determination has occasionally placed Stoute at odds with other Hip-Hop luminaries. In 1999, Puff Daddy (and his crew) famously attacked him with baseball bats and champagne bottles for refusing to remove a clip of a crucified Puff Daddy from a rap video.[4] The rapper Cormega claimed that his refusal to agree to the management terms offered to him by Stoute led to him being thrown out of Hip-Hop supergroup The Firm (a group Stoute conceived of to improve the commercial prospects of the constituent rappers) and a stalling of his career.

But Steve Stoute isn't just a shark-like vessel of aggression and ruthlessness; he is a true Hip-Hop business visionary. He sees (and helps realise) potential where others see pitfalls. An example of his magnitude as a marketing and business visionary? Nas.

Russell Simmons, the godfather of the Hip-Hop business and founder of Def Jam, scoffed at the idea of signing Nas, dismissing him as a Kool G Rap soundalike, 'and G Rap ain't selling no records'.[5]

Where Russell Simmons saw a cheap replica of a highly respected but commercially underwhelming 1980s rapper, Steve Stoute saw a more lyrically advanced, charismatic and marketable prospect altogether. He saw a diamond in the rough and decided to cut and polish it.

After Nas's iconic debut album *Illmatic* was released to the best critical reception in the history of Hip-Hop, but mediocre sales, Stoute made his way to Queensbridge projects (a place Nas has helped make something of a Hip-Hop tourist attraction) and asked to manage him. Within eighteen swift months of being managed by Steve Stoute, Nas went from a critically acclaimed but badly selling rapper to a critically acclaimed and multi-platinum selling rapper. Indeed, *It Was Written,* Nas's sophomore album – a career-ending pitfall for many a rapper – became his bestselling record. Stoute helped Nas strike that fine balance between commercially viable records, records that appeal to the core audience and a presentation that would broaden his audience. Without his union with Stoute and the business vision that came with it, there is a great chance Nas would have enjoyed the type of career Kool G Rap has enjoyed: high on respect, low on sales.

With his teeth firmly cut managing Kid 'N' Play, Nas and others, Stoute transitioned from manager to record executive – meaning he went from looking after the interest of the artists and protecting them from the excesses of the label to looking after the interests of the label. After that, Stoute broke into advertising, where he established the appropriately named agency Translation (a company that 'provides strategic, creative, and contextual rigor for brands to thrive by leading, not following, contemporary culture'). He is now working on a company that may disrupt or evolve the prevailing business model of the music industry – United Masters.[6]

Stoute's ideas, foresight and instincts for positioning, promotion and product development, as well as his sheer hard work, helped him cultivate a reputation that would help Hip-Hop develop much closer ties to the corporate world. He brokered deals between Hip-Hop artists and corporations that were once inconceivable. Along the way, he helped guide the careers of Mary J. Blige, Will Smith, 50 Cent, producers The Trackmasters and more.

JIMMY HENCHMAN: MY NAME IS MY NAME

What do the following have in common?

- Academi, the private military company;
- Accenture, the multinational professional services corporation; and
- James Rosemond, the Hip-Hop executive.

Answer: precious little other than the fact that they all had to change their names in a bid to save their continued business operations from their soiled reputations.

Academi changed their name from Blackwater following an endless stream of scandals emanating from their involvement in the Iraq War. Accenture was once known as Andersen Consulting, the business and consultancy arm of the now defunct scandal-plagued accountancy firm Arthur Andersen. And James Rosemond, principally known by his street name Jimmy Henchman, was known as 'Hip-Hop's ubervillain'.

In the same way Steve Stoute acted as the bridge between the corporate world and Hip-Hop, Jimmy Henchmen was often the bridge between Hip-Hop and the criminal underworld (a milieu many a rapper claims to represent). The art is from the street, so it follows that you need people who understand and are respected in the street to help navigate and maintain it – Henchman specialised in this.

As far as earning and managing reputations are concerned, Henchman presents a unique case study, as he had not one but two well-earned reputations.

First, as a hugely successful, highly respected, super-savvy and powerful entertainment executive. A reputation he earned by managing the likes of The Game (originally to the disgust and distress of his label heads, Dr. Dre and Jimmy Iovine), Sean Kingston, Akon, Wyclef Jean, Brandy, Gucci Mane, Salt-n-Pepa, Groove Theory and more.

Second, as a triple-A-rated gangster who specialised in extortion, robbery and drug distribution. A reputation solidified by allegedly orchestrating the life- and career-altering 1994 shooting of Tupac Shakur and the 2005 shooting of Suge Knight at Kanye West's VMA party. The famed Hip-Hop photographer Johnny Nunez was allegedly positioned by Henchman to get the perfect picture of Suge Knight getting shot at the bar during the latter incident. Once Suge blew a circle of cigar smoke in his face, Henchman supposedly signalled for the shooter and the photographer to get to work, and a split second later there was a 'BOOM!' followed by 'snap snap snap'.

The Tupac allegation did the most to shape Henchman's reputation. On 'Against All Odds', the eery final track on the first of his many posthumous albums, *The Don Killuminati: The 7 Day Theory*, Tupac – from the grave – scornfully accused Henchman of orchestrating his shooting. Being accused of attempted murder by one of the most popular and celebrated people to ever walk the earth is not going to shower stardust on your reputation. Despite his sullied reputation and criminality-peppered past, Henchman still yearned for what many a 'former' gangster craved: a legitimate job. Speaking in a prison interview on the Michael K. Williams fronted *Unjust Justice* podcast, he explained: 'My dream was always to become corporate. To have a travel and expense account. To be on the board of something instead of just a consultant.'[7]

In 2007, his dream nearly came true when he got the tap on the shoulder to head up the rap division of Virgin Records. Speaking, again, on the *Unjust Justice* podcast, he explained:

A guy like me, who comes from the projects of Brooklyn, is being offered to run the rap department of Virgin Records. But the first thing when I go in for the meeting for the job – the execs look at me and say, 'This Jimmy Henchman name, oh my god.' I am in the building and there's whispers all over the place . . .

Needless to say, he didn't get the job. His reputation screwed him. In a bid to salvage his reputation, the man born James Rosemond decided Jimmy Henchman had to go:

> I had to put out a press release stating: 'That is not my name, do not call me that any more.' Cos I didn't like the connotations that came with it. It was hindering me from becoming who I wanted to become.

Jimmy Henchmen was dead. James Rosemond was reborn. Taking matters into his own hands, Rosemond then decided to do a full profile interview with *Vibe* magazine to put the Tupac allegations in particular to bed. This proved disastrous. The opposite happened.

Far from cleaning up his reputation, it made matters worse. The article labelled him as the music industry's 'ubervillain', linked him to various criminal cases, coloured him as a shadowy underworld figure and all but ensured he'd forever be who he had been in the past.

Or maybe Jimmy Henchman *was* just who James Rosemond really was? The federal government certainly believed so. In 2010, Rosemond was arrested on charges of cocaine trafficking, money laundering and witness tampering. In 2012, he was found guilty and sentenced to life in prison for drug trafficking, obstruction of justice, firearms violations and other financial crimes associated with his position as head of a multimillion-dollar transnational cocaine-selling organisation. Upon sentencing, Loretta E. Lynch, the then United States Attorney for the Eastern District of New York, offered her opinion on Rosemond:

> Rosemond styled himself a hip-hop mogul, bringing the music of the streets to a wider audience and expanding opportunities of artists. In reality, his image as a music impresario was a cover for the real Jimmy Rosemond – a thug in a suit who flooded those

same streets with cocaine, and shuttled drugs and money from coast to coast. Today's life sentence is a fitting end to the Henchman's two-faced machinations.

In 2015, Rosemond faced an entirely separate trial, conviction and life sentence (plus twenty years) in a murder-for-hire case related to a rap rivalry between The Game and 50 Cent's G Unit crew.[8] A member of G Unit and an affiliate (Lowell 'Lodi Mack' Fletcher) assaulted Rosemond's then fourteen-year-old son James Rosemond Jr (today the manager of the hugely popular rapper Ice Spice), and Rosemond Sr responded by having Fletcher murdered.

Where James Rosemond, the Hip-Hop executive with corporate yearnings, started and Jimmy Henchman, the 'thug in a suit', ended is anyone's guess.

Reputation Management Lessons from Jimmy Henchmen/James Rosemond

1. Choose any pseudonym/business name carefully — it may be used against you.

2. Your reputation is your future — it literally precedes you.

3. Journalists (like the police) are not your friends.

4. Don't call a journalist when what you really need is a public relations officer.

5. What happens in darkness will destroy your good name when it eventually comes to light.

HOW TO TURN YOUR REPUTATION INTO A BRAND

A brand is an identity for a product or service that distinguishes it from the competition. It is a name, term, design, symbol, quirk or any other feature that comes to define the identity of a person, brand or business. In modern business, brand identities are often spoken of in a manner similar to human personality traits: Nike is 'really cool', Mercedes is 'proper bougie', Apple is 'slick', Wu Tang Clan 'ain't nuthing ta fuck wit'.

A brand adds value to a company and/or the products and services it provides, and could eventually be worth more than the company itself. For example, based largely on the strength of their iconic brand, Wu Tang were able to sell the only copy of their unheard 2015 album *Once Upon A Time In Shaolin* for $2m – making it the single most expensive piece of music in history.[9] It sold again as a non-fungible token (or NFT, meaning a digital token or identifier denoting ownership and authenticity) in 2021 for $4m. By comparison, their 2017 follow-up, *The Saga Continues*, didn't generate anywhere near the money or buzz generated by *Once Upon A Time In Shaolin*, an album that remains unheard by all but a handful of people on the planet.

With their follow-up compilation album, they were no longer able to attract current top-tier talent, elite performance spots, lucrative advances, major record deals, expensively produced videos, etc. Had they had a strong reputation for great music but a poor brand (like practically anyone you love and respect in underground Hip-Hop) they probably would have struggled to sell *Once Upon A Time In Shaolin* for such a lofty price, and the rest of their music would have hung around on the shelf too. What *Once Upon A Time In Shaolin* makes clear is that the Wu Tang brand remained strong and valuable, even as interest in their core offering, their actual music, waned. James Lindsay, founder and CEO of Rap Snacks, and former manager of Meek Mill, helped prepare a young Meek Mill for where Wu Tang is now with the following advice: 'Your career will not last for ever; your brand, if managed well, might.'

BRAND VS REPUTATION

Brand and reputation are like lemon and lime. Or rappers and R'n'B singers. They complement each other to such an extent that they are often mistaken for each other and often used interchangeably. It is essential that the difference between the two be properly understood.

Brand	Reputation
How the customer perceives the quality of a product or service	How all stakeholders (employees, rivals, investors, regulators, etc) perceive a company, entity or person
Creates credibility	Creates relevance
Can be purchased through, say, advertising spend	Must be earned through persistent delivery of good or bad results
Establishes competitive uniqueness	Establishes competitive legitimacy
Most closely related to awareness	Most closely related to performance
Results of a promise of quality made	Results of a promise of quality kept
A strong brand does not equate to a good reputation	A strong reputation does not equate to a good brand

Table 3: Brand vs Reputation

A good reputation is the basis for a good brand. A good brand, however, can mask the constituent features of a bad reputation or bad practice in general – but only for so long. Without the delivery of great performance, firmly kept promises and good service, a brand will eventually ring hollow. As will any goodwill or financial cache associated with it. At that moment, the brand becomes valueless – possibly going from an asset to a liability.

Suge Knight, for example, founded one of Hip-Hop's most

iconic brands – Death Row Records. At the label's helm in the early to mid-1990s, Suge Knight developed a reputation as a great music executive – delivering hit after hit after hit to the tune of hundreds of millions of dollars. Yet he also developed a reputation for using violence as a means of getting his way. Following the 'if it bleeds, it leads' mantra to its logical conclusion, Suge's more shocking and violent behaviour became his brand. After a while, his reputation as a music executive was eclipsed by his brand as a deeply fearsome and often violent man who happened to be a music executive. Logically, his brand as a violent man decimated his reputation as a gifted music executive.

Suge Knight eventually leaned into his brand's notoriety and attempted to use it to break into reality TV. In March 2008, a trailer for a Suge Knight reality show called *Unfinished Business* emerged. The premise for the show appeared to be Suge attempting to rebuild his music empire. Suge is depicted vetting artists (sometimes laughing in their faces as they try and prove how tough and similar to him they are), humble-bragging about 'hanging out' with Vanilla Ice (see p. 74) and, as you would expect, there are various moments of violent commotion. Even though it looked rather blood-rushing and interesting, *Unfinished Business* either failed to get picked up or failed to air. It's not clear why, but one can only speculate on how much insuring such a production would cost, given Suge Knight's brand.

Interestingly, one of the most enduring and best monetised brands in Hip-Hop remains the house that Suge Knight built, Death Row Records. T-shirts, hoodies, films, TV shows, jewellery – even red wine – are all sold off the back of the Death Row brand and its menacing logo: a man in chains with a bag over his head strapped into an electric chair. Following a 2022 purchase, the Death Row brand is now owned by Death Row's once marque artist, Snoop Dogg (who himself happens to be one of the best-managed brands in Hip-Hop).

THE HIP-HOP BRANDING ONION

A branding onion is a simple mechanism used to define and provide a 'layered' holistic overview of a brand identity in order to maximise the profits of the brand as well as perpetuate and protect it. Each layer of the branding onion observes a different part of the brand identity, what complements it and what corrodes it.

Branding in Hip-Hop (and many other industries) can be broken down into three layers.

1. The Core: the main commercial activities that constitute the brand of the rapper or organisation. It is the main identity and activity of the rapper's brand (and their crew or label). For rappers, regardless of how far their business empire extends, the core is of course the music, around which everything else revolves.
2. The Complement: every commercial, charitable or even personal activity or interest that stands to enhance, complete or improve a rapper's core activities.
3. The Corrosion: any activity or business interest that contradicts (and therefore corrodes) the core activity of the rapper and would damage the rapper's brand.

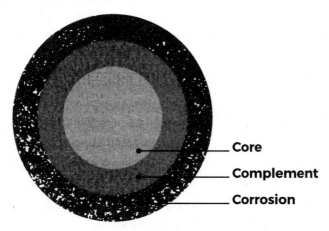

Core

Complement

Corrosion

Figure 3: The branding onion

N.O.R.E. and Lyor Cohen

In several interviews, N.O.R.E., a hardcore street rapper from Queens, tells a story about being scolded by then Def Jam CEO Lyor Cohen for attempting to make Ja Rule-like radio-friendly 'popcorn' music. Cohen's fear was that N.O.R.E. (his asset) was washing his brand down a very predictable drain by deviating too far towards things that would damage it. According to N.O.R.E., an interesting conversation ensued between the two men in a recording studio, one that was submerged in brilliant managerial metaphor and spoke to the core of branding.[10]

Cohen: Nore, if I cut you right now, what would you bleed?

N.O.R.E.: I would bleed blood.

Cohen: OK. Ask me the same question.

N.O.R.E.: Lyor, if I cut you right now, what would you bleed?

Cohen: 'Sucker MCs' by Run DMC [a pioneering and massively influential song by the group Cohen cut his teeth in the music business with, when he managed them in the mid-1980s].

[Silence]

Cohen: So, I am going to ask you again: if I cut you right now, what would you bleed?

N.O.R.E.: 'Superthug'. [Nore's Pharrell Williams-produced breakout hit]

Cohen: Exactly, Pharrell is in Virginia waiting for you, the car service is downstairs – GO!

N.O.R.E. promptly made his way to the session with Pharrell Williams and made 'Nothin'', the biggest hit of his career.

Core

Hardcore punch-you-in-the-mouth street Hip-Hop – which somehow fills the dance floor. Making songs and telling stories about his life in the street, his father (a boxer), his family and being Latino.

Complement

Finding a second career in reggaeton with hits such as 'Oye Mi Canto' and 'Mas Maiz'. Launching Drink Champs, a one-of-a-kind drunken podcast in which Hip-Hop legends are interviewed and given their just dues. Roles in movies that are dear to street life – such as *Paid in Full*. Giving Pharrell Williams his break.

Corrosion

Attempting to make Ja Rule-like radio-friendly 'popcorn' music.

Figure 4: N.O.R.E.'s branding onion

More critically, Cohen taught N.O.R.E. a strong lesson in understanding and standing by your core. In asking N.O.R.E. 'What would you bleed if I cut you?', he forced him to return to his essence – to what made him a success and what made his brand appealing.

Intangibly, a rapper's core is what they stand for (i.e. their reputation), the stories they tell, the demeanour they give off, the aura surrounding them. And it is the same for pretty much any professional or business.

Once a core is established to an audience, client or customer base, it will prove very difficult and risky to move away from it – as that is the basis of everything they come to you for. However, it does not mean that you cannot complement it, which is exactly what N.O.R.E. did, as shown in Figure 4.

Jay-Z

It became clear in the late 1990s that establishing clothing brands complemented a rapper's music career. Doing so helped push their brand further by turning their legions of fans into brand ambassadors (who were happy to pay for this privilege) as well as broadening their fan bases. It was good for the bottom line. Starring in movies and TV shows that are aligned with a rapper's core identity also complements their brand.

Where Hip-Hop diverges from the rest of society is in the fact that 'street credibility' complements the brand of many a rapper, whereas it would ruin the brand of most other professionals.

Case in point: on 30 November 1999 (just days before his thirtieth birthday), Jay-Z went to Q Tip's album release party at the Kit Kat Club in Times Square and stabbed fellow former drug dealer turned record executive Lance 'Un' Rivera for bootlegging his album an entire month before it was scheduled to be released. He was arrested, charged and faced fifteen years in prison if convicted.

Core
Grown-man Hip-Hop. Rapping about his life experiences as a drug dealer who happened to be a talented rapper. And then rapping about being a successful and politically connected businessman and family man.

Complement
Clothing line, sports agency, basketball team, vodka line, champagne brand, record label, starting a luxury wine bar and club, stabbing a bootlegger, texting with Obama, marrying Beyoncé.

Corrosion
Working with the NFL to move beyond the Colin Kaepernick boycott ('we gotta get pass the kneeling'), inadvertently assisting the gentrification of Brooklyn, starting an affordable sports shoe line.

Figure 5: Jay-Z's branding onion

Ever the businessman, Jay-Z spent the interim fifteen months between charge and trial protesting his innocence on hit records like 'Guilty Until Proven Innocent' featuring R. Kelly (who, to put it very mildly, faced his own gravely serious legal challenges). When he finally took the stand, Jay-Z looked the judge dead in the eye and pleaded guilty. He was sentenced to three years' probation.

This would have spelled ruin for most other people – for Jay-Z it upgraded his credibility. It also made it abundantly clear he was not to be trifled with. In terms of record sales its effect was beyond golden – it was platinum.

Stabbing someone and pleading guilty as charged complemented his core activity, it reaffirmed his on-record persona and ultimately strengthened his brand. In fact, in a 2023 interview with VladTV, Lance Rivera revealed that, despite his guilty plea, Jay-Z was *not* the person who actually stabbed him. It was an associate of Jay-Z. Rivera repeatedly refers to Jay-Z as a 'nice guy' in the interview.[11] In the meantime, of course, Jay-Z's brand has since become one of the most significant in entertainment and beyond, but that doesn't mean it's completely corrosion-resistant, as shown in Figure 5.

A Jay-Z-inspired Branding Tip

Violence in pursuit of career or brand enhancement objectives is entirely counterproductive and more likely to land you in prison . . . unless you are an elected (Western) politician, a gangster or at least a gangsta rapper. And even then, you're on very thin ground (except the politician).

Rick Ross

Miami's own William Leonard Roberts II, known to the world as the bearded, effortlessly charming and endearing rapper Rick Ross, is today renowned as 'the biggest boss the game has ever seen'. He made his brand explicitly clear on his highly addictive 2006 breakout single 'Hustlin'':

- He was not only 'the boss' but *the fucking* boss
- He was a major international narcotics smuggler
- He was powerful to the extent that deposed and incarcerated former de facto Panamanian leader Manuel Noriega (best friend of many a money-laundering drug baron) was in personal debt to him
- A mere glance at the wheels on his car was enough to seduce any attractive woman

He looked the part, sounded the part and played the part. So, everyone proceeded on the assumption that the role was his. A major rap star was born.

In 2008, a serious threat to Rick Ross's brand emerged. The Smoking Gun (an investigative news site) revealed that Rick Ross, *the fucking* boss, was actually . . . a former prison warden: 'Florida Department of Corrections records show that the 32-year-old hip-hop star (real name: William Leonard Roberts) worked as a correctional officer for 18 months, until he resigned his $25,794.34 post in June 1997.'[12]

Ahem. Understanding the potentially terminal impact such a revelation would have on his brand as a rapper, Rick Ross vehemently denied that he had ever worked as any kind of law enforcement officer. No matter what evidence emerged (and there was a mountain of it) he kept dismissing it as fake. When a picture came out showing him graduating as a prison warden, he said:

Online hackers put my face when I was a teenager in high school on other people's body. If this shit was real, don't you think they would have more specifics, like dates and everything?

With his customary verbal effectiveness, he added:

Fake pictures are created by the fake, meant to entertain the fake.[13]

Alas, 'more specifics' emerged: the Florida Department of Corrections handed over Rick Ross's eighty-six-page file (which ironically and impressively revealed he had also spent a year at Georgia's Albany State College . . . studying Criminal Justice). Nevertheless, he maintained his innocence/guilt with the tenacity of a Trump-era press secretary.

In the end, everyone either decided to disbelieve their eyes or just let the great music speak for itself while accepting that it could all be an act. Rick Ross's career was not damaged. His brand remains firmly intact. In 2010, he released the appropriately named album *Teflon Don*: nothing sticks to him. Certainly not the truth.

In the same way tobacco companies once marketed cigarettes as healthy and Mars chocolate bars were marketed as something that can help you 'work, rest and play' (as opposed to make you fat), Rick Ross is to be admired for standing his ground and protecting his brand by using the most corporate tool known to man: the blatant lie. This is possibly the first time in the history of his family that they've had the opportunity to create transformational wealth. You, dear reader, have probably lied for much less. Rick Ross, like all great brands, did exactly what he needed to do to protect his brand and its related earnings pipeline.

Core
Rapping about being a boss, drug dealing, being irresistible to women, the good life, good food, exotic locations, etc.

Complement
Starting a record label, owning a chicken wing franchise (Wingstop),  opening a vast eighteen-room mansion previously owned by boxing champ Evander Holyfield, bestselling author, assaulting a journalist who reported on his previous life as a prison warden, etc.

Corrosion
Previous life as a law-abiding citizen and prison warden, studying criminal law (arguable), getting sued by the person you named yourself after.

Figure 6: Rick Ross's branding onion

Rick Ross-inspired Branding Tips

- Brand perception is brand reality. Once you've decided who and what you are going to be, i.e. what your brand is, who or what you were is entirely irrelevant. Make sure it remains so: protect your brand (even if it is built upon a falsehood) no matter the cost

- Street credibility, like many a form of reputation-moulding credence (or professional qualification) can be a straitjacket for a brand. For 'Jimmy Henchmen', the inability to shed his 'qualifications' in the street proved catastrophic. For Rick Ross, the threat to his brand from his previous professional experience in the criminal justice realm was only averted by his supreme talent, oozing appeal and the convenient 'blindness' of the masses

---

Not long after Rick Ross had survived the prison warden unveiling, he was sued by an actual former drug baron called Freeway Rick Ross (a man who pretty much really lived everything the rapper Rick Ross had rapped about) for impersonating him. In short, this was the case of the reputation owner vs the brand owner: who gets to lay claim to the name Rick Ross?

Rick Ross (the rapper) won. Teflon, indeed.

A Final Rick Ross-inspired Branding Tip

Your brand must shape your history, not the other way round – unless convenient.

MONETISING A BRAND

On paper, it doesn't make sense. Why would an artform rooted in the pain and cultural traditions emanating from the debasement, underprivilege, undereducation and enslavement of a beleaguered population become one of the key drivers of success, popularity and brand recognition for many a major multinational corporation?

In the past, practically every company pitch person had to be cleaner than clean and, of course, whiter than white. The few Black company endorsement figures who did exist were generally (in public at least) comforting, deracialised saints who certainly didn't counter prevailing popular culture. Think Uncle Ben (a fictional house negro waiter whose comforting features were finally removed, in 2020, from the rice he made famous following the murder of George Floyd) and Aunt Jemima (a vaudeville 'mammy' character who helped a syrup and pancake mix become one of the most recognised brands in US history, also dropped in 2020 following the murder of George Floyd). Or O.J. Simpson before he became *O.J. Simpson* – in 1975, Simpson became the first African American man to be the face of a major corporation's advertising campaign; he was even on the board of several companies, including a Swiss Army Knife importer, when he was arrested and charged with murdering his ex-wife in 1994. Or, in fact, think of either MJ: Jordan or Jackson.

For an example of how brands feel the need to protect themselves against association with Black people, let alone rappers, we don't have to go too far back. In the medieval days of 2013, Marilyn Booker, Morgan Stanley's then Diversity Chief, suggested that the company create a mutual fund with a low minimum buy-in of $5,000 that could be marketed to Black communities with the help of the beloved, entirely wholesome (he is heavily moustachioed, for goodness' sake) and family-friendly Black daytime TV host Steve Harvey. The bank's Chief Marketing

Officer shut the idea down, informing Ms Booker that Harvey was not 'consistent with our brand or our audience'.[14]

While Hip-Hop has a unique relationship with brands and companies today, once upon a time it was considered toxic to the brands of major multinational corporations – even in the entertainment field. Time Warner's 1995 political pressure-driven fire sale of their 50 per cent stake in Death Row Records' parent company Interscope is a perfect example of this.

Bowing to public and political pressure over gangsta rap (led by Tipper Gore, the wife of Vice President Al Gore, and as civil rights activist C. Delores Tucker), Time Warner divested its share of Interscope in the belief it would protect the Time Warner brand. They sold their 50 per cent share in the company back to its founders – the media mogul, entrepreneur and film producer Ted Field and record executive Jimmy Iovine – for $115 million.

A matter of months later, MCA Records (now absorbed into the Universal Music Group) would buy 50 per cent of Interscope for $200m – $200m that would ultimately earn them billions and a dominant stake in popular culture. Even today, Interscope remains a major profit centre for Universal Music Group. And Hip-Hop is the main profit driver for Interscope, Universal and much of the music business.

THE THREE Es OF HIP-HOP AND BRANDS

Today, for many a company, Hip-Hop is the difference between banking billions and going bust. To understand what changed, we need to look at the Three Es of Hip-Hop and Brands:

1. Endorsement
2. Empowerment
3. Equity

Endorsement

Hip-Hop's relationship with huge companies and brands started with normal product placement – a mere shoutout on a song or the use of a product in, say, a video or at an awards show. This would result in free items and/or a fee (sometimes minuscule, sometimes mammoth) for the rapper . . . and often a fortune for the company. A few examples:

- In 1986, Adidas truly bridged the gap between sportswear and street fashion and culture when Run DMC released 'My Adidas'. The song led to a groundbreaking $1m endorsement deal, the first between a musical act and a sports clothing company. Sales of Superstar trainers hit nearly half a million in the first year of the deal, and a wider Run DMC range was soon released[15]
- Tommy Hilfiger was far from the major success it came to be until, in the late 1990s, Grand Puba of Brand Nubiuan, Mary J. Blige, a smoking-hot Snoop Dogg (then at the pinnacle of youth culture) and Aaliyah helped make his fashion label a phenomenon beyond its preppy origins[16]
- The Notorious BIG immortalised DKNY, Versace, Moschino and Coogi by prominently name-checking them in a verse of his track 'Hypnotize', the lead single off of his prophetically and tragically named sophomore album *Life After Death* (which was released just weeks after Biggie was murdered). In doing so, he made the boards of these companies look like geniuses. As with the artists mentioned above in regard to Adidas and Tommy Hilfiger, he helped expand, extend and enhance their brand – especially with 'urban' and youth audiences
- Timberland were a manufacturer of workwear and boots until Wu Tang, Biggie, Jay-Z and other (predominantly) East Coast giants got hold of them, made them super-fashionable and helped them generate annual revenues in excess of $1bn
- In the UK, So Solid helped make the Audi TT synonymous with young urban success (and the Metropolitan Police and media in turn subsequently helped make it synonymous with criminality – no fees payable for this one)[17]

Empowerment

Around the early to mid-90s, Hip-Hop gradually adopted a more self-contained and self-owned approach to brands, culminating in the explosion of Hip-Hop native brands in the late 1990s. The Hip-Hop figures behind these brands went from being workers to owners, and the companies they embraced were more reflective of Hip-Hop's core constituents. These native Hip-Hop brands often competed with more established brands or, in some cases, were subsidiaries of more established brands.

- Hip-Hop embraced Black-owned companies such as FUBU (For Us By Us), Karl Kani and Cross Colours
- In 1992, Russell Simmons launched his Phat Farm clothing label, an idea that was firmly ahead of its time. Then, in 1995, following the success of *Enter The Wu-Tang (36 Chambers)*, the Wu-Tang Clan, in collaboration with Oliver 'Power' Grant, released Wu Wear. Not all members of the Clan were pleased. Despite the line raking in money, Method Man dismissed some of the items as 'shoddy'.[18] Simmons' idea's time truly came in 1998, when Puff Daddy launched Sean John, a Hip-Hop-native fashion lifestyle company. A year later, Jay-Z (and his then business partner Damon Dash) quickly followed Puff Daddy's lead by establishing Roc-A-Wear
- From there it snowballed: along with a platinum plaque came a clothing line. Missy Elliott teamed up with Adidas to bring Respect ME to the world. Outkast, DMX and LL Cool J respectively all launched their extremely creatively titled offerings: Outkast Clothing Co, DMX Signature Clothing and the LL Cool J Collection. Fat Joe had the plus-sized line FJ560 by Fat Joe, follicly challenged legend Common had a hat line called Soji (named after his next-door neighbour), and Beanie Sigel created State Property. Reviving the concept for the Instagram age in 2020 and 2021 respectively, Lil Kim and Dababy both launched clothing lines with fast fashion retailers PrettyLittleThing and BoohooMAN (both part of the Boohoo group, a British company)

Equity

At the turn of the millennium, Hip-Hop's relationship with large companies and brands evolved into owning a slice of the company, partnerships, stakeholdings and co-dependency. For example, between 2015 and 2019 Kanye West's joint venture with Adidas, Yeezy, sold over $1.3bn worth of footwear. On his first album, *College Dropout* (2004), Kanye had rapped about being the 'token blackie' when he worked in a Gap store as a fifteen-year-old retail assistant. When it was announced in June 2020 that Gap were entering a ten-year partnership with Kanye, their share price shot up 42 per cent (to a ten-year high) in a single day.[19]

Reputation, Branding and the Video Vixen

Perhaps the most vivid example of how reputation is leveraged into a brand, then how that brand is monetised, comes from the least convenient of places in Hip-Hop: the video vixen.

The job of the video vixen is to provide sex appeal, to make the video look like something you just must watch, to generate excitement that will be emulated in real life and, above all, to help make a rapper look like a star. There have literally been thousands of rap videos and more than likely tens of thousands of video vixens. Many of them have great reputations. Yet, arguably, only one of them enjoyed a great brand that she was able to monetise in spectacular fashion: Karrine 'Superhead' Steffans, the video vixen turned bestselling author.

The family friendly nature of *The Hip-Hop MBA* does not permit it to go into how or why Karrine developed and enjoyed such a strong brand, but her eye-opening bestseller *Confessions of a Video Vixen* offers vivid details.

Through these three methods of brand comingling and association – endorsement, empowerment and equity – Hip-Hop thoroughly penetrated and then helped change the world of corporate branding by making it more diverse, edgy and, at times, more progressive. Yet, most critically, Hip-Hop helped brands become more profitable – while simultaneously the culture itself became more visible, buoyant and profitable.

6.

RISK AND REWARD

K ool & The Gang, one of the most sampled funk bands in Hip-Hop history, offer an inadvertent yet interesting insight into what risk is and why you should take it in their 1981 dance-floor packer 'Get Down On It'.

The chorus is a set of rhetorical questions about the ability to get something done when not participating. The juxtaposition is clear: you're guaranteed defeat if you don't try to win. For practically all of the song the questions are about dancing. However, twice in the song they tweaked the chorus from not wanting to dance to not taking a chance.

In that tweak, Kool & The Gang offered a subtle yet sharp explanation of the options you face when it comes to taking risk: you have to 'get your back off the wall' and take a chance to attain your intended reward. And even if you do, you might still fail. But at least you tried, right? Participation is what counts, right?

Participation breeds palpitation, panic attacks, embarrassment and, in some situations, podium places.

In many a walk of life, especially business and professional life, the difference between an utter clown and an absolute genius often boils down to one thing: the success or failure of a risk taken. Sometimes standing against the wall and not confirming yourself an 'utter clown' may not be a bad idea; you're reducing exposure to risk. Nevertheless, standing against the wall is a risk in itself: the wall could collapse on you.

In Hip-Hop, risk could not be more of a serious factor.

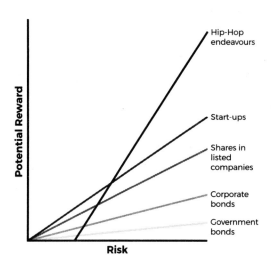

Figure 7: Hip-Hop Risk vs Reward

Risk Explained

What do God and (good) risk managers have in common?

Simple: they both giggle at your plans.

God and, to a slightly lesser degree, risk managers, know that things will not go as smoothly as you've elaborated so beautifully in your business, career or project plan. Risk is simply the anticipation that things do not turn out as expected, that something unforeseen, uncalculated or unintended – negative or positive – will happen.

On an undesirable day this could be something bad, dangerous or terminal. On a good day this may prove lucrative, or at least make things easier than expected. Understanding risk requires the anticipation of some degree of failure . . . or success. The major concern is, of course, potential failure. It is not a negative or a positive; it is a fact of life and a cost or benefit of doing business. Where there is no risk, there is no reward. The higher the risk of failure, the higher the anticipated rate of return, and vice versa.

RISK AND REWARD IN HIP-HOP

Pursuing a career or endeavour in Hip-Hop is nearly always a high-risk, potentially high-reward and low-security endeavour. The likelihood of failure is very high, but when success strikes, it can be very rewarding indeed.

For rappers themselves, it can also be quite personally dangerous:

- In one study of the deaths of over 13,000 musicians across genres, the leading cause of death for rappers was murder (51%)[1]
- Since 1987, more than 84 of the roughly 2,000 people recognised as professional Hip-Hop musicians in the United States have been murdered.[2] By comparison, in 2018 in the United States, 5 people were murdered per every 100,000 of the general population
- Only 21 of the over 84 cases of murdered US rappers have been solved[3]
- The average age of a murdered rapper is just 26. Coincidentally, 26 is also the average age of Americans who were killed in the Iraq War (it is unclear what the average age of an Iraqi killed during the Iraq War was).

There are a range of social, economic and political factors why this may be the case: the age and demographic of rappers (i.e. they are mainly young, Black and male), the age of the genre (Hip-Hop is a young genre performed in the main by young people who are yet to reach the age where they are at high risk of diseases such as cancer or heart disease), relationships with the state, the nature of competition in Hip-Hop and so on. Plus, rappers are a reflection of the cheapness of economically challenged Black life in general.

Embarking on a rap career is thus an entrepreneurial act as well as an artistic one – but with highly unusual up- and down-side risks.

The love of the art aside, the key appeal of the high-risk and high-reward nature of Hip-Hop is financial. Those who do 'make it' stand the unique chance of garnering wealth – and possibly even power – that can last for generations. Rap is truly black gold, and, just like oil, when you strike it, everyone loves you (except environmentalists), and when you don't, everyone remembers you as the clown who left a massive hole in the ground.

The profits are potentially vast. In the 2007 lawsuit brought against the LAPD, blaming them for the wrongful death of the Notorious BIG, Biggie's estimated life earnings lost as a result of his death were $500m.[4] This figure would now be recognised to be a huge underestimate – some of his peers are worth double that today.[5]

Financially speaking, even people in Hip-Hop who don't become wild successes are able to live comfortable lives that many a corporate leader would consider highly prosperous. Rappers who fail to even chart once in their careers can cultivate followings that keep them financially afloat as touring artists for the rest of their lives. Fiscally, the risk certainly seems worth it.

Let's go back to the example of 50 Cent.

50 CENT: MAN OF RISK

Curtis '50 Cent' Jackson has lived a life synonymous with risk-taking. From his origins to his market entry strategy (see Chapter 4), from his failures to his successes, he typifies the boom-and-bust nature of risk and reward:

- Aged 8: Sabrina Jackson, his (single) mother – who worked as a drug dealer – is murdered
- Aged 12: starts selling crack cocaine to make a living – his first major foray into risk-taking; he is arrested for it at 13
- Aged 21: meets Jam Master Jay and commences journey to becoming a rapper
- Aged 23: makes debut professional appearance on Onyx's 1998 single 'React'
- Aged 24: leaves Jam Master Jay and signs with Sony through the Trackmasters, a super-successful production duo; records his unreleased debut album *Power Of The Dollar* and releases the underground singles 'How To Rob' and 'Ghetto Quran'
- Still aged 24: nearly dies after being gunned down; dropped by Sony/Columbia and blackballed from the industry
- Aged 26: releases his comeback mixtape *Guess Who's Back?* It catches the ear of Eminem
- Aged 27: signs a $1m deal with Shady/Aftermath/Interscope (Eminem, Dr. Dre and Jimmy Iovine); releases his bestselling and record-breaking debut *Get Rich Or Die Trying*
- Aged 28: global superstar, sex symbol and Hip-Hop executive

In his 2020 book, *Hustle Harder, Hustle Smarter*, 50 Cent attributes his legal and illegal success to two qualities: having the heart of a hustler and fearlessness.[6]

50 Cent highlights fearlessness as a driver of his success. Interestingly, Jimmy Iovine – his one-time ultimate boss –attributes fear as a motivator of his own success. Whereas 50 Cent does not fear the consequences of a risk not working out, Jimmy Iovine fears the consequences of not taking a risk. Though they have opposing views, both men reveal that a clearly understood relationship with fear is an essential ingredient of risk management and, therefore, their success.

As a global superstar, 50 Cent exhibited these attributes – fearlessness and the heart of a hustler – in a way that was unique for Hip-Hop. The norm for many a top-of-the-game rapper is to move into areas with a proven high Hip-Hop Elasticity of Demand. This has traditionally included things like record labels, clothing lines, strip clubs and alcoholic beverages. Not so for 50 Cent. Ever the innovative, fearless and thoughtful hustler, he decided to take a risk by betting on an area with a remarkably low Hip-Hop Elasticity of Demand and extremely high supply: water.

As the story goes, in 2004, inspired by the huge price differences between different water brands in a supermarket, 50 Cent decided he wanted a piece of the action. Chris Lighty, 50 Cent's manager, happened to be old business acquaintances with the Zambian-born, British-educated (he went to Harrow, a grooming ground of the British elite), Indian-American marketing genius Rohan Oza, a man who is probably best known to the American public as a recurring judge on the entrepreneurial game show *Shark Tank*.[7]

In 2004, he was working for a privately owned New York beverage company called Glacéau. Their key product was Vitaminwater, which boasted 50 Cent, a poster boy for health, fitness, body positivity and street violence, as a fan.

A meeting was set up between Lighty, 50 Cent, Oza and his somewhat wary bosses at Glacéau. Wary because fan, fitness or body positivity aside, Vitaminwater – literally flavoured water packed full of vitamins – was not a brand associated with 'urban demographics'. 50 Cent helped assuage any nerves by demonstrating himself to be a smart and savvy business-focused man. For instance, he suggested that having a grape flavour would make Vitaminwater more appealing to the audiences he could help them attract.[8]

With initial fears of 50 Cent potentially being gunned down assuaged and the vision expanded upon, a deal was struck.[9] 50 Cent would become Vitaminwater's main brand ambassador in exchange for a reported 10 per cent minority stake in Glacéau. Let's break down the risk to both parties to the deal.

Risk to 50 Cent	Risk to Glacéau
Failure to meet a sales quota would be financially damaging	Could alienate existing customer base – worth $100m at that point
Brand alignment – would advertising a healthy-living brand complement, corrode or add to the core of the traditionally hard-living brand of a gangster rapper?	Potential to ruin the perception and positioning of Vitaminwater as a wholesome, healthy-living brand
Time – 50 Cent would not be blazing hot for ever. Capitalising on his popularity was important and urgent	Likelihood of their main brand ambassador being involved in a violent incident
Getting dropped for moral or behavioural reasons. As a brand, 50 Cent at this time was akin to a stuntman – he had to do controversial and crazy stuff to remain relevant. There was a chance this would place him at odds with Glacéau and Vitaminwater	Brand ambassador has a history of occasional lapses in 'conventional' professionalism

Table 4: Risk to 50 Cent vs Risk to Glacéau

The risk taken by both parties helped yield huge reward. With Vitaminwater sizzling in part due to 50 Cent's relentless endorsement, sales increased an estimated 600 per cent from $100m in 2004 to $700m in 2007.[10] The deal really paid off in May 2007, when Coca-Cola purchased Glacéau for $4.1 billion. According to the *Washington Post*, 50 Cent's 10 per cent stake in Glacéau netted him an estimated (but not disclosed) payday of between $60m and $100m. Not a bad return.

THE $75,000 CHEQUE

Timing is everything. Leaving a successful band or organisation is a bit like leaving the nest too early . . . or too late. It is a serious commercial risk that could have lifelong implications. O'Shea 'Ice Cube' Jackson could have been another Eddie Kane (of the film *The Five Heartbeats*), Ringo Starr or Geri Halliwell – a famed member of a popular group who will probably die regretting the day either they left or the group broke up. But Ice Cube was more to NWA than Geri Halliwell was to the Spice Girls or Ringo Starr was to The Beatles. Ice Cube was the group's soul, the A in NWA. The anti-establishment worldview that defined the group was largely his. He was the voice, the visionary and the writer of the collective, and therefore a godfather and populariser of gangsta rap. Perhaps above all, he was an inspiration for generations of rappers and young people thanks to his wit, wisdom, wickedness (in a good way) and business prowess.

MC Ren and DJ Yella were both supremely talented in their own right and played critical supporting roles, but the fact that NWA counted both Ice Cube and Dr. Dre, another once-in-a-lifetime talent, as members was the equivalent of winning the lottery twice in an evening. Adding Eazy-E – who Bryan Turner (CEO of Priority Records) described as the marketing and imaging genius behind NWA – into the mix was taking your double lottery winnings straight to the roulette table, betting on black and doubling your loot.

Ice Cube was the youngest member of the group, but he was also the only one to have had any tertiary education and a stable two-parent background. He was also the savviest. During the 1989 *Straight Outta Compton* tour, as other members of NWA were, in manager Jerry Heller's words, 'fucking any and all pieces of strange that came their way',[11] Ice Cube was working to improve his profile by speaking to the press. Heller described this as a 'good move' and said that by the end of the tour his profile was 'almost as high as his ego'.[12]

At the height of NWA's success, the constituent members were still all unsigned artists. The group was not contractually bound together or to Eazy-E's record label, Ruthless Records. This meant getting paid was not a contractually organised affair and anyone could leave as they pleased. Given the sheer volume of records they were selling, the lack of formal contractual arrangements was an unbelievably huge risk in its own right. Attempting to rectify this, each member of the group was offered $75,000 and a contract tying them exclusively to Ruthless Records.

Dangling cash and a contract (often predatory) in front of talent is a well-worn concept in showbusiness. To economically challenged young people, $75,000 is almost indistinguishable from a million and would easily be the biggest single payday of most people's lives.

Ice Cube had to make a decision:

- Sign the contract, take the $75,000 and remain a fifth of the 'Black Beatles' – the seemingly low-risk option
- Refuse to sign the contract, leave the group and walk into the big unknown of trying to successfully establish himself as a solo artist – the high-risk option

With his characteristic extreme integrity, Ice Cube picked the high-risk option. After running the contract by his lawyer, he refused to sign it. It was probably one of the wisest decisions he ever made.

Proving that the 'low-risk' option is often the high-risk option in disguise, signing the contract placed Dr. Dre on a business rollercoaster that would last for well over a decade, forcing him to partner with less conventional businessmen, such as Suge Knight, in order to get out of the deal.

Ice Cube took the right steps in determining whether or not the risk of signing the contract and taking the money was the right thing for him to do. Perhaps unknowingly, he took those steps by assessing three key considerations:

1. Was he *willing* to take the risk?
2. Was he *able* to take the risk?
3. Did he have a full *understanding* of what the risk was/risks were?

Risk consideration	Translation	Ice Cube's likely position
Willingness	'You sure you want to do *this*?'	Hell yeah
Ability	'You sure you have what it takes to handle *this*?'	Likely
Understanding	'Do you even know what "this" is?'	Ice Cube clearly did not understand the risk. He sought legal advice and decided against it

Table 5: Ice Cube's risk assessment

Though both Ice Cube and Dr. Dre have flourished post-Ruthless Records, the short-term thinking that led Dr. Dre to take the $75,000 cheque and sign the contract cost him an enormous amount of money, energy, security issues and emotional baggage.

Dr. Dre – signed the contract	Ice Cube – refused to sign the contract
Contractually obliged to stay with NWA and Ruthless Records	Left NWA free as a bird
$75,000 richer	Still broke
Did a deal with Suge Knight to get out of his Ruthless Records contract	Did a deal with a New York production crew to produce his first album
Founded Death Row Records with Suge Knight and enjoyed major international success but had to pay Eazy-E's Ruthless Records a percentage of his earnings – which cost millions	Founded Lench Mob Records and enjoyed success but didn't have to pay Eazy-E a copper penny

Table 6: Risk and reward outcome comparison for Dr. Dre and Ice Cube

BIRTH OF A RISK-WARY HOLLYWOOD MOGUL

In 1986, eighteen-year-old John Singleton included a script called *Summer of 84* in his application to film school. In 1990, on graduation, Singleton sold the complete script of *Summer of 84* to Columbia Pictures. The key difference was that *Summer of 84* was then called *Boyz n the Hood*, named after the 1987 record written by Ice Cube and performed by Eazy-E.

Boyz n the Hood – in which Ice Cube played a starring role – was shot with a budget of $3.5m and debuted in cinemas in July 1991. It went on to gross over $60m in the United States, and Singleton, then only twenty-three years old, was nominated for two Oscars: best screenplay and best director.

Boyz n the Hood was a critical moment in Ice Cube's career. He was paid $35,000 for his acting services (by comparison, Ruthless Records was paid $50,000 for the use of the title of an NWA record. Jerry Heller only charged Singleton so much because he was eager not to get out-negotiated by a 'punk-kid like Ice Cube'), but beyond the pay cheque the experience would set Ice Cube up on a new creative path.

Singleton told Ice Cube 'if you can write a vivid record that can make me see it in my mind, you can write a script'.[13] With those wise words, Ice Cube commenced the painfully lonely process of scriptwriting. The third script he wrote was the first to get the green light: *Friday*, a comedy set on a single day in the hood.

Friday was a venture fraught with nothing but risk:

- The screenwriters (Ice Cube and DJ Pooh) were unknown, untested and inexperienced
- The director (F. Gary Gray) was unknown, untested and inexperienced
- The producer (Patricia Charbonnet) was unknown, untested and inexperienced

- The lead comic role was to be filled by an unknown, untested and inexperienced actor (DJ Pooh – playing opposite Ice Cube)
- The supporting actors were a mixture of underappreciated veterans and largely unknown, untested and inexperienced performers
- They only had twenty days to shoot the film

By all estimations, *Friday* had 'WILD CRITICAL AND COMMERICAL FLOP' written all over it. Ice Cube and Mark 'DJ Pooh' Jordan, a renowned west coast Hip-Hop producer who also got his break in film on the set of *Boyz n the Hood*, considered self-financing the film. New Line Cinema, who had found previous Hip-Hop related success with the *House Party* series (starring Kid 'n' Play), offered to invest. Here, faced with the two financing options, Ice Cube, once again, had to weigh up the risk and potential for reward:

- Self-finance: Ice Cube would own the lion's share of the profits . . . or losses
- Corporate finance: New Line Cinema finances the film and Ice Cube owns a rather small portion of the profits. Additionally, New Line had another stipulation – that a more established comedian or comic actor play the starring comedic role alongside Ice Cube

Ice Cube and DJ Pooh agreed to New Line Cinema financing the film, and DJ Pooh was replaced on-screen by up-and-coming *Def Comedy Jam* favourite Chris Tucker. They were granted a shoestring budget of $3.5m, and the film went on to gross well over $60m. Nevertheless, measuring the risk and reward in monetary terms alone would have been an error. Yes, Ice Cube could have made more money on *Friday* if he had self-financed it, but by doing the deal with New Line the film reached a much wider audience, has had a significantly greater cultural impact than it otherwise would have had (partly through VHS and DVD sales, of which Ice Cube received a share), and made household names of many of its stars, not least Tucker – the film's most energetic presence. It also granted Ice Cube the chance to learn the business from the inside.

The key lesson emerging from Ice Cube's approach to risk is that dollars and cents may not always be the best measure of risk and reward. Sometimes dollars and sense may be a better metric. Never discount the value of the learning capital in losses.

Hip-Hop Lessons on Risk and Reward

1. Before taking any risk, always question if you are truly willing, able and knowledgeable enough to take it. If the answer to any of these stipulations is no, find the appropriate counsel before making a final decision.

2. 50 Cent's entire life (and near lack thereof) is testimony to the fact that where there is no risk there is no reward, and the greater the risk of failure, the greater the potential for reward.

3. Take that risk . . . but, like Ice Cube, ensure you understand it and are able to withstand it if it doesn't go according to plan.

4. Paraphrasing Nas: even buying a bottle of cheap brew is an act of risk-taking. That same dollar could have purchased a lottery ticket – which would probably be a waste of money. But at least there is some chance that it would win you a huge return.

7.

NEGOTIATION

'If it came from Compton, it came through me.'

The 'I went to Harvard'-like mantra of never knowingly modest Alonzo 'Lonzo' Williams: DJ, producer and founder of World Class Wreckin' Cru – a Godfather of West Coast Hip-Hop and the first person to truly bank on the talent of Dr. Dre.

Speaking on the *Gangster Chronicles* podcast, Lonzo shines a torch on the music business:

> *The record business is run by suit and tie gangsters – for real. Understand this: when you walk into a deal you own 100 per cent of everything. You walk out and you only own 10 per cent – if anything. Any artist that walks into a record deal owns 100 per cent of everything – publishing, masters, everything. If you walk out and, nigga, you got 15 per cent? Nigga, you a bad* [meaning good] *motherfucker.'*[1]

Lonzo is not exaggerating. It is customary for record deals, or any form of commercial deal, to benefit the more established party. Everything from 'standardised' contracts to 'standard' terms of business and 'standard' business protocols – all operate firmly in the interest of those who established and gain advantage from the 'standards'.

These standards enshrine power, lock in privilege and help

increase the likelihood of profitability for businesses. But for artists, employees and other junior partners they do the opposite. They enshrine powerlessness, lock in disadvantage and increase the likelihood of pauperism, or at least perpetual dependency on the more senior party.

The argument to justify this goes:

- The more established party is taking more risk and is therefore deserving of more reward
- The more established party is bringing more to the table (a concept often referred to as 'I am the table-ism')
- The likelihood of the success of the venture is more reliant on the input of the more established party
- Or, in simple terms: *'Bitch, you ain't shit without me'* – the more established party (which is the exact language every pimp eventually uses with his exploitees)

Finally, Lonzo was even right about percentages. On an industry 'standard' deal – 10 per cent of profit on sales for the artist is common, and 15 per cent would be a good deal. In both cases, advances would be a subjective judgement by the label, and can vary widely. However, there are some exceptions to the rule: No Limit's 1996 deal with Priority Records was for 80 per cent, with an advance of $375,000 per album; in 1998, Cash Money secured a deal with Universal for 85 per cent of royalties, 50 per cent of publishing revenue, 100 per cent ownership of masters and a $30m advance.

If the 'standards' are so rigid, how do deals like those made by Cash Money and No Limit happen?

Cash Money and No Limit have three things in common:

1. Both originate from New Orleans, Louisiana.
2. Both were deeply rooted in the tradition of African American family businesses.
3. Both of their landmark deals were negotiated by Wendy Day.

The last is the key to those unusual deals. A synonym for 'bad motherfucker' as used by the great Lonzo Williams is 'good negotiator'. And when it comes to Hip-Hop, any discussion on negotiation should have one name front, back and centre: Wendy Day, Hip-Hop's chief 'bad motherfucker'/'great negotiator' or, as Birdman from Cash Money called her, 'the bitch that negotiated the No Limit deal'.

LEVERAGE: POWER BROKER, BAD MOTHERFUCKER

Wendy Day, a woman with a personality that falls perfectly somewhere between effortless charm and invading army, is Hip-Hop's secret negotiation weapon. She is the founder and CEO of Rap Coalition, a not-for-profit artists' advocacy organisation founded with the aims of educating, informing and unifying rap artists, producers and DJs. As a result of the deals she has helped secure, Day has helped build more intergenerational wealth within African American communities than almost anyone you can think of.

If you extract Wendy Day from Hip-Hop, the entire landscape is very different and significantly more exploitative.

Wendy was raised in an economically challenged Christian household in a wealthy, middle-class Jewish area. This childhood experience of being 'the other' helped her normalise the feeling of being different, of being a fish out of water. Which perhaps explains Wendy's career as a white woman in a Black male-dominated industry.

Over the course of her career in Hip-Hop, Day has worn three hats:

- deal breaker: getting countless rappers out of bad deals
- deal maker: getting countless rappers into good deals
- record breaker: securing some of the biggest label deals in Hip-Hop history

Wendy's secret sauce of negotiation can be summarised as leverage, more leverage and even more leverage.

Leverage Defined

Leverage is simply anything that gives a party the upper hand in a negotiation and is therefore the main influence on the outcome of any negotiation. The party with the most leverage is the most likely to walk away from a negotiation with terms favourable to them.

Synonyms: bargaining chip, advantage, the upper hand, 'the nigga behind the trigger', etc.

Wendy Day swears, lives and breathes leverage. In our interview, it quickly became clear that she considers leverage as the basis of any business discussion. In her view, without leverage you're wasting your time walking into any negotiation: you've already lost. In her own words:

When I started Rap Coalition in 1992, very quickly I realised that just pulling people out of bad deals was not enough. Just educating people was not enough. I needed to take what I was learning about bad deals and put them into good deals. So, I started doing 'leveraged deals'.

What that means is that as an artist builds their fan base and starts to make money out of their music, the labels become very interested in them. And the more leverage they have, the more power they have. And they can translate that power into making the lion's share of the money and having control. And the first deal I applied that to was Master P's initial No Limit deal [with Priority].

LEVERAGE-DRIVEN NEGOTIATION AND THE RISE OF SOUTHERN HIP-HOP

Hip-Hop as the cultural package the world knows today is indigenous to New York. Given that New York is both the home of Hip-Hop as well as a global epicentre of culture, media and finance, the New York Hip-Hop scene was unsurprisingly the first to achieve established status and then uncontested dominance.

But from the late 1980s onwards, New York's 'uncontested dominance' over Hip-Hop started to get contested by West Coast Hip-Hop – Ice T was the first to break out, but NWA really took West Coast Hip-Hop to levels previously unseen. Acts like Compton's Most Wanted, WC & The Maad Circle, DJ Quik and Too Short helped maintain that level. By the mid-1990s, Dr. Dre and Suge Knight's Death Row completed the West Coast takeover of rap music.

Reeling from the threat of alienation and loss of privilege that comes with the loss of dominance, some New York rappers (and Hip-Hop journalists) openly poured scorn over West Coast Hip-Hop. The most famous diss track was probably Tim Dogg's 'Fuck Compton' (1991).

West Coast and East Coast Hip-Hop dominated much of Hip-Hop's first decade and a half of existence. The sounds and stories permeating from different areas reflected the lifestyles and life stories of each area.

Throughout this West and East Coast-dominated period, there were green shoots of major potential from Southern Hip-Hop – 2 Live Crew in Miami; the Geto Boys, DJ Screw's Screwed Up Click, UGK (and Rap-A-Lot records in general) in Houston; 8-Ball and MJB and Three 6 Mafia in Memphis; Jermaine Dupri's So So Def and, of course, Outkast and Goodie Mob (and the Dungeon Family) in Atlanta.

From Gospel to the Blues, Soul, Rock 'n' Roll, Country, Jazz and Rock, Zydeco and R 'n' B – all find their roots in the South.

126

Nevertheless, despite having the most deliciously rich musical heritage on the face of the earth, the stigma associated with the brutal history and politics of the South more generally extended to Southern Hip-Hop. The drawled accents and country living; the Southern hospitality-rooted charm (a deeply loaded concept) and the history of Black people in the South often left Southern Hip-Hop open to stereotypes of being less savvy and sharp than its coastal brethren.

The thinking was that Southern Hip-Hop was 'slow' or 'backwards' – in terms of intellect, actual pace (notably in relation to chopped 'n' screwed remixes) and certainly in business practices. The Wendy Day-negotiated emergence of No Limit and then Cash Money in New Orleans helped shatter this perception. It also helped propel Southern Hip-Hop into a dominant position where it has enjoyed the longest run of any of the regions.

NO LIMIT AND CASH MONEY

The biggest hurdle facing both Cash Money and No Limit became their biggest asset: they were not located in major record label, entertainment or financial hotspots. All of the major and main record labels (both those indigenous to Hip-Hop and establishment players) were located on either of the main coasts. So for No Limit, Cash Money and other non-coastal upstarts, selling records independently was their only option. As a result, they sold their albums however they could – mom 'n' pop stores, local retailers or even from the trunks of their cars. As Master P put it:

> See, I watched the Avon lady in my hood. She popped her trunk and sell her products. So, I put all my CDs and cassettes in the back of my trunk and I hit every city, every hood.[2]

Master P and his business partner, Tobin Costen, were driving the No Limit tank – a family microbusiness founded with a

$10,000 cheque from the founder's grandfather's insurance settlement – full steam to major success.

No Limit was selling over 100,000 copies per release – independently, with no nationwide presence, no radio airplay, limited infrastructure and no formal distribution network. A phenomenal achievement made only more interesting by the fact that the main artists on No Limit at the time were:

- Master P (founder)
- Sonya C (founder's wife)
- C Murder (founder's brother)
- Silk the Shocker (founder's other brother)
- TRU (a group consisting of the founder and his two brothers)

There wasn't a groundbreaking or uniquely brilliant lyricist or musician amongst them. But what they lacked in technical skill on the microphone, No Limit made up for in business acumen, work ethic and an industrialist mindset. No Limit released albums at a remarkable rate – a business practice that would go on to become a trademark for them. They also carefully cultivated a brand, with a tank logo and fatigues. The inspiration for the army regalia was Master P's grandfather, a military veteran. As Master P revealed on Solange's 2016 album, *A Seat At The Table*, his grandfather urged him to start his own army, as America would always neglect them. And that is what he did.

Army	No Limit
Highly productive, efficient, motivated and disciplined unit with bankable levels of professional competence	Highly productive, efficient, motivated and disciplined unit with bankable levels of professional competence
Lives in a barracks together	Lived in a luxury estate together
Enjoys a buoyant budget	Enjoys a buoyant budget

Army	No Limit
Staffed principally by deprived country folk	Staffed principally by deprived country folk
Led by a highly respected, principles-guided, duty- and honour-bound leader	Led by a highly respected, principles-guided, duty- and honour-bound leader

Table 7: The Army and No Limit compared

The No Limit brand, sound and work ethic helped them develop a loyal following, a sales track record and buoyant profitability. In short, they developed a huge amount of leverage – they were super-successful as an independent record label. Master P, ever the industrialist, wanted to expand – billions were his objective. Through associates, they found out about and made contact with the person who knew exactly what to do next: Wendy Day, the 'rapper's guardian angel'.

Numbers speak louder than words. Thanks to the leverage Master P and No Limit had accrued, Wendy was able to negotiate a truly groundbreaking press and distribution deal with Priority Records (famous for distributing Ruthless Records, home to NWA). After looking over the contracts for tell-tale signs of pitfalls and business malpractice, Day got down to the business of negotiating terms. What she came back with were headline terms and conditions truly worthy of headlines:

- 80 per cent of all profits
- Creative control
- Ownership of masters
- Press [manufacturing] and distribution services to be provided by Priority
- Billing and collection services would be conducted by a professional agency – payment for this would come from Priority's share of profits
- An advance of $375,000 per album

What Wendy Day negotiated was beyond a blinder, it was an affront to the supposed natural order of business. The deal was fantastically in favour of the party who would be considered less established: No Limit. Bryan Turner, CEO of Priority Records, the more established party on the other side of the No Limit negotiation deals, pours a little lukewarm water on the deal while affirming the size of the numbers:

> It was more of a straight P & D [press & distribution]. The advances really reflected the amount of records he was selling independently. The money was big because the money warranted those numbers. Every deal, no matter how common they looked, had to be blown up into something that was extraordinary for the brand and the label and the public opinion of what these deals were. They had to be positioned as something 'bigger than life'. And the story just blossomed and became ... part of the lure. But the deal was a solid deal – we all made a lot of money.

They did indeed make a lot of money, as the *New York Times* chronicled in 1998:

> *Two years ago, Priority sold $114 million in music; last year sales climbed to $175 million, and this year the company expects to take in over $240 million. These increases can be attributed primarily to a distribution deal with the phenomenally successful No Limit Records, the Louisiana-based rap label run by Master P. Priority now accounts for 3.2 percent of the American record market.*[3]

Master P's first album after the deal (which happened to be the eighth album he would release either as a solo act or as part of Tru in under five years) was the first of his albums to go platinum. From there, awash with cash, No Limit and Master P exploded into full-blown industrialists in the truest sense of the term. He signed an army of talented local rappers, including

Mystikal, Mia X, Kane & Abel, Fiend, Tre-8 and Mr. Serv-On. As Suge Knight's Death Row Records imploded (following the exit of Dr. Dre, the murder of Tupac Shakur and the probation violation-related incarceration of Suge Knight himself) – Snoop Dogg, Death Row's remaining highly bankable figure and a globally recognised rap star, was 'sold to the country boy' (as Reggie Wright, former interim president of Death Row, put it). From there it snowballed: they signed a figurative army of artists.

By comparison, Sean 'Puff Daddy' Combs' Bad Boy Records, the toast of the music business at the time, would release no more than four albums a year – usually two or three. No Limit were at times releasing more albums per month than Bad Boy would in a year. And as No Limit had fantastically better deal terms than Bad Boy (thanks, in part, to Wendy Day's negotiation), it can be safely assumed that Master P earned more money than Puff Daddy, even though Puff Daddy, a city slicker, projected wealth more than Master P.

Master P quickly diversified into other areas: sports management, films (he struck a similarly favourable distribution deal with Harvey Weinstein's Miramax for the No Limit-produced film *I Got the Hook Up*),[4] a real estate company (No Limit built a luxury housing estate to house their talent), a Foot Locker outlet and a gas station, a clothing line, a phone-sex company and more. As busy as he was, Master P even found time to become a professional basketball player. Success in the areas he diversified into varied.

No Limit had built up enough demonstrable leverage in terms of a sales track record to snag a great deal; Cash Money, a rival New Orleans label, had built up the cultural capital – but not the sales. No Limit was selling hundreds of thousands independently, Cash Money were selling a fraction of this.

At a 1997 music conference in New Orleans, Wendy Day popped into Peaches, a local record store, and picked up a CD by a popular local artist called Pimp Daddy. She flipped it over and saw the Cash Money logo. She started asking around about the company and quickly found out about the cultural significance (i.e. the impact of the music they were releasing), local following and respect within New Orleans. They had released thirty-one independent albums in a six-year period.

Cash Money had the best leverage I had ever seen. I tried to find them to try and get them a deal. I was a little shocked they didn't already have one. But I could not find them. So, I kind of gave up. That was in May of 97. In August of 97 I got a call from a street-team guy in Houston and he said: 'I have these two brothers, they have a record label and they want to meet you.' I said, 'Oh God, please be Cash Money'. I asked, 'What's their name?' and he said, 'Cash Money.' I said: 'PUT 'EM ON THE PHONE!' They sought me out as they saw what I did for No Limit – they saw No Limit as their competition. To quote them, they said they wanted 'the bitch that did the Master P deal'.

As much cultural leverage as Cash Money's catalogue of thirty-one albums in six years had built up – they were selling 5,000, 6,000, at most 20,000 units. In short, they were No Limit without the numbers. You could say No Limit, with some limits. Perhaps as a result of their limited numbers, the first offer Day attained when she opened up negotiations with the major labels was $75,000 – for their artist Juvenile only. So how did Day manage to negotiate her way up from $75,000 to $30m, with 80 per cent of profits going to Cash Money and retention of masters, just nine months later?

Simple: leverage.

I had already been working with Twista and Do or Die out of the Midwest, so I had relationships in the Midwest. So, what I did was I brought Cash Money into the Midwest. My lawyers were also the lawyers for Three 6 Mafia, so we were able to put Cash Money on a Three-6 Mafia tour . . . all through the Midwest. So we expanded their market. And by expanding their market they went from selling 5,000–25,000 CDs to selling 75,000, 80,000, 100,000, 125,000 – so as I am shopping their deal, they are getting bigger and stronger. It is not like they stayed the same and the money climbed, they were climbing as the money was climbing, and the money was a reaction to what they were doing.

Leverage-driven Negotiation and Tupac Shakur

In 1995, Tupac Shakur was simultaneously in heaven and hell: the top of the charts and solitary confinement in Clinton Correctional Facility, a maximum-security prison (his incarceration resulting from a sexual assault conviction). Financially destitute – despite having one of the bestselling albums of the year – and following the universal principle that desperate people do desperate things, Tupac reached out to Suge Knight to strike a deal that would finance his bail pending appeal and get him signed to Death Row Records. What is little known, however, is that at the same time, discreetly, Shakur also reached out to Wendy Day to help him negotiate the deal.

Day felt her closeness to Death Row could present a conflict of interest, so she was unable to negotiate the deal from the driving seat (as fate would have it, Death Row did not suffer such ethical proclivities – see Chapter 17). Unknown to Knight and his lawyer, David Kenner, she did advise Tupac from the back seat – informally. Knight and Kenner repeatedly flew to New York to see Tupac and negotiate the terms of the deal with him – in prison. After they left, Tupac sent the handwritten terms of the deal to Wendy Day for advice and feedback.

Confirming or dispelling a nearly three-decade-old myth: did Tupac really sign a record contract written on toilet paper (or a kitchen towel), as has long been rumoured? According to Wendy Day: 'That was real. They could not bring the contract into the prison so they sat there and negotiated with him face to face and they wrote things back and forth – just like I was writing back and forth to him.'

Tupac signed a three-album deal with Death Row, who in turn paid the whopping $1.4m bail to get him released from prison.[5] The first release was *All Eyez On Me* – the first double album in Hip-Hop. It would go on to sell over 10 million copies, marking a commercial high of 1990s Hip-Hop. It catapulted Tupac to even greater superstardom. Critically, it also granted Tupac an enormous amount of leverage for a post-Death Row deal, a deal he would not live long enough to complete.

Negotiation Tips from Wendy Day

1. **Leverage is the ultimate trump card.**

If properly understood and carefully used, leverage is significantly more important to the outcome of a negotiation than great negotiation skills.

2. **The pursuit of leverage never stops.**

By expanding Cash Money's market presence while she was in active negotiation, Day was able to secure an unprecedented deal. If she had remained stagnant, with the numbers they previously had, they would probably have settled for what Alonzo Williams described as 'bad motherfucker' deals (15 per cent royalties, etc). It is essential, especially when the chips are down, to continue to add value to yourself or your endeavour, value which can be transformed into leverage.

3. **The pursuit of leverage is a 360° endeavour.**

Wendy Day was able to help Cash Money make good on their leverage – however, she had no leverage over Cash Money. Proving once and for all that even earth-shattering favours don't go unpunished, despite all of her assistance and reducing her $3m fee (10 per cent of the advance of the deal) to $150,000, Cash Money did not pay her. They did, however, pay the lawyer she introduced them to as he still enjoyed leverage over them — thanks to the paperwork.

In a 2014 interview with the rap blog NahRight, Wendy Day revealed a different type of 'leverage' emerged to attain payment:

'At one point, one of my artist friends bumped into Birdman and put a gun to his head and made him call and apologise to me, which he did. [Birdman] called me up and said, 'Oh, your friend just pulled me out of Hot97 and I'm here on the street, on my knees and I want to apologize to you.' I really didn't care about the apology. I wanted to know, why would somebody s— on someone that changed their life for the better?'[6]

Eventually everything was settled in a more calm and amicable manner.

'I filed suit, and we settled out of court. I was finally paid in March of 2000. As to 'why' [Birdman didn't pay Day] — no, I was never given an explanation, but time showed that not paying people was a common theme in their business model and a common complaint against them.'

4. **Know when to just say no.**

Wendy Day took nine months to negotiate her deal for Cash Money. She chalks part of the success in the negotiation up to the fact that the Cash Money brothers let her say no to offers and continue the negotiation. Be prepared to walk away . . . or to at least create the impression you will do so.

5. **Learn from masters.**

Great negotiators are made, not born. Day developed her expertise as a negotiator by learning from hedge-fund traders and studying the former president of the Walt Disney Company and founder of the Creative Artists Agency (CAA), Michael Ovitz.[7]

6. **Or defer to the masters.**

Corporations hire the best of people to go and negotiate on their behalf. Had Cash Money, for example, negotiated with Universal directly, there is a great chance they would have walked away with $75,000 as opposed to $30m. By hiring Wendy Day, they made a fortune.

If negotiation is not your strong point, it would be a great idea to attain the services of a master of negotiation, such as Wendy Day, to lead the endeavour for you. Beware of conflicts of interests and pay the negotiation master.

7. **Money is a short-term goal of any negotiation.**

Money is a motivator but not the key driver of a negotiation. As Day puts it: 'The goal was never to get somebody money, my goal was to build a career. A record deal is not the goal, a record deal is just the first step in achieving success.' Though money is a reflection of the value placed on your leverage, negotiating skill or what the other party feels they can get away with, getting the money is only the first step. Attaining a career, power, establishing a market presence or reputation or building a brand is the lucrative long-term goal.

8. **Winner should not take all.**

According to Day: 'It is not a good deal if everyone is not earning money.' Though the Cash Money and No Limit deals would prove highly profitable for Cash Money and No Limit, it was also good for everyone that the deals proved highly profitable for Universal and Priority, respectively. Take the steak, leave some salt.

8.

PROMOTION

In what may be one of the greater rebounds of all time, not long after being sacked by Uptown, Puff Daddy had secured an elusive distribution deal with industry veteran Clive Davis's Arista Records for his newly minted record label, Bad Boy Entertainment. The first two artists signed to the label were Craig Mack, a highly melodic and rather simplistic (by New York standards) funk-laden rapper – who became a brutal yet persistent punchline due to his supposed unattractiveness – and the Notorious BIG, a once-in-a-lifetime, uniquely super-gifted rapper, who famously labelled himself 'ugly'.

Looks do a lot of heavy lifting in most areas of showbusiness, for obvious reasons, but principally they make the job of endearing someone to the public so much easier. Good-looking no-talents regularly outperform people who are somewhat challenged in the sex-appeal department. By betting on two artists who were arguably not considered a delight to look at to launch his empire, Puff Daddy was betting on talent over tin labelling, substance over sheen. As a result, he needed a super-duper watertight marketing and promotions plan. Thankfully, that is one of his key talents.

In a stroke of the marketing genius that would come to define him as an executive, Puff Daddy came up with the idea of leveraging one of the most popular products in the world, McDonald's

Big Mac– an artery-clogging product so loved it is an indicator of global inflation – to introduce his artists, his label and himself to the world.

Like the best ideas, it was imaginative yet simple: he took the last names of both artists, BIG and Mack, and started what came to be known as the 'B.I.G. Mack campaign'. They created a sampler mixtape (then still physical cassettes) with songs by Craig Mack on one side and songs by the Notorious BIG on the other, placed them in 'B.I.G. Mack' branded burger boxes and handed them out. The B.I.G. Mack campaign was punctuated with a print media advert shot by famed Hip-Hop photographer Chi Modu in a makeshift 'McDonald's' (which actually happened to be a Burger King branch – the real McDonald's had nothing to do with it). The advert showed Puff Daddy, flanked by Craig Mack and the Notorious BIG, stood behind a 'McDonald's' counter. The customary fast-food menu behind them had been photoshopped into adverts for the Notorious BIG's *Ready To Die* and Craig Mack's *Funk Da World*, both debuts. The banner on the bottom read 'Bad Boy Entertainment: Born to Make Noise'. The campaign worked a treat. It created a buzz, helped propel both albums to success and effectively introduced Puff Daddy and his new label to the world.

Puff Daddy-inspired Promotion Tip

Where symbiotic or even parasitic promotional opportunities with large corporations present themselves, consider exploiting them, mercilessly. What is peppercorns to them could spell a fortune to you.

Promotion often marks the difference between being really great at what you do and being *recognised* for being really great at what you do. The difference between fame and anonymity.

And in many cases, it can spell the difference between 'moving forward' or remaining stagnant, success and failure, rags and riches, rapidly increasing sales and no sales at all. Happiness and deep-fried misery. All of which is why promotion forms a quarter of the marketing mix, otherwise known as the four Ps: Product, Price, Place (distribution method), Promotion.

As illustrated by Puff Daddy's B.I.G. Mack campaign, promotion is an area where Hip-Hop has distinguished itself as a force to be reckoned with, as both a business and culture. From its commercial inception in the late 1970s till this very day, Hip-Hop's business minds have innovatively promoted Hip-Hop from the bottom of society's barrel to the very pinnacle of society's champagne glass. Along the way, Hip-Hop has created and revealed geniuses who have left their stamp on marketing, advertising and promotions for ever.

THE REMIX OF THE MARKETING MIX

Born to an African American mother and an Eritrean father, Ermias 'Nipsey Hussle' Asghedom was a special human being. Softly spoken, measured and entirely focused at all times, he was gifted with a personality that by nature commanded respect and conveyed seriousness. And where respect was wanting, the repercussions were instant. A parking valet at the 2018 BET awards show learned this the hard way when his face met the back of Nipsey Hussle's hand during a belligerent exchange over where Nipsey should park.[1]

Critically, Nipsey Hussle was a shrewd, savvy and determined businessman who also happened to be a rapper (and a lover of Black people). As his Nipsey *Russell*-inspired stage name suggested, he was someone who was determined to make the most of opportunities – whether they were given to him or not. He was a hustler in the best Hip-Hop sense of the term: a person focused on economic betterment by any means necessary.

As a result, Nipsey Hussle was razor-focused on business from a young age. At eleven, he shined shoes for $2.50 a pop; in his early twenties he (reluctantly) signed a record deal; in his late twenties he founded All Money In Records. He was an early evangelist for cryptocurrencies, investing in tech and creating tech hubs. In one of his earliest interviews (with legendary Bay Area DJ Davey D), he made it clear that he was much more interested in buying real estate and other assets than buying jewellery. He paid $2.5 million for his own shopping mall, the Marathon Clothing Store, situated on the intersection of Slauson Ave and Crenshaw Boulevard in LA – an area synonymous with gang violence (as originally immortalised by Kurupt on Dr. Dre's 'Stranded On Death Row' track) and not far from where he grew up. Tragically, Nipsey Hussle brutally murdered in 2019, right outside his own shopping mall, in broad daylight.

Nipsey Hussle's main contribution to business innovation was in relation to the marketing mix in a time of market volatility. By 2010, when he released *Crenshaw*, his first official mixtape, the market for music as a physical commodity had collapsed due to the rise of online consumption habits – legal and illegal. The barcoded compact disc was being chased out of the market wholesale by the cowboys of the freely downloadable MP3. At this time, Nipsey Hussle was in his ascendancy and had to make a name for himself . . . and a living. So, he did what all great hustlers do: he hustled innovatively.

The marketing mix for the music business had been altered as shown in the table below.

Marketing mix element	Established	Change due to technology
Product	Music	Nil[2]
Price	$15 an album	Widely available for free

Marketing mix element	Established	Change due to technology
Promotion	Traditional media and advertising	Online and social media
Place	Bricks-and-mortar retail stores	Online

Table 8: Changes to the music marketing mix

Nipsey Hussle responded to the change in the marketing mix by making price the promotional point. He merged price and promotion into one element.

As it was no longer possible to sell his mixtapes for the traditional price of, say, $10, he released a limited edition of 1,000 copies of his mixtapes priced at an eye-watering $100. This resulted in:

1. Generating $100,000 in a single day on the sales of a tape that would otherwise have been free.[3]
2. Generating significantly more interest and press coverage than the project would have received otherwise.
3. Catching the attention and respect of Jay-Z, who immediately ordered 100 copies and promptly sent Nipsey $10,000.
4. Improved Nipsey Hussle's stature and significance in Hip-Hop and grew his fanbase.
5. Demonstrated Nipsey's prowess as an enterprising rapper to be taken very seriously.

In Ermias 'Nipsey Hussle' Asghedom's own words: 'As an artist, my goal is to inspire . . . entertain . . . motivate . . . and most importantly INNOVATE.'[4]

THE STREET TEAM

'Word of mouth' has long been considered the ultimate promotional tool. It is likely to be an honest reflection of the feelings of a customer, it conveys genuine excitement and enthusiasm, it is free of charge and it cannot, at least directly, be purchased. It can, however, be influenced.

The problem with 'word of mouth' is that it is no guarantee of success: it can take a lot of time to manifest and it may not happen. It is part good product and service, part good luck. Luck and hope are about as reliable as the rain dance in terms of corporate strategy. So how does one remove the luck element from word of mouth?

In every population there are tastemakers and leaders who are the key drivers of 'word of mouth'. You could call these people the 'Queen Bees'. These arbiters of 'cool' are the people who drive popular culture and help shape the tastes of the masses. In fact, it is estimated that the actions and tastes of 90 per cent of the population are influenced by the actions and tastes of 10 per cent of the population.[5] Following this logic, as opposed to waiting for the word of mouth to cascade, what if you could:

1. Identify these Queen Bees.
2. Keep them at the cutting edge of culture by making them insiders on your products.
3. Package them into a branded team surrounded by other similar bees.
4. Get them to 'hit the street' professionally and pass the 'word of mouth' about your product around.
5. Attain feedback on what (or who) audiences and consumers connect with.
6. Charge a fee for all of the above.

Steve Rifkind, a second-generation successful music executive, is credited with creating this very type of promotional service – which was eventually dubbed 'the street team'.

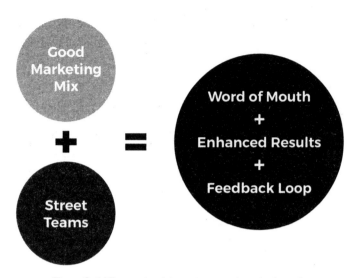

Figure 8: Adding a street team to a good marketing mix

Rifkind's main contribution to marketing, however, was his idea to transform cool kids who happen to be connoisseurs of the culture and key drivers of word of mouth into a commercially viable, street-based legion of brand ambassadors, who often spelt the difference between the success and failure of a project.

Today, the concept of street-team marketing underpins influencer marketing on Instagram and further afield.

'PIMP THE SYSTEM'

Countercultures and large corporate machines external to the entertainment business are mostly like oil and water: they *usually* don't mix. But sometimes they have to; sometimes they need each other. Corporations need, say, rappers in order to help them connect with younger consumers, stay relevant and look cool. Rappers, on the other hand, need corporations to get paid.

CORPORATIONS   **RAPPERS**

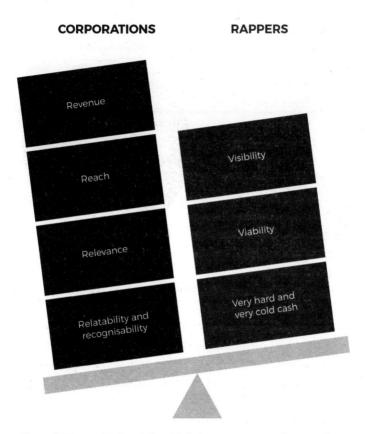

Figure 9: The symbiotic relationship between rappers and corporations

Every faceless corporation needs one thing: a face. The Gap is a classic faceless corporation – they make clothes principally for swagger-free corporate people. It is the exact sort of organisation that needs someone to make it more cool, more hip. In steps Hip-Hop.

In 1997, Gap inadvertently created a corporate need for culturally savvy people thanks to an advertising campaign they ran with the Hip-Hop icon and pinnacle of cool, James Todd 'LL Cool J' Smith. In the ad, LL Cool J wore classic Gap clothes: loose-fitting, light-blue, soft denim jeans with a matching light-blue denim shirt wrapped around his waist topped off with a white T-shirt – with the right sleeve rolled up to reveal a tattoo of a microphone on a chiselled bicep. In what should have set off alarm bells, LL Cool J wore a baseball cap with the logo 'FB' on it in graffiti font. The hat was designed by FUBU (pronounced 'foo-boo'), a then little-known Black-owned Hip-Hop apparel company.

The advert was simple, straightforward and entirely in line with Gap's minimalistic brand: LL Cool J rapping about Gap in front of a plain white background. A single camera angle captures all of the action.

The critical part of LL Cool J's Gap advert: 'Jeans popping in every mall and town and city / G-A-P, gritty / Ready to go / For us, by us, on the low'.

'For us, by us' is the Black empowerment-drenched meaning of the acronym FUBU. Context: in the middle of a prime-time advert for a major multinational corporation, LL Cool J took a moment to subliminally advertise a Hip-Hop apparel company he had a relationship with. It was the ultimate countercultural *screw the man and pimp the system* moment. But in this moment of 'on the low' corporate marauding, something beautiful happened. FUBU's Daymond John (now famous for being a judge on *Shark Tank*) remembers it:

Gap calls him [LL Cool J] up to do a commercial, they don't care that he can wear a FUBU hat, they don't even know what FUBU is. All of a sudden he slips 'for us, by us' in the commercial. We couldn't make enough product so the kids start going to the Gap for FUBU. Gap finds out almost three weeks after the commercial is airing. They spent about $30m on this commercial. They pull the commercial. All of a sudden, they found the target market they were trying to hit increased 300% because the kids thought they could get FUBU at the Gap. Gap blows up, FUBU blows up, LL Cool J remains the superstar who slipped FUBU in a Gap commercial. Forget about the

Starbucks cup in Game of Thrones, *this is probably history's biggest advertising coup. FUBU baby.*[6]

In 1998, the year after the hijacked Gap advert, FUBU grossed over $350 million in annual worldwide sales. Gap, on the other hand, benefited more from the advert than they would have otherwise. Gap evolved in its appreciation of Hip-Hop. Twenty-three years after the advert with LL Cool J – in a bid to essentially save the company – they announced a ten-year partnership with Kanye West, a former Gap shop floor assistant, in 2020.[7] In 2022, Gap also announced that they were going into a partnership with famed Hip-Hop fashion disruptor Dapper Dan. They also ran several commercials with Missy Elliot, Future, Sza, Nas (and his father, the jazz musician Olu Dara), Metro Boomin and other rap luminaries.

The Gap were hoodwinked, bamboozled and led astray . . . all the way to the bank. It turns out that everyone can derive profit and pleasure from those occasions when Hip-Hop attempts to screw the man – including the man himself.

LL Cool J-inspired Tip

No matter what capacity you may work for or with them in, large organisations will love you as long as they can use you. When you're out of uses you're out the door. Ensure you use them while they're using you. And use them to help empower and promote people like you, who in turn will help you when doom and gloom start to loom.

GOOD DEEDS MAKE GOOD PROMOTION

From the Good Samaritan to Band Aid to Drake's 'God's Plan' video – the good deed has been a consistent source of promotion going back millennia.

In early September 2014, a video of Atlanta rapper Jay 'Young Jeezy' Jenkins' appearing at a press conference was posted on a YouTube channel owned by the influencer and internet-based, real-estate entrepreneur, Jay Morrison. In the press conference, Jeezy gifted a giant $1m cheque to Jay Morrison's for-profit, internet-based, real-estate training firm, the Jay Morrison Academy.

The stated aims of the Jay Morrison Academy include: to teach students 'what the wealthy don't want you to know' and, more convincingly, to 'provide affordable, high quality wealth education to the masses with a special interest in minority and low-income students who have typically not been afforded this invaluable information due to reasonable access and cost'.

These commendable aims (especially the latter) make Jeezy's decision to gift the Jay Morrison Academy $1m admirable . . . if mildly perplexing, given that it is not a real academic institution (in the conventional sense), it is not a charity (but a for-profit business) and it is not able to issue qualifications with any respected or verifiable indicator of skill, knowledge or intellectual prowess. Either way, it is hard to argue against the idea that a $1m donation to enhance the skills of young people was a generous gesture.

The donation was reported widely and warmly in Hip-Hop, Black media and wider (i.e. whiter) media. However, there was one small issue: the entire arrangement – from press conference to giant cheque – according to former insiders, was a promotional mirage.

There didn't appear to have been a $1m donation at all. What is alleged to have happened is a convenient convergence of interest that brought together a rapper in need of good public relations with an album to promote, an influencer in need of clout to market his real-estate course and a brilliant Hip-Hop dark arts practitioner (a fixer) after a payday.

Whistle-blowers, including a former girlfriend, a former business manager and a former business partner of Jay Morrison, all revealed that it was a public relations stunt posing as a society-enhancing endeavour.

At the press conference, Jay Morrison, a charismatic and well-groomed fake-it-till-you-make-it character, stated that real-estate investing helped him turn from a life of crime (he had several convictions and custodial sentences) to a life of legitimate wealth. Jeezy spoke rather fleetingly. The press conference enjoyed the enthusiasm and elation of a baby's funeral – to the point that Jeezy himself felt the need to say 'this is a great thing – y'all can be happy' to try to arouse some form of joviality in the room.

The giant $1m cheque was dated 2 September 2014 and was issued by Young Jeezy's charity, Street Dreamz Foundation. In 2021, Jayson M. Thornton, a licensed financial advisor and accountant who runs a financial investigations platform called Pocket Watching with JT, forensically and publicly reviewed Street Dreamz Foundation's tax filings. There was no mention of or allusion to Jay Morrison Academy or a $1m donation.

It should be noted that Jeezy did quietly donate over $200,000 to at-risk students returning to conventional schools during the same period.

By all indications, Jeezy did not donate $1m to the Jay Morrison Academy. As it often does outside Hip-Hop, philanthropy as a promotional stunt worked beautifully. Jeezy looked 'like a hero to the hood' right on time for his album to be released and the enrolments for the Jay Morrison Academy reportedly went through the roof.

Morrison and Jeezy used the good deed in the exact way most corporations use it: as a means of suggesting you are doing good, when in reality you're doing quite well.

Jeezy- and Jay Morrison-inspired tips

1. The corporate feel-good story and the average generic promotional tactic are designed to do the same thing: make you feel good, excite you and make you aware of something or someone.

2. There is seldomly such a thing as a no-strings attached 'donation'.

3. The press conference/press release is where charity stops and promotion starts.

9.

VISION AND MISSION

Part prayer, part propaganda, part corporate pornography: there is often nothing emptier, more uninspiring or more pretentious than a company's vision and mission statement. Below are a few of the good, the bad and the not-so beautiful.

- Johnson & Johnson: *'We will delight our consumers, treating each person who contacts us as if they are our only consumer, providing them with a response which is evidence of our interest and that leaves them with the clear understanding that they are important to us.'*
- BBC: *'Our mission is to act in the public interest, serving all audiences through the provision of impartial, high-quality and distinctive output and services which inform, educate and entertain.'*
- Disney: *'The mission of the Walt Disney Company is to entertain, inform and inspire people around the globe through the power of unparalleled storytelling, reflecting the iconic brands, creative minds and innovative technologies that make ours the world's premier entertainment company.'*

(You can wake up now.)

- Death Row Records: *'Bow wow wow yippy yo yippy yay – Death Row's in the motherfuckin' hooouse!'*

According to the powers that be, a powerful mission and vision statement must radiate the following qualities:

1. Conciseness
2. Clarity
3. Future orientation
4. Stability
5. Challenge
6. Abstractness
7. Desirability or ability to inspire[1]

If this is to be believed, then one of the single greatest company mission and/or vision statements ever conceived and proclaimed didn't come from the mind or mouth of a Harvard, Wharton or Oxford-educated business magnate or marketing guru. It came from Juvenile, a gold-toothed rapper who speaks exclusively in Magnolia Projects ebonics, in his 1999 track 'Back Dat Azz Up':[2]

> *'Cash Money Records taking over for the nine-nine and two thousands'*

Not only do they robustly meet every criteria of a good mission and vision statement, those words were the birth of one of Hip-Hop's longest-lasting dynastic reigns.

If you were born after 1999, there is a chance you may owe your existence to this vision and mission statement. Most importantly, 'Cash Money Records taking over for the nine-nine and two thousands' was not an empty brag. It did exactly what the very best of vision and mission statements are supposed to do: it motivated, empowered, aligned energies and helped set strategy.

Perhaps partly as a result, Cash Money's vision and mission became real. Very real. And it remains real. Of all the major Hip-Hop record labels that existed in 1999, Cash Money Records is the one that still exists in buoyant form. Drake, Nicki Minaj and Lil Wayne were all signed to them. Their reign at the top of the business has been significantly longer than that of even Motown Records, a byword for music-industry dominance.

Cash Money Records was founded (and is still owned and run by) the Cash Money Brothers (a name taken from a drug-dealing crew in the 1991 crime thriller *New Jack City*), the New Orleans natives Ronald 'Slim' Williams and Bryan 'Birdman' Williams.

Orphaned at a preciously young age, Slim and Birdman are two of twenty-three siblings (eleven boys and twelve girls). Their mother died when Birdman (who is five years younger than Slim) was two, and their father died when he was five. As a result, they grew up in some of the worst boys' homes in America and eventually ended up homeless and selling drugs. Before he passed away, their father instilled entrepreneurialism into his young sons: 'My dad always told us that we need to start our own business and be entrepreneurs. He put that in my head,' said Slim in a 2019 interview with *Forbes* magazine.

Similar to their approach to mission- and vision-setting, their entrepreneurialism bucks a trend. In a 2013 paper, Berkeley economists Ross Levine and Rona Rubenstein analysed the shared traits of entrepreneurs, and found that most were white, male, highly educated and from moneyed families. 'If one does not have money in the form of a family with money, the chances of becoming an entrepreneur drop quite a bit,' Levine told *Quartz* magazine.[3]

Noticing the burgeoning popularity of bounce music (a bass-heavy, sex-drenched, call-and-response-style music native to New Orleans), Slim and Birdman decided to get into the music business as a means of escaping poverty and crime.

They founded Cash Money Records in 1991, tapped into the local sound and became magnets for local talent. As we have seen, from 1991 to 1997 they released dozens of albums with various local acts (some of whom they would eventually take international) before signing a groundbreaking deal with Universal Music Group in 1998 (see Chapter 7).

Birdman reflected on their early ambitions in *Forbes*:

Well, if you grew up in New Orleans . . . whatever you get into you'll just be a beast about it, you're going to be very aggressive about it. If you're a hustler, you're going to be aggressive. If you play sports, you're going to be aggressive. I just took the street life and converted it into the aggressiveness of being a hustler. Finding ways of turning one to 10. 10 to 100. I wasn't about just being kosher with making a few dollars, we really wanted to make some real money in this game.

And that they did. Since 1998, they have sold over 130 million albums and generated nearly $2 billion in revenue.

The first major hit (and second single) Cash Money Records released after signing their deal with Universal Music Group was 'Back Dat Azz Up', the mother of all twerk records (and 'the greatest love song ever wrote' according to its producer, the great Mannie Fresh)[4] . . . which starts with that ideal company mission and vision statement: 'Cash Money Records taking over for the nine-nine and two thousands.'

'Back Dat Azz Up'-inspired Vision- and Mission-setting Tip

Your vision and mission statements are your clarion calls, not your funeral sermons. It is unforgivable if they do not:

- Arouse excitement, attraction, commitment and determination. Preferably they should help get hearts racing.

- Feel more '5 p.m. Friday' than '9 a.m. Monday'. They must evoke warmth, happiness and snap people out of their slumber.

- Appeal to most demographics.

- Stand the test of time.

- Help shape the direction of travel and progress of your organisation.

- Complement your organisational goals.

SECTION 3

MOVING UP

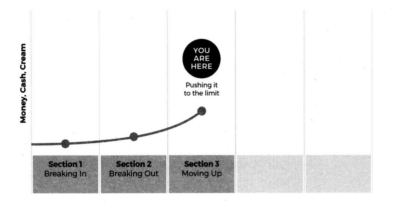

10.

LEADERSHIP AND CORPORATE MANAGEMENT

THE MAKING AND BREAKING-UP OF ROC-A-FELLA

Jay-Z had a rather interesting exchange with MTV in a 1998 interview.

MTV: *What kind of boss do you think you are?*

[Jay-Z looks sideways, smirks and smiles throughout his response. He never looks at the camera or the interviewer.]

Jay-Z: [sarcastically] *I think I am too nice, need to start being more stern. Get a couple of people out of there. Nah, but really – I like to think of myself as being a pretty cool person to work with. Pretty easy-going. I don't argue so much. That is my other partner – I leave that for him.*

From their earliest days as co-chief executives of their then independent label, Roc-A-Fella Records (originally distributed by Priority Records but from 1997 a subsidiary of Def Jam), Jay-Z and his then business partners Damon 'Dame' Dash and (figurative as well as often literal) silent partner Kareem 'Biggs' Burke worked hard to ensure that their artists were given every possible chance to succeed. From disproportionately prominent spots on tours, albums, compilations and radio appearances to ensuring they featured in magazines, films and adverts – Jay-Z, Dame, Biggs and their staff worked hard to help craft careers for the people they invested in. The self-interest was of course clear: the success of the artists meant a return on investment for Roc-A-Fella. Nevertheless, it is far from uncommon for labels to sign, shelf, exploit for tax write-off reasons and eventually drop artists without giving them much light or a shot at success.

The corporate leadership structure and strategy that drove the success of Roc-A-Fella was:

- Jay-Z focused on delivering hit records – otherwise loosely known as product development
- Dame Dash focused on the day-to-day running of the business – otherwise loosely known as corporate management
- Both were very public ambassadors of the brand

It worked. With everyone playing to their strengths, the company grew stronger and stronger. By 2002, Roc-A-Fella was on fire. They had fingers in all sorts of pies: clothing lines, TV shows, films, alcoholic beverages and an electronics brand. Thanks to Jay-Z, they were pretty much guaranteed a platinum album annually, and as far as attracting talent was concerned, they stood a fantastic shot at getting whoever they wanted. And they hoovered up talent. Roc-A-Fella was a Black dynasty, an iconic lifestyle brand and a symbol of the good life. Not bad for a seven-year-old company run and founded by three school dropouts in their early thirties.

But at the height of their popularity, discontent within the partnership at Roc-A-Fella brewed. Dash, who was the very definition of an assertive executive, made a series of hires, fires and promotions that fell somewhere between irritating and insulting Jay-Z.

In 2003, Jay-Z announced his 'retirement album' – the *Black Album* (although, like many a sporting great, the game pulled him right back). With Jay-Z 'retired' from making albums, Roc-A-Fella Records had to stand on its own two feet.

Rumours of a potential split intensified. These rumours became *Death of a Dynasty*, a 2003 indie comedy film parodying rumours of a Roc-A-Fella split (the film gave early career breaks for future superstars Kevin Hart and Rashida Jones). And, in 2004, the rumours became reality.

Having 'retired' at the top of his game, Jay-Z was off to become the president of Hip-Hop's main indigenous label: Def Jam (a role Dame Dash probably would have been the more obvious fit for; however, Dash is famously and vehemently opposed to having a boss or working for anyone).

Def Jam also happened to be the parent company and 50 per cent owner of Roc-A-Fella. After becoming president of Def Jam, Jay-Z had the option to buy out the remaining 50 per cent of Roc-A-Fella Records, an option he decided to exercise. With the buyout complete, Jay-Z controlled both Def Jam and Roc-A-Fella Records. Meanwhile, Dame Dash and Kareem 'Biggs' Burke left to establish the Dame Dash Music Group, a partnership with Universal (in turn the parent company of Def Jam).

This meant that the artists on Roc-A-Fella had to make a decision: stick with Jay-Z or leave with Dame Dash. This was essentially a choice between two very distinct, personality-driven management styles: which was better situated to steer their ship in a direction that would increase their likelihood of success?

The table below looks at key indicators of leadership quality and analyses how Jay-Z and Dame Dash performed against them based upon their widely perceived mannerisms and history at the time.

Leadership quality	Dame Dash, 33	Jay-Z, 35
Mastery of business field	You could not pull the wool over Dame's eyes	More the creative lead than the business lead
Temperament	Prone to huge yet usually entirely rational outbursts	Smooth as silk
Vision	Emphatic business visionary with a tendency to overextend himself	Calculating and cautious
Communication and presentation skills	Highly captivating and unorthodox communicator	A more reserved communicator when not performing
Managing internal conflict	Prone to making decisions that can create internal conflict	Likely to decisively fire any source of internal conflict
Attracting high-potential talent	Exceptional	At that time: questionable
Manageable (maintains good relations with bosses)	A virtual zero	Jay-Z adopted a more diplomatic and approachable relationship with his bosses
Gravitas	In an alienating manner	Enough to make British royalty feel like hippies
Special sauce	Fearlessness	Machiavellian

Table 9: Jay-Z and Dame Dash's 2005 leadership qualities compared

Jay-Z's biggest appeal at that time was himself: he was well established as a highly professional and influential music man with a consistent track record of strong sales. Jay-Z's biggest shortcoming was his lack of track record as a businessman.

Dame Dash's biggest appeal was his track record as a fearless and innovative businessman with a demonstrable catalogue of success. His biggest shortcoming was himself: his personal qualities – loudness, brashness, cockiness, over-assertiveness (which often spilt into rudeness) – made it hard for him to build and maintain relationships.

So, who did the artists, i.e. the assets, flock to? The proven businessman or the unproven one? The great rapper or the man with no musical ability (though he would attempt to establish a rock band at forty-eight)? The business brilliance *ying* or the creative genius *yang*?

It was a split: artists who stayed with Jay-Z and the new Roc-A-Fella/Def Jam included Kanye West, Memphis Bleek, Freeway, Young Gunz, Foxy Brown and DJ Clue. Artists who left with Dame Dash included Beanie Sigel (incarcerated at the time) and Ol' Dirty Bastard (who had died the previous year). Cam'Ron and his crew, The Diplomats, went their own way.

Having left only with one incarcerated and one deceased man, it is a fair summation that Dash did not get the pick of the litter. In many of the post-Roc-a-Fella interviews with the artists, a theme emerged: most who stayed with Jay-Z proclaimed Dame Dash to be the more effective/better executive (the exception is Memphis Bleek, who stuck with Jay-Z for tribal reasons),[1] but the other thing that they kept highlighting was that Jay-Z was a 'smoother' and nicer person.

August 2005. Jay-Z, newly minted president of Def Jam, appears on a special fold-out cover of *XXL* magazine. The theme for the cover was a White House administration with Jay-Z sat presidentially in the oval office, surrounded by his 'cabinet'. 'Leader of the Rap World – President Carter's Cabinet' was the headline.

There were a total of eleven people on the cover: Jay-Z, Kanye West, Foxy Brown and LeBron James were on the front. Freeway, the two members of Young Gunz, DJ Clue, Peedi Crack and Tierra Mari appeared on the fold-out. They were all dressed conservatively in black – almost as if they were at a funeral. Eight of them arguably were . . .

Fast-forward just a few years, and of the ten musicians on the cover only two were still viable artists with lucrative careers: Jay-Z and Kanye West, both of whom were nurtured to success by Dame Dash. With that said, no one who went to the Dame Dash Music Group flourished to become bigger than they were on Roc-A-Fella. The Dame Dash Music Group soon folded, and Dame Dash walked away from Def Jam.

To the artists on the label, Roc-A-Fella Records was stronger together.

Side question: why was basketball star LeBron James on the *XXL* cover with Jay-Z? *XXL* asked Jay-Z, and he responded in an interesting manner:

> **XXL:** What's happening with LeBron James? Are you trying to get into business with him?

> **Jay-Z:** No, he's a friend of mine. That's it, nothing more. A young guy coming up, grew up looking up to me, and that's it. I give him advice like I would give everyone else. I can't do nothing with him. I have a stake in the Nets. I can't do nothing with LeBron James, nothing. It's silly to even say. It's silly. There's no such thing as Def Sports Management. There's no such thing.

If it sounds like Jay-Z 'doth protest too much', it may be because he did: in 2013, Jay-Z established Roc Nation Sports, a major new challenger in the sports management business. Jay-Z is now one of the most renowned managers of talent in the world – thanks to Roc Nation. Most management organisations remain faceless corporations whose names remain entirely unknown to the public, never mind those of their executives – Roc Nation Sports' clients are proud to instruct people to 'call Roc Nation', almost as mantra, and almost as if it adds cool points to them and their personal brand (which it does).

LeBron is not a Roc Nation client, but the many athletes who have signed with them would have seen LeBron James on a magazine cover with Jay-Z a swift decade beforehand. It would, of course, be purely speculative to suggest that the cover may provide some degree of insight into Jay-Z's strategic, Machiavellian and long-term calculating approach to leadership.

Jay-Z-inspired Leadership Tips

- The punch from the hidden fist hits harder: never let anyone see you coming.

- A degree of unpredictability adds to the armour of the great leader – too much of it, however, could result in chaos.

- Unpredictability and unreliability could not be more different.

TWELVE LEADERSHIP RULES FROM SO SOLID'S MEGAMAN

At the turn of the century, UK Hip-Hop was largely ignored, derided and commercially irrelevant. And then Dwayne 'Megaman' Vincent, an incarcerated seventeen-year-old, had a dream. A dream in which he saw flashing lights and money.

A few years, a not-guilty verdict and a burning desire to prosper on a legitimate basis later, and that dream became So Solid Crew, the pioneering thirty-five-person-strong garage and Hip-Hop collective he founded.

Twenty years after So Solid's groundbreaking success, rap music is today a dominant force on the United Kingdom's cultural landscape, complete with a commercially vibrant domestic scene. At the root of this success is Megaman and his dream, and he has more than his fair share of tips on leadership. Below are a few.

1. Leadership development starts at home

Growing up in a multi-generational Caribbean household in Battersea (at the time an economically challenged multicultural area) taught Megaman how to take care of other people's interests. 'Their dreams,' he explains, 'become your dreams, their ambitions become your ambitions. These values stay with you as you leave the house. It taught me how to listen to people and how to build the skills and traits I needed to achieve.'

2. Lead those willing to follow; build with those wishing to build

Megaman took the leadership values and skills he learned in the nurturing environment of his family home into founding So Solid. Specifically, he wanted to build a successful company with a 'family' of his own, his friends – many of whom happened to be street guys. 'Your friends will upset you, your friends will offend you. But they all have a different skillset. If you bypass that skillset because of something that happened in a different part of your life, you probably won't get together and build something special.'

3. Be a sponge for knowledge, wisdom and information

When he got the opportunity to work at Supreme FM, a local community radio station, Megaman used this small opening to study how everything worked on the business and creative side of music. 'I was always looking for a window to accelerate [success]. I would ask questions like: what does it take to run a radio station? I'd ask how and where vinyl was pressed up. I don't know what other MCs and DJs did. Maybe they came to MC lyrics and get girls. And that was my ambition too – but my deepest ambition was to learn how everything worked.'

4. Keep learning: understand everyone else's assignments

As a leader, the more you understand everyone else's jobs, the safer you are and the more successful you are likely to be. In building So Solid, Megaman had to 'think like the promoter, the club owner, the radio guy, the studio guy, the club guy, the label'. In order to think like them, he had to master their jobs too.

5. Play to people's strengths

Believing that everyone had particular gifts, Megaman worked to ensure he understood everyone's strengths and assigned them to work where they were most likely to prosper and stay out of trouble. 'I tried to piece everyone together. If you were not a good rapper, you could do the business side. If you were good on the tech side, you could do the radio stuff. Everyone had some sort of expertise – so why were we in the streets doing illegal activity?' Megaman adds that it is critical that everyone gets the opportunity to learn how to do something new.

6. Results are the ultimate motivator

How did Megaman ensure over thirty people were where they needed to be at the right time and performing to optimal ability? By 'giving people the belief that as a team we can achieve things quicker than as individuals. And then them actually seeing this happen. That is the proof in the pudding.' Results breed results. Let them see what they can be.

7. Spread a business philosophy

To ensure the crew was razor-focused on achieving their dreams, philosophically (business-wise) on the same page and spiritually fulfilled, Megaman set up 'So Solid Sundays' – a weekly meeting in which he played inspirational, affirming and enriching audio-books to members of So Solid.

8. Display key leadership qualities

In the eyes of Megaman, leadership qualities are a cocktail of 'a little bit of talent, a little bit of knowhow, a little bit of faith as well as having strong morals and keeping your emotions in check'.

9. Make sacrifices

Leadership is a sacrifice. 'The captain of the ship cannot party on the ship. He must focus on navigating. That takes a hard mindset. Every successful leader has had to look back with regret at the discipline they had to undertake to achieve it. And the enjoyment they had to miss.'

10. Effectively manage and settle disputes

Disputes were avoided by ensuring everyone knew 'they were part of something bigger' than themselves. There were 'scuffs, arguments and stuff but they always sorted it with respect'. Megaman laid down one golden rule: 'no throwing around of egos'. In situations where things fell apart and could not be resolved internally, he would seek arbitration by bringing in 'people from other business areas or people from the streets to bring balance and calm. We also surrounded ourselves with respected elders.'

11. Measure your own success

'Anyone [or any leader] who leaves this earth and people cannot point to you and say "he changed my life" is a leader who has not achieved anything.'

12. Rewards come in many forms

Being rewarded for success is 'not just about the money', advises Megaman. 'Enjoy the process. If I cannot enjoy the process, I won't do it.'

11.

PEOPLE MANAGEMENT

According to former Republican presidential candidate and businessman Mitt Romney, 'corporations are people'.[1] And as Jay-Z acknowledged when he proclaimed that he was not a businessman but 'a business, man', people with high-value asset- and service-based careers (such as him) are indeed corporations. It logically follows that rappers are corporate entities. And what is considered a rapper's crew (often mockingly described as a posse) is actually the mirror image of the executive and board leaderships of a major company.

Role	Corporate equivalent	Job description
Rapper's career	Corporation	The source of all wealth and the basis of the entire operation
Rapper	CEO	The leader, the face, the front office and voice box of the organisation
Manager	Chief Operating Officer	Responsible for overseeing the day-to-day administrative and operational functions

Role	Corporate equivalent	Job description
Bodyguards	Safety, Security & Resilience	Responsible for the safety of the organisation. Likely to be former security and intelligence officials
Goons	The police	Pumped-up amateurish thugs who are able and willing to get their hands dirty
Lawyer	Head of Legal Affairs	Responsible for ensuring the company (especially the principals) stays out of legal problems and prison
Recently freed 1980s street legend	Chairman of the Board	Provides ultimate leadership. Occasionally the seed financier of the operation
Spiritual Adviser	Head of Compliance	Independently minded and morality obsessed adviser with a supposed direct line to authority figures. Often ignored
Token Woman[2]	Human Resources	Responsible for bringing calm, order and compassion to the organisation. Or at least the appearance thereof. Often ignored
Hype Man	Chief Brand Officer/ Director of Communications	Responsible for amplifying, protecting and improving the brand and image of the company

Role	Corporate equivalent	Job description
Shooter	Chief of Staff	Shadowy figure who reports directly to the CEO. More 'operational enforcer' than 'gatekeeper'
Accountant	Chief Finance Officer	The numbers person, responsible for filing accounts and monitoring the financial health of the organisation
Second Accountant	Auditor	Person watching the numbers guy to ensure the organisation doesn't go broke
Driver	Chauffeur and/or executive assistant to the CEO	Super-trustworthy person hired by the rapper/CEO to ensure they are where they need to be at all times, to extract them from sticky situations and to guard some of their deepest and dirtiest secrets
Weed Handler and Charge Taker	Chief Risk Officer[*]	Takes the criminal charge when wrongdoing is uncovered. Rewarded with a promotion if everything blows over

Table 10: Leadership comparison:
the rapper's crew and the corporation's board

So, with the personnel perhaps not as far apart as you might imagine, what can we learn from Hip-Hop's moguls about human

---

[*] Or any senior leader who no one knows what they do.

resource management? Over the course of this chapter, we'll look at how rap moguls deal with three key pillars of people management:

1. Recruitment
2. Management
3. Support

RECRUITMENT

Recruitment – getting the right people into the right jobs – is an enormous industry that has itself spewed subsidiary industries. According to the Society for Human Resource Management, companies spend $4,129 to recruit for an 'average' job and multiples more for 'above average' – i.e. more senior – roles. The *Harvard Business Review* estimates that collectively corporate America spends $20bn a year on hiring and firing. That is roughly the equivalent of the gross domestic products of Barbados, Sierra Leone, Montenegro, Belize, Liberia and Aruba – combined. Putting it mildly, getting the right person in the right job is big business.

Recruitment innovation lessons from Puff Daddy

It is often suggested that, despite his huge success in music, technical musical talent (on the microphone, boards or instruments) is not Sean 'Puff Daddy' Combs' true gift. One thing that is not in doubt is his ability to recruit and assemble world-class talent into a creative and commercially conducive environment and nurture them to success.

For example, most Hip-Hop record labels are centred around the musical production talents of one key person or duo. At Death Row it was Dr. Dre, at Startrack it was the Neptunes, at early Def Jam it was Rick Rubin, and so on. In an early sign of his gift for talent spotting and recruitment, Puff Daddy departed from previous business protocol and recruited various talented producers as in-house producers at his own label, Bad Boy Entertainment – he called this highly successful ensemble the Hitmen.[3]

Puff Daddy had a slightly different role to play. He sits in the ranks of Steve Jobs, Elon Musk, Jay-Z, Sir Richard Branson and Sir Martin Sorrell – hyper-visible senior executives who are synonymous with their companies and form a critical part of the value of their company brands. Provided the boss is not a barrel of toxicity and inappropriateness, one of the benefits of having a celebrity boss includes making it easier and cheaper for the company to attract and retain talent. It also has its downside: the celebrity of the boss could overshadow the efforts and achievements of staff. Suge Knight certainly thought this may be the case with Puff Daddy and used this 'weakness' as a recruitment call at the 1995 Source Awards:

'Any artist out there that wanna be an artist, stay a star, and won't have to worry about the executive producer trying to be all in the videos . . . all on the records . . . dancing: come to Death Row!'

Suge Knight-inspired Recruitment Tip

Where you sense the hint of dissatisfaction in a lucrative star employee at a rival organisation, exploit the source of dissatisfaction as a potential recruitment perk. Where you don't sense a hint of dissatisfaction, attempt to create it.

Despite Suge's disapproval, Puff Daddy, who himself worked as an unpaid intern for over two years at the start of his career, has always been ahead of the curve in modern recruitment.

In 2007, when YouTube was still a relatively new wonder of the world, Puff Daddy used it as a recruitment tool for a new assistant. His requirements for hopeful applicants were simple:

A three-minute explanation as to why they deserved the job, and a college degree.[4]

His own pitch ran as follows:

Why you should be my personal assistant? What better job than to have me scream at you, go crazy, keep you up long hours, have you sleep deprived? If this job interests you, upload your video interview saying what makes you my perfect assistant.

Viewers of the video would pick the finalists; however, Puff Daddy would pick the winner. Skewed democracy in action. Game on.

This highly unorthodox pitch, application and selection process attracted over 600 applicants in a matter of days, a decent number for its time. In the end it boiled down to three people, and they had to make their final pitch directly to Puff Daddy on the *Oprah Winfrey Show*. Heather Joy Thompson, a lawyer (who is, like Puff, from Harlem), sealed the victory with these words:

I think I should have this job because my experience as a lawyer, a Returned Peace Corp volunteer and my wide scope of professional experiences I believe make me uniquely qualified to serve Mr Combs. And I am very humble and not unwilling to take the role of assisting him because I understand who the star is in this relationship. And I am willing to support him in the way that he needs.

In this process, Puff Daddy not only found a world-class assistant, he also attained publicity money could not buy – an Oprah Winfrey special and a 2008 VH1 spin-off show called *I Want to Work for Diddy* (the actress Laverne Cox, best known for starring in *Orange Is the New Black*, got her first major break on TV on this show). Critically, Puff Daddy found a way to monetise what is usually an expensive cost base – the recruitment process.

His innovation in recruitment did not catch on, though. Had

this Pontius Pilate-isation of recruiting staff been refined and attained a hold, Puff Daddy could have been the inventor of a much more efficient and streamlined recruitment process, one with positive and negative outcomes (see Figure 9).

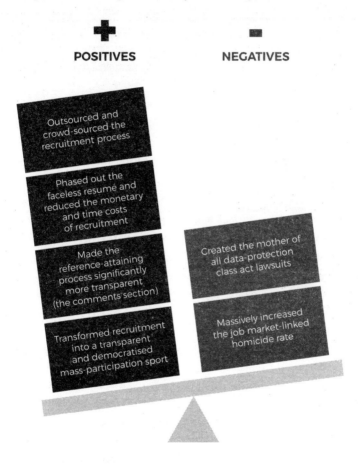

POSITIVES   NEGATIVES

Outsourced and crowd-sourced the recruitment process

Phased out the faceless resumé and reduced the monetary and time costs of recruitment

Made the reference-attaining process significantly more transparent (the comments section)

Created the mother of all data-protection class act lawsuits

Transformed recruitment into a transparent and democratised mass-participation sport

Massively increased the job market-linked homicide rate

CAUTION
The weightings on the diagram above imply an equality of impact which may not be the case in practice.

Figure 10: Outcomes of Puff Daddy's Pontius Pilate-isation of recruitment

175

Key things Heather Joy Thompson, Esq., learned from Puff Daddy

Employees tend to leave bad managers for a million reasons. Employees tend to leave good managers for one reason: growth-related success. After working for Puff Daddy for a year, Heather Joy Thompson left to become a United States diplomat, a role she remains in today.

Below are some of the key skills she took from her time with Mr Combs:

1. Reject all forms of assimilation and show up as your full authentic self. Never ever conform. However . . .
2. . . . expect to be underestimated if you don't conform. 'Puff, to me, was sometimes underestimated by the suits at the table because they expect talent to show up and sound one way. They expect you to speak the Queen's English at all times, be attired a certain way and conform to their expectations of what an intelligent person sounds like. But he is an impresario: he comes to the table looking and sounding like a Hip-Hop star and he doesn't come to the table unless he wants to. Yet, at every table I went to with him: he was the smartest person there. He really just outsmarted, outclassed and outfoxed every group of people I saw him with.'
3. You become the smartest person in the room by considering every single angle possible for a deal or situation beforehand. 'Puff would think through their [the suits'] equations and then fifteen more before he ever sat down.'
4. Know the value you bring to the table. 'Puff is from Westchester but he is really from Harlem. He had a fully Black upbringing. He understands his Black and Latino Harlemite and worldwide audience in a way that may not be captured by the metrics these corporations may use. They think they understand us: he really does.'

5. Appreciate the details. According to Heather Joy, Puff Daddy would personally go to mom and pop stores to ensure his products were positioned prestigiously.

6. Build dynamic organisations that are bound by talent as opposed to artificial barriers such as academic qualifications. But . . .

7. . . . work your way around nepotism by being results-orientated: elevate the people who get things done.

8. Consider if being process-driven really works for you. Puff Daddy is more driven by personality, feel and creativity.

9. Embrace diversity by surrounding yourself with people different to you. Puff Daddy's most trusted counsel and business partners are intentionally drawn from a range of professional and personal backgrounds.

Puff Daddy and *Making the Band*

In 2000, MTV debuted *Making the Band*, a reality show in which budding musicians vied for a position in a group. In season two, the ante was upped when Puff Daddy was brought in as both an executive producer, mentor and ultimately the boss of the label the successful contenders would be signed to. In a moment of advanced creativity, the first group to win the Puff Daddy-fronted *Making the Band* golden ticket went on to be called Da Band.

In *Making the Band*, Puff Daddy also seized an opportunity to debut another alternative recruitment innovation. He simply asked the contestants to go and buy him a slice of cheesecake on foot . . . from a shop that was a mere three-hour walk away. In doing so, as opposed to *asking* the contestants why they wanted the job, he made them *show* him. He made them demonstrate their ambition, determination, humility and desire to go places. He made them prove that they were the right people for the job.

....

Puff Daddy-inspired Recruitment Tip

Somewhere between humility and humiliation lies an indication of ambition and job suitability . . . in some situations. In other situations, the thin line between humility and humiliation is known as an ambulance-chasing no-win, no-fee lawyer; the recruiter should tread carefully when pulling Puff Daddy-style recruitment stunts.

....

MANAGEMENT: HIP-HOP'S SUPERMANAGER

Bad management is corrosive and super-costly. It kills morale, productivity, ingenuity, balance sheets and, most seriously, it kills people. It is simultaneously a super-expensive and super-needless cost. The *HR Review* estimates that bad management costs the UK an estimated $106bn (£84bn) a year.[5] Estimates of the cost of bad management seep into trillion-dollar territory in the United States.[6]

But what makes a good manager? Darrell 'Chris' Lighty had the answers.

Chris Lighty's life, as Hip-Hop historian and author of the *Big Payback* Dan Charnas noted, is itself a Hip-Hop life story. Born in the South Bronx, the birthplace of Hip-Hop, he was the eldest of six children and raised by his mother, who instilled independence, dependability and loyalty in her young. These personal qualities would prove essential in Chris Lighty's professional development as a manager.

Lighty's personal qualities and street smarts proved valuable in helping him attain an early career break in rap: carrying records and providing 'muscle' for the legendary New York radio jock Kool DJ Red Alert in the late 1980s.

Red Alert believed in Chris Lighty to such an extent that he made him road manager for the Jungle Brothers, a group he was developing. Granted a millimetre of an opportunity, Chris Lighty grabbed the length of the equator.

After the Jungle Brothers, Lighty went on to manage the seminal rap group A Tribe Called Quest. Noticing his talents, Rush Artist Management and Def Jam's Russell Simmons and Lyor Cohen attempted to recruit him. Lighty began working for Rush Artist Management, which was famous for guiding the careers of the Beastie Boys, LL Cool J, Public Enemy, Run DMC and Whodini. After working for Rush for over half a decade, Lighty, alongside Mona Scott (who would later go on to create the hugely successful Hip-Hop reality TV series, *Love & Hip-Hop*), left to form his own management company, Violator.

Violator in time became Hip-Hop's pre-eminent management company, managing the careers of the likes of Warren G, Ja Rule, Mobb Deep, Missy Elliott, Fat Joe, Q-Tip (originally of A Tribe Called Quest), Busta Rhymes, LL Cool J, Noreaga (aka N.O.R.E.), 50 Cent, Mariah Carey, Sean 'Puff Daddy' Combs and others.

The story of Chris Lighty, Hip-Hop's most revered and respected manager, offers great insight into four critical areas of management, namely:

- Opportunity creation
- Bespoke management
- Being a critical friend
- Commercial nous

Opportunity creation

A good manager adds clear value to their clients, and there is no more demonstrable value added to a career than creating new and unique opportunities. Here, Chris Lighty shone bright.

LL Cool J: One of Lighty's most important clients was Hip-Hop royalty – indeed Hip-Hop's Prince Charming, LL Cool J. LL Cool J became a professional rapper in the mid-1980s at the tender age of fifteen. Decades later, he is Hip-Hop's equivalent of

Kellogg's, Levi's, the British Royal Family or Colgate: a highly successful and carefully managed entity, brand and establishment cornerstone. By the mid-1990s, most of LL Cool J's peers had fallen by the wayside as a new generation arrived to take over. In what could have been a period of managed decline, Lighty carefully ensured LL Cool J withstood the winds of change and remained at the forefront of the culture. He did this by:

- Pairing LL Cool J with Trackmasters, a go-to production duo who specialise in making monster hit records, and acting as executive producer on LL Cool J's return-to-form album, the double-platinum-selling *Mr Smith* (1995)
- Securing a landmark 1997 Gap advert . . . which LL Cool J turned into a joint Gap and FUBU advert (see Chapter 8), further solidifying LL's legend
- Helping LL Cool J navigate his (non-violent) beef with then smoking-hot upstart Canibus. Canibus's excellent '2nd Round KO' (featuring 'Iron' Mike Tyson) could have dented LL Cool J's career. Instead, LL Cool J's retort, 'The Ripper Strikes Back', elevated his own career and ended Canibus's altogether
- Though LL Cool J had been in film and TV since 1985 (long before Lighty broke into Hip-Hop), Violator's success in managing LL Cool J helped elevate his Hollywood career with hugely successful roles in *Deep Blue Sea*, *Any Given Sunday* and *In Too Deep*

Missy Elliott: One of the most captivatingly creative artists ever. From her music to her videos to her own presentation, she was always someone who moved in a different direction to the pack. Her creativity made her an advertiser's dream. Chris Lighty was there to help those dreams come true. She starred in adverts for three separate major soft drink brands – Coca-Cola, Pepsi and Sprite (though Sprite is owned by Coca-Cola). Missy also starred in adverts for Gap, Doritos, Virgin Mobile and MAC Cosmetics and provided the soundtrack for an advert for Chrysler's Jeep campaign. In 2004, Missy Elliot launched 'Respect ME', her own clothing line with Adidas.

A Tribe Called Quest: Sprite had embraced Hip-Hop since the mid-1980s. However, the norm was for them to work with popular, poppy and photogenic rappers (e.g. Kurtis Blow, LL Cool J and Kriss Kross). Lighty helped Sprite become the staple soda of urban young by pairing them up with less chart-friendly but culturally cutting-edge artists such as A Tribe Called Quest to be the face of their 'Obey Your Thirst' campaign. This helped deepen Sprite's relationship with Hip-Hop and ultimately with consumers. Along the way, it also made Sprite the epitome of a cool soft drink. For A Tribe Called Quest, the ad presumably helped deepen their pockets.[7]

Foxy Brown: Foxy Brown had all the ingredients needed to become a popular rapper – confidence on the microphone, the sound, the looks (of a top-tier supermodel), the swagger, the background, the streets and the alliances but she lacked one thing: the ability to write radio hits. Chris Lighty was able to pair her with Jay-Z to write her singles, a match made in Hip-Hop heaven that produced records like 'Get You Home' (featuring Blackstreet), 'Big Bad Mama' (featuring Dru Hill) and 'I'll Be' (featuring Jay-Z) and Jay-Z's own first hit record, 'Ain't No Nigga'.

Foxy would also go on to become a Calvin Klein model.

In his own corporate bio Lighty explained the role opportunity creation plays in his management style:

My whole philosophy is to try and get the best product from my artists, get them the best opportunities. It's a serious venture, because you're dealing with peoples' lives and their livelihoods and you want them to have something to stand on.[8]

Lighty worked to maximise the earning potential of his clients while simultaneously ensuring he delivered enhanced returns for any business they did deals with. Critically, he ensured the deals were not just financial in nature – they complemented the brand and integrity of the client.

Bespoke management

In a rare elaboration of the wildly overquoted 'checkers not chess' mantra, the *Harvard Business Review* states that great managers:

> *discover what is unique about each person and then capitalize on it. Average managers play checkers, while great managers play chess. The difference? In checkers, all the pieces are uniform and move in the same way; they are interchangeable . . . In chess, each type of piece moves in a different way, and you can't play if you don't know how each piece moves. More important, you won't win if you don't think carefully about how you move the pieces. Great managers know and value the unique abilities and even the eccentricities of their employees, and they learn how best to integrate them into a coordinated plan of attack.*[9]

Chris Lighty lived and breathed exactly what the *HBR* suggested here: bespoke management. Recognise the individual as an individual with unique strengths and weaknesses and address their needs to get the most out of them. The management needs of Chi Ali (who was charged with murdering his girlfriend's brother, went on the run for over a year, became subject of a huge manhunt complete with an appearance on *America's Most Wanted* and was ultimately convicted of manslaughter) must have been quite different to the needs of, say, Mariah Carey, the queen of Christmas.

Likely management needs of Chi Ali	Likely management needs of Mariah Carey
• Keeping him off the streets while simultaneously retaining street credibility • Protection – when you're a rapper telling the stories of the street, the street may occasionally 'test' your knowledge • Retaining the services of a reputable, respected and highly effective lawyer	• The careful protection and perpetual nurturing of their brands • Career perpetuation • Partnership selection • Status improvement and maintenance • Iconography • Legacy preservation

Table 11: Bespoke management: Chi Ali vs Mariah Carey

The highly personalised micro-needs of all the artists Lighty managed – in addition to his own needs – were all challenging. The personal lives of many of his clients were often highly chaotic, but each presented their own set of strengths, weakness, opportunities and threats that had to be properly taken care of – all in accordance with the needs of the client. Rapidly adapting and adjusting his management style and strategy would likely have been a daily challenge for Chris Lighty.

Being a critical friend

There is nothing more appealing to the ego than someone who will tell you you're always right, your ideas are always good, your missteps are golden steps and your farts smell like top-drawer Paco Rabanne. As a result, Yes Men (and women) simultaneously:

• Rule the world and make the best friends
• Ruin the world and make the worst friends

In contrast, the Yes Man's opposite, the critical friend, offers:

- Encouragement and support
- Honest and, where needed, forthright and difficult feedback
- Critical honesty about shortcomings, problems, weaknesses and emotionally charged issues
- A thorough g-checking and/or gut checking where necessary

A good manager is the very definition of a critical friend. An inadvertently bad manager is likely to be a Yes Man. Chris Lighty and Shotti, CEO of Tr3yway Entertainment and a member of the Nine Trey Gangsters, offer an interesting comparison of the critical friend and Yes Man approaches to artist management.

Chris Lighty started his career as a tough street guy. Even while he worked for Rush Artist Management he supplemented his earnings with dealings in the street. Lyor Cohen gave him an ultimatum: 'Do you want to be this guy or that guy?'.[10] Lighty had to decide: did he want to be a street guy or a music executive? Lighty walked away from the streets, put on a business suit and went on to elevate Hip-Hop as a creative and commercial force and managed some of the biggest names in the business.

Not so for Kifano 'Shotti' Jordan.

'6ix9ine can talk shit because I say so, he got the OK sanction and he one of the niggas that's really with the shits,' said Shotti in an Instagram live post, offering an insight into his management philosophy.

The line between even corporate-level Hip-Hop and the streets has always been blurred. For the Nine Trey Gangsta Bloods (a subset of the Blood Nation, a gang founded in Rikers Island prison in the early 1990s)[11] and Tr3yway Entertainment, that line did not exist at all. Shotti was the CEO of Tr3yway and therefore de facto manager of Daniel 'Tekashi 6ix9ine' Hernandez, a travel-sized, eccentric, rainbow-haired Mexican-American rapper with tattoos all over his upper torso.

Tekashi's music has an almost electric kind of energy. It is wild, super-violent and utterly shocking. Solely off the strength of his music, he became a super-hot star. Every single song on his debut mixtape, *Day69*, became a chart hit – a monumental achievement.

The video for Tekashi's breakout single, 'Gummo', featured a couple of dozen Blood gang members (or people posing with red bandanas) throwing up gang signs, flashing guns and alcohol, and posing with enormous bags of marijuana while sat on the bonnet of an SUV. Even the NYPD makes an inadvertent cameo – offering further credibility in the process. Neo-minstrel concrete Tarzan meets *Law & Order: Organized Crime*. As it was designed to do, it went super-viral and made Tekashi something of a star.

Tekashi was not a gang member or a street guy or a tough guy – he was a financially destitute young man who understood the power and appeal of internet trolling. Trolling garnered him an audience on Instagram, but not much money. When his girlfriend became pregnant, he did what many a financially desperate person does, he prayed: 'Please, God, change my life. Please, God, make me famous,' as Tekashi told it to Power 105's Angie Martinez.

Through 'Gummo', which has now been viewed over 400 million times on YouTube alone, his prayers were robustly answered. It was also on the late summer 2017 set of the 'Gummo' video that Tekashi met Shotti.

Shotti (then thirty-six) and Tekashi (then twenty-one) saw something in each other.[12] In Shotti, Tekashi saw street credibility, protection, access to video props and subject material for his music, career advancement and collateral damage in waiting.

Shotti saw a cash cow.

Shotti became Tekashi's unofficial manager, and Tekashi became Tr3yway Entertainment and the Nine Trey Gangsta Bloods' main legitimate revenue source.

Emboldened by his new backers – a violent street gang – Tekashi became an ever-more vocal, confident and belligerent troll. Tekashi and Tr3yway/the Nine Trey Gangsta Bloods went on what can only be described as a trolling-driven promotional run, which was often indistinguishable from a brazen crime spree.

They got into a needless fight at Los Angeles Airport, were embroiled in a shooting at the Barclays Center and the choking of a fan in Houston, and Tekashi invited serious people, including serious gangsters, to meet his genitals (and not in a nice way).[13]

In a moment that was shocking by anyone's standards, Tekashi – on crystal-clear 4K camera – offered $30k to anyone who would shoot Tadoe, the cousin of Chief Keef, a rival rapper from Chicago, following a squabble with Tadoe on FaceTime. Days later, Chief himself narrowly escaped a shooting in New York, Tekashi's hometown. Interestingly, as Tekashi is squabbling on FaceTime, Shotti, complete with a lit joint, attempts to offer Tekashi tips on what to say to escalate things. As he is doing so, someone off-camera attempts to pull Shotti himself away from the conversation. The should-be critical friend is himself being pulled away by an *actual* critical friend. With every misstep along the way, every crime, attempted crime and every 'SUCK MY DICK', Shotti enabled and egged Tekashi on.

The streets eat their own. Tekashi was a big-mouthed civilian entertainer surrounded by serious gangsters. A seal surrounded by sharks. The predictable ensued: Tekashi alleged that Tr3yway/ the Nine Trey Gangsta Bloods exploited, defrauded and extorted him to the tune of millions. That they violently kidnapped him and threatened his mother's life. Specifically, Tekashi accused Shotti, his own unofficial manager, of sleeping with his girlfriend, the mother of his daughter (she denied it). He took to the Breakfast Club to fire Shotti and everyone else from Tr3yway.[14]

The other predictable thing happened too: the feds were investigating them all. Tekashi, Shotti and a host of other Tr3yway/ Nine Trey Gangsta Bloods were arrested by the Bureau of Alcohol, Tobacco, Firearms, and Explosives, in concert with the NYPD and Homeland Security. During their initial joint court hearing, Shotti, under oath and in the presence of a (white) judge, shouted out: 'We don't fold, we don't bend, we don't break. It's Tr3yway.'

Shotti had 'managed' Tekashi all the way to a potential life sentence in prison.

After hearing wiretap recordings in which Shotti and other Nine Trey Gangsta Blood members spoke on 'super-violating' him, Tekashi did one of the few things that is still taboo in Hip-Hop: he snitched. According to TMZ, 'the day after he was arrested', Tekashi broke a street code he only ever pretended to abide by for entertainment reasons and agreed to cooperate with the government.

An example of how little honour there is amongst the Nine Trey Gangsta Bloods – Tekashi testified against Kooda B for shooting at Chief Keef . . . even though he ordered and paid for the hit (he offered $30k on camera, promised $20k in real life and only paid $10k in the end). In 2019, a mere year after he began managing Tekashi, Shotti was sentenced to fifteen years in prison after pleading guilty to one count of firearm possession during a crime and one count of firearm discharge during a crime.

Tekashi, on the other hand, pled guilty to nine charges, including conspiracy to commit murder and armed robbery. He was sentenced to two years in prison . . . and released early due to the COVID pandemic.

In the end Shotti was the real-life embodiment of when management's attempt to be down with the kids goes wrong; Tekashi was the embodiment of when an artist's attempt to keep it gangsta goes wrong.

Chris Lighty and Shotti were not apples and oranges; they were in the same business but adopted very different strategies and achieved very different results.

Chris Lighty (Violator)	Shotti (Nine Trey Gangstas)
Played a background role with no discernible star ambitions (despite having the fourth verse on the demo version of A Tribe Called Quest's 'Scenario')	Front and centre with a clear desire to be a star, occasionally served as a video prop
Plugged weaknesses	Exacerbated weaknesses

Chris Lighty (Violator)	Shotti (Nine Trey Gangstas)
Capitalised on strengths	Exploited strengths
Compendium of good ideas	Compendium of needless criminality
Reserved personality	Energetic personality
Professional	Reckless
Managed his clients to major success	Managed his only client to a prison sentence
Left the streets	Stayed in the streets
Critical friend	Yes Man
Helped his clients to make good commercial decisions	Aided, abetted and at times executed his clients' crimes
A manager	An enabler

Table 12: Management comparison: Chris Lighty and Shotti

Commercial nous

Put simply, commercial nous is the understanding of how an industry operates and makes money and the ability to translate this understanding into performance as well as tangible and demonstrable outcomes. A manager without commercial nous is a manager in job title only – taking up space as opposed to making their presence felt. Thankfully, it is a learned skill.

A good manager doesn't just have commercial nous but recognises how to compound and when to swoop on commercial opportunities. They should also be aware of how best to sell those opportunities to other people within an organisation. Preferably externally too.

Chris Lighty was clearly dripping with commercial awareness – almost everything in this section demonstrates it – and his commercial and cultural nous proved pivotal in a moment of crisis for his organisation.

By 1994, Death Row was on cruise control. Suge Knight and his band of merry men ruled the airwaves. Between 1992 and

1994, Death Row, with just two records and two soundtracks, sold a total of 11 million records in the US alone – grossing somewhere in the region of $140–180m.

Meanwhile, Def Jam, Hip-Hop's most established label, released 18 albums, of which only one went multi-platinum. They sold 8 million records.

As the truism states: *'Statistics are like bikinis, they reveal a lot but conceal the more crucial parts.'* And the more crucial part of the statistics listed above is that the only artist to go multi-platinum between 1992 and 1994 on Def Jam was Warren G, a Death Row reject. Roughly half of Def Jam's 8 million records sold over the period in question came from Warren G's *Regulate . . . The G Funk Era*.

Given his track record with NWA, Dr. Dre was clearly Death Row's talent magnet, but Warren G, Dr. Dre's stepbrother, was the person who helped place the 'talent metal' in Dr. Dre's magnetic field. In 1990, best friends Warren G, Snoop Dogg and Nate Dogg formed 213 (vocalised as Two-One-Three), a rap group named after the telephone area code for Long Beach, where they were from. Warren G was the DJ and producer, Snoop was the rapper, and Nate Dogg, a one-of-a-kind, highly addictive gospel crooner but gangsta, sang the choruses.

They recorded a demo tape at Long Beach's VIP Records. Warren G passed the demo to Dr. Dre, who quickly expressed interest in working with them. In an interview in *Welcome to Death Row*, a documentary chronicling the rise and fall of Death Row Records, Nate Dogg recalled being summoned to the studio where Dr. Dre was working on the second NWA album, *Niggaz4Life*: 'At that time, it was a dream just to be in the same room with Dr. Dre. Dr. Dre wants us to come to the studio where he is? I'd have jogged up there if I didn't have a car.'

In their early days, Death Row got a million things right. They established a heavenly creative, corporate and street ensemble which collectively bred a rap dynasty. Everyone played their role to perfection. And to their mutual credit (and disadvantage), the one area early Death Row appeared to be poor on was the corporate cancer of nepotism.

Death Row was a meritocracy to a fault – and for this one rare moment in corporate and human history, it was quite a fault. As a result, they turned down the very person who should have been a shoo-in: Warren G. As a member of 213, he helped Death Row secure two of their superstars (Snoop and Nate Dogg) and he was, perhaps above all, Dr. Dre's stepbrother. Speaking on the *Mogul* podcast, Warren G explained why he didn't end up on Death Row:

> I felt left out, I felt kind of hurt. There was a meeting we had one time and everyone got a Death Row jacket and I didn't get one. I spoke to Dre and I said, 'Damn. What's up, man – how come I didn't get a jacket?' I was really pissed off. He said, 'Warren, this is what – I want you to be your own man and just handle your business. I don't want you to be involved in this.' I was hurt.[15]

Warren G further explained that when they arrived at the airport for a trip with all of the Death Row entourage, he discovered he did not have a ticket. Death Row literally and figuratively waved bye-bye to a crushed Warren G.

This aborted trip would have been the first time Warren ever boarded an airplane in his life. With a broken heart and significantly diminished prospects – all while his stepbrother and childhood friends were becoming household names – Warren did the opposite of what many of us would do:

> I went back to Long Beach and slept on my sister's apartment floor and just took my drum machine, which Dre gave me (an MPC 60 – and I still got it till this day), and laid it on the floor, my turntable and my drum machine and just put beats together. Next thing I know I got a call from Tupac and – BOOM – I did 'Definition Of A Thug Nigga'. Paul Stewart [A&R for Delicious Vinyl and others] hit

me and – BOOM – I did 'Indo Smoke' [by Mista Grimm, featuring Warren G and Nate Dogg] and it kept rolling after that and then Lyor came in and Russell came in . . .

Though his bosses Lyor Cohen and Russell Simmons are credited as the visionary leaders who called the shots, it was Chris Lighty who did the heavy lifting of signing Warren G.

Whereas everyone else saw a producer in Warren G, Chris Lighty saw a rapper, a great personality, alluring looks, a childhood friend of rap's biggest stars, backdoor access to rap's biggest label, Dr. Dre's stepbrother *and* a producer. More importantly, in Warren G, Chris Lighty saw a star.

Chris Lighty-inspired Management Tip

A key area of expertise for all good managers is making their bosses look like geniuses.

To this day, it remains customary for West Coast rappers to sign with West Coast labels and East Coast rappers to sign with East Coast labels. Same as Southern rappers and even UK rappers. There are many reasons for this: proximity to home, understanding of culture, familiarity with professional networks, loyalty and, sometimes, good old-fashioned 'fuck-the-other-side-ism' (otherwise known as tribalism).

So, wooing Warren G to Def Jam, the ultimate East Coast label, would be no easy feat. Chris Lighty did the deed in the most music-executive way known to man: exposing the talented boy from the ghetto to the good life. Lighty took Warren G out for a classic champagne, shrimp and caviar dinner. And then put him on his first flight ever – to New York. There, rap legend and Def Jam's marquee artist LL Cool J showed him the town and how he got down. Successfully wooed, Warren G signed with Def Jam and recorded the hugely successful single 'Regulate' with Nate Dogg.

'Regulate' was irresistible. A deeply melodic and therapeutic rap song that just made the listener relax and feel good . . . despite being about a robbery, a mass shooting and an orgy. The song served as the first single of Death Row's soundtrack for *Above the Rim* (a movie about a basketball star and his violent drug dealer friend – played by Tupac) and the first single of Warren G's debut album, *Regulate . . . The G Funk Era.*

Regulate . . .The G Funk Era became Def Jam's first multi-platinum success in twelve successive quarters. It went on to sell roughly four million copies, generating between \$50–60m. The leather jacket and airline ticket that Death Row refused to buy for Warren G belongs in a missed opportunity (and opportunity cost) hall of fame.

If it was not for twenty-six-year-old Chris Lighty's remarkable commercial awareness driving him to sign Warren G, there is a chance Def Jam would be a distant memory today. Lighty's actions teach us that commercial nous is the ability to:

1. Identify high-potential growth opportunities, especially in places where others may be blind to them.
2. Spend as little as possible to accrue as much as possible.
3. See beyond and circumvent customs, rules, culture, the law or any other artificial parameter to make good on an opportunity.
4. Recognise the difference between an inducement and a bribe and then recognise that they can be just as effective as each other in securing deals.
5. Build deep relationships that can be called on to win future business.

On 30 August 2012, Darrel Steven 'Chris' Lighty died from a self-inflicted gunshot wound to the head. He is survived by his family, friends and a good portion of Hip-Hop's elite.

SUPPORT

There are three types of gangsta rappers:

1. Gangstas who happen to be rappers and vice versa. This concept is best described as authenticity.
2. Rappers who attempt to be gangstas and vice versa. This concept is best described as wannabe.
3. Civilians pretending to be both of the above for commercial purposes (otherwise known as studio gangsters). This concept is best described as tragic hilarity and, quite often, runaway profitability.

Dwight 'Beanie Sigel' Grant quite comfortably falls into the first category.

Beanie Sigel is an immensely versatile, skilled and fierce rapper. Bar for bar, line for line, he is – without a shadow of a doubt – one of the best of his generation. One of his key skills as a rapper is the unique way he makes every single line in a verse end with the same word or the opposite of the word the previous line ended in. 'Look At Me Now' (2005) is a perfect example of this – as is his show-stealing verse on 'Adrenalin' by the Roots (1999).

In addition to technical rhyme skill, he is deeply introspective and philosophical well beyond his years – often casually throwing life advice worthy of a centenarian – see 2005's 'Feel It In The Air'.

These skills made him as adept at battling as he was at making really great records. In 2001, Beanie Sigel found himself in an intense beef with Jadakiss, de facto leader of the Lox, a celebrated and highly respected New York street-rap group. As a rapper, Jadakiss was (and still very much is) feared on the microphone. Beanie Sigel, then a new entrant to the market working on making a name and carving a niche for himself, was not someone anyone would have thought would provide competition for someone of Jadakiss's magnitude and prowess.

Jadakiss subliminally insulted Beanie Sigel on a range of songs, most notably on the DMX featured track, 'Un-Hunh! (Here We Go Again)':

> I'll give you a Reason why I'm the Truth for real,
> ... Had to stop eating red meat cause I ate too many Beanie-Macs

This was vintage Jadakiss – thinly veiled yet super-tight bars littered with subliminals. *The Reason* and *The Truth* were the titles of Beanie Sigel's first two albums – it is easy to see who Jadakiss was coming for. By the time he got to the final line above, it was all but explicit.

Dropping all pretences and subtlety, Beanie Sigel hit back with the self-explanatory 'Fuck Jadakiss', a scathing diss track insulting everything from Jadakiss's prowess as a musician to his reputation as a businessman and as a man – all over the instrumental to Jadakiss's single 'Put Your Hands Up'. Jadakiss responded in a similar manner with 'Fuck Beanie Sigel (AKA Son Of A Kiss)'. To most people's surprise, Beanie Sigel arguably edged out a victory.

With victory in battle secured, victory on the charts was now within his grasp. Siegel was a couple of good songs and moves away from becoming a major success. Unfortunately, what granted Beanie Sigel his legitimacy as a *gangsta* rapper also meant his finger was never far from the self-destruct trigger.

Beanie Sigel derives his stage name from his grandmother's nickname for him – 'Beanie' – and Sigel Street, a street in the deprived part of South Philadelphia that he comes from. As a nineteen-year-old in 1994, Beanie Sigel and a friend, Calvin Saunders, got into a shootout with a Philadelphia police officer they claimed was harassing them.[16] For most people, that experience with the police would spell chapter and verse for a lifetime; for Beanie Sigel it was merely a comma. Lamenting Beanie Sigel's wasted potential and, as a result, Philly's lack of a hometown rap mogul, his hometown publication, *Philadelphia Magazine*, elaborated:

Beanie Sigel backs up his big talk. Beanie has been accused of attempted murder; Beanie led Philadelphia police on a high-speed chase through South Philly; Beanie has dodged child support; Beanie has been caught with drugs; Beanie has violated parole; Beanie has committed tax fraud. Beanie has done hard time. Beanie has mortgaged his future to satisfy a lust for realness unseen in today's hip-hop superstars . . . While the lack of realness among our hip-hop heroes may be pitiful, it's not as sad as Beanie's commitment to it.[17]

As extensive as it may feel, *Philadelphia Magazine*'s laundry list of Beanie Sigel's legal transgressions was not exhaustive. He was an unpredictable and unstable poetic genius with a streak of violent crime. He was high potential, high value and therefore worthy of investment – Beanie Sigel had everything it takes to be in Hip-Hop's mogul class. But he was also exceptionally volatile and high risk.

One simple question: how does a manager support someone like Beanie Sigel?

How do you get the most out of someone so rooted in the street, so accustomed to the harsher aspects of life that they risk wasting their highly lucrative potential? How do you support someone so seemingly intent on self-destruction? How do you help a person make good on their undeniable potential – for them, you and any broader organisation, especially once you've exhausted the usual support mechanisms (coaching, mentoring, exposure, education opportunities and so on)?

In 1998, Jay-Z and Dame Dash's Roc-A-Fella Records signed Beanie Sigel. Below are some of the ways they attempted to support him.

Soft intervention

On 'Momma Loves Me', from Jay-Z's 2001 album *The Blueprint*, Jay expressed an uncustomary degree of public brotherly and cautionary love for Beanie Sigel, which he delivered in a sombre tone. Paraphrasing, he said that he was attempting to help Beanie

Sigel move from being a street guy to being a legitimate star in the field of entertainment. Key message: he needed to change his ways.

This was a soft intervention. A means of saving someone from themselves, disrupting a downward spiral and rescuing a potentially lucrative yet troubled asset in the process.

The then thirty-two-year-old Jay-Z revealed to the world, but most importantly to twenty-six-year-old Beanie Sigel himself, that if he didn't successfully make that transition from 'the street' to the vast prospects he had in Hip-Hop, things could end badly. Which would, of course, mess his money up (home is where charity starts). In his own way, Jay-Z was informing Beanie Sigel, his mentee and artist, that he had a small window of opportunity to really change his life. To do so he would have to walk away from the evils (D'Evils?) plaguing him.

Soft interventions have to be conducted in just such a manner: softly. In order for them to be effective, it needs to be clear that the intervention, the interruption of a downward spiral, is coming from a place of care, concern and love. The 'you're dropping the ball' element has to remain implicit.

As touching and heartfelt as Jay-Z's public intervention would be to the average non-gangsta, Beanie Sigel saw it differently. Speaking to N.O.R.E.'s *Drink Champs* podcast in 2021, twenty solid years later, Beanie Sigel revealed that he initially took umbrage with the line.

> When he said that, I was totally offended. Because we didn't have that conversation. When did you try to give me the game? But it took me a minute ['a minute' in this instance is slang for 'a while'] to realize that was the game on that record.[18]

Perhaps for the reasons Beanie Sigel alluded to, the intervention did not succeed. Beanie would continue along the path he was already on.

A sense of belonging

The second way in which Roc-A-Fella supported Beanie Sigel was to make him feel like he was part of something bigger than himself. Once they, i.e. the asset, feels part of something bigger, the prayer is that they behave in accordance with the stated behavioural aims of the organisation.

For the same reason that families have traditions, armies have standards, and religions have commandments, corporations create 'values'. They all serve the same purpose – they influence behaviour and therefore outcomes from members. They foster stability, a code of ethics and, hopefully, help pave the way for enhanced performance and camaraderie. Those who fail to live within the designated parameters tend to be eventually ousted.

In October 2000, Jay-Z released his fifth album, *The Dynasty: Roc La Familia*. It was originally intended to be a compilation of Roc-A-Fella artists but was eventually marketed as a Jay-Z album with all but four of the sixteen tracks featuring Roc-A-Fella artists. Beanie Sigel featured on half of the songs, while Memphis Bleek – Jay-Z's long-term protégé – featured on five. It was also the first album to include production from future Roc-A-Fella go-to producers Just Blaze and Kanye West. *The Dynasty: Roc La Familia* was a critical and commercial success, selling over two million copies.

Its additional impact was the creation of the concept of 'Roc La Familia'. In the eyes of Beanie Sigel, Roc-A-Fella was now beyond a record company, it had become a family. It made him feel part of something that was bigger than him and near sacred to him:

> *Roc-A-Fella Records was the only thing that I have ever been a part of that I thought was honest. I never looked at me having a career, I never looked at the business – it was la Familia, la Familia, la Familia. We're a family.*

**Benefits of Labelling a Cold Corporate
Profit Machine a 'Family'**

1. Breeds camaraderie, goodwill and a collegiate atmosphere.

2. Encourages company and brand loyalty.

3. Attracts additional talent and followers.

4. Tricks staff to work harder for less pay or no pay.

5. Enhances professional values and upholds standards.

Beanie Sigel demonstrated supreme loyalty to 'la Familia'. La Familia's beefs were his, their successes were his, and his successes were theirs. Where they faced danger, he was happy to risk it all to protect them.

But the honour of 'la Familia' didn't necessarily improve Beanie's behaviour or help further transport him from the street to fame. Actually, things got worse.

In early July 2003, while on tour with Jay-Z, Beanie Sigel was arrested and charged with attempted murder, aggravated assault, simple assault and possession of a criminal instrument. He was alleged to have fired six shots at a man in front of a Philadelphia strip bar, hitting him in the stomach and foot.

The alleged shooting occurred in the early hours of Tuesday, 1 July 2003, not long after Beanie left the stage after performing with Jay-Z. With the benefit of hindsight, this was the equivalent of a Microsoft executive facing charges for shooting someone at a strip club after leaving the on-stage celebration for the launch of Windows 95 with Bill Gates.

While being part of 'la Familia' did make Beanie Sigel feel like he was part of something bigger than him, it didn't alter his street ways.

Despite victim and eyewitness testimony, he would go on to face a hung jury at his first trial and was found not guilty of all charges in the subsequent re-trial. He was sentenced to a year and a day in prison for a separate firearms charge. While in prison, he released his best ever work, his third album *The B Coming*.

During the first trial, Jay-Z offered another lesson in management support, namely:

Withdrawal of support

'If yu cyaan 'ear, yu mus' feel' is an old Jamaican saying. Translated, it means: if you cannot hear, you must feel. In sweet and simple Queen's English: people who fail to learn from caution tend to learn from consequences.

Roc-A-Fella Records saw to it that Beanie Sigel's attempted murder trial was in line with the brand: one of the most glamorous ever. Each day, A-list celebrities were ushered in, often by helicopter, to attend. Jay-Z, Beyoncé, Kanye West, Freeway, Mariah Carey and others all showed up. Beanie Sigel himself dressed in suits and a fedora worthy of a mafia boss. But the real people-management lesson took place during one of the pre-trial bail hearings rather than the actual courtroom showdown.

Jay-Z, Dame Dash and others served as witnesses to Beanie Sigel's good character. However, according to Beanie Sigel, the judge asked Jay-Z if he would be willing to vouch for his mentee's whereabouts. To Sigel's shock, Jay-Z, the Don Corleone of the Roc-A-Fella 'Familia', declined.

Jay-Z-inspired People-management Tip

Manage your own emotions – especially when on the stand. No matter how much you may love or like them, do not risk your career and good name by vouching for someone who cannot be trusted to live up to expectations.

The disappointment Beanie Sigel felt was understandable, but in that moment the following should have dawned on him:

1. Roc-A-Fella was a business, not a family (or even 'la Familia').
2. Roc-A-Fella was a business, not a mafia.
3. Roc-A-Fella was a business rooted in the streets, but it was not the streets.

The juxtaposition of Beanie Sigel's unpredictability, temperament and refusal or inability to transition from the streets and Jay-Z's vast business ambitions meant it would have been mad for him to vouch for Sigel. It probably would have been bad for Sigel too.

If Jay-Z's actions teach anything here, it is that in some situations removing help can be a necessary if painful type of support. It may have cost Jay-Z nothing to vouch for Beanie Sigel; it may have cost him a lot. One thing seems certain: had Jay-Z done so, Sigel would have learned nothing. He took the support he was offered by 'la Familia' for granted, assumed it was unconditional and felt crushed when he learned that the support it offered had limits.

On the *Drink Champs* podcast, Beanie explained his initial thoughts:

Cos I'm like: damn, that's my man. And I looked at it like, all right – what if I had to get the fuck out of there? I'm in jail, I'm stood tall – but what if I needed to go? Bro – I had attempted murder in the state and a federal gun charge . . . I was facing forty years. What if I needed to roll? What if I really needed to roll and be on the run and go? I'm shackled round the waist, ankles and everything and my man was like 'nah'. That fucked me up. That took away a lot of shit that I thought that we had. That was [my] big bro.

Ambition is something that cannot be trained into people. Jay-Z, for example, was driven by a desire to go somewhere special in life. To get to the very pinnacle of business and society. He had a laser-sharp focus on that ambition in word and deed for over three decades. Beanie Sigel, arguably an even more gifted rapper than Jay-Z, either didn't or couldn't see himself in such a position.

As people-managers, Dame Dash and Jay-Z faced what was essentially an impossible task: to help elevate Beanie Sigel's God-given talent above all of the setbacks he faced — childhood instability; poverty and the hopelessness that often accompanies it; an inability to trust people or systems; societal ruthlessness and mercilessness; police brutality; betrayal — and make him the major prospect he was.

With the benefit of hindsight, Beanie Sigel himself conceded that he was 'the perfect example of when keeping it real goes wrong'. The very authenticity that helped propel him to greatness was the same authenticity that kept dragging him away from it.

Beanie Sigel-inspired Management Tips

When an employee is blowing it, let them know they're blowing it. Tell them:

- If you fail to learn from mistakes, ensure you learn to fail – well.

- The window of opportunity will be open only for so long and only so far. If you fail to climb through the window while it is open, someone else will.

- Do not let your future become a victim of your past.

In the end, Roc-A-Fella's main breakout star (other than Jay-Z) wasn't Beanie Sigel, the great lyricist dripping with authenticity and credibility in the street, but his absolute opposite, Kanye West.

12.

DIVERSITY

D iversity. Far too often a corporate punchline delivered with a remarkably straight face. It is spoken of endlessly but rarely remembered once the words have left the lips. Frequently promised but rarely, if ever, delivered. Fashionable but hardly ever worn or displayed. A huge industry that doesn't really produce anything other than more diversity professionals. It garners huge sums of 'investment' with no discernible desire for a return (not dissimilar to a Ponzi scheme). It is simultaneously a means and a meme to an end. Nevertheless, its pertinence (not so much its pretence) is critical to any business.

Perhaps owing to its roots in poverty and the streets, Hip-Hop as an industry and artform has been exemplary in terms of diversity. It is a rare industry in which people (admittedly usually men) with educational qualifications compete on a par with people without them. In Hip-Hop, you win or lose on true merit. Having a criminal record could boost your chances of employment rather than hindering them. Whether you've got the body of a Greek god or the body of someone who diets exclusively on Big Macs and milkshakes is unlikely to determine your fortunes and access to opportunity (again, sadly only if you're a man, as this book shows). Hip-Hop is probably one of the few artforms in which a performer with dwarfism, such as Bushwick Bill of the Geto

Boys, is not reduced to a punchline but is taken seriously as a commanding voice.

Capitalists, super-hyper-capitalists, communists, socialists, anarchists, hoteps (of course), pan-Africanists . . . even people who have revealed white-supremacist tendencies have found their way into Hip-Hop.

The diversity of sound, thought and presentation of the actual music also easily tops any other genre. The genre that gave the world acts and sonics as diverse as Missy Elliot, Snoop Dogg, Jay-Z, the Migos, Skinnyman, Shaybo, the Pharcyde, Bone Thugs-N-Harmony and countless more cannot seriously be compared to, say, indie, pop or heavy metal. Additionally, as much of this book chronicles, Hip-Hop has itself had a diversifying impact on the corporate and business worlds, as well as society more broadly.

While the overwhelming number of successful businesspeople in Hip-Hop have been men, and despite what you might think if you watch any number of rap videos, Hip-Hop's moguls have often proved more advanced on gender diversity than much of the corporate world.

STORMZY: INVESTOR IN DIVERSE PEOPLE

Lean in with me: the best case for gender diversity ever made was not the thoughts of a Fortune 500 or FTSE 100 CEO or senior politician (feminist or otherwise) or, giggle at the silly thought, a diversity officer. It was made by Stormzy in 2020, a British-Ghanaian Hip-Hop mogul in the making, from the podium of an awards show where he had just been named Best Male Artist:

> To be the Best Male, I've got the most incredible females on my team . . . I love you lot. You are the greatest. The best male is nothing without these incredible females. I love you.

Stormzy was all of two years old when Tupac Shakur was assassinated. Yet Tupac's diversity-drenched formula for making popular music with enough appeal to make you wealthy is one that has served Stormzy well.

Tupac's Formula for Leveraging Gender Diversity

'Yo, if you wanna make your money, you gotta rap for the bitches, do not rap for the niggas . . . the bitches will buy your records and the niggas want what the bitches want.' – Tupac Shakur in a 1996 interview with Sway Calloway

Translation: Appealing to women is a faster and more certain route to profitability and profit maximisation than appealing to men, because men want what women want – either for peace of mind or other reasons.

Caveats: By 'bitches' in the formula Tupac means women, and by 'niggas' he means men. Tupac's gender and sexuality politics can be comfortably assumed to have been fairly binary in nature.

Part of what separates Stormzy, Tupac, Lauryn Hill, LL Cool J, the Notorious BIG, Megan Thee Stallion, Nas, Nicki Minaj, Cardi B and others from many other significantly less successful rappers was their ability to appeal to women. Mainly through their music, but through other qualities too (their look, sex appeal, aura and so on). In fact, other than marketing prowess and saying what the powers that be wish to hear, a key difference between what is 'mainstream' and what is 'underground' often boils down to whether or not it appeals to women.

As Tupac alluded to in his own unique way, in Hip-Hop, business and, especially, in economies, the difference between major success and mediocre success or even success and failure is often the ability and willingness to appeal to and include women (in particular). And Tupac did this very well – he made music that made women want to dance ('How Do You Want It'), think ('Just Like Daddy'), celebrate ('Dear Mama'), conquer ('Keep Ya Head Up'), emote ('Brenda's Got A Baby') and get angry ('Wonda Why They Call You Bitch').

From the outset of his career, Stormzy went beyond this formula. He recruited women into critical roles in the development and management of his burgeoning #Merky empire – his brand manager, publicist and team manager are all women. Much of the staff at his publishing company, #Merky Books, are women too. His words about women making him the Best Male were true.

Stormzy's music and diverse recruitment patterns demonstrate an advanced understanding of the need for gender diversity, and his success demonstrates the benefits of it. Without the women in his team there is a great chance he'd be yet another excellent yet little-known rapper performing before small sausage factories.

DIVERSITY AT DEATH ROW

In his heyday as CEO of Death Row, Suge Knight made his thoughts on ethnic diversity as a critical barrier to success very clear. He was much more concerned about being exploited by the older Black men (presumably the ones who helped put him in business and he subsequently double-crossed) than he was scary white men:

> 'There is really a lot of prejudice in the business and people think it is black and white. A lot of it is young and old. Older guys – the only thing they want to do is sit you down and say: 'OK, Suge, you say you're a young entrepreneur, this is what we're going to do. Give me all the stuff you got, give me your tapes, give me your masters, give me your groups, and I'll go over there and make you

a deal.' But, you know, my opinions was: 'Look, I ain't no punk. You don't got to talk for us, we gonna go there and . . . speak for ourselves. Instead of getting a dollar, we want five. And our masters and our ownership.'

And that is exactly what he did. As determined, detailed and destructive to anything that stood in his path as ever, Suge got the money, masters, ownership and power he craved. But it would be wrong to suggest that Suge didn't have an understanding of, and appreciation for, diversity. He actually built and sustained Death Row by carefully assembling and balancing a different kind of 'colour diversity'.

Suge may not have seen the world in racial terms, but he understood the power and importance of colour. Specifically red, blue, dark blue and, presumably, black (not included in this list are the parent company, Interscope, who were predominantly white).

A Broad Breakdown of Diversity at Death Row Records

On the face of it, this looks like a recipe for disaster. Putting civilians to one side, the executive, creative and security – bloods (red), crips (blue) and the police (dark blue) – do not traditionally enjoy collegiate relations. They're better known for exchanging gunfire than Christmas cards. However, there appears to have been a method to this madness. Suge Knight's approach to diversity is comparable to that of another great American leader: Abraham Lincoln. The two men have quite a bit in common.

Abraham Lincoln	Suge Knight
Both were light-skinned, 6 foot 4 and looked good in a beard	
Both enjoyed a groundbreakingly successful four-year run	
Both enjoyed successes that helped bring in sweeping reforms that changed the world	
Neither was afraid to use violence when needed	

Abraham Lincoln	Suge Knight
Robustly tackled white supremacy: abolished slavery	Robustly tackled white supremacy: abolished Vanilla Ice's career
Both led one side of the nation to war with the other side	
Made an eternally memorable speech at Gettysburg Address	Made an eternally memorable speech at the 1995 Source Awards
Both were knocked off at the peak of their powers	
Both belong to the ages	
Both appointed a team of rivals	

Table 13: Abraham Lincoln and Suge Knight: a comparison

In 1861, Bro Abe Lincoln was inaugurated as the sixteenth President of the United States. Perplexingly at the time, to push his agenda through seamlessly, enjoy broad support, ensure the nation was competently run and to maintain the confidence and unity of his party, Lincoln appointed all of his former main rivals for the Republican ticket into his Cabinet. In doing so, he appointed people many deemed intellectually superior and more suited to the presidency than him. And he did it for just that reason. In Lincoln's own words:

We need the strongest men of the party in the Cabinet. We needed to hold our own people together. I had looked the party over and concluded that these were the very strongest men. Then I had no right to deprive the country of their services.

Lincoln's Cabinet would go on to be labelled the 'team of rivals', a concept which is by nature one with diversity at its core, to a near adversarial level. Death Row was a record label of rivals – complete with an adversarial approach to business.

The 'record label of rivals' and 'colour diversity' at Death Row could and should have:

- Fostered an environment of competition and therefore efficiency
- Ensured all bases were covered by engraining diversity of thought
- Ensured all of LA's key 'elements' were reflected and represented
- Ensured Death Row was not synonymous with one set or crew but a rainbow company welcoming to all
- Provided a united front to the world
- Ensured the label was connected in all critical walks of life
- Balanced power amongst the various factions
- Assisted with operational optimisation, bolstering creativity and maximising profits
- Protected Death Row's long-term dominance
- Ensured that only the strong survived in the company

To some degree it probably did achieve many of these things – Death Row did, after all, rapidly grow to become one of the most successful companies in music. Everyone played their role. The diversity 'strategy' was a risky yet good one – it paid off massively, for a while. The problem and ultimate downfall of this approach was the old corporate idiom: 'culture eats strategy for lunch'.

In this case, gang culture devours corporate culture for pudding.

The company was selling 'gangsta rap', so a limited amount of the gangsta element was a necessity to capture and convey authenticity, create a myth and the profits that come with it. Nevertheless, given the balance of diversity (of rivals), there had to be some kind of professional framework to ensure it worked, didn't spiral out of control and the organisation could continue to operate effectively. As there wasn't, coupled with the fact that Suge Knight declined in executive seriousness and discipline (as he grew in success), what could have been an exemplary business template was consumed by a triple whammy of destructive forces: violence, gang culture and operational incompetence.

Suge Knight's Diversity Policy

... Three to get ready, and fo' to hit the switches,
In my Chevy – '64 red, to be exact ...

The above is Warren G's rather strange contribution to Snoop's 'Ain't No Fun (If The Homies Can't Have None), a stellar cut from his 1993 debut album *Doggystyle*. Strange because Warren G is thought to be a member of the Rollin' 20s Crips, a gang that sports the colour blue as their flag. By nature, Warren G would not be caught dead in a red car. Suge Knight is said to have insisted that the lyric be included on the song, providing an insight into the inner workings of Death Row.

Putting Dr. Dre (who was not gang-affiliated) aside, the creative core of Death Row at the time was dominated by Snoop Dogg and his affiliates: the Dogg Pound (which consisted of Snoop's cousin Daz and Kurupt); the Long Beach Crew (otherwise known as the Long Beach Crips); and close friends such as Nate Dogg and the aforementioned Warren G, all of whom were Crips.

Complete with a fierce dog named Damu (which is Swahili for 'blood'), the executive core was led by Suge Knight, who was famously a MOB Piru Blood, as were most of his inner circle and muscle, who provided what Reggie Wright, Death Row's former Head of Security, dismissively described as 'homeboy security'. Post-imprisonment Tupac himself is rumoured to have become a MOB Piru Blood – hence him often shouting, 'Money over bitches' or just 'M-O-B'. Non-homeboy security was provided by off-duty police officers (several Death Row-affiliated police officers were part of the Rampart police corruption scandal), whereas much of the rest of the company activities was conducted by civilians, many of whom lived quite nervous lives.

> The rapper DOC – who was one of the writers for much of Death Row's heyday material, especially on *The Chronic* – described the working conditions at Death Row as being worse than being in an actual prison.[1] Reports of seriously violent incidents – such as beatings (including of women and unsigned artists), shootings and making people drink urine – were widespread. A 2001 story in the *Guardian* typified the ongoings:
>
> > Knight relished his role as in-house muscle – bringing in an army of gang affiliates to extol summary punishments. He quickly established a ruthless reputation for himself: one writer from the *New Yorker* magazine, on asking the wrong question, was beaten up. Knight and his henchmen, dressed in the red insignia of the Bloods, later tried to bundle the writer into a fish tank filled with piranha. Knight admits that 'sometimes things get out of hand. But we never messed up anyone who didn't deserve it.'[2]

THE IRON LADY OF RAP

Diversity is a balancing act of beauty and duplicity. Every movement towards diversity has a person who represents the before and after, the person who 'smashes the glass ceiling', 'falls the wall' or leads their protected characteristic group to the 'mountaintop'. That's the theory, anyway. In reality, that lauded ceiling smasher often reinforces the status quo – inadvertently or otherwise. And how could they not? To do otherwise would be to bite the hand that pulled them up. They often get to where they are because they pose minimal threat to the status quo. According to the *Harvard Business Review*, in the 'conventional' corporate world only people from the most powerful segment of society (white men) are rewarded for promoting diversity. Women and minorities tend to be penalised for it. As a result, in many areas, when a woman or ethnic minority makes it to the top, it tends to lead to a closing of ranks and a drying up of opportunities for people who share their protected characteristic.

Margaret Thatcher, the UK's first female prime minister, is a laboratory example of this effect. As the first female leader of one of the world's most powerful democracies, she was a major ceiling-smasher for women. However, she did not do much to advance the cause of, say, feminism or women's equality in general, and certainly not women in politics. By her own design, she was the only woman at the top table of her own government.

In terms of diversity, the opposite of Margaret Thatcher is Virginia native Melissa Arnette Elliott, professionally known as 'Missy Elliott'.

Margaret Thatcher	Missy Elliott
Conservative icon	Hip-Hop icon
Key policy quote: *'The problem with socialism is that you eventually run out of other peoples' money.'*	Key policy quote: *'If I didn't have some kind of education, then I wouldn't be able to count my money.'*
Led Britain to victory in the Falklands War	Led women to victory on Lil' Kim's 'Not Tonight'
Key ally: President Ronald Reagan	Key ally: producer Timbaland
Deregulated and privatised much of British industry	Helped 'alternise', feminise and commercialise much of Hip-Hop and R'n'B
Had very limited diversifying or empowering impact on her field or wider society	A one-woman diversity machine. Indeed, the embodiment of full spectrum diversity

Table 14: Margaret Thatcher and Missy Elliot: a comparison

There's no getting around the male domination of the culture and business of Hip-Hop. From affinity, unconscious and beauty biases to the Dunning–Kruger effect, conscious and cognitive biases – there is barely a bias that women in Hip-Hop do not have to overcome. Add rap's 'One Woman Syndrome' (see Chapter 14 on Competition) and you have very difficult terrain – characterised by extremely high barriers to entry, rapid obsolescence and low barriers to exit, all hallmarks of intense competition. And all more intense for women.

It should therefore come as no surprise that going all the way back to the Roxanne Wars in the mid-1980s,[3] women in Hip-Hop have long been pitted against each other. Lil' Kim was up against Foxy Brown (a rivalry that led to an exchange of gunfire through proxies and, subsequently, a perjury conviction and prison time for Lil' Kim). More recently, Nicki Minaj was pitted against Cardi B (which led to an exchange of blows and shoes – see Chapter 14).

Missy Elliott is that rare rapper who has never been forced to compete with anyone. And there is a good reason for that: she is without rival. Thanks to her super and unrivalled creativity as a sound-smith (she may be the only female producer most people can name in Hip-Hop), performer and in presentation, Missy Elliott was truly one of one in Hip-Hop. There is zero similarity between her and anyone else. She is in her own lane, one she paved for herself.

In a period where to be a woman in rap was to be hyper-sexualised, clad in the most expensive of Italian designer clothes and dominated by samples of 1980s pop hits, Missy offered something that slapped the prevailing order round the face. Her use of indescribable sound effects (for example, 'Hee-Hee-Hee-Hee-How' and 'Ti esrever dna ti pilf nwod gnaht ym tup i ' from 'Work It'!*) helped her stand out even more.

In the video for 'The Rain (Supa Dupa Fly)', her debut single,

---

* Which is the preceding lyric, 'I put my thang down, flip it and reverse it', in reverse.

she defied every single 'standard' expected of female rappers. She flipped the script entirely: rather than looking like a mafioso widow, she wore what appeared to be an inflated dustbin bag. Missy's creative uniqueness made her a compulsory listen, and her talents went beyond her own career to impact many others.

Instead of engaging in cut-throat competition, along with fellow Virginia native, Timothy 'Timbaland' Mosley, she found success in collaboration, which in turn made her more powerful. Missy could have used this power any way she wished, but, to the benefit of many in the business, she predominantly used it to aid the cause of female inclusion.

Missy helped launch and nurture the careers of the likes of Gina Thompson, 702, Total, Jazzmine Sullivan, Nicole Wray, Lil Mo, Tweet and Aaliyah (post her creative and predatory relationship with R. Kelly) – all of whom she wrote and/or produced star-making and star-elevating material for.

Critically, at a time when most female rappers did not collaborate with other female rappers, Missy Elliott went out of her way to collaborate with practically all of the main female rappers of the age, including Da Brat, Lil' Kim, MC Lyte, Lisa 'Left Eye' Lopez, Eve, Foxy Brown, Queen Pen and so on.

Rappers on the come-up, especially those different to the norm, had a near automatic friend in Missy, who would be there to offer them a hand up – as exhibited by her collaborations with early career Eminem ('Busa Rhyme', 1999) and Ludacris ('Gossip Folk', 2002). Her ability to adapt and adjust to fit any mould makes her an essential ingredient in the diversity of Hip-Hop.

Missy is living proof that standing out from the crowd, setting as opposed to following trends and embracing diversity pays and pays well. She is the highest-selling woman in Hip-Hop history and has earned four Grammy awards, as well as a spot in the songwriter's hall of fame.

THE RISE OF THE GAY RAPPER

Despite the fact that the dress sense of many of Hip-Hop's pre-Run DMC pioneering rap crews was often indistinguishable from, say, the Village People (a group synonymous with gay men), Hip-Hop was far from a rainbow flag-friendly culture. Thanks to the often hypermasculine nature of the culture (which itself is rooted in the overcompensated reassertion of denied masculinity in Black men), for decades the concept of a gay rapper floated on a scale that ranged between punchline to whispered rumour to outright insult.

An episode of the razor-sharp satirical Hip-Hop cartoon, *The Boondocks*, explored the hysteria around the idea of a gay rapper and the impact it would have on the culture to hilarious yet profoundly thought-provoking effect. In the episode, a fictional, pink-wearing, successful studio-gangster[4] rapper/fashion designer called Gangstalicious (voiced by Mos Def) is outed as gay by a video vixen turned international bestselling author (thought to be based on the real-life video vixen turned international best-selling author, Karrine 'Superhead' Steffans). The episode ends with rappers once desperate to associate with Gangstalicious hiding from him (proving them to be homo-*phobic* in the most literal sense) and a teary, confused eight-year-old Riley, one of his most loyal young superfans, begging Gangstalicious to tell the truth: was he gay or not? After careful consideration, an isolated, lonely, rapidly falling from grace Gangstalicious denied his sexuality . . . in a way only a child could believe.

Real life was no better or less strange than fiction. During this period of intense homophobia in rap, wearing pink was very risky (until Cam'Ron and Kanye West absorbed the risk by making it fashionable), and if his jeans were too tight it could cost a rapper their place in a crew.[5] One rap icon was long suspected of being gay – principally because he had naturally green eyes. Lyrics or statements that could be interpreted as 'sounding gay' were suffixed with 'gay neutralising' terms such as 'pause' or 'no homo' or, for the absence of all doubt: 'NHJIC' (meaning: no homo just in case). Homophobic slurs and slang were commonplace in rap songs – even progressive rap songs by rappers who are today left-wing icons.

With this backdrop, it goes without saying that it would be career suicide for a (male) gay rapper to reveal their sexuality. Even women whose sexuality was an open secret performed as straight women.

Homosexuality (male in particular) was a 'taboo' too far in rap music . . . until Montero 'Lil Nas X' Hill emerged.

Lil Nas X's life followed the usual poverty to poetry to penthouse pipeline of many of Hip-Hop's superstars. He grew up with his single father in the rougher parts of the outskirts of Atlanta. Born in 1999, Lil Nas X is part of a younger generation that has never really known a world without high-speed internet and social media. Not only was he a digital native, but he also carefully studied the lucrative science/art of going viral. And as cannot be repeated enough: in the attention economy, virality is currency. And in the virality space, Lil Nas X displayed what can only be described as genius, which he transformed into hard currency to the tune of millions.

After a period of sharpening his skills across multiple social-media platforms, he found his virality feet running a popular Nicki Minaj fan page on Twitter. Here he was able to go viral again and again in support of Minaj. Eventually, following his gospel-singer father's advice, he started making songs of his own and began independently releasing music. In the process he made a unique sort of Hip-Hop record: a country-rap song called 'Old Town Road'.

The song immediately connected with a lucrative demographic Hip-Hop often struggles to reach: very young school children. They could not get enough of it. Lil Nas X would show up in schools to perform 'Old Town Road' and children as young as four or five would go nuts after hearing just the first few notes of the song.

But although children loved it, the country music vanguards didn't. They refused to accept it as a country song – despite the fact that it had already reached number nineteen on the *Billboard* country charts.

In time-honoured fashion, the rejection meant 'Old Town Road' got bigger and bigger, as it went from being a child-friendly country-rap song to being a lightning rod for the chatterati. In defiance of the establishment of his genre, the country music legend Billy Ray Cyrus hopped on a remix of 'Old Town Road' – once again helping the record grow. The song was certified platinum – in some places a dozen times over – in a total of twenty-two countries. It became the longest-leading number one in the history of the *Billboard* Hot 100 and currently sits at number forty-one in the *Billboard* tally of the all-time best charting songs.[6]

Given the enormous and unique success of 'Old Town Road', Lil Nas X was widely expected to be a one-hit wonder. Then, on 30 June 2019, the last day of Pride Month, he tweeted: 'Some of y'all already know, some of y'all don't care, some of y'all not gone fwm [fuck with me] no more. but before this month ends i want y'all to listen closely to c7osure.'[7] The tweet, which contained a micro video for 'c7osure', a song about freedom, was punctuated with a rainbow flag.

And just like that, the mythical idea of the gay rapper – once an unspeakable taboo in Hip-Hop – became a reality. Heart-warmingly, the culture didn't show its ass, it showed love. Most of Hip-Hop happily embraced Lil Nas X for who he is. Signifying this, the original Nas, who is the pinnacle of artistic credibility in Hip-Hop, performed a remix of Lil Nas X's 'Rodeo' with him at the Grammys. The Nas and Lil Nas X collaboration was then released as a single, complete with a *Matrix*-themed video.

Once Lil Nas X came out, he came *out-out*. He created a sub-genre that was – again – once unthinkable in Hip-Hop: LGBT rap songs complete with Satan-saluting hypersexual videos. In his hit single 'Industry Baby', a collaboration with the white rapper Jack Harlow, Lil Nas X dances naked in a prison shower with a group of Black men. Critics argued that it was a crass, inadvertent celebration of the slow genocide that is the mass incarceration of Black men. In fairness to the critics, the same argument was made against 50 Cent's '21 Questions' video nearly two decades earlier – for the same reason: the glorification of Black prison life.

In terms of dollars and cents, similar to Missy Elliott, Eminem, Post Malone and various female rappers, Lil Nas X proved himself a case study in the benefits of diversity. He helped make Hip-Hop become much more representative and reflective of society, and as a result he:

1. Opened rap music up to an often ignored and hard to capture audience and therefore broadened the customer base of the culture.
2. Extended the maturity phase of the collective product life cycle of Hip-Hop to yet another generation. This ensures Hip-Hop will remain a leading force in popular culture for the foreseeable future.
3. Upped the sales ante of Hip-Hop. Prior to the arrival of Lil Nas X, it looked as if Hip-Hop had reached its commercial zenith as the leading genre. Lil Nas X helped elevate this peak even further.
4. Improved Hip-Hop's market share. The sheer volume of records Lil Nas X was selling helped expand Hip-Hop's share in various markets. In the UK, rap music accounted for a fifth of all streams in 2019. By 2021, it was accounting for a third.

Missy Elliott and Lil Nas X-inspired Tips

Wherever there is a lack of diversity there is an abundance of opportunity.

A lack of diversity is more often than not proof of the presence of bigotry – which in turn places a limit on financial viability.

In a business sense, the true opposite of diversity is conformity. Conformity is a tax on creativity, a war on innovation and, therefore, a limit on profitability and sustainability. Diversity, at its core, although often mistaken for a burden, when leveraged properly is a money-printing superpower.

13.

INNOVATION

In a 2018 interview with *Variety*, Adam Levine (lead singer of the pop-rock band Maroon 5) cited a major reason for the commercial decline of rock music: innovation in Hip-Hop. He explained:

All of the innovation and the incredible things happening in music are in Hip-Hop. It's better than everything else. Hip-hop is weird and avant-garde and flawed and real, and that's why people love it.[1]

Mr Levine is of course right, for Hip-Hop is a culture of innovators. From the techniques of making the music to the marketing and business of Hip-Hop itself, every element is built on an innovative spirit rooted in poverty and alienation from the mainstream.

Unable to afford a club to contain the audience, at the first Hip-Hop concert, Kool Herc, Hip-Hop's founding father, innovatively powered his turntables and other equipment with electricity from a lamp post. He built the music itself around breaks in soul, jazz and funk records. The record player was repurposed as turntables, nano sections of old soul or disco records became gold mines for sampling – which itself was a result of being unable to afford instruments.

Subversive Hip-Hop Media Innovations

Locked out of traditional mass media, Hip-Hop artists innovatively produced street DVDs to document the culture and give voices to people who would otherwise go unheard and people trying to build careers.

Locked in prison in mass numbers, Hip-Hop artists innovatively produced Hip-Hop-themed prison and street magazines, such as *FEDs* and *Don Diva*, which told the stories of the streets and people behind the wall.

Locked in during a pandemic, Hip-Hop artists innovatively produced a series of wildly popular live online shows to keep everyone's spirits up. These included:

- *VERZUZ*, originally an Instagram Live-based nostalgia extravaganza, created by Timbaland and Swizz Beatz, in which classic artists go head-to-head in a competition of their biggest hits.

- DJ Cassidy's *Pass the Mic* series, a celebration in which an R'n'B or Hip-Hop legend performs a few lines of their greatest hits from their living rooms . . . and then 'passes the mic' onto someone else.

- *#NS10v10* – Black British radio station No Signal's sound clash series, in which the ten best tracks of two artists are pitted against each other on a round-by-round basis. The winner of each round is decided by the public via a Twitter poll.

- *Quarantine Radio*, Tory Lanez's frequently banned Instagram-based freakshow.

Innovation is the practical implementation of ideas that result in the introduction of new goods or services or improvement in offering goods or services.[2] Where there is great innovation there is often genius. There also happens to be a thin line between genius and mental health issues. There is no one in Hip-Hop who has consistently embodied this thin line like the innovative genius that is Kanye West.

KANYE: THE APPLE INC. OF HIP-HOP

Now I could let these dream killers kill my self-esteem,
Or use my arrogance as the steam to power my dreams

Words that made the world fall in love with Kanye West. The exact sort of mind-play that has become his signature and selling point: most would view arrogance as unappealing and unattractive – Kanye presented it as his superfuel. But the words themselves are not entirely accurate: it wasn't arrogance that fuelled his dreams, it was outside the box thinking-driven innovation. Kanye West is Hip-Hop's most successful innovator, the Apple Inc. of Hip-Hop. His knack for innovation lay not in being consistently original, but in his ability to build on the originality and ideas of others and out-innovate everyone else.

Kanye's innovations in . . . product creation

Starting at the bottom and behind the scenes, Kanye West emerged as a go-to producer in the early noughties following Jay-Z's classic 2001 album *The Blueprint*, on which he produced a third of the fifteen tracks, specifically 'Takeover', 'Momma Loves Me', 'Izzo Hova', 'Never Change' and 'Girls, Girls, Girls (Part 2)'. At the time, he was equivalenced with Justin 'Just Blaze' Smith, the other main producer on *The Blueprint*, as the production duo of the day. 'Kanye West and Just Blaze' became names that could help generate interest and excitement in almost any project.

Showing early signs of his mindset as an innovator, West crafted his own signature sound which in turn was advancing the sound of rap itself. His process and sound was as effective as it was addictive: he'd identify a few potent seconds of old soul records, speed them up slightly (or alter them) and place the sample on his own soul-slapping drum pattern. This production method came to be known as 'chipmunk soul' (named after the high-pitched voices of the *Chipmunks* cartoon series). His productions served as a near heavenly compliment to even remotely competent rappers, let alone great ones like Jay-Z, Beanie Sigel, Talib Kweli, Common, Twista and Scarface – all of whom he helped elevate.

Whereas most rap producers, even the great ones, would create a sonic loop (a short instrumental sound that repeats itself) as a beat – Kanye would create what could be described as a sonic experience. His productions were characterised by being more of a journey, one characterised by dramatic build-ups (see 'Nothing Like It' by Beanie Sigel or 'Father Stretch My Hands' by Kanye himself), deconstruction and then reconstruction (see 'Slow Jams' or 'Overnight Celebrity' by Twista) and climatic completions (see 'Two Words', again by Kanye). Kanye just kept on innovating, kept pushing the potential of what a rap song could be and how far it could go sonically.

Just Blaze embraced Kanye's chipmunk-soul sound and created his own equally appealing version of it. Just Blaze, however, never went beyond being a producer, whereas for Kanye being a producer was just the start. Becoming a rapper is what really propelled him into greatness.

Starting with his emphatic debut, *The College Dropout* (2004), as a rapper Kanye was a super-refreshing break from the norm. He wasn't a gangster, trapper, hustler, baller or shot caller. He was not a Hip-Hop stereotype-affirming entity. He made normal guy Hip-Hop, stuff the average person could relate to – and it sounded much better than anything else. But his music was not one long complaint letter; it sounded exciting, complex, comical and triumphant. In short – he made it sound like Phonte . . .

To understand how Kanye West became truly great as a rapper, we must become familiar with the name Phonte Coleman, lead rapper of the seminal North Carolina rap group Little Brother.

Kanye: using innovation to secure competitive advantage

In *Foundations of Corporate Success*, John Kay points out that the history of innovation in business is full of stories of firms which successfully innovated but failed to turn that innovation into a sustainable competitive advantage. EMI, for example, were innovators in the fields of television, computers, radiology and the music business. But it was principally in the music business that their innovations were able to attain a competitive stranglehold that they leveraged into sustained profits.

Apple, in contrast to EMI, is a company that regularly built on the innovation of other companies. For example, there was nothing original about the hardware concepts of, say, the iPod, the iPhone and the iPad. They were all innovatively upscaled, heavily branded versions of existing products. Nevertheless, Apple were able to leverage their 'secondary' innovation all the way to becoming the first trillion-dollar company.

Phonte is Hip-Hop's equivalent of EMI (in television, computers and radiology). He did the heavy lifting of the research and development that drove innovation in modern Hip-Hop, and a key beneficiary of Phonte's heavy lifting was Mr Kanye West.

Much of what the world loved about Kanye's work as a rapper (especially on his initial albums) was rooted in Phonte's innovation. This ranged from making songs principally about subjects an ordinary law-abiding person could relate to, such as: hating your job (see 'Speed', 'First Day/Last Day'), expressing raw emotion about family (see 'Far Away from Me'), introspective and brutal honesty about his vulnerabilities (see 'Expensive Genes'), skilled satirical humour (see 'Whatever You Say',

'Cheatin'') and astute social analysis ('Black Magic'). Additionally, he often spilt into occasional sultry melody and in some places full-blown singing. There is a direct line of innovative influence between Little Brother's debut *The Listening* (2003) and Kanye's debut *The College Dropout* (2004); a similar umbilical cord exists between the highly innovative *Connected*, the debut album of Foreign Exchange (Phonte's R'n'B group formed with Dutch musician Nicolay)[3] and Kanye's *808s & Heartbreak*.

In 2019, Uproxx, a Hip-Hop website, opined: 'By the time the group [Little Brother] officially announced their breakup in 2010, the game was overrun by artists with their DNA.'[4]

Asked by Hip-Hop DX in 2016 who the 'little brothers to Little Brother' were, Phonte responded – absolutely credibly – with a who's who of cutting-edge modern Hip-Hop: Wale, J. Cole, Kendrick Lamar, Drake (who publicly credited Phonte with inspiring him as he picked up a songwriting award in 2011) and, of course, Kanye.

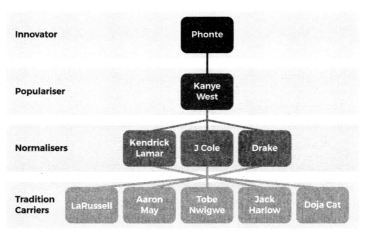

Figure 11: Phonte's sphere of transformational innovation influence

The 'gods' of innovation and competitive advantage conspired against Phonte and conspired for Kanye. But why? The full spectrum of the marketing mix (product, price, place and promotion) are where Kanye West was able to attain a competitive advantage for his music and where Phonte's commercial appeal has thus far not taken off as it should have done. From marketing and machine support, media coverage, audience engagement (Kanye appealed to multiple audiences, including backpackers, students, the street element, ballers and pop-music fans; Phonte appealed principally to backpackers), sonic advancement and market timing – Kanye had the bases covered.

It is a truism in business as well as in wider life, intrinsically linked to the idea that the early bird gets the worm, that the first mover will be the one to reap the rewards, or the commercial advantage of early innovation. The story of Kanye and Phonte lays bare the fallacy of this thinking. In fact, going all the way back to Kool Herc in New York or Big Oomp Records in Atlanta, many of the first-move innovators in Hip-Hop did not attain the commercial advantage the concepts of 'justice' and 'nature' suggest they should have.

Kanye- and Phonte-inspired Tips

Innovation often attracts in hard cold cash what originality attracts in social cache and respect. However, rarely does the first person to build something build the most advanced and impressive version of that item.

Just because someone does something first, doesn't mean they'll do it best. In fact, the first-move innovator is in many situations a sacrificial lamb.

The much-lauded first mover advantage is often a disadvantage in disguise.

Kanye's innovations in . . . product releases

Product launches are a carefully crafted and highly expensive art. Getting it wrong can ultimately mean a good product doesn't attain the commercial value it otherwise would have. It can spell the difference between a product popping or flopping.

'There is only one Steve Jobs and now there is only one Kanye West and I am just like Steve.' So said the ever-humble Kanye West in 2013.[5] And in his own way, especially when it came to launching products innovatively, Kanye West may have a point.

The purpose of the product launch is to ensure everyone – in an entire 360° radius – is aware of the product. But awareness is not enough. Excitement, enthusiasm and intrigue are more rewarding goals. In order to achieve those things, a degree of innovation is needed to wrestle attention away from the infinite number of other things people can be focused on. At this, Kanye is a master; he is indeed the Steve Jobs of Hip-Hop.

The Apple CEO approached his launches with trademark seriousness. They were safe, sound, yet charming affairs – they remained highly professional and somewhat corporate. In contrast, Kanye threw all of his chips on the table with highly innovative strategies that were sometimes high-risk. These included:

Free samples: Named after Kanye's record label, GOOD Music's (GOOD standing for Getting Out Our Dreams) GOOD Fridays were a weekly free music giveaway, which were used to support the launch of his fifth studio album *My Beautiful Dark Twisted Fantasy* (2010). Every Friday, fans would be gifted a rare track, new remix or new song on the new album. It worked an absolute treat, helping propel the album to the top of the *Billboard* charts, selling 496,000 copies in the first week alone.

Broadening elite access: Listening parties are normally intimate affairs attended by the elite of the entertainment business to get a chance to listen to an album before it goes out to the world. For his tenth studio album, *Donda* (named after his deceased mother), Kanye innovated the hell out of the listening party concept. He did a series of listening parties . . . in stadiums packed full of tens of thousands of people . . . all while the album itself was still in development. He upgraded the listening party from a literal party to a stadium tour, raking in an estimated $10–12m on the rough draft of an album.

Politics as promotional theatre: It is hard to determine where Kanye's true political heart lies. Over the last two decades, he has swung from far left to far right, seemingly touching on everything in between. He was supportive of LGBT issues long before his fellow Chicagoan, President Barack Obama, and he chastised President George W. Bush's deadly amateurish Hurricane Katrina rescue efforts, famously declaring on live TV that 'George Bush doesn't care about Black people'. Taking an unexpected turn to the far right, he later embraced President Donald Trump, compared the abolitionist superhero Harriet Tubman to a recruitment agent who never actually freed enslaved Africans, declared hundreds of years of African American enslavement to have been 'a choice' and toured TV studios with outright white supremacists, some of whom even had Black skin (such as Candace Owens). Through all this, he continued to release new music and fashion lines, initially without a negative effect on sales. In fact, Kanye would often become more politically vocal and erratic when he had a product to sell.

Competition: In the late noughties, Kanye and 50 Cent were giants of the music industry. Nevertheless, these two towers of Hip-Hop went head-to-head when they both released their third albums on 11 September 2007. The fact that they both represented a different vision of rap music seemed to force fans to take a side. 50 Cent was an unashamed street rapper; Kanye West was, at that point, still something of a reflection of the ordinary person. Kanye's *Graduation* won the battle with a staggering 957,000 units sold in the first week, while 50 Cent's *Curtis* topped out at 691,000 units. Both were clearly winners, as was the Universal Music Group, the parent company of the labels both were signed to.

Fear of missing out: Following in the vein of GOOD Fridays, Kanye expanded his product release innovation to include albums by other people. In 2018, he produced five albums from head to toe, each one containing seven tracks. He called this period the Wyoming Sessions, named after his ranch in Wyoming where the albums were recorded. The albums were: *Daytona* by Pusha T, *Ye* by Mr West himself, *Kids See Ghosts* by Kid Cudi and Kanye, *Nasir* by Nas and *K.T.S.E.* by Teyana Taylor.

The albums were released in successive weeks. Although innovative, audacious and, in some places, splashed with the creative genius you would expect from Mr West's production and the artists involved, the commercial results were poor. None of the albums were big sellers, and it would be the first time in Kanye's music career that he didn't sell over a million records domestically.

Media rounds: When Kanye West does media rounds, every stop is an unpredictable event. It would be wrong to compare this process to a car crash; it is more like a rocket launch. Fascinating to watch on a good day, on a bad day the imagery sticks with you for life. His radio appearances can be both steady and highly provocative. In interviews and public appearances, he has: revealed that he was $50m in debt; asked Facebook founder Mark Zuckerberg for a huge amount of money; screamed 'YOU AIN'T GOT THE ANSWERS, SWAY!' at a respected radio DJ; revealed deeply personal information about his wife; snatched the microphone from Taylor Swift (a rapidly rising starlet) as she was about to pick up an award; randomly developed a faux British public-school accent; been prone to unexpected and entirely needless swearing (on daytime TV) . . . and this is just a selection of his hard-to-categorise approach. This may or may not have something to do with Kanye's confirmed bipolar diagnosis, as well as the fact that he appears to be grief-stricken following the sudden death of his mother.

There does seem to be calculation to Kanye's methods: as strange as all of the above are, the media rounds associated with Kanye's product-launch strategies are usually highly effective. Unique, unpredictable, exciting and memorable. The routine itself is now predictable: Kanye is releasing something; we expect a wild ride. But the specifics remain entirely unpredictable. He repeatedly manages to cut through the noise and therefore generate the awareness, interest and anticipation needed to sell a product. Critically, his product launches are usually fairly cost-effective (perhaps not including personal, family and, latterly, reputational costs).

Kanye-inspired Innovation in Product Launch Tips

A product launch that does not capture imagination or attention is a waste of time and money. It is critical that you identify unique and shocking ways to wrestle attention for yourself and your product – be merciless and shameless.

In the midst of any mayhem and madness associated with your product launch, do not let your antics overshadow your product.

Kanye's innovations in . . . conquering closed industries

Kanye didn't stumble into becoming a billionaire. He researched, plotted, planned, worked meticulously and screamed it into existence – quite literally into the ear of anyone who would lend him one. He found immense wealth not in his core career, making music, but in his complementary career, fashion (see Chapter 18).

The initial problem for Kanye was that what should have been complementary paths – his music and his sense of fashion – were widely considered to be corrosive to each other. As a result, neither industry was an open door for him. On 'Last Call', the closing track of *College Dropout*, Kanye chronicled how his refusal or inability to behave or dress in a manner that was conventional or expected for rappers resulted in him struggling to get a deal.

From his fashion sense to the subjects he tackled in his music to his route into a career in rapping (as a producer), pretty much every step of the way, Kanye West faced a firmly shut door. He was trapped in a box while thinking outside the box. And as much as 'outside the box thinking' is spoken of, only a few really do it, can do it or can afford to do it. Most people believe what they see and proceed from there. Perception was Kanye's prison. Innovation was his liberation. He used a range of innovative methods to break out and then occupy the world.

Unique offering: Starting clothing lines in Hip-Hop has been an established route to generating wealth since Russell Simmons launched Phat Farm in 1992. The difference between Kanye and 'traditional' Hip-Hop clothing line owners was that Kanye West, 'The Louis Vuitton Don', was truly a fashion connoisseur. By comparison, Jay-Z (who owned Roc-A-Wear) and Puff Daddy (who owned Sean John) never publicly spoke with immense passion and high emotion about the 'feel and texture' of textiles; they never struck anyone as deep-dive fashionistas. When Kanye West is at fashion shows, you can see the world's most famous college dropout looking like a highly attentive, teacher-pleasing student in the front row of the class, paying preciously intense concentration to every detail.

West had no intention of making 'traditional Hip-Hop clothing'; he was not set on competing with Sean John, Roc-A-Wear, Phat Farm, Wu Wear or Outkast Clothing. The products he brought to the fashion market, through his Yeezy brand and other ventures, were a unique offering: to the lay person, some of the clothes looked like literal rags, some of the shoes looked like something you'd expect to see an astronaut wearing, and the fashion shows looked like a crisis advert for homelessness. However – all proved to be immensely popular. Critically, the uniqueness of his offering helped him knock doors down.

Ambitious targets: His intention was quite clearly to compete with the absolute elite of the high-end global fashion market. Speaking with Sway Calloway in an unforgettable 2013 *Sway in the Morning* interview (on Eminem's Shade 45 radio station), he revealed an advanced understanding of the landscape of the fashion world and his competitors:

> Francois Pinault owns Balenciaga, Puma, Saint Laurent, Stella McCartney. [Bernard] Arnault owns Louis Vuitton, Céline, Givenchy. Renzo Rosso owns Margiela, Diesel, Marni, Viktor & Rolf. These guys got factories! These guys have factories. They run that!

Pinault, Arnault and Rosso are estimated to be worth $52.1bn, $181.4bn and $4.2bn respectively. Kanye West had fashion's European establishment in his sights. As he was announcing his arrival to his billionaire would-be competitors, Kanye happened to be '$53m in debt'.[6] He turned to the nouveau riche of the American tech world to invest in him – Mark Zuckerberg and his ilk. To his disappointment, they were apparently more interested in less consequential stuff . . . like 'building schools in Africa'.

Back to school: By 2009, Kanye was a multi-platinum-selling, multi-millionaire rapper and one of the most recognisable people on Earth. So he did the most logical thing possible: he became an intern at a fashion label.

From the inception of his career, West was unshakeable in

his ambition to become a transformational success in fashion. At the pinnacle of his fame (and the beginning of his Taylor Swift-related infamy), he – along with future fashion megastar, the late, great Virgil Abloh – went to intern for Fendi. Many would consider this an embarrassment or a huge step backwards – especially for someone with an ego the size of Kanye's. In reality, it was a million steps backwards in order to make a giant leap forward.

Speaking to the *New York Times* about their time interning with Fendi, Michael Burke, CEO of Louis Vuitton, said:

> I was really impressed with how [Abloh and West] brought a whole new vibe to the studio and were disruptive in the best way. Virgil could create a metaphor and a new vocabulary to describe something as old-school as Fendi. I have been following his career ever since.

Kanye saw their time at Fendi differently; according to him, they 'didn't do shit' during their internship.

Kanye-inspired Tip

A step back should never be mistaken for a setback. A setback itself should be seen as an opportunity for a get-back.

Whether they did or didn't 'do shit', the internships paid off. Years later, Michael Burke would go on to hire Virgil Abloh as the artistic director of Louis Vuitton and Kanye himself would go on to become one of the most bankable people in high fashion, clothing retailing and sportswear. He started at the very bottom so he could shoot for the very top.

By interning, Kanye attained an opportunity to understand

the very nature of the business, to listen and learn at no cost. As a result, when he speaks of fashion he speaks with much greater depth and clarity than any of his Hip-Hop peers. He knew when he was, as he put it, getting 'Kanye Wested on price' (i.e. overcharged due to who he is), he understood exactly how he had to be positioned to break into the elite of the fashion world, he knew all the runners and riders. Critically, he became an actual fashion designer, as opposed to a figurehead or a pitch man.

THE HARD WIRING OF A GREAT INNOVATOR

In addition to drive, motivation and his undeniable creative genius, the characteristics below explain how and what makes Kanye West such a great innovator.

Opposes consensus

From the prevailing order of music, fashion and politics: wherever popular perspective, political properness or perceived wisdom may be – you won't find Kanye West there. You'll find him trying to identify different, often contrarian, ways of seeing, doing or thinking about things.

Fearlessness

West is clearly not captured, regulated or coerced by fear. Be that fear of failure, embarrassment, shame or unpopularity. For example, most people with ambitions of being a serious player in the sports apparel business would not daydream of falling out with Nike – even when they're in the wrong. But, feeling under-valued by the biggest sportswear brand on the planet, Kanye publicly derided them, ended his partnership with them and took his innovations in footwear to the second biggest brand, Adidas – where they became a money-printing machine.

Continuous reflection

Most product creators only reveal their products to the world when they're finalised and polished. On several albums, Kanye West would reveal a handwritten track listing on social media. As he continued to work on the album the handwritten list would be continuously updated – to the point where the piece of paper is filled with jottings. This reveals a mindset of someone who is continuously reflecting on their work and therefore continuously innovating.

Attention craving

West clearly craves attention – most would consider this a negative, but Kanye spun this clear need for attention into a creative and commercial boost: to attract attention, he keeps pushing the boundaries of convention. And innovation in all of the areas he operates in is his overarching method of pushing boundaries.

Putting ideas into action

As the old saying goes, an idea without action is just that: an idea. Innovation without action is hallucination. No matter how left-field they may have been, Kanye always made sure his innovative ideas became a reality.

Willingness to break the rules

One thing is certain with Kanye West: whatever the rules are, he is going to robustly break them. Not just break them for the sake of it, but as a means of further pushing and propelling his ideas and himself to greatness. While most rappers would shudder at the thought of revealing that they relied on ghost-writers – Kanye (similar to his production peers turned rappers, Dr. Dre and Puff Daddy) openly assembled an all-star team of writers. His objective was clearly not artistic purity, but global artistic success rooted in innovative boundary pushing.

WHEN BOUNDARY-PUSHING INNOVATION TAKES YOU OFF A REPUTATIONAL CLIFF

A willingness to break the rules, oppose consensus, crave attention, alongside his clear mental health issues, the qualities that drove Kanye West as an innovative genius have taken him into deeply dark and truly alarmingly racist and antisemitic territory. From proclaiming that the enslavement of millions of Africans was a choice to expressing heartfelt admiration for Adolf Hitler and Nazis, to publicly harassing his ex-wife, West alienated and sacredly offended millions of people.

As a result of a sustained campaign of extremely and unashamedly antisemitic media appearances, Kanye became persona non grata in the business. From Adidas to Gap to his agents, practically everyone cut ties with him. In the process, he immediately lost billions of dollars, his good name and any affection large parts of the general public once had for him.

Everything he is has now made Kanye West everything he is not . . . and once was.

14.

COMPETITION

'Hip-Hop is based on competition, on the battle . . .
I'm Hip-Hop.'
– Elliot 'Yellow Nigga' Wilson, former editor of *XXL*

Where there is efficiency, excellence and innovation, there is competition. And from its inception, strident competition has polished Hip-Hop into a shining jewel. Artistry required meticulous practice, research, originality and boundary pushing. Stylistic plagiarism was strictly forbidden. Rappers had to write their own rhymes, and DJs had to come up with their own routines to be taken seriously. And then to be crowned, to attain a place, let alone a leading position in Hip-Hop, the artist had to prevail in battle. Explicitly or implicitly. Whether lyrically or stylistically, the best and most enduringly successful rappers fought like hell to make it to the top.

With sweet success (often) comes the bitter root of all evil, the secret sauce of everything that makes life worth living and the melting point of meritocracy: money.

From the moment Hip-Hop began to evolve from a solely cultural phenomenon in clubs and neighbourhoods to big business, the main principle of rap as an artform began to be violated. For example, the very concept of meritocratic lyrical skills began to compete with deep pockets. This idea was crystallised most beautifully by Puff Daddy (or his ghost-writer) in 'Bad Boy For Life' (2001): 'Don't worry if I write rhymes / I write cheques'.

Nevertheless, the big business of Hip-Hop has mirrored its once flawlessly meritocratic creative side to the point of almost becoming a blood sport. In fact, at times, it has been bloodier than a blood sport. It is incomparably more competitive than any other genre of music, and ruthlessly so. The level of competition in Hip-Hop has boosted its capitalist prowess, creativity, ambition and global influence to such an extent that it is comparable to another empire that has made good on its global ambitions.

Goldman Sachs	Hip-Hop
Founded and headquartered in New York; now enjoys huge global reach	Founded and headquartered in New York; now enjoys huge global reach
Key champion and component of American capitalism	Key champion and component of American capitalism
Leading entity in its industry	Leading genre in its industry
World-beating alumni – including US Secretaries of the Treasury Steven Mnuchin, Robert Rubin and Henry Paulson, Prime Minister of Italy Mario Monti, Bank of England Governor Mark Carney, British Prime Minister Rishi Sunak and many more	World-beating alumni – including ESPN presenter Max Kellerman, actor and Hollywood executive Mark 'Marky Mark' Wahlberg, Leader of His Majesty's Most Loyal Opposition Moses 'Shyne' Barrow, Oscar-winning actors Will Smith and Mahershala Ali, ostrich farmer Norman 'Terminator X' Rogers, daytime TV presenter Eve and . . . Miley Cyrus
Despised and blamed for much that is wrong in the world by left-wingers	Despised and blamed for much that is wrong in the world by right-wingers
Eye-wateringly unequal worker–boss pay ratio and significant gender-equality issues	Eye-wateringly unequal worker–boss pay ratio and significant gender-equality issues
A white man sits at the very top	A white man sits at the very top

Goldman Sachs	Hip-Hop
Leverages competitive means to mercilessly rid itself of worst performers	Leverages competitive means to mercilessly rid itself of worst performers

Table 15: Goldman Sachs and Hip-Hop: a comparison

Despite lapses, inefficiencies, the odd bit of nepotism and corruption, both Hip-Hop and Goldman Sachs maintain a rifeness of competition, which helps ensure they retain a special place in the hearts and minds of customers, staff and rivals, attract and retain the best staff, remain at the forefront of their industries, provide the best products and services possible, and remain profitable.

When it comes to separating the wheat from the chaff, Hip-Hop is merciless. Even more unforgiving than Goldman Sachs, who are famous for hiring no one but the very best and firing the worst performing 5 per cent of their workforce annually.[1] As similar as they may be, competition exhibits itself quite differently in Hip-Hop than an old-money industry such as banking or a new-money industry such as tech. There is a reason for this.

HIP-HOP COMPETITIVENESS

All industries fall into one of the following categories: perfect competition, monopolistic competition (sometimes described as imperfect competition), oligopoly and monopoly.[2] Dry as they may sound, you gotta know the ledge. So, here is the breakdown:

- **Monopoly** (one king) – occurs where there is 'only room for one don dada', where a market is dominated by a single provider. Examples of this include search engines (Google), the UK's railway infrastructure

(Network Rail) and certain utility providers (Thames Water is just one UK company that has a monopoly on local water supply)
- **Oligopoly** (two or a few kings in a ring) – occurs when a market or industry is dominated by just a few large participants selling competing products. Examples of this include mass media, soft drinks, supermarkets, cereals and mobile phone network providers
- **Perfect competition** (a royal rumble where all kings are equal) – occurs in an industry or market where the products are virtually the same thing, regardless of which provider you buy them from. Examples of this include foreign exchange (a dollar is a dollar), shares in a particular stock (a share in Netflix is a share in Netflix), and agricultural produce (full fat milk is full fat milk)
- **Monopolistic competition** (all kings are different and every king enjoys a peaceful kingdom) – occurs where there are many producers in a market potentially selling the same thing, but the products are different. Examples of this include restaurants (a bowl of spaghetti Carbonara in one place is never the same as in another), hair salons (it is not every hairdresser you trust with your hair) and clothing

Competition in Hip-Hop, however, presents a unique situation – one that is often not well defined in traditional business thinking. At a granular level, the artist level and even Hip-Hop-label level (but not major parent-label level), in terms of the product in the hands of the consumer, the industry naturally falls into a monopolistically competitive environment – the products offered are not perfect substitutes nor are they interchangeable. Competition is highly imperfect. A Tupac album, for example, is not really a substitute for a Biggie album, nor vice versa. A Drake album is not a substitute for a Kendrick Lamar album. They're all rap albums, but they are vastly different in terms of sound, feel, soul, flow and production. And the same goes for any two albums or songs.

Despite being monopolistic, the business of Hip-Hop often operates with the intensity and ferociousness of a bitter oligopoly in a death-match competition for monopoly power. The cut-throat nature of the competition between Puff Daddy's Bad Boy Records and Suge Knight's Death Row Records went much further than, say, Coca-Cola and Pepsi would ever have dreamt of taking their rivalry. In fact, it arguably went further than any business in the legitimate realm. One of the key reasons for this is because competition in Hip-Hop is actually dominated by two intense forms of competitiveness: hyper-competitiveness and deprivation-driven competitiveness.

Hypercompetitiveness

Hypercompetitiveness is said to exist in industries that offer similarly priced products and are subject to rapid and regular obsolescence due to, say, advances in innovation, and where competitive advantage can therefore often prove very temporary. The businesses in these industries have to consistently and quickly evolve and move fast in order not to lose relevance or market share. Sounds like rap music.

Hip-Hop is a classically hypercompetitive industry – it is fast-moving, with similarly priced products, swift innovation and unstable competitive advantage.

Those who prevail in hypercompetitive markets tend to be people who are:

- blessed with foresight and intuition
- willing and able to swiftly adapt and adjust with the times while retaining authenticity and credibility
- financially buoyant enough to buy out or withstand the risk of threats, or shore up their weaknesses
- mercilessly competitive (of course)

Jay-Z, for example, foresaw the 2002 rise of 50 Cent – then a true underground king – and the seismic change it would bring. Reminiscing on the *Breakfast Club* in 2013, he recalled that he urgently advised his protégés (and roster of artists), Beanie Sigel, Memphis Bleek and others to flood the market with music immediately because '50 Cent is coming'. Proving that his foresight was 20:20, 'four months later "In Da Club" [50 Cent's breakout single] came out and it was over.' 50 Cent, a fascinatingly edgy and entertaining rapper with a bulletproof back story, an alliance with Dr. Dre and Eminem and irresistibly delicious debut album (*Get Rich Or Die Tryin'*) cast a shadow over any potential competitor.

The sound, style, structure and stars of rap change so quickly that to be near the peak of relevance in the game for, say, five years, is to have performed something of a miracle. The likes of Jay-Z, Nas, Nicki Minaj, Kanye West, Snoop Dogg, Dr. Dre, Eminem, Puff Daddy, Missy Elliot, Rihanna and others who have managed to last decades and remain on the cutting edge of the culture have as good as moonwalked on water.

Deprivation-driven competitiveness

Deprivation-driven competitiveness is competition rooted in what the British rapper Skinnyman labelled 'the science of social deprivation' on 'Council Estate Of Mind'. Poverty, ambition and limited opportunity make an explosive cocktail. It can bring out the best or the worst in a person – and usually it's both. When you take a person from an economically destitute background who really wants to go places in life and give them an opportunity, there is an enhanced likelihood that they will do whatever it takes to make good on that opportunity and to defend themselves against losing it.

Largely due to their lack of an economic safety net and limited access to opportunity, when two or more people (or parties) from harsh and economically disadvantaged environments compete for opportunity or dominance of a sector, the competitiveness compounds to potentially dangerous levels, as the parties have a clear understanding and fear of the stakes if shit sails south. As a result, all business is likely to be seen as a high-risk and high-stakes endeavour. So, when two or more poor and ambitious people compete for a rare yet highly lucrative opportunity, what you'll see is . . . well, what you often see in Hip-Hop:

- Highly impressive levels of innovation and creativity
- Excessive and lopsided risk-taking
- The personalising of business rivalries and disputes
- Flexibility with the law
- Emotional instability
- Ruthless determination

With the above in mind, the sections below examine competitive strategies and outcomes in Hip-Hop, and how competition has been used as a promotional tool.

DIVERSITY AND COMPETITIVE INTENSITY: THE TOKEN WOMEN

The threat of new entrants into a market is an issue everyone has to contend with. When a new product is released, it will be compared to and compete with existing products already out there. When a new employee joins a department, she will be compared to and compete with existing employees. When that new entrant is similar to you in product, service or presentation, there's more reason to toss, turn and sweat at night. For women, already a brutally underrepresented group in Hip-Hop, this competition, indeed Hip-Hop competition, is much stiffer. The reasons:

One Woman Syndrome

There is often seemingly only space for one woman in the top tier of Hip-Hop performers, compared to multiple men. Unsurprisingly, the available opportunities for women are far fewer. Most rap crews only have room for one woman. In Ruff Ryders it was Eve, in Bad Boy it was (arguably) Lil' Kim, Roc-A-Fella had Amil (for a while), at Death Row it was Lady of Rage. Murder Inc. and Three 6 Mafia are two of the only crews to have more than a single woman in a leading position.

Glass ceiling

There is no glass ceiling for men in the business of Hip-Hop. However, there is one for women and they hit their heads on it rapidly. Most (if not all) of the moguls, top producers (Missy Elliot may be the only real exception to the rule here) and executives (with the honourable exception of Sylvia Rhone) in Hip-Hop are men.

Looks

Men in Hip-Hop can look however they wish and still stand a shot at making it to the top. Top-tier women in modern rap music have to look like voluptuous supermodels (often requiring dangerous surgery to do so). Men are allowed to age and remain at the pinnacle of the business. Not so for women (with the exception of Missy Elliott, Lady of Rage and Queen Latifah).

Twice as hard, twice as good

The requirements for excellence in presentation and performance are much higher, and so women are often expected to demonstrate a rap skill level comparable to or, preferably, superior to the elite of their male peers.

NICKI MINAJ AND CARDI B: A FORCED COMPETITION

Trinidadian New Yorker, Onika 'Nicki Minaj' Maraj-Petty ticked all of the boxes and then some. For close to half a decade, she worked tirelessly through the mixtape circuit, releasing three well received projects – *Playtime Is Over* (2007), *Sucka Free* (2008) and *Beam Me Up Scotty* (2009). She also became a queen of the fairly wild early to mid-noughties 'street DVD' era (the predecessor to the Hip-Hop YouTube documentary channel), with critical features on the *Smack DVD* and *On the Come Up* series. It was in these street DVDs that she would get noticed by her future boss, Lil Wayne, who wrote the following on Nicki in a 2016 article for *Time* magazine:

> You know, in New York they used to have these street DVDs. It just so happened that I appeared in one, and when I looked at the finished product, Nicki Minaj was on a part of the DVD. I was like, 'Woooooow!' She was just being Nicki without the glitz and glamour. When I heard the first two and four bars, it wasn't even about her rapping better than any female rapper. It was about, man, she's rapping better than other rappers – period.[3]

With her buzz reaching deafening levels, Minaj signed with Lil Wayne's Young Money Records in 2009. It was in 2010, however, that she broke through with a show-stealing appearance on 'Monster', a single from Kanye West's very highly regarded fifth album, *My Beautiful Dark Twisted Fantasy*.

Over the course of thirty-one exceptional bars, she demonstrated a supreme mastery of lyricism as well as rapping in multiple accents and personalities. Her verse on 'Monster' was the birth of a monster. In a feat that many would have considered impossible, she outshone Jay-Z, a persistent contender for the greatest rapper ever, and Kanye West on the song. In 2013, *Complex* magazine hailed Nicki Minaj's verse on 'Monster' as the best in rap music from the prior five years.

Nicki Minaj-inspired Competition Tip

While still an underdog, whenever you're in head-to-head competition with the best in the business, remember they have little to win and you have nothing to lose – operate accordingly: do your best to bury them.

Later in 2010, Nicki would release her debut album, *Pink Friday*, which would go on to sell over three million copies – solidifying her as a leading light in Hip-Hop, a global star and the undisputed First Lady of rap music. She was also a fashion and beauty flagbearer – she helped change the landscape of Western beauty standards from stick-skinny to voluptuous. Along the way, she saw off early competitive rivalries from more established female rappers, specifically Lil' Kim and Remy Ma.

And then came Cardi B, a stripper turned social media and then reality TV star . . . armed with one of the greatest elevator pitches of all time: 'People be asking me like, "What do you does? Are you like a comedian or something?" Nah. I ain't none of that. I'm a hoe. I'm a stripper hoe. I'm about this schmoney.'[4]

Cardi B-inspired Tip

Your elevator pitch is a critical part of your competitive arsenal. People hear multiple pitches (subliminal and otherwise) a day: ensure yours is absolutely memorable.

Cardi B has a super-infectious personality. This, plus her fearless authenticity and her thorough understanding of practically all media – but especially social media and reality TV – helped her to grow a mass following. And eventually she came to conquer the rap world – despite the fact that she is not, unlike Nicki, an organic and highly skilled rapper. In fact, Cardi B was not really anything like Nicki Minaj at all.

Nicki Minaj	Cardi B
Born: 1982	Born: 1992
Career commenced circa 2005 when she released her first mixtape	Career commenced circa 2015 when she was cast on the reality TV show *Love & Hip-Hop*
Developed an audience through the mixtape and street DVD circuit	Developed an audience through social media (Instagram and Vine) and by appearing on reality TV shows
Highly respected as a rapper	Beloved as a media personality who raps
Unique selling point: super-abilities as a rapper and a very quirky set of personality traits and alter egos	Unique selling point: super-brutal honesty; a deeply alluring personality and back story
Writes her own raps	Proudly admits to using the assistance of a ghost-writer

Table 16: Nicki Minaj and Cardi B: a comparison

All they really had in common is that they were female New Yorkers of Caribbean descent who rapped for a living. Nevertheless, Hip-Hop's one-woman syndrome made them competitors. And the stakes were high. The normal subliminal (and not so subliminal) insults and social media digs commenced. In terms of insight into the profitable nature of competition, perhaps the most interesting of all these exchanges came from Nicki Minaj on Katy Perry's May 2017 single 'Swish Swish', in which she rapped about how rap beefs only served to enrich her further, before wittily offering:

My life is a movie, I'm never off set
Me and my amigos (no, not Offset)

She ended the verse alluding to the fact that she got 'them', assuming Cardi B, 'upset'.

Breaking this down for the uninitiated: 'Offset' is the name of Cardi B's then boyfriend (now husband), a member of the rap group The Migos. Most importantly, Nicki Minaj was right – the nature of the beef, the competition, was indeed making her richer – but if she lost, it could have damaged her financially in the long-term.

In February 2017, Cardi B signed to Atlantic Records. In August 2017, on her single 'No Flag', Minaj made reference to record labels trying to emulate her success and addressed a nameless woman whose success she says is down to her own. Even though the disses were as subtle as a volcano erupting, Nicki and Cardi B would deny that they were rapping about each other. In September 2018, the denials could no longer hold. At perhaps the least likely ever place for a rap beef to turn violent – *Harper's Bazaar*'s Icons Party during New York Fashion Week – Nicki Minaj and Cardi B, dripping in couture regalia, came to blows. *Cosmopolitan* got the scoop:

Sources from inside the event, where a crowd of party-goers were waiting to watch a performance by Christina Aguilera, say Nicki was taking a photo with Kelly Rowland and La La Anthony when Cardi walked past. Reportedly, Nicki deliberately stepped on Cardi's train [of her gown], *which led to a scuffle – Cardi got hit and part of her wig was pulled off. Then Cardi* [with her naked bottom on full display] *threw her shoe at Nicki – yes, you can see a shoe being removed in the video above, and hear a 'thwack' noise as it makes contact with its intended target, or some poor security guard who had to take it.*[5]

Cardi B walked away with a lump on her head; everyone walked away embarrassed. Lady B took to Instagram to offer her rationale for the rumble at the fashion jungle:

> I've let a lot of shit slide! I let you sneak diss me, I let you lie on me, I let you attempt to stop my bags [money], fuck up the way I eat. You've threaten other artists in the industry, told them if they work with me you'll stop fuckin with them!!! . . . I've worked too hard and come too far to let anybody fuck with my success!!!![6]

In a separate situation, Remy Ma made similar allegations about Nicki Minaj's alleged use of behind-the-scenes skulduggery to maintain her position in the business and protect her from competition.[7]

Nicki Minaj took to her radio show, *Queen Radio*, to speak her mind on the New York Fashion Week rumble:

> You came into my fucking culture! I never had to bang [sleep with] a DJ to play my fucking songs. You call Black women roaches. Real bitches never attack a woman. You're angry and you're sad. This is not funny. Get this woman some fucking help. This woman's at the highest point in her career and she's throwing shoes?

She went on to allege that Cardi B's career was built on 'sympathy and payola', an allegation Cardi B's team released a statement to describe as 'absolutely false'.[8]

Spitting in the face of the very notion of justice in the world, in 2019 Cardi B became the first woman to win a Grammy for Best Rap Album for her debut *Invasion Of Privacy*, beating albums by highly respected rappers – Pusha T, Travis Scott and the late greats Mac Miller and Nipsey Hussle. In this moment of Cardi B euphoria, a tweet by Black Entertainment Television (BET), tweeted a news article stating: 'Cardi B Is the First Solo Female

Rapper To Win Best Rap Album, And Fans Are Weeping', and added in a caption, 'Meanwhile, Nicki Minaj is being dragged by her lacefront [wig]'.

BET's cheap shot proved to be quite expensive. Nicki Minaj calmly struck back, hitting them where it really hurts: the pocket. She took to Twitter and informed the world that: 'Young Money will no longer be a part of the BET Experience or award show. Summer Tour dates dropping soon.'[9]

Young Money is home to Lil Wayne, Drake and Nicki Minaj herself. With those three pulling out, the BET Experience would be far inferior, less popular and lacking a cutting edge.

> ### Nicki Minaj-inspired Competition Tip
>
> Whatever you possess that may help you win or defend competitive advantage – be it weapons, connections or financial prowess, etc – use it. In a bout for survival or supremacy, all is fair game.

Nicki Minaj deserved her place at the top, and so did Cardi B. But Cardi B was not worthy of taking Nicki Minaj's place in Hip-Hop as a musical artist; she was just the woman most likely to do so. Nicki Minaj read the threat of competition from Cardi B correctly. And she acted appropriately to protect her interests, her esteem and her position in the business. All is fair in love . . . and Hip-Hop. In a just world, however, there would be space for more than one woman at the top table of Hip-Hop.

In 2020, the Cardi B and Nicki Minaj beef/competition seemed to have fizzled out altogether. This may or may not have something to do with the fact that 2020 marked the year where Hip-Hop's One-Woman Syndrome eased up and became the year of the female rapper. Competition gave way to cooperation. Nicki and Doja, Cardi and Megan Thee Stallion all scored their first number-one hits – by working with each other in those duos, as opposed to just competing against each other. Noname, Mullato, Bbymutha, Flo Milli, Hook, Rico Nasty, Ivorian Doll, Saweetie, SU'lan, Chika, City Girls, cupcakKe, Deetranada, DreamDoll, Junglepussy, Ivy Sole, Jozzy, KenTheMan, ppcocaine and Yung Baby Tate all made splashes in what turned out to be a stellar year for female rappers.

A popular tweet pondered what men in Hip-Hop would do now that women were taking over. One of the most retweeted responses was rooted in the reverse of what women had been subjected to in commercial Hip-Hop for as long as anyone can remember: 'Shake something, nigga.'

Pitch, Presentation and Development Lessons from Battle Rapping

The honesty, immediacy, brutality and demands for high standards found in battle rapping offer several important lessons, especially in the realm of presentation, pitching and development:

1. Confidence – even when conveyed through naked arrogance – is appealing, indeed sexy, especially when you can back it up. In presentation, humility can be ugly.

2. Throw gentle customs and caution out of the window. Carefully study your opposition to effectively crush them. Do not shy away from highlighting the flaws of your opposition.

3. The audience is persistently offering you feedback. In battle rap the response is audible ('ooooh', 'boo', 'braaap', etc), but in traditional business areas, feedback is often just as clear. Early dismissal 'Erm, I have an unexpected meeting: any chance we can make this a much quicker interview?', wandering eyes,

---

uneasy hand gestures, etc are often signs that things are not going well.

4. Humour is an immensely powerful weapon. It disarms, endears, conquers and impresses. Always ensure your presentations and pitches are loaded with the three Ws of pain: wit, wisdom and wordplay.

5. To excite is to ignite. A boring presentation will always be trumped by a lively, entertaining and invigorating one.

JAY-Z'S MARKET LEADERSHIP STRATEGIES

There always has to be a chief, a king, a standard-bearer, a market leader. In Hip-Hop the market leader proves themselves worthy of their position through victory on the battlefield, i.e. through sustained success in competition – in sales, credibility and consistent creative ingenuity. From 1998 till today, Jay-Z has been a clear and consistent market leader in Hip-Hop.

It is virtually impossible to sustain yourself as a market leader in a hypercompetitive business environment, such as rap, by being passive. Simultaneously, being recklessly aggressive is likely to distract, damage and dethrone a market leader. Over the last few decades, Jay-Z faced challengers of various competence from practically all angles; in order to defend his position as market leader he adopted a range of slick competitive strategies (see Figure 12).

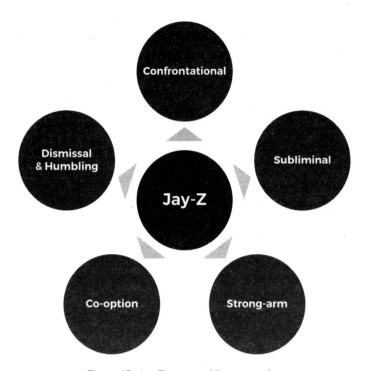

Figure 12: Jay-Z's competitive strategies

Jay-Z competitive strategy I: Subliminal taunts (or cold war tactics)

Jay-Z's opening salvo in most forms of competitions is strikingly similar: it starts with subliminal taunts. From music to business, from Noel Gallagher, Nas, Robert De Niro, The Game and Mase right the way down to the comedian Faizon Love – Jay-Z always taunts the competition/opposition to step up or step away from the danger zone. Part caution, part invitation – but it is almost always, at least inadvertently, promotion.

Accepting taunts as a subliminal 'invitation' (as opposed to a caution) can lead to dire business consequences, for he will not hesitate to use his power as market leader against a rival.

Whether soft, sweet, hard or sour, the taunts themselves are often effective in distracting or provoking a potential competitor to reveal their hand, their thoughts and feelings. This is valuable, as it provides some insight into what their subsequent actions or reactions might be. For Jay-Z, a market leader, how the competitor responds reveals the potential threat they pose to his position and, ultimately, assists him in making optimal decisions on how he defends his position against them.

Jay-Z-inspired Competition Tip

Identify soft ways to attain an understanding of how a potential competitor views your position and how they will act or react to moves made by you.

For Jay-Z, this is a win-win strategy. The stories, speculation and excitement created by his subliminal taunts have helped generate and sustain interest in Jay-Z's thoughts, fears, ideas – and therefore albums – for over two decades. It also adds to the Machiavellian mystique of Jay-Z as an executive. It enhances his legend, bolsters his brand and adds to his allure.

Jay-Z competitive strategy II: Confrontation (or hot war tactics)

Whatever goes on in darkness eventually comes to light. Jay-Z's cold war taunts often turn hot. And they usually turn hot when it best serves his own strategic business interests.

By 2001, Nas was pound for pound and line for line the most perfect and supremely talented rapper in the game, and the only person in Hip-Hop who posed a remote threat to the idea of Jay-Z as market leader. Highly presentable and photogenic, commercially solid and strategically gifted – Nas was a uniquely tricky rival. His fellow Queensbridge native, Prodigy of the respected rap group Mobb Deep – also had issues with Jay-Z at the same time. Jay-Z decided to make a meal of both of them (inconvenient plot twist: Prodigy and Nas also decided to make a meal of each other at the same time). In terms of competition, Prodigy was the starter; Nas was the main course.

What looked like a mere rap squabble was actually a competition for supremacy and industrial dominance by two leading multi-million-dollar entities, operating under the brands 'Jay-Z' and 'Nas'.

Ever the excellent corporate strategist, Jay-Z picked the moment most strategically beneficial to his interests to make his move. He launched his open head-to-head competition with Nas and Prodigy at Hot 97's Summer Jam (an annual Hip-Hop festival) – premiering 'Takeover', a diss track aimed at both men, before revealing a giant picture of Prodigy, a highly respected hardcore street rapper – as a child ballerina. Jay-Z claimed the picture was taken in 1988, when Prodigy was fourteen and Jay-Z was 'pushing weight' (selling drugs). Prodigy claimed it was taken in the early 1980s.

Moments after this stunt, Jay-Z did something magical: he brought Michael Jackson, *the* Michael Jackson, onto the stage. The king of rap and the king of pop, twin market leaders, stood side by side. The moment was engrained into popular culture and Hip-Hop history. All of this created the perfect appetiser for his upcoming album, *The Blueprint*, which was released on 11 September 2001 and debuted at the pinnacle of the charts.

Jay-Z-inspired Competition Tip

Refrain from being drawn into any form of competitive endeavour that does not benefit your economic or business interests.

Nas skilfully and robustly responded to Jay-Z's 'Takeover', first with a freestyle called 'Stillmatic freestyle' (also known as 'Nastalgic freestyle') and then, more extensively, stingingly and conclusively on 'Ether'. Jay-Z responded to 'Ether' with 'Supa Ugly', a song so graphically below the belt that his own mother demanded he apologise for it. Nas would go on to be crowned the victor of the on-wax competition between the two of them. Jay-Z, however, remained market leader.

Jay-Z competitive strategy III: Co-option

The absence of hostility should not be mistaken for an absence of competition (or the presence of it either). Regardless of the approach – hot or cold, vertically, or horizontally, direct or through proxies, sideways or 'straight ways' – Jay-Z always ensures any competition works to his advantage.

As a result, any emerging serious competitor is forced to consider and contend with where they're stood in relation to him. Where there is no hostility, Jay-Z tends to co-opt would-be competitors into his powerful network. Traditionally, he has used what could be described as his Three Ss of Co-option: Sign, Sing and Supper.

All three areas of co-option have an overarching effect: they shift competitors and potential competitors to complements and dependents.

Sign: Neutralise competitors by acquiring them. Or, in Jay-Z's own famous words from the *Backstage* documentary:

There's a nigga right now somewhere he at the table with a bowl of Apple Jacks and he's reading the back of the cereal. And in between eating the Apple Jacks he's writing some shit. And he wants my spot. I'mma find him though, I'mma sign him ... I don't want no problems.

In October 2005, Jay-Z was the headline act for New York radio station Power 105.1's Powerhouse concert. He titled his performance 'I Declare War', promising to 'air out' some rivals in a manner similar to his theatrical 'airing out' of Nas and Prodigy at the 2001 Summer Jam. But the event turned out to be yet another classic Machiavellian Jay-Z business move. Instead of war, Jay-Z and Nas took to the stage together and declared peace – much to the delight of the 20,000-strong crowd. Three months after the concert, Jay-Z, then president of Def Jam, signed Nas – a proven bestselling artist – in a multi-album, multi-million-dollar deal. This was not a one-off. Many of Jay-Z's past competitors – notably Fat Joe, The Lox and Jim Jones – are now signed to his management company, Roc Nation. He also signed would-be competitors such as Jay Electronica, J Cole and Meek Mill.

Also in 2005, Lil Wayne, a jewel in the Cash Money Records crown, had fully shed his image as a child rap star and had grown into something of a cultural phenomenon – the leading light of a new generation of rappers. He was a clear emerging competitor for Jay-Z. Of course, Jay-Z attempted to sign him . . . but was robustly rebuffed through a legal threat of 'tortious interference' from 'his friend' (and rival executive) Cash Money CEO Bryan 'Birdman' Williams (Lil Wayne's adopted father).

Jay-Z-inspired Competition Tip

Where an opportunity to turn a potential commercial competitor into a commercial asset presents itself – snatch it. Where it does not present itself – seek it.

Sing: Neutralise competitors by co-operating with and complementing them. Though Jay-Z was unable to sign Lil Wayne, he embraced him and co-opted him into his powerful network by making prominent songs with him, which curtailed any threat of competition to Jay-Z while helping Lil Wayne maintain the threat of competition for his services – Cash Money knew Roc-A-Fella/Def Jam were eagerly interested.[10] This is similar to the approach he would adopt with a slew of would-be competitor rappers – including Eminem, Young Jeezy, Drake, Wale, Rick Ross, 50 Cent (despite the occasional squabble) and Jay Electronica.

For three years in the aftermath of Tupac's 1996 murder, West Coast Hip-Hop remained stagnant and quiet compared both to the East Coast and the emergent but buoyant Southern Hip-Hop scene. Fresh from finding Eminem and transforming him from a talented battle rapper into a global superstar, Dr. Dre, the brain behind much of the success of West Coast rap, was back in the studio in album mode. This made it clear that there was likely to be a West Coast re-emergence. To Jay-Z, at that point an uncontested market leader, this was the Hip-Hop equivalent of the emergence of a re-energised post-Cold War Russia.

In the past, West Coast and East Coast Hip-Hop competed at levels once unthinkable. This time around, Dr. Dre and Jay-Z made it different. Dr. Dre hired Jay-Z to write his comeback single, 'Still D.R.E.' (featuring Snoop Dogg) – an act of co-operation that would have been considered unconscionable just half a decade before. It helped ensure that both coasts no longer saw themselves as rivals but as complementary – curtailing the threat of destructive competition.

Supper: Neutralise competitors by socially absorbing them. Every year, Jay-Z hosts the ultimate networking event for the great and good in Hip-Hop (and its periphery): the Roc Nation Brunch.

An invitation to the Roc Nation Brunch has become a signal of success in Hip-Hop. In addition to super-lucrative networking opportunities, it offers attendees the opportunity to attain a critical clout stamp and mark of arrival amongst the elite: a picture with Jay-Z and/or Beyoncé.

So what does Jay-Z get in return? Well, there is no such thing as a free brunch – even less so a Roc Nation Brunch. Everyone who attends pays him the supreme compliment of recognising his leadership in the market that is Hip-Hop – making him a magnet for opportunities and deals. It keeps him at the epicentre of the culture, once again curtailing the threat of serious competition.

One thing is for certain: Jay-Z is meticulous in maintaining his ground. Ultimately, if Jay-Z cannot sign you, sing with you or supper with you, there is a great chance he is going to use his other S: he will *sting* you . . . but only if you're worthy.

Jay-Z competitive strategy IV: Strong arm of business

How does the $400-a-bottle tipple of the European old-money super-elite become the favoured champagne of the Hip-Hop generation? Answer: through the influence of a deeply working-class former drug dealer from the Marcy Projects.

Jay-Z was a pioneer in popularising Louis Roederer's flagship champagne, Cristal. Thanks in part to the repeated mentions (promotions) of Cristal by him and other popular Hip-Hop figures in their music, the champagne developed a degree of a Hip-Hop elasticity of demand. The 'gold' bottle wrapped in an additional layer of 'gold' material (orangey-yellow plastic) became the beverage of choice for Hip-Hoppers at the pinnacle of the good life. Jay-Z's product placement was extensive:

- In the opening scene of Jay-Z's first solo video, 'In My Lifetime' (1995), he is seen opening up a bottle of Cristal before pouring it over the camera – signifying the ground – as a tribute to his deceased friend Danny Dan.
- In the 'I Just Wanna Love You' (2000) video, Beanie Sigel is seen pouring Cristal over a beautiful woman as Jay-Z raps 'might buy you Cris but that's about it'. Jay-Z and Lil' Kim are also seen sitting next to bottles of Cristal as Jay-Z raps.

- In the 'Big Pimpin'' video, he and then business partner Dame Dash are portrayed living their absolute best lives in Brazil on a yacht with models and Cristal.
- And then, suddenly, in the video for 'Show Me What You Got' (2006), Jay-Z is shown spurning an offered bottle of Cristal and in place is delivered – in a secure metal briefcase – a bottle of champagne called 'Ace of Spades'.

Why the shift? Until 2006, Cristal managed to straddle being the tipple created for the Tsar of Russia and favoured by the King of New York. And then came an *Economist* article titled 'Bubbles and Bling', featuring the paragraph:

> . . . the attitude of the house of Roederer to the unexpected popularity of Cristal among rappers is considerably more circumspect. Frédéric Rouzaud, who took over from his father as managing-director of the winery in January, says that Roederer has observed its association with rap with 'curiosity and serenity'. But he does not seem entirely serene. Asked if an association between Cristal and the bling lifestyle could actually hurt the brand, he replies: 'That's a good question, but what can we do? We can't forbid people from buying it. I'm sure Dom Pérignon or Krug would be delighted to have their business.

Jay-Z, a loyal and voluntary Cristal brand ambassador for well over a decade, a man who had made millions upon millions upon millions for Cristal (with no return or payment) thanks to free advertising and credibility, considered this statement racist. In his 2010 book *Decoded*, he explained his objections to Rouzaud's comments:

> That was like a slap in the face. You can argue all you want about Rouzaud's statements and try to justify them or whatever, but the tone is clear. When asked about an influential segment of his

*market, his response was, essentially, well, we can't stop them
from drinking it. That was it for me.*

In pursuit of supremacy-laden cultural 'purity', Cristal foolishly
blew it. In response to Rouzaud's comments, Jay-Z launched one
of the most unusual acts of corporate activism known to man:
he led a boycott of a super-luxury champagne brand, despite the
fact that most people could only dream of buying $400 cham-
pagne. A brand that even the producer made clear only targeted
the top '3–5% of wine drinkers who really know wine, and who
take the time to taste it correctly'.[11]

On his great recession-era 2009 record 'Onto The Next One',
Jay-Z made it explicitly clear that he considers Cristal to be racist
and therefore abandoned the beverage. After his line labelling
Cristal racist came one that spoke to the competitive genius and
business strong arm of Jay-Z: ' . . . so I switched gold bottles
on to that Spade shit'.

If Jay-Z was a simpleton, a game goofy businessperson or, even
worse, a social media influencer when he led the boycott of Cristal
he would have directed everyone to an existing rival brand.
Instead, he created his own brand of champagne, Ace of Spades
– official description: 'The Armand de Brignac Ace of Spades
Brut Gold NV, the brand's flagship cuvée, is a singular example
of the Brut Champagne tradition.' Cased in a starker opaque gold
bottle than Cristal and priced even more expensively, it instantly
became the champagne of choice for Hip-Hop.* Gradually, Cristal
faded into insignificance in Hip-Hop. Jay-Z used his art as a
strong arm of business to take on and take out a market-leading
brand in a hard-to-penetrate market.

Ace of Spades served as the realisation of prophecy for Jay-Z:
the cover of his first single, 'In My Lifetime' (1994), was an

---

* I would offer a perspective on the difference in taste between Cristal and
Ace of Spades, but a writer's salary does not stretch far enough to afford either.

illustration of a bottle of champagne with his name on it. In February 2021, French conglomerate LVMH (Moët Hennessy Louis Vuitton) announced it had purchased a 50 per cent stake in Jay-Z's champagne house, Armand de Brignac – producer of Ace of Spades — earning Jay-Z a reported $300m.

Jay-Z competitive strategy V: Dismissal & humbling

Jay-Z (aka Jay-Hova) occasionally adopts a competition tactic that arguably finds its roots in Matthew 23:12: 'For those who exalt themselves will be humbled, and those who humble themselves will be exalted.'

Dismissively humbling competitors and reminding them of their place is Jay-Z's approach to less than worthy competitors.

Speaking to the August 2001 edition of *XXL* magazine after the West Coast rapper Jayo Felony made a diss record about him, Jay-Z insisted that it was a 'pure business move . . . he might want a gold album or something' (selling half a million records, at the time, was something Jay-Z would almost effortlessly achieve in a week). When Jim Jones, a flamboyant street rapper from Dipset (a Harlem rap crew once signed to Jay-Z's Roc-A-Fella Records), came for him, Jay-Z mockingly suggested that there should be a qualification requirement of 'at least a classic verse' before people could engage him in competition.

COMPETITION AND MARKET SHARE: *THE SOURCE* VS *XXL*

The Source magazine was rap's bible. It was not the first magazine dedicated to Hip-Hop, but it was the first to gain and maintain widespread appeal – largely as a result of being the best thought-through and the best product. It provided the presentation and representation of the culture, business, politics and the music. It provided structure, demanded respect, offered clear and authoritative information, encouraged and highlighted commercial possibilities, improved visibility, upheld integrity as well as standards and established an intellectual basis for the culture. It helped solidify the culture *as* a culture.

So essential to me personally was the publication that, during my own financially destitute university days, in the non-battle between spending my few remaining pounds on transportation and food (i.e. fries and a bus ride) or buying *The Source*, it didn't matter if it was raining or snowing – *The Source* was easily winning.

Founded in 1988 in a Harvard dorm by Dave Mays, who would hire his Harvard contemporaries Jonathan Shechter, James Bernard and Ed Young as the initial employees, *The Source* was truly a market-moving magazine: a favourable mention in its pages could attain a rapper a lucrative record deal; a good review was the groundwork of great sales. Readers, rappers and the rank and file of the industry respected and revered *The Source*. As a result, from the early 1990s onwards, the magazine enjoyed a stranglehold on Hip-Hop publishing. Indeed, the entire concept of in-depth Hip-Hop journalism (as opposed to public relations) was synonymous with *The Source*. Many competitors rose – even the great Quincy Jones himself established *Vibe* – but none could really topple *The Source*. And then came 'double XL'.

Founded in August 1997, *XXL* was owned by mammoth publishing house Harris Publications. For their debut issue, they had soon-to-be moguls Jay-Z and Master P (both label owners distributed by Priority Records) on alternative covers.

XXL's sales tagline was 'Hip-Hop on a Higher Level'. And they lived up to it. The magazine was very well put together – intellectually robust, witty, confrontational and street. They clearly followed the blueprint laid out by *The Source*. Nevertheless, for their initial years, *XXL* remained firmly an underdog against the giant that was *The Source*, trailing the sales and cultural impact of the larger and more established company.

At the recommendation of Jon Schechter, a departed founding

editor of *The Source*, in late 1999 *XXL* hired Elliot 'Yellow Nigga' Wilson, a razor-sharp, highly confrontationally competitive and energetic former *Source* music editor, who left the magazine disgruntled that they had changed the coveted rating he gave to an album by Kurupt (then a former Death Row artist). In a November 2017 interview on (Hip-Hop journalist turned record executive) Noah Callahan-Bever's online interview series, *Blueprint*, Wilson was asked what his mission was at *XXL* as far as *The Source* was concerned. Wilson responded: 'Destroy them! Kill them! Bury them! Burn 'em to the ground!'[12]

> ### Elliot Wilson-inspired Tip
>
> Humour can serve as an immensely effective weapon in competition, but only when it is backed up by serious strategy, sound-mindedness and effective execution. Without the backup, the joke will end up on the joker.

Fuelled by scorn and a burning desire for revenge, Wilson approached *XXL*'s competition with *The Source* like a prize-fighter in his prime (or a battle rapper vying to get signed). He was super-aggressive, often deeply personal but always entertaining (unless you were on the receiving end of his disses). He transformed the normally dour editor's note section into a unique selling point for the magazine. Finding out in what deliciously creative way Elliot Wilson would mercilessly mock his rivals became a merchandising and motivation point. From the safe space of his column, he attacked and attacked and attacked *The Source*, month in, month out.

Asked in a 2003 interview with the *New York Times* what caused *XXL*'s beef with *The Source*, Wilson, like al-Qaeda in its prime, stridently claimed responsibility: 'I've been going at them since day one, every month . . . Hip-Hop is based on competition, on the battle . . . I'm Hip-Hop.'

Despite the monthly royal roasting at the hands of the editor of a very worthy rival, *The Source* remained *The Source*. And for a long time, they, wisely, did not respond to Elliot Wilson's taunts. Nevertheless, Wilson's relentless competitive nature did improve the standing of *XXL* in the eyes of the public, in Hip-Hop and on the stand. In 2002, *XXL*'s circulation grew 33 per cent to 216,445, whereas *The Source* grew 5 per cent to 487,425. Strong growth from *XXL*, but the gulf remained.

It was a set of separate yet related competitions that would ultimately help Wilson achieve his desire to 'destroy them, kill them, bury them and burn 'em to the ground'.

Eminem vs *The Source*: The Great Hip-Hop Race War

In addition to being the establishment, *The Source* had another ace in its pocket that gave them a stronger hand than *XXL*: access to the biggest crossover rapper in the world – Eminem. And access to star talent was the lifeblood of magazines.

The Source had championed Eminem ever since his days as a down-on-his-luck underground battle rapper. As he began to blow-up in 1998, pre-Wilson *XXL* and Eminem had fallen out over *XXL* printing a picture of Eminem showing his naked bottom at an awards show. Additionally, according to Eminem, this earlier *XXL* regime had implied that he was a 'culture stealer and a Ku Klux Klan member'.[13]

Eminem was one of the biggest names in music at the time (still is), so it was certainly not in *XXL*'s interest to be at odds with him. The fact that they were gave *The Source* an immense additional built-in commercial and competitive advantage. Then, in the blink of an eye in 2002, things suddenly and almost inexplicably changed: Raymond 'Benzino' Scott and *The Source* launched what is probably best described as 'The Great Hip-Hop Race War' against Eminem and Interscope.

The Source, through their co-owner Raymond 'Benzino' Scott (who also happened to be a rapper . . . as well as father of the rapper Coi Leray), launched a vicious fight with Eminem. Though their reasons for this were never properly, calmly and clearly articulated, it appeared to revolve around several things:

- *The Source* gave Eminem's album a lower rating than it should have been given
- Benzino was gearing up to release an album of his own and may have been attempting to drum up competition to drive attention to his album. Benzino – a journeyman MC at best – released several diss tracks against Eminem (including the very personal 'Die Another Day', which Eminem, a battle-rap icon, responded to with 'Nail In The Coffin'). In fairness, in the David vs Goliath rap battle that was Eminem vs Benzino, Zino performed much better than anyone could have expected
- *The Source* accused Eminem of being a culture vulture and a racist who was inhibiting the sales of Black artists by crowding them out

In support of the latter, somewhat dubious charge, *The Source* unearthed 'Foolish Pride', an old song in which Eminem made shockingly racist statements about Black women, calling them 'bitches and gold diggers' and cautioning fellow white men not to date them.

The revelation of 'Foolish Pride' was a defining moment in the competition between Eminem and *The Source* (as well as in Eminem's career). Benzino (and his journalists) had secured definitive and undeniable audio of the biggest name in a Black artform making a piercingly racist song – with no sign of satirical intent. The gloves were off; there was no turning back: this had all the hallmarks of the business equivalent of a death match.

Having stumbled on a tactical nuclear weapon in 'Foolish Pride' (which Eminem sued *The Source* for releasing)[14] Benzino and *The Source* decided to rain a racial nuclear shower on Eminem. They included a 'special editorial audio supplement' (a mixtape in the form of a compact disc) in their February 2004 edition. On the tape was a judge-permitted twenty seconds of 'Foolish Pride', a poem by Nikki Giovanni, a speech by Malik Shabazz (of the New Black Panther Party) and another speech by Bob Law, an activist and talk radio host. There was no room for subtlety: *The Source* was attempting to paint Eminem as a rapping Klansman. In fact, Benzino went as far as calling him 'the rap Hitler' in 'Die Another Day'.

Alas, it didn't work.

Eminem apologised and ascribed his comments to youthful indiscretion permeating from a Black woman dumping him and . . . that was that. Despite Benzino calling a press conference and explicitly demanding that media treat Eminem as they did the scandal-clad 'R. Kelly and Kobe Bryant', the unearthed tape did not have the intended effect. *The Source*, a small, independent yet highly influential company, had entered into a needless existential competition with the main cash cow of a mammoth market-leading international corporation. Making matters worse, they fired their ultimate missile . . . and it proved to be a dud.

The Source-inspired Competition Tip

If you come for the king, don't miss. If you aim to topple a market leader, don't fail, for they will crush you.

In the process of launching their missile (and missing), *The Source* handed a key component of competitive advantage in Hip-Hop media to *XXL*: exclusive access to Eminem. Making matters worse, *The Source* had now created a Voltron of a coalition against them. One that facilitated their demise.

The Source vs *XXL*, Eminem, 50 Cent, Dr. Dre and Interscope/ Universal

In late 2002, Eminem and Dr. Dre signed a then smoking-hot and raring-to-go 50 Cent, an artist *XXL* had long championed, even when he was down on his luck, even as his body lay bullet-ridden on the floor.

With the hottest name in music (Eminem), the undisputed king of the street who was certain to be a mainstream monster (50 Cent) and Hip-Hop's premier icon (Dr. Dre) in their Interscope-backed camp, Eminem's manager, Paul Rosenberg, made his move against *The Source*.

In a strategy best described as 'Eminem's enemy is my enemy', Rosenberg made peace with *XXL* and organised for 50 Cent, Eminem and Dr. Dre to appear on the cover of the magazine together. Elliot Wilson predicted that this copy of *XXL* would 'sell like crack in the eighties'.[15] He was right. For the first time in their history, *XXL* outsold *The Source*.

Making matters worse, *The Source* became increasingly light – advertisers had clearly deserted them. According to their own advertisers' index, in September 2003 sixty-eight companies ran adverts in *The Source*. This number had dropped to twenty-eight by February 2004, when they painted Eminem as a racist. The competition and mocking from Elliot Wilson led to Benzino personally storming *XXL*'s offices in an attempt to intimidate him.

Fast-forward a few years, and Dave Mays and Benzino lost ownership and control of *The Source*. Elliot Wilson was himself let go from *XXL* to cut costs. But was the juice worth the squeeze? Did *XXL*'s competition with *The Source* improve their standing and market share? Without a shadow of a doubt. The numbers speak for themselves.

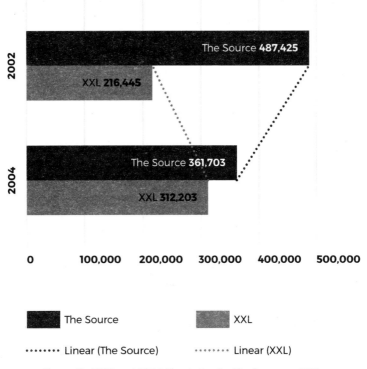

Figure 13: 2002 and 2004 Circulation for *The Source* and *XXL*.
Source: Complex

But as entertaining and exciting as it was, this tale of rival rap mags ended in catastrophe. Ultimately, there was no winner in *The Source* and *XXL* competition. It turned out they were tearing chunks out of each other at the very moment they should have pulled together to identify a way to contend with the existential threat they collectively faced known as 'the internet'. While both publications exist today, they are zombified, largely online-only versions of their former selves. *The Source* is occasionally still available in print, after its precipitous fall from being the bestselling music magazine on American newsstands in 1999 to filing for bankruptcy in 2007.[16]

With the collapse of *XXL* and *The Source* came the collapse of quality Hip-Hop journalism, a once lucrative middle-class career (popping with future opportunities) and disproportionately populated by working-class Black and brown people. The competition between *The Source* and *XXL* (aligned with Eminem, 50 Cent and Interscope) proved a particular adage to be right: 'When elephants battle, the ants perish.'

Benzino-inspired Tip

Before embarking on any type of competition – but especially any form of confrontational competition – consider carefully if the spoils of victory are worth the risk of defeat.

In his battle with Eminem, Benzino would have at best personally gained a gold album. In the process he lost one of Hip-Hop's crown jewels: *The Source*.

COMPETITION, INFLATION AND MARKET SHARE: THE INDIES VS THE MAJORS

'*Yesterday's price is not today's price*' – the immortal words of Fat Joe.

Despite being portrayed in the movie *Straight Outta Compton* (he was the record executive Ice Cube visited with a baseball bat and whose office he destroyed), Bryan Turner is one of those behind-the-scenes people in Hip-Hop who most people have never heard of. But without him, most people would not have heard of Hip-Hop.

The softly spoken yet sharply considered white Canadian visionary who founded and led Priority Records – and helped bring NWA, Jay-Z, Master P (and many more) to the world – is one of the main reasons why Hip-Hop has become the commercial juggernaut it is.

When asked why Hip-Hop did not become the fad it was predicted to be, Bryan ascribes it to Hip-Hop's rocky relationship with the vanguards of music – the major record labels – as well as competition between the indies and the majors. He breaks it down into three phases

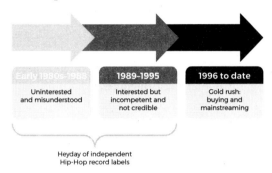

Early 1980s-1988	1989-1995	1996 to date
Uninterested and misunderstood	Interested but incompetent and not credible	Gold rush: buying and mainstreaming

Heyday of independent
Hip-Hop record labels

Figure 14: The Bryan Turner timeline of Hip-Hop's relationship with major labels

Phase 1: No competition (early 1980s–1988)

Turner recalls the major label sentiment at the time: 'It is not even music because you're sampling other people's music and you're not even singing – you're talking . . . so when guys were shopping artist deals all of the major labels said no . . . and thank God all of the major labels said no.'

If the major labels had embraced Hip-Hop from its inception, there is a significant chance it would have become a fad because the avenue independent record labels occupied may not have existed. The independents, such as Priority, Profile, Def Jam, Tommy Boy and so on, kept overheads low and were able to move quickly.

'There was no economic formula for why we should put something out and why we shouldn't. We were totally comfortable putting something out that would sell 40–50,000 units – because that was enough money to pay overheads and keep everything going.' By comparison, at the time, selling 40–50,000 units in a debut week would be considered a flop by major labels and would get an artist dropped.

The major labels are motivated by the prospect of profit maximisation; the independents were happy to meet overheads – as a result, the majors would not have given Hip-Hop the time and space to grow.

Phase 2: Incompetent competition (1989–1995)

Where there is opportunity there are opportunists, where there are dollars there are capitalists and where there are capitalists in pursuit of an easy quick dollar – there are blunders. As Bryan Turner explained: 'After two or three years they [the major labels] looked and then they go: "Look, we were wrong – this is being sustained." They decide to compete with us [independent labels] and they hired A&R staff to go out and compete and sign acts.'

The acts the major record labels signed were far from dripping with credibility – though they did, in some cases, sell lots of records. Turner elaborates: 'If you're a West Coast hardcore rapper – you want to be on Priority. Because NWA was there, we had the Geto Boys, we had Master P – we were the label you wanted to be on. You weren't going to sign with Capitol Records – they had MC Hammer. So you're not going to sign with them. And the exact same scenario was happening on the East Coast.'

The pursuit of profit maximisation led to the major labels lacking cultural credibility. This in turn rendered them ineffective competitors against the independents.

Similar to love and happiness, money cannot buy competence or competitive advantage.

Phase 3: Acquisition and consolidation (1996 to date)

According to Bryan, by 1996, the major labels waved the white flag and the cheque book. 'Now they decide that they can't compete [on a credibility basis]. What happens is that we [independents] have five, six years of complete control – as independents – of an entire culture. So, now they [the majors] decide that "the market share is growing" and they are all about market share, [and] we [the majors] still can't compete with them so now we have to go and buy them.'

Play time was over. The major labels, the self-appointed traditional custodians of popular music, decided to muscle the little man out and take his lunch.

'Now the majors say "OK – we're going to buy up these different artists [and labels]." And they still are signing acts, because of their egos, they have to continue to try to develop music that is popular – so they start outpricing all of the independent labels. They come into it and they say, "OK, we're going to spend a million dollars on your video." And my guys are coming to me going, "I want to spend a million dollars on my video" and I go, "You're out of your mind: who can do that?" And they say, "Well, that guy did that," and in that space [in Hip-Hop] it is all about who does what and I want to be as popular and I want a billboard on Sunset . . .'

The third point is perhaps the most critical. In a bid to win the market away from the independents, the major labels threw money at Hip-Hop. The intention was to squeeze them out by one of two means: buy them out or price them out. As a result, competition in Hip-Hop became more financial and superficial as opposed to musical and lyrical. And this had a major inflationary impact. It needlessly pushed the price of everything up. It also had a cultural impact.

Suddenly, the hood was no longer the focal point of the rap video – jumping out a helicopter or being chased by police in helicopters or flying around in a helicopter overlooking your mansion became the standard. Big-budget videos were increasingly the norm.

Hype Williams: The Major Labels' Weapon

Harold 'Hype' Williams, a young graffiti artist turned music video director, became the go-to man for huge-budget videos. There was a point where seriousness and legitimacy in the business was near synonymous with having a budget-busting video directed by Hype. He became a star vehicle, and there was a very good reason for this: from story to lighting, speed, black and white or colour (or both), contrast, resolution, angling to location selection, Hype Williams' perfectly executed imaginings upped the ante for music videos (and album sales). His videos served as the perfect complement and signal of ambition not just to rap songs but to Clintonian economic expansion.

Williams directed many of the great and groundbreaking videos of the era — 'California Love' (Tupac and Dr. Dre), 'Woo Hah!! Got You All In Check' (Busta Rhymes), 'If I Ruled The World (Imagine That)' (Nas & Lauryn Hill), 'Loungin'' (LL Cool J), 'I'll Be Missing You' (Puff Daddy), 'The Rain' (Missy Elliott), 'Gettin' Jiggy Wit It' (Will Smith), 'Get Me Home' (Foxy Brown), 'Mo Money Mo Problems' (The Notorious BIG), 'Big Pimpin'' (Jay-Z) and many, many more. They were amazing to watch, but they were even more impressive as a tool in winning market share.

Before the invasion of competition from the majors, an average video would cost $50k; an expensive one would cost double that. The video for Busta Rhymes' 1999 single 'What's It Gonna Be?!' cost an estimated $2.4m. As the videos were not cheap, Hype Williams became a weapon only the majors could afford. It follows that he became a critical part of how the majors snatched Hip-Hop market share from the indies.

The competition for market share amongst the major labels, as well as their intention to push the independents out, had a huge inflationary effect. Hip-Hop had become a pissing contest, and for independents this was not sustainable or viable. So how does the poorly endowed compete in such circumstances?

Bryan Turner explains: 'Rawkus [who were distributed by Priority] wanted $250,000 for a [Mos Def] video. I said to Mos Def: "Everybody is doing that; everybody is making all these videos for all this money. The thing to me that will stand out to MTV or BET is something that is so creative . . . the creativity is what will set you apart from everyone else. And that doesn't take a lot of money."'

Mos Def took the advice and shot a stunning yet highly creative and indeed minimalist video for the deeply soulful 'Umi Says' (from his 1999 debut album *Black On Both Sides*). It cost $20,000 and became one of the more memorable videos of the time – especially after the song was picked up by Nike's Jordan brand for a major advertising campaign starring Michael Jordan. Interestingly, in the advert version of the song, the lyrics 'for black people to be free' and 'for my people to be free' were altered to 'for the people to be free'.

From Russell Simmons (Def Jam) to Bryan Turner (Priority) to Tom Silverman (Tommy Boy) – most of the owners of original independents founded in the 1980s sold their companies to the majors for major sums. In 2005, independents enjoyed a 28.4 per cent market share of the music industry – the biggest force in the sector. By 2011, that number had fallen to 12.11 per cent – a large part of this change boiled down to who had control of Hip-Hop.

COMPETITION AS THEATRE

What came first: 50 Cent's prowess as a competitor or his God-given talent for theatre? Odds are they arrived at the same time. Case in point: much to Hakeem 'Chamillionaire' Temidayo Seriki's dismay and confusion, despite them enjoying a cordial relationship, 50 Cent kept making disparaging remarks about him. Going high when 50 Cent went low, the Texan Nigerian rapper turned tech guru didn't respond. Instead, he confronted 50 Cent in person when he saw him at MTV's offices. Purposefully creating the impression that he was about to manhandle him, 50 Cent dragged Chamillionaire into a room and calmly said:

'Listen, man, you're a cool dude, you know we're cool . . . you could have said "50 Cent needs to shut the hell up!" If you go to Mumbai, India, and sit on a train, on the back of the seat there is a newspaper. When you take that newspaper out and you look at it . . . you would have been on the front page of that newspaper – if you would have said that back to me. Because I'm the biggest . . .'[17]

'I was just like, "Man, this dude crazy," added Chamillionaire.

The main point of competition is to win the sweet spoils of bitter victory, to beat the opposition into providing the best product or service and awareness of it. The sweet spoils? Money, cash and moolah. Customers, market share and prestige. Rappers have long leveraged a unique route to the spoils of victory – theatre.

The creation of great theatre, of a great story, is a critical part of the business of popularising rap music. The theatre and theatrics are essential components of what separates stars from 'studs'. Great competition generates great theatre. Great theatre sticks in the memory and generates sales. For 50 Cent, a Hip-Hop field marshal in this realm, competition through the prism of combative theatrics have earned him unspeakable riches. As demonstrated in his exchange with Chamillionaire, 50 Cent clearly understands that in the all-lucrative and hypercompetitive attention economy, virality is hard currency.

SECTION 4

STAYING UP

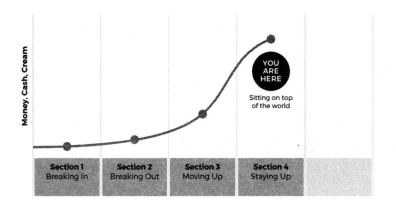

15.

EVOLUTION

'Change is the only constant in life.' So said the Greek philosopher Heraclitus. The African American philosopher Tupac Shakur said the exact same thing on his posthumous record 'Changes', only with more style, passion and rhythm (and existing copyright protection). Nevertheless, Pac and Heraclitus were great minds thinking alike: life and success often boils down to the illusion of two choices: change or die. In reality, they're not really choices at all, because whether you like it or not, you're going to do both. In terms of change, the question is whether you're going to:

- Choice 1: Be passively changed by the times
- Choice 2: Actively change with the times
- Choice 3: Aggressively change the times

Success in Choice 1 is often overreliant on luck or circumstance conspiring in your favour. It hardly ever yields longevity. Luck always runs out eventually.

Hip-Hop's success stories have been good at actively changing with the times and aggressively changing the times. They have done this principally, although not always successfully, by looking to the future. Dr. Dre, Jay-Z, Jermaine Dupri and others are in a persistent state of discovery and evolution, and, by extension, they ensure the culture and business evolves with them.

DR. DRE: EMBRACING THE NEW

On 'Deeez Nuuuts' from his debut album *The Chronic*, Dr. Dre rapped rather prophetically that things won't change until he

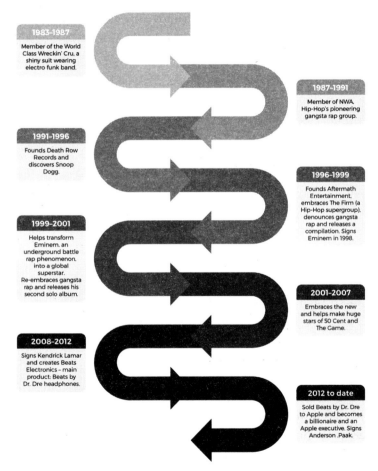

1983-1987
Member of the World Class Wreckin' Cru, a shiny suit wearing electro funk band.

1987-1991
Member of NWA. Hip-Hop's pioneering gangsta rap group.

1991-1996
Founds Death Row Records and discovers Snoop Dogg.

1996-1999
Founds Aftermath Entertainment, embraces The Firm (a Hip-Hop supergroup), denounces gangsta rap and releases a compilation. Signs Eminem in 1998.

1999-2001
Helps transform Eminem, an underground battle rap phenomenon, into a global superstar. Re-embraces gangsta rap and releases his second solo album.

2001-2007
Embraces the new and helps make huge stars of 50 Cent and The Game.

2008-2012
Signs Kendrick Lamar and creates Beats Electronics – main product: Beats by Dr. Dre headphones.

2012 to date
Sold Beats by Dr. Dre to Apple and becomes a billionaire and an Apple executive. Signs Anderson .Paak.

Figure 15: Dr. Dre's Evolution

changes them. Dre's trajectory over the past twenty years has proven these words to be no empty brag. What stands out from a cursory look at his career timeline is how he has both actively changed with the times and aggressively changed the times. On occasion, he has also misread the times, but one thing is clear: he always embraced and championed the new.

Embracing the new in a manner that was authentic to him, while allowing the new to thrive in and of itself, was a critical part of Dr. Dre's success. The artists he introduced to the world were a fairly diverse set of characters: Eazy-E, Ice Cube, Snoop Dogg, Eminem, Truth Hurts, 50 Cent, Game, Kendrick Lamar, Anderson Paak. However, as Dr. Dre evolved he complemented each of them in terms of sound, brand and, therefore, career advancement. As the culture evolved, he evolved – and eventually a good slice of the culture was evolving around him.

JAY-Z: THE TIMES ARE A-CHANGING

Jay-Z's rap career is a near perfect example of each of the three modes of change detailed at the start of this chapter. Going back to the start of his career in the late 1980s, his first decade is arguably an example of being moulded by what was going on around him in the culture.

1988–1998: Changed by the winds

'Excitin the mic much to the delight of millions of Nubians / And Amorites just can't understand the groove we're in' – Jay-Z's lyrics from the 1990 single 'Originators', his introduction to the world, was a reflection of what was popular in Hip-Hop at the time: rapid-tongue wordplay and Black nationalism. In the late 1980s, when Hip-Hop embraced various types of Black nationalist aesthetic (including the Nation of Islam, Nuwaubianism and the Black Hebrew Israelites), Jay-Z and his mentor Jaz-O (both of whom were known followers of Dr Malachi Z. York of the

United Nuwaubian Nation of Moors, aka the Nuwaubian Nation), also did so. But when the culture moved on, so did Jay-Z.

In the mid-1990s, when Hip-Hop embraced a more glamorised mafioso demeanour – with stories of dealings in the street – Jay-Z not only joined in but arguably created the magnum opus of the era in his debut album, *Reasonable Doubt*. The intro to *Reasonable Doubt* is a recitation of a Tony Montana speech (Al Pacino's character in *Scarface*). On the greyscale album cover, Jay-Z is dressed like a mafia kingpin.

By 1997, the Puff Daddy-led bling and corporate influx Hip-Hop era was in full effect. Large money, jewellery, shiny designer clothes and remade 1980s hits had captured Hip-Hop – and Jay-Z became an essential proponent of it.

Throughout this period, Jay-Z was being blown in the direction of the wind. In 1998, Jay-Z 's relationship with the winds of change changed.

1998 to date: Changing with the winds and changing the winds

By 1998, Jay-Z continued to move with the times but, as he assumed a market-leading position following the release of *Vol 2 . . . Hard Knock Life*, he started to aggressively change the times. He went from someone who was influenced by what was popular to the very person who was aggressively influencing what was (and is) both relevant and popular. The direction of change, of evolution within the culture, was shaped by Jay-Z.

When he started wearing, say, jerseys or button-up shirts, the culture followed. When he stopped, so did the culture.

Jay-Z wasn't the first to work with the Neptunes, Kanye West, Just Blaze or – to a much lesser degree – Swiss Beatz and Timbaland, but he certainly helped mainstream their sound and made them go-to producers.

In 2003, Jay-Z became the first person who was not a sports star to get a deal for their own line of sneakers from an athletic shoe company – 50 Cent, the Game, and, perhaps most notably, Kanye West followed suit.

As music distribution evolved from physical audio formats to downloads to streaming, in 2015 Jay-Z attempted to move with and control the winds of change by purchasing Tidal, a small Norwegian streaming service, for $56m. His aim was to compete with Apple and Spotify on a basis that was more friendly to the artist. At the launch of Tidal, Jay-Z was joined on stage by a slew of 'artist stakeholders' made up of the brightest stars from a range of genres – Usher, Rihanna, Nicki Minaj, Madonna, Deadmau5, Kanye West, Jason Aldean, Jack White, Daft Punk, Beyoncé and Win Butler. In 2021, Jay-Z sold his stake in Tidal to Twitter CEO Jack Dorsey's Square for $302m.

Like Dr. Dre, with every move and change he made, Jay-Z remained complementary and largely true to his character and brand. You could say he *kept it real*.

MC HAMMER: BLOWN OFF COURSE

Oakland's own Stanley Kirk 'MC Hammer' Burrell was a true Hip-Hop phenomenon unlike anything seen before or since. Hammer was an electrifying performer. In Hip-Hop, there is a super-thin line between novel and novelty, so conveying cool while being entertaining is a balancing act. Most rappers err on the side of cool, MC Hammer erred on the side of being a showman dripping with charisma, sweat and – eventually – money.

While many rappers steered clear of dancing or hired back-up dancers to do the heavy lifting for them, MC Hammer embraced it. He released a single called 'Dancing Machine' and lived up to its title in the video. In fact, he not only had no issue with dancing, but he brought in Broadway-worthy choreography with glittering costumes that would make Michael Jackson blush, and those super-baggy 'genie' trousers. He was comfortable with making rap-based mega-pop songs ('U Can't Touch This'), rap-based crooning love songs (such as 'Have You Seen Her') or rap-gospel songs ('Pray'), and turned them all into major hits.

He also started out as an astute businessman. As a 1990 *Ebony* article revealed:

> In 1987, after a record deal went sour, Hammer borrowed $20,000 each from former Oakland [Athletics baseball] players Mike Davis and Dwayne Murphy to start Bust It Productions. He kept the company going by selling records from his basement and the back of his car. Bust It spawned Bustin' Records, the independent label of which Hammer is CEO. Together, the companies have more than 100 employees.

His debut album *Feel My Power* was released on Bustin Records in 1986 and sold 60,000 copies. Before *Feel My Power* came out, Hammer had declined offers from major labels. With 60,000 copies sold independently, Hammer was swimming in leverage. Capitol Records, a major label, approached him and offered him what, at the time, was a mega-deal: a multi-album recording contract with a reported $1.75m advance. By contrast, thirteen years later in 2003, 50 Cent – then the hottest thing on the underground – signed to Shady/Aftermath/Interscope for a reported $1m.

In 1988, Hammer released his major label debut, *Let's Get It Started*. It included the energetic hit single, 'Turn This Mutha Out' and went on to sell two million copies, grossing circa $20m–30m. An impressive success by any measure, and more than enough to cover Hammer's advance. But what would come next was unthinkable and almost unbelievable. And it helped expand Hip-Hop's audience massively.

In February 1990, MC Hammer released his third album, *Please Hammer Don't Hurt 'Em* – an absolute monster of a success. The album was supercharged by the runaway success of the enormously popular Rick James-sample-powered hit 'U Can't Touch This', a song so infectious the label decided to limit its supply as a $2–3 standalone single in order to maximise demand for the $15–20 album of which the song would form a part.

MC Hammer-inspired Tips on Demand and Supply

- Where demand is insatiable, adjusting supply in order to enhance the price may be a possibility. Where it is: pounce on it.

- Consider if your appetiser offering may cannibalise your main course offering.

- Carefully analyse whether your loss leaders are prohibiting your ability to maximise your revenue.

Please Hammer Don't Hurt 'Em would swiftly become Hip-Hop's first diamond-selling album. By June the following year, it had sold over a million copies – it would go on to sell over 17 million.

Too Legit To Quit, the 1991 follow-up album, sold a highly impressive 5 million copies. Hammer's record company, Capitol Records, considered it a flop. They had spent over a million dollars in advertising and millions more on other promotional tools such as videos. In terms of promotional budgets, this was Michael Jackson territory. In the star-cameo-heavy, super-high-budget mini-movie that was the video for '2 Legit 2 Quit' (one of the most expensive videos ever made), Hammer humorously made it clear that he had Michael Jackson in his sights as a rival by casting someone to satirically play MJ (via his diamond-gloved hand) and a record label boss scared stiff by the prospect of Jackson competing with Hammer. Capitol spared no expense in promoting *Too Legit To Quit*. Its 'failure' was only seen as such in comparison to his previous success; in reality, *Too Legit To Quit* sold as many units as Jay-Z's highest-selling album.

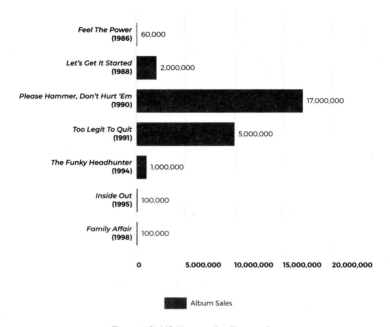

Figure 16: MC Hammer's album sales

A pop megastar in Hip-Hop was bound to face immense criticism from his peers. Ice Cube, then a solo artist at the artistic and business pinnacle of 'conventional' Hip-Hop, mocked Hammer in the video for his 1992 single, 'True To The Game', a song about selling out. A man assumed to be portraying Hammer (played by the brilliant DJ Pooh) is shown in traditional West Coast Hip-Hop garb at a photoshoot posturing as a hardcore artist, before suddenly, as the camera starts flashing, transforming into a smiling and dancing performer wearing a shiny red outfit eerily similar to what Hammer would wear at the time.

Until that point, MC Hammer was successfully ignoring the times, and any winds of change. He stayed in his own lane without any real rival (other than, perhaps, Vanilla Ice). A true one-of-a-kind with one foot firmly in Hip-Hop and the other in pop. A seemingly difficult balance to maintain, but he managed it comfortably.

And then, out of the blue, Hammer decided to respond to the winds of change. In 1994, he returned from a three-year hiatus and released *The Funky Headhunter*. His videos became quite explicit (especially for a part-time spiritual rapper) and more aligned with what was going on in new jack swing and gangsta rap.

In the initial video for 'Pumps And A Bump', the sexually charged lead single from *The Funky Headhunter*, Hammer is shown gyrating with bikini-clad women at a mansion pool party. An oiled-up Hammer himself wears nothing but a micro thong, a gold chain, fingerless black thermal gloves and what look like a pair of Loakes (shoes more aligned with business attire). Though it may have had something to do with Hammer's appearance of at least slight arousal, this rare moment of gender equality in rap videos (for once everyone was scantily clad) was deemed too explicit for MTV and banished. Hammer shot another video for 'Pumps And A Bump' (under the guise of a 'remix'), and this time around he went full-blown conventional gangsta rap video – seemingly endless rows of tough-looking men in gang colours and dark sunglasses, and beautiful women with hardly any clothes on. This, however, was a gangsta rap video with a key difference: choreographed dancing. Lots of it.

Even though *The Funky Headhunter* sold over a million copies, Hammer's attempt to evolve with the times and embrace the new did not work because it never seemed true to who he was. It felt opportunistic and looked much more novelty than novel. Evolving from pop-rapper to energetic dancing gangsta-rapper was an evolution too far – and it didn't sell.

MC Hammer-inspired Evolution Tip

With every attempt to evolve, it must be carefully considered if the change will complement or cannibalise any existing customer base, brand, operations or relationships.

The basis of gangsta rap was authenticity – or at least the believable appearance thereof. The audience had to believe you were the part. It was hard to see Hammer as some form of gangsta after all the success he had enjoyed as a pop star. Even more perplexing was Hammer's decision to sign with Hip-Hop's most gangsta label ever during its most turbulent period – Suge Knight's Death Row – right around the time Tupac was murdered.

Perception is not always reality, of course. Although he may have appeared to be a gentle and lovely pop-rapper, MC Hammer was, without a shadow of a doubt, much more 'gangster' than most gangsta rappers. Getting on his bad side could have very serious consequences. MC Serch, one third of the New York rap group 3rd Bass, found out about Hammer's ire the hard way. His group inadvertently insulted Hammer's mother on a song. According to Serch, Hammer responded by putting a $50k bounty on his head with the Rolling 60s Crips. The hit was only called off when Russell Simmons was able to negotiate a 'peace treaty' through Mike Concepcion, a wheelchair-bound (due to a gang shooting in 1977), highly respected triple OG Crip. Concepcion's price? Tickets to the American Music Awards, where he'd be sat next to Michael Jackson.

Speaking to VladTV, Serch revealed that he only took the hit seriously after he was approached by two obviously armed men – one masked – who informed him that they had been planning 'to smoke him' but didn't because Mike Concepcion's associate (who was with 3rd Bass) gang-signalled for them not to. The armed gentlemen politely complimented his music and asked for autographs . . . instead of murdering him. MC Hammer has publicly denied ever putting a hit on MC Serch.

The winds of change blew in a direction that made it more straightforward for the likes of Dr. Dre and Jay-Z to evolve, move with the times and embrace the new than it was for Hammer. As they remained true to their ethos and enjoyed continued success, Dr. Dre and Jay-Z were eventually able to influence the direction of those winds themselves. With *Please Hammer Don't Hurt 'Em*, Hammer enjoyed more sales than multiple Jay-Z and Dr. Dre albums combined, but he was unable to control the direction of travel of the culture. He was a market leader with no influence over the market. He was not being followed – perhaps partly due to his magnitude as a performer. His attempt to align himself with the market resulted in him being laughed out of it. Hammer's critical mistake was his attempt to evolve in the direction of a market he was not fully in: hardcore Hip-Hop. As a result, he rendered himself irrelevant in a market in which he was dominant and where he *was* breaking new ground – pop-rap.

PURITY AND PROFITABILITY: AN INVERSE RELATIONSHIP?

Evolving with the times comes with risk and cost. But not evolving at all comes with, arguably, even greater risk and cost.

Many rappers and moguls from Hammer's heyday didn't even attempt to evolve, embrace the new or move with the times. It could be argued that they defined 'keeping it real' by remaining true to the culture, sound and tradition of Hip-Hop when they met it. Purity was their laudable pursuit, but purity and profitability often, possibly even usually, have an inverse relationship. When one goes up, the other tends to go down. Consult your local drug dealer or dairy farmer for further insight.

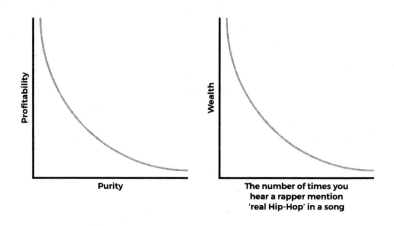

* For illustrative purposes only

Figure 17: Purity vs Profitability and 'real Hip-Hop'

Had Dr. Dre refused or been unable to evolve beyond his World Class Wreckin' Cru or NWA era or stuck with it in the name of 'cultural purity' or 'keeping it real' or 'keeping the golden age alive', he might be a long distant memory today. If he hadn't continuously embraced what was young, fresh and new – be it Ice Cube, Snoop Dogg, Eminem, 50 Cent, The Game or Kendrick Lamar – he'd be gathering dust in a museum.

Evolution and the Rapper-founded Record Label

For practically any forward-thinking rapper, with even mild success comes a record label. Bad Boy, Hoo-Bangin, Disturbin Tha Peace, G Unit, Ruff Ryders, Aftermath, October's Very Own, Shady, Black Wall Street, GOOD, Dream Chasers, Thugged Out Murder Unit – the list of Hip-Hop record labels is extensive. In fact, in her first 40 years of existence over 400 record labels were established to serve, preserve and nurture rap music. And, of course, to capitalise on the growth of the culture. These labels have helped turn Hip-Hop into the industry it is today – many of them get rich along the way and create employment opportunities.

In addition to everything listed above, evolution is a critical part of why rappers establish record labels. The infrastructure, money and promotional power of the label attracts young, hungry and raw talent in search of an opportunity to expand. It is a process that is akin to when large companies purchase start-ups: the hope is that the start-up brings the future to the table.

What Yahoo, for example, saw in twenty-two-year-old Mark Zuckerberg when they offered him a billion dollars for Facebook, is what Fat Joe saw in Big Pun, Jay-Z (and Damon Dash) saw in Kanye West and Beanie Sigel, and Lil Wayne saw in Drake.

As a result, many of the young artists signed to a rapper-led record label often serve the subtle purpose of perpetuating and elevating the label owner's rap career. They help craft and create new sounds and songs and bring the latest ways of thinking or speaking to the foreground. They also potentially bring a degree of credibility with a younger audience, and as a result they form an essential component of how older, richer and more established artists remain in tune with what is emerging at the grassroots of popular culture: i.e. the streets.

Hate to preach, but the world is in a persistent state of change. In a changing world, moving with the times is critical. However, retaining your authenticity, remaining true to who and what you are, what you stand for and are known for, is equally essential. It's a hard balancing act to perfect, and the stakes are high.

Evolve or die: the choice is (not really) yours, *youngsta*.

16.

UNDERVALUED ASSETS AND CUSTOMERS

The value in a cut, polished and glittering diamond is self-evident. The value in a dull stone pulled out of the ground and coated in earth is not. It requires someone to search and dig for, then polish that dull stone to bring its value to the surface – before it can be presented to the world as a gem.

With this logic, the likes of Logic, Nicki Minaj, Kanye West, Megan Thee Stallion, J Cole, Eminem and Cardi B are all very easy investment choices today. They are Hip-Hop's equivalent of oil companies in the noughties, 'defence' (weapons) manufacturers in the time of war or chocolates, roses, diamonds and contraception around Valentine's Day. In short, they're a sure bet. It is a no-brainer to invest in them; they will make you money.

However, it is the astute gambler or investor who is able to spot a bargain, to recognise a good buy when it is yet to attain popularity and/or is undervalued. Astute investors are the likes of Joe '3H' Weinberger – who saw value in Kanye West before he became Kanye West; Jas Prince – who saw value in Drake before he became Drake; and Bryan Turner – who saw value in industrialising West Coast Hip-Hop before anyone else. The ultimate astute investor is someone who can see value where no one else does – perhaps in a stock that is being deserted because it appears to be in decline. When a stock is in decline most sophisticated investors go short (bet against it) so they can make money as it crashes. It takes bravery, confidence and perhaps a degree of insanity (or inside information) to bet against the direction of the market. The ability to ignore the noise, shun the direction of travel, trust their contrarian convictions and stay the course – only to be proven right – is the mark of extreme astuteness.

In 1995, Tupac Shakur was a high-value stock in rapid decline. Even though he was a successful rapper and actor, he had become a magnet for controversy of the most serious nature. His social baggage alone would be enough to scare most potential investors away. And it did.

As Tupac languished in prison, convicted of the sexual assault of Ayana Jackson (a charge he denied until his dying day), his third album, *Me Against The World*, shot to the top of the charts and remained there for over a month. Nevertheless, in a hyper-competitive market such as Hip-Hop, where things change rapidly, eighteen months to four and a half years in prison is a very long time. Certainly long enough to render a rapper near obsolete. Out of sight, out of mind. Additionally, given all of the controversy, revolutionary tendency, craziness and criminality surrounding Tupac, it was a legitimate question to ask whether or not he was truly out of his mind.

Although he was entitled to bail pending appeal, Tupac, a man who was generating tens of millions of dollars in album sales, was unable to raise the $1.4m needed to secure his release. As he sat in prison for nine months, his stock price and star value plummeted. He was a seriously undervalued and distressed asset, figuratively and literally. Given what was coming next, putting up Tupac's $1.4m bail money was one of the bargains of the century.

Marion 'Suge' Knight had long dreamt of signing Tupac.

What made Tupac scary and too risky for many was what made him appealing to Death Row. Tupac was the exact sort of controversial star, one with icon potential, who would complement and be complemented perfectly by the brand, image and methods of Death Row Records. So, when Tupac called on him for help, Suge swooped in on a distressed asset he had long had in his sights. The terms of the deal were handwritten on prison scrap paper:

1. Tupac would be managed by Suge Knight and represented legally by Suge Knight's high-powered criminal attorney turned entertainment lawyer, David Kenner.
2. A $1 million signing advance.
3. $120,000 for the acquisition of a car.
4. $124,000 monthly expenses allowance.
5. 18 points on every album plus a one-point bump when the album sold a million copies.
6. $250,000 legal fund to be spent with a specified law firm at Tupac's direction (we shall return to the law firm the deal in Chapter 17).

Within two weeks of being bailed out of prison, Tupac recorded his Death Row debut album, *All Eyez On Me*, a twenty-seven-song thrill of a record (with twenty-nine songs left to spare) that would serve as Hip-Hop's first double album. It sold over 10 million copies, generating over $150m in revenue, and helped elevate Death Row even further within a business where they were already dominant. Suge Knight's investment in and rehabilitation of an undervalued asset paid off massively.

Suge Knight-inspired Tip

Always look under the bonnet. What you find may shock you or may reveal one hell of a bargain.

Suge's approach to investing in undervalued assets was laudable. His philosophy could best be described as: 'a diamond in the gutter doesn't stop being a diamond'.

APPLE BOTTOM JEANS

'Does my bum look big in this?' was once a staple comedy catchphrase, thanks to a *Fast Show* sketch. They're also seven simple words that would be likely to prompt different answers depending on the era or culture you're living in.

For much of its recent existence, the fashion industry's key target demographic was women who fell into the traditional twentieth-century Western standard of beauty: the slimmer, the more beautiful. A woman who was not stick-skinny was generally not portrayed as a figure of beauty, and other body shapes were totally underrepresented in terms of clothing and fashion.

And then, in 1992, a man called Anthony L. Ray took a defiant stand. Performing under the name Sir Mix-A-Lot, he released the groundbreaking pro-curves anthem, 'Baby Got Back'. The songs starts with two women – who may as well have been *Vogue* writers or fashion industry executives – in conversation, condemning a socially 'unacceptable' body. Specifically, they suggested that the woman they were critiquing looked like a 'prostitute' or a rapper's girlfriend, because she had a large bottom. And then, our hero, Sir Mix-A-Lot, comes in with his considered point of view to 'save' the big-bottomed lady in distress:

'I like big butts and I cannot lie . . .'

And just like that, curvaceous women (with 'an itty-bitty waist') made one giant step forward. As time went on, Hip-Hop increasingly (often inadvertently through tropes that would themselves be considered sexist) helped transform the standard of Western beauty from skinny to curvy to super-curvy. Increasingly, curvaceous women started to become celebrities as a result of appearing in Hip-Hop videos. Long before Ashley Graham and Kim Kardashian, there were the Hip-Hop video vixens, such as Buffy the Body, Melyssa Ford and Ki Toy Johnson.

Case Study: Kim Kardashian vs Gwyneth Paltrow

REDACTED

Sorry.

The days in which 'does my bum look big in this?' elicited a mandatory 'no' were replaced with a mandatory 'yes'. Nevertheless, to a large extent the fashion world remained stubbornly committed to skinniness. Which resulted in curvaceous women being a hugely underserved customer base. Where there are underserved customers, there is opportunity.

In 2003, Cornell 'Nelly' Iral Haynes Jr and his partners Yomi Martin (Nelly's cousin), Nick Loftis and Ian Kelly stepped up. Nelly founded Apple Bottoms Jeans. *Essence* magazine described Apple Bottoms Jeans as: 'Jeans that catered to Black women with curves who struggled to find form-fitting denim for our naturally curvy physique. A pair of pants that wouldn't give you the annoying gap in the back of your jeans like most.'[1]

With a clearly defined unique selling point, a well-designed product, a gaping hole in the market and a deeply underserved yet highly accessible customer base, Apple Bottoms Jeans hit the ground running. The promotions process was stellar; it included:

- Nelly himself – a muscular, handsome and wildly popular multi-platinum selling rapper at that point – was the perfect pitch man (yep, man) and co-owner. He often appeared topless and biting a red apple handed to him by a lady in the Adam and Eve-influenced print adverts

- *Nelly: The Search for Miss Apple Bottoms*, an *American Idol*-style reality TV contest to find a 'booty model' to be the booty of Apple Bottoms Jeans. The show was broadcast on VH1. A 'New Yorker by way of Philadelphia' called Jasmin Watkins won. Of the finalists she was the shortest and curviest – the opposite of who tends to prevail in conventional modelling
- The jeans, which naturally had a high Hip-Hop elasticity of demand, became the subject of multiple popular rap songs, including Flo Rida's breakthrough single 'Low' (which came to be better known as 'Apple Bottoms Jeans'). 'Low' sold over 10 million units and would go on to become the most downloaded song of the noughties

According to Yomi Martin, Apple Bottoms Jeans were projected to do '$60 million in wholesale business' in 2005 alone.[2] From 2003 to 2010, the company had a fantastic run, but 2010 was the year Apple Bottoms Jeans ran their last advert, and then, like many a Hip-Hop clothing line – it inexplicably faded to black.

Purely coincidentally, following two years of plummeting incomes, 2010 was the year Levi's, then a 157-year-old company, decided they could no longer ignore the 68 per cent of the market who purchased clothes above size 12. As a result, they launched Levi's Curve ID jeans – i.e. jeans that target all women, including curvy ones. According to Levi's: 'The line was created as a result of studying more than 60,000 body scans and listening to women around the world – from ultra-curvy to stick straight and everything in between.'

Levi's Curve ID jeans were classic soccer mom jeans; for many, they lacked the style, swag, sexiness and stitching that was the hallmark of Apple Bottoms. In 2020, Nelly hinted on Twitter that Apple Bottoms may be on the verge of a comeback.

Nelly and his partners saw a phenomenal opening that should have been apparent to practically everyone in fashion but was certainly visible to anyone in Hip-Hop: the women in Calvin

Klein posters were not a reflection of the women most people see in real life. Nelly made jeans for 'real women', women who would normally not be represented on the runway, the TV screen or the magazine page. And it did not take him 60,000 body scans to realise the blindingly obvious.

17.

FINANCE AND LEGAL

Lawyers and accountants may be back-office bores to many of us, for rappers and rap moguls in particular, but these bean counters and contract experts are the signal bearers of the bad times, the good times and the great times. You can tell how things are going by how much you hear from them.

Number of times you hear from your lawyer or accountant	What it signifies	What the lawyer or accountant is doing
Under six times a year	You're on top of your taxes, and your criminality does not extend beyond parking tickets	Stomaching you
Six to fifty times a year	Money is flowing in; you are a magnet for business opportunities that require sophisticated negotiation and your criminal prowess is either celebrated or yet to be detected	Kissing your ass

Number of times you hear from your lawyer or accountant	What it signifies	What the lawyer or accountant is doing
Fifty times a year and above	You are drowning in deep shit. Broke, on the brink of bankruptcy and probably held in a rat-infested cell on serious charges with bail repeatedly denied	Milking your desperation for every copper penny they can – before the ship inevitably sinks

Table 17: My lawyer/accountant wants to talk: should I be worried?

The careers of many of Hip-Hop's moguls demonstrate that managing your legal and financial affairs is key to maintaining any success, wealth and freedom that you've accrued. It is often the difference between making yourself wealthy or financial servitude.

MC Hammer is Hip-Hop's most famous case of financial downfall. As chronicled in Chapter 15, he was a super-success – Hammer's 'flop', *Too Legit To Quit*, sold as many copies as Jay-Z's bestselling album, *Vol 2 . . . Hard Knock Life*. By the early 1990s, Hammer was a dancing, money-printing machine. From 1988 to 1991, he sold in excess of 24 million copies of three albums. By comparison Jay-Z sold 27 million units over the course of thirteen albums between 1996 and 2017.

The odds are Jay-Z made more money because he was a label owner, but this gives an indication of the commercial popularity of Hammer in a window of time. It is widely acknowledged that Hammer made tens of millions of dollars between the late 1980s and mid-1990s. The problem Hammer had is the problem that anyone who runs into financial difficulty has: he spent much more money than he made. The key question is: what did he spend his money on? Reports suggest:

- A $30m mansion (the highly personalised nature of mansions means they often struggle to sell)
- Transportation – including private jets and luxury cars
- Racehorses – a stable of them (according to racehorse owner, Jon Roberts, an 1980s Miami cocaine cowboy, it costs in excess of $50,000 a month to feed a racehorse)
- Lawsuits – Hammer was sued by Rick James (and others) for sampling their songs without permission
- Staff – Hammer employed over 200 people

The last point, staff, is where Hammer's story is most heart-breaking. Speaking to the radio hosts Opie and Anthony in 2009, he explained that he had felt compelled to hire so many people from Oakland, his home town, because of the levels of deprivation and violence in the area, much of which was related to the crack epidemic.

We were dying. Go and look at the murder rate in my city at the time. My city became very famous for being in the top three in homicide. That is where I lived, that is where I grew up my entire life. Some of the people that were dying were my classmates, my neighbours.

Hammer went on to explain how he recruited people struggling in the community – in order to save their lives:

Well – the amount of money . . . was worth the lives to me . . . if I had to do it all again I would absolutely put some of that money in the bank but the real truth is: not in exchange for the lives that lived.[1]

Hiring over 200 people is a huge undertaking. Each person requires a salary, of course, but then there are also vast additional expenses.

The tragedy of MC Hammer's bankruptcy was that he lost such a big chunk of his money in pursuit of humanitarian betterment. Even down, he should have been seen as a hero. Instead, he became a global punchline for going broke.

Hammer's laudable error was turning his profit-seeking endeavours into a de facto charity under the continuing assumption that he was earning enough (and would continue to do so) to keep it all afloat. Based upon Hammer's figures, paying a salary of $30,000 per annum to over 200 people meant he was paying at least $500,000 a month in salaries – that's $6m a year before taxes, benefits and expenses. Given this level of expense, directed mainly at people who had no means of helping him generate profits or attracting larger crowds – it ended predictably and sadly.

Hammer's management of business was actually quite good – he made the wealth. It was in the management of personal money where he fell flat, combined with the desire to help more people than he possibly could.

MC Hammer became wealthy at a rapid rate. His sales were concentrated in a three-year window of his life. Jay-Z's sales have been lower than Hammer's but more consistent over the last twenty years. Hammer's manner and speed of earning make him comparable to a lottery winner.

When people who don't come from money and don't have access to strong financial advice somehow stumble onto a huge windfall, there is a great chance that they will soon be separated from this windfall. This can be due to a lack of budgeting and planning for the future, poor impulse control and generosity. This is a common theme for athletes and musicians, but can also operate at governmental level, especially in natural-resource based economies.

As admirable and honourable as his intentions may have been, this is likely what happened to MC Hammer. The fact that Jay-Z came from a street pharmaceutical background may have helped him learn about financial planning, budgeting and re-investing profits.

The one thing Hammer, Jay-Z and all people of means need is a solid pair of hands to manage their business affairs and provide sound financial advice. Which is not as straightforward as it sounds.

RIHANNA: THE NECESSITY OF GOOD FINANCIAL ADVICE AND REPRESENTATION

In an interview with MTV, Dr. Dre once offered a cautionary note on legal affairs and money management: 'As hard as you work for your money there are at least two or three people out there working just as hard to get it from you.'[2]

As a result, you need people working hard to help you keep your money, save your money and make your money work for you. And even then, you can still get stung. Rihanna nearly had to learn this the hard way.

Robyn 'Rihanna' Fenty is today a global beauty and singing icon, estimated to be worth over a billion dollars. But rewind to 2009 and she was on the verge of bankruptcy.

In 2003, Rihanna was a fifteen-year-old Barbadian in a three-member aspiring girl group when she met and performed for Evan Rogers, one half of a successful New York-based songwriting duo, alongside Carl Sturken. Rogers was immediately blown away by Rihanna's charisma, but suspected she wouldn't be able to sing. With renditions of Destiny's Child's 'Emotion' and Mariah Carey's 'Hero', she robustly proved him wrong.

Lord Andrew Lloyd Webber, the undisputed king of musicals, also spotted Rihanna around the same time singing karaoke in a resort in Barbados. Webber failed to follow his instincts and didn't bring Rihanna back to the UK, but Rogers didn't think twice – he signed Rihanna to a production deal with his company, Syndicated Rhythm Productions. Over the course of the next year, he recorded a demo tape with Rihanna, which would include her future breakthrough hit 'Pon De Replay', and sent it to newly minted Def Jam President, Jay-Z.

In early 2005, she was flown to New York to perform for Jay-Z. He was convinced on the spot and was so adamant about signing her she was not allowed to leave the building until he had her ink on the page. The contract was eventually signed at 3 a.m. in Jay-Z's office, and Rihanna also signed a contract with Peter Gounis of Berdon LLP, an accountant, to take care of her finances.

With her affairs taken care of, in August 2005 Rihanna's debut album *Music Of The Sun* was released. Five months later, she was a seventeen-year-old platinum-selling artist and a global success story. It seems inexplicable that four years after her initial flurry of success she was on the verge of bankruptcy.

The financial affairs of a teenager raking in millions require the utmost fiduciary responsibility of any client. Rihanna was too young to smoke, drink or vote at this point. She was still a child. Nevertheless, in 2012 Rihanna sued her accountants for $35m, alleging negligence and gross financial mismanagement, specifically citing:

1. Tens of millions in losses.
2. Shoddy bookkeeping.
3. Failure to recommend she trim expenses when her 2009 Last Girl on Earth tour was losing money (despite revenue increasing).
4. Failing to inform her that her 2009 Last Girl on Earth tour was losing money.
5. Taking 22 per cent of the Last Girl on Earth tour's total revenues while paying Rihanna only 6 per cent.
6. Failing to advise her against buying a run-down Beverly Hills mansion for $7.5m – despite the fact that they knew she could not afford it.
7. Failing to ensure she was being paid song royalties properly.
8. Failing to properly litigate her international tax affairs.

All of the above resulted in Rhianna staring down the barrel of bankruptcy and being subject to an audit by the Internal Revenue Service (aka The Notorious IRS) in the US. After initially defending themselves and claiming, in court, that she squandered vast sums on shoes and clothes, in 2014, Berdon settled Rihanna's lawsuit against them out of court for a reported $10m. By that point, her specific accountant, Peter Gounis, and his partner (i.e. boss) Michael Mitnick, had left the firm.

In response to this turbulent experience, Rihanna released 'Bitch Better Have My Money', the video for which was an all-out revenge fantasy about kidnapping, torturing and eventually murdering an accountant (aka 'the Bitch') and his trophy wife. The video ends with Rihanna sitting in a trunk full of money, naked and covered in her fictionalised financial handler's blood. The song sold over two million units and, despite becoming the first age-restricted video on Vevo-certified video, it has been viewed over 160m times on YouTube. She had turned near financial tragedy into a money-making triumph.

Rihanna is one of the lucky ones – too many like her have been unable to escape dubious financial management like she did. Joseph 'Fat Joe' Cartagena was an artist burnt by his accountants – with severe consequences. It resulted in him spending four months in prison. In a 2021 interview with the podcast *Earn Your Leisure,* Fat Joe described the experience as 'the one time I didn't do the crime'.[3]

WHO WATCHES THE WATCHERS?

So how does one deal with the issue of dodgy accountants and bad lawyers? The Notorious BIG had an idea. He said he had 'lawyers watching lawyers so I don't go broke'.[4]

Dame Dash, at a 2004 urban music seminar in London, said something similar: he hires an accountant and then hires a better accountant to observe the initial one.

What Dash and Biggie were describing was multiple tiers of defence. Three lines of defence is a widely practised approach to curtailing the threat of bad financial representation:

- The first line of defence is to watch what you make and spend and then retain a record of all your spending and transactions. No one is going to watch your back like you are going to watch your back. The first line is otherwise known as risk taking
- The second line of defence is to hire a reputable accountant and lawyer to advise on your business affairs and ensure you comply with all filing and regulatory requirements. Otherwise known as risk oversight
- The third line of defence is to hire an even more reputable accountant and lawyer to quietly oversee the work the second line of defence accountant is doing for you. This is risk assurance

There is a clear cost associated with this strategy: paying for two teams is more expensive than paying for one. However, if you are running an organisation or are a high net worth individual, it may not be a bad idea at all. It certainly beats going to prison, paying a large fine or entering expensive litigation because of a corrupt or incompetent son of a three-legged bitch you hired to do the work for you.

LAWYERS, LAWSUITS AND LAWLESSNESS[5]

The poverty to poetry to penthouse pipeline of Hip-Hop's elite sadly has another stop that they may experience: prison. The December 2005 edition of *The Source* magazine featured a dozen rappers on the cover – all of whom were, at that time, in prison.

Given the large number of rappers and Hip-Hop figures who end up entangled in the long arm of the law, the list could have been significantly more extensive. There are multiple reasons for this, but here's the main one: there is possibly no legitimate career under more intense law-enforcement scrutiny than being a rapper, especially one who tells tales of the street.

For Death Row Records, the ability to keep people out of prison despite serious criminal charges and/or convictions became a selling point to attract talent. In their heyday they managed to keep Snoop, Dr. Dre and Suge himself out of prison and managed to get Tupac released – all despite serious charges and convictions. All of the above is credited principally to one lawyer: David Kenner.

David Kenner: Defending Death Row

Kenner was an enigmatic figure. A quietly spoken, rather awkward and seemingly introverted older white man who stood out like a gangrene-riddled finger in the midst of Death Row's young and thuggin' predominantly Black staff. He passed the bar when Suge Knight was three years old but still dressed like a rap executive – complete with the company medallion.

Despite being a criminal lawyer, it was in his role as Head Counsel for Death Row Records that he really became a figure of major importance. In the *Who's Who of North American Attorneys*, Kenner cited 'sincerity, focus and dedication' as the keys to his success.[6] His one time-opponent, Ruthless Records' Jerry Heller, saw it differently and was less impressed. He described Kenner as a 'greasy haired, ponytailed scumbag'.[7] Michael 'Harry-O' Harris, the client who brought Kenner and Suge Knight together, described him as 'smooth as you want to be or as vicious as you want to be given the scenario'.[8]

According to investigative journalist Sam Gideon Anson, between 1995 and 1997, Kenner's 'smoothness and viciousness' earned him and his offices $13m from Death Row, roughly 17 per cent of their total earnings.[9]

Stellar as he was on the criminal defence side of things, initial cracks began to appear in the critical legal grey area of conflicts of interest.

Kenner and Death Row: contracts and conflicts of interest

After his death, Tupac's estate sued Kenner, Suge and Death Row, saying the famous hand-written contract Tupac had signed in prison may not have been legally binding, principally because it was riddled with conflicts of interests and Tupac didn't have appropriate representation. Tupac's mother and inheritor of his estate labelled Death Row a 'criminal enterprise' in the process. As reported in 1997 by the *LA Times*:

> *The lawsuit names Death Row attorney David Kenner as a defendant, accusing him of malpractice and contending that his representation of Shakur was in conflict with his personal financial interests and obligations to [Suge] Knight and Death Row.*
>
> *That contract is invalid, according to the lawsuit. The estate contends that Shakur did not have proper representation and signed the agreement primarily because he was unhappy and had been incarcerated for months on a sex abuse charge before Knight showed up with a promise to bail him out.*
>
> *In addition, the lawsuit contends, there is no language in Shakur's contract to support Knight's claim for a 20% management fee, which is twice what an artist of Shakur's stature would typically be charged.*
>
> *Kenner said on Friday that he, Knight and Death Row did not violate any law or mishandle Shakur's account, blaming the rapper's debts on his extravagant spending habits.*[10]

Kenner's management of conflicts of interests was, to put it mildly, rather relaxed. For example, the handwritten prison contracts Kenner drew up for Tupac Shakur necessitated that he:

1. Sign with Death Row Records.
2. Appoint Suge Knight, the CEO of Death Row Records, as his manager.
3. Appoint David Kenner, the lead attorney of Death Row Records, as his attorney.

This may not be the mother of all conflicts of interest, but it would certainly qualify as a close aunt. It was a clear and obvious situation in which a conflict of roles facilitated a financial benefit – there should have been a firewall segregating competing interests (the person representing the company's interests should have been different to the people representing the client's interest).

David Kenner and Tupac-inspired Tip

No matter the deal, there is no substitute for your own representation. And even then, your advisers advise, you decide.

Death of a dynasty: Kenner and the downfall of Death Row

From the day Tupac died – Friday, 13 September 1996 – Death Row Records, once the dominant force in rap music, rapidly descended into an existential crisis. Despite Kenner's efforts to keep him out of prison, Suge Knight, the head of the company, had violated his probation by jumping into a post-Mike Tyson fight melee between Tupac and a reputed South Side Crip gang member called Orlando Anderson (a man who was being investigated for four separate murders when Tupac attacked him. Tupac's would be the fifth murder he was widely believed to have committed).

Dr. Dre had already left. Snoop Dogg requested to leave not long after, and lesser-celebrated stars followed them. As the game dried up, Death Row took several measures to shore up their finances. They:

- Reined in spending and abolished all perks, including company cars and other benefits
- Fire-sold assets: for example, Snoop Dogg, one of the biggest names in music, was 'sold' to Master P's No Limit Records for a reported $4m and a profit-share arrangement

- Traded on the glory days: Death Row's main income sources became re-issues, remixes or rip-offs of their heyday artists and albums. They released several posthumous Tupac records, a gangsta Christmas album, multiple Death Row greatest hits compilations and diss record compilations targeting their heyday artists. Additionally, they signed soundalikes and lookalikes of Tupac and Snoop (Top Dogg and Tha Realest respectively)
- Stripped back head count to an essential minimum. Perhaps in a bid to ensure they didn't end up in an MC Hammer-type of situation, Death Row cut, cut and cut to the bone. Even David Kenner himself became surplus to requirements and was eventually let go – which proved to be a critical mistake

The ultimate collapse of the half-a-billion-dollar house Suge Knight built is directly linked to the final point above. In the early noughties, Suge Knight was sued (for $107m) by then incarcerated drug baron Michael 'Harry O' Harris and his then wife Lydia Harris for failing to provide a return on an alleged $1.5m seed investment which the Harrises claimed granted them a 50 per cent ownership stake in Death Row.

In 2005, a Kenner-less Suge Knight failed at the most elementary of legal affairs – showing up in court to present your side of the argument. As a result, the Los Angeles County Superior Court Judge, Ronald Sohigian, ruled against Suge and Death Row by default.

In two falls of the gavel, Suge Knight plunged from king to pauper. All the fruits of the (quite literal) blood, sweat and tears: gone. He lost literally everything. And Death Row, a company with the potential of one day becoming a Black version of Disney, crumbled to dust.

Suge Knight and David Kenner-inspired Tip

In the event of an emergency cutting of costs to bare essentials, ensure that you do not create an even greater emergency. Carefully understand, estimate, challenge and stress test your definition of bare essentials. Cutting your own tailored legal and financial representation costs may prove an even more costly mistake.

Suge Knight soon returned to his original ways of doing business – bullying, extortion and intimidation – but without the success. Kenner, on the other hand, still represents rappers and Hip-Hop figures to this day. In 2023, he represented Tory Lanez,[11] who was convicted of assault with a semiautomatic handgun, having a loaded and unregistered firearm in a vehicle and gross negligence in discharging his firearm following the shooting of Megan Thee Stallion. In 2023, he also unsuccessfully represented Prakazrel 'Pras' Michel of the Fugees, who was convicted of illegally taking tens of millions of dollars to lobby the United States government on behalf of a Malaysian financier and the Chinese government.[12]

Kenner made mistakes along the way, and Death Row clearly needed much more legal structuring, but his presence and then his absence demonstrated the critical nature of solid legal affairs management and representation. No matter how much Kenner cost Suge and Death Row, it would have ultimately proved cheaper to keep him.

Representation Tips from a Hip-Hop Lawyer

Wallace E.J. Collins III is an attorney in private practice in New York specialising in entertainment and intellectual property law, handling both transactional and litigation matters. He also happens

---

to be a man who speaks with a persistent and very welcoming warm smile.

From the early 1990s until the magazine's decline in the noughties, he advertised his services in the classified section of *The Source* (right beside the Black porn adverts and knock-off jewellery). His adverts brought him to the attention of a very young Puff Daddy and an equally young Jay-Z, who would recommend that their artists approach him for representation. As a result, he negotiated and agreed the legal aspects of record deals for the likes of Craig Mack (the first artist signed to Bad Boy Entertainment), Faith Evans, Beanie Sigel, Freeway and others. Those micro adverts cost Wallace a few hundred dollars a quarter and, in his words, earned him a 'better return than Apple stock' over the period. Context: had he invested $100 in Apple stock in 1991, it would be worth nearly $300,000 right now.

Below, Wallace offers some tips to help ensure you don't get burnt and make the most of your representation.

1. Do not sign anything – other than an autograph – without running it by a lawyer.

2. Never negotiate without a lawyer.

3. The biggest lawyer may not be the best lawyer: make sure you have a lawyer that is right for your needs.

4. Your lawyer's experience is essential. Do not hire a real estate lawyer for an entertainment deal. And vice versa.

5. A good lawyer can form part of your leverage in negotiations.

6. Ensure you can trust and clearly understand your lawyer. If you can't, keep searching until you find the right representation for you.

7. Know your business: the lawyer can only advise; you decide.

8. Stay on top of your business: the people who get screwed often get screwed because they were not paying attention.

9. Find good people [professionals] and listen to what they say. But always remember – you have to live with the deal you sign, not them.

SECTION 5

SPREADING OUT

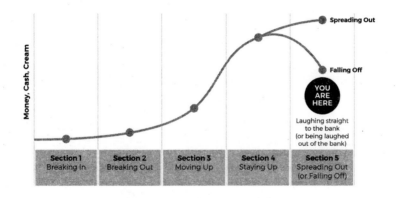

Money, Cash, Cream

Spreading Out

Falling Off

YOU
ARE
HERE

Laughing straight
to the bank
(or being laughed
out of the bank)

| **Section 1**
Breaking In | **Section 2**
Breaking Out | **Section 3**
Moving Up | **Section 4**
Staying Up | **Section 5**
Spreading Out
(or Falling Off) |

18.

DIVERSIFICATION

The music stops, the lights come on, and the DJ shouts, 'You ain't gotta go home but you can't stay here!' The party is officially over: what do you do next? Go home or go somewhere else?

Nothing lasts for ever. Eventually your carefully planned winning streak will come to a slow halt or, even scarier, a sudden one. At this stage there are two options: fall off and fade into oblivion or spread out. What differentiates Hip-Hop's enduring success stories from most mere mortals is their use of the good times to plan, prepare and pounce on future-proofing opportunities before they are over. They do this by leveraging success in one field into even greater success in another field and transforming any accrued soft power into hard political influence.

This is the final frontier of *The Hip-Hop MBA*.

In an interview with Mass Appeal (owned by Nas and other investors), Nipsey Hussle said:

As an artist, there's a business model that exists in the music industry to prevent you from having ownership, to prevent you from being a partner in the lion's share of the profit. The value is created in content, so when I think of us as hip-hop artists, we create content . . . but we don't have a wide product line. You go to Disneyland, they got tons of products. Ears, Mickey everything. And so that's the vision behind The Marathon [Clothing] store.[1]

The Marathon Clothing store was one of Nipsey Hussle's several business ventures. As mentioned in Chapter 8, in 2019 he was murdered right outside it. Today, it stands as a testimony of much of what he stood for and spoke about: especially the co-mingled mogul-making areas that are ownership as related to diversification.

Diversification is a business-expansion and risk-management strategy in which an entity develops or forays into new products and services, or enters new markets, beyond its existing ones. Diversification can help make a company a greater success, it can rescue a company from failure and, in some situations, it can be the tombstone of a company.

Diversification, especially when it comes with ownership, is what separates the rap star from the rap mogul. The rap star sticks to rapping and the periphery benefits and opportunities that come with it – the thinking being that this limits their exposure to risk. But the reality is that it may increase their exposure to risk – especially should their rap career, their main income source, turn sour. The rap mogul aggressively diversifies into other areas of economic opportunity and business expansion, which is often considered a high-risk endeavour, but the potential rewards are infinite.

The rap mogul leverages everything they have gained from their primary career into promotional tools, steady income streams and seed investment as a springboard into opportunities outside their primary careers.

DIVERSIFICATION AND HIP-HOP

Diversification traditionally comes in three types:

1. **Concentric diversification:** Occurs when a company exploits similarity in product, production or presentation in order to add similar products or services to the existing business. Examples: Dell, a desktop computer manufacturer, starts making laptops; Facebook, a social media firm, purchases Instagram, a picture-focused social media firm; Coca-Cola, soft-drink leviathan, purchased Vitaminwater; Roc-A-Fella, a rap label, signs Kanye West – a 'producer-rapper'.
2. **Horizontal diversification:** Occurs when a company adds new and unrelated products or services to an existing consumer base. Examples of this include Apple, traditionally a computer manufacturer, expanding into MP3 players (iPods) and smartphones (iPhones) or Roc-A-Fella – a rap label – signing Victoria 'Posh Spice' Beckham, a pop star.
3. **Conglomerate diversification:** Occurs when a company adds new products or services that are significantly unrelated to their current offerings (in terms of product, production or presentation) and with no technological or commercial similarities. For example, Virgin, initially a record store, expanding into rail travel, an airline, space, telecoms, TV, healthcare, etc. Or Birdman and Slim, the owners of Cash Money Records, establishing Bronald Oil – an oil exploration company.

Hip-Hop has helped introduce what could be argued to be a different kind of diversification – one that is open to people as much as it is to corporations. It is best described as Clout-driven Diversification (CDD).

The best way to describe this form of diversification is as a process in which clout (as opposed to expertise, technological prowess or capabilities) acquired and accrued in one industry, profession or product type becomes the driving force of diversification into another industry.

Clout-driven diversification has resulted in a highly lucrative situation in which rappers are able to exploit the credibility, marketability, popularity, reputation, relationships and/or financial prowess accrued in their primary career to establish a secondary career or pursue other ventures. What they lack in expertise, technological prowess or capabilities, they make up for in clout.

Gone are the days where revenue maximisation for an artist was a T-shirt with their band's name on it or the endorsement of a product. Hip-Hop figures now regularly diversify into multi-billion-dollar opportunities, and it all centres around clout. Depending on the ownership structure, the secondary career (or venture) the rapper diversifies into – where it is calculated, well-executed and successful – often proves more financially rewarding than their music. As a result, as Nipsey Hussle's statement above suggests, the one thing practically all rap moguls have in common is that they earn a large portion, if not the bulk of their wealth, outside rap music.

CASE STUDIES: CLOUT-DRIVEN DIVERSIFICATION IN MOTION

Dr. Dre

Dr. Dre is to the art of crafting sound what Pablo Picasso was to the art of painting and sculpture. For over four decades, Dre repeatedly advanced the very concept of music, shaping popular culture as he went along. He was the key driver of advancements in music ranging from West Coast electro-Hip-Hop and gangsta rap to g-funk. From the World Class Wreckin' Cru, NWA and Snoop Dogg to Eminem, The Game and Kendrick Lamar, Dr. Dre built a global reputation for being blessed with a unique gift to make sound undeniably delicious to the human ear. In terms of clout, Dr. Dre had it all, but it was his reputation as a true sonic wizard that served as his most lucrative clout-driven diversification opportunity.

Google named its now discontinued photo-organising software, Picasa, after Picasso. Dr. Dre didn't wait until he was in a coffin to make good on his CDD. Alongside his long-term business partner, Interscope Records supremo Jimmy Iovine, in 2006 Dr. Dre founded Beats by Dr. Dre, a premium headphone company. Despite murmurs of poor quality from the audio press, their signature product, the Beats by Dr. Dre Studio (Beats) headphones, were launched in July 2008 and proved to be an instant hit – everyone from rappers, college kids and athletes to conservative politicians was seen proudly wearing them (and therefore became a cyclical part of the marketing for the product).

The perception of the quality of Beats headphones – drawn from Dr. Dre's good name as a soundsmith – was high enough to justify the high price for what was truly a mass-audience product. By 2011, according to American market research firm the NPD Group, Beats by Dr. Dre enjoyed a 64 per cent market share for headphones that cost over $100 and generated $1.5bn in revenue in 2013.

Dr. Dre was clearly not the first sonic wizard the world has ever known and he was also far from the first musician or celebrity to slap their name onto an electronics brand. But in terms of CDD, he was the one who best epitomised 'cool', technological advancement and staying power in modern popular culture. Therefore, he had the marketability, popularity, crossover appeal and (street) credibility to properly implement a CDD plan into a successful product line that became worth billions.

By comparison, headphones by Phil Spector would probably have been a hard sell – regardless of how sonically advanced the 'wall of sound' was (and the small hurdle of being in prison for murder). In fact, Iovine himself was a music man, a mega-successful producer and highly respected music executive but a headphone line under his own name – imagine 'Iovinenient Audio' – would almost certainly not have exploded in the same way

Beats did. He lacked the necessary clout with consumers and the public to pull it off.

As an icon in the business, Dre is a star to stars. As a result, he also enjoyed relationships that could be leveraged for marketing purposes. Puff Daddy and Lady Gaga both had their own line of Beats headphones. Compound clout meant Beats became a brand that would add to the celebrity of the person endorsing it, as opposed to just the other way round.

In 2014, Beats by Dr. Dre was purchased by Apple for over $3bn – netting Dr. Dre and Iovine a reported payday of somewhere between half a billion to a billion dollars apiece.

Rihanna

Miss Fenty's appeal as a fashion and beauty figure was instant. In 2009, *The Cut* opined:

> Rihanna is known for her looks, style, and makeup as much as her singing abilities. Indeed, few young stars possess the ability to shift looks so dramatically and with such ease. With the snip of a scissor or a new lipstick shade we see a new side to the singer, and, as time passes, she becomes edgier, chicer, and more on trend.[2]

This was fertile ground for Rihanna to create a CDD plan. Her initial foray was in the well-trodden ground of perfumes. She released a total of eleven different fragrances, struck an endorsement deals with Secret Body Spray, became the face of Nivea, collaborated with MAC cosmetics and was the first Black woman to become the face of Dior. Her role as creative director of women's clothing at Puma saw her release her own shoes – which sold out within hours. In 2014, she was given a fashion icon award by the Council of Fashion Designers of America – high praise indeed, but all this was only a warm-up. Rihanna's real money-spinning CDD came when she launched her own fashion and beauty lines.

In 2017, twenty-nine-year-old Rihanna Robyn Fenty entered into a reported 50/50 venture with the luxury goods mammoth LVMH (aka Moët Hennessy Louis Vuitton) and created the diversity- and inclusion-focused cosmetics brand Fenty Beauty.[3] Unlike traditional cosmetic brands, Fenty catered to over fifty skin tones including previously overlooked complexions – notably darker-skinned Black women. Fenty changed the make-up game for ever. And when the game changes, players who wish to remain in the game change too, so everyone had to scramble to meet the new standard: the Fenty standard.

Diversity and inclusion became Fenty's unique selling point. Rihanna herself was Fenty's marketing, popularity and credibility point. She was the brand's clout. In 2018, its first full year of operations, Fenty is reported to have generated over $550m in revenue.

Rihanna's reported 50 per cent stake in Fenty is now estimated, by *Forbes*, to be worth $1.4bn.[4] Owing to this well-thought-through and executed CDD, Rihanna is currently the richest female musician and richer than most of the British Royal Family combined. Not bad . . . for a 'bad girl' from 'the colonies'.

In a 2019 discussion with *Oceans 9* co-star Sarah Paulson for *Interview* magazine, Rihanna spoke about how her primary career, music, led to her CDD:

> . . . the thing that keeps me alive and passionate is being creative. With every business outlet, I'm making something from a vision to a reality, and that's the thing I really enjoy. Music had led me to these other outlets, and to things that I genuinely love.[5]

Music gave Rihanna the clout; her CDD gave her the wealth.

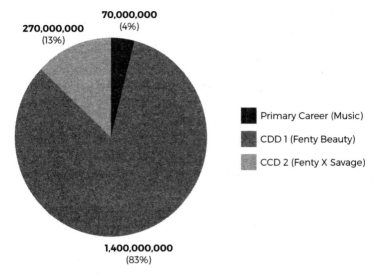

Figure 18: Rihanna's estimated earnings. Source: *Forbes*

Puff Daddy

If the concept of CDD in Hip-Hop had a patron saint, it would be the one-man luxury brand that is Sean 'Puff Daddy' Combs. Since he was a teenager, the man has been the perfect human actualisation of clout.

No matter what he did – transforming rough-round-the-edges young people into global sex symbols, running his record labels, posting on social media, running a marathon, acting, hiring staff, fleeing from a nightclub after a shootout, going to court, beefing with rivals, conquering competitors – he made it look alluringly amazing. Sexy even.

As a consequence, when it comes to marketing, credibility, reputation, popularity, finances and relationships – he has it all in abundance. Starting in his late 1990s heyday, with music properly conquered, he began exploiting his high CDD potential – to near perfection.

Puff Daddy is to style and suavity what Dr. Dre is to sound.

In 1998, Puff Daddy leveraged his reputation for style and quality, his popularity in the culture and his marketing genius as well as his marketability to create Sean John, a clothing line bearing his real names. At its peak the company was grossing over $500m in revenue a year. Puff Daddy sold Sean John in November 2016 for an estimated $70 million[6] (a far cry from the reported $204m Jay-Z sold Rocawear for in 2007),[7] retaining a 20 per cent stake in the company.

Launched in 2003, Cîroc, the British-distributed French vodka brand, had struggled to gain a foothold in the United States, barely selling 40,000 crates per annum in its first few years on the market. In 2007, Diageo, the distributor, struck a marketing deal with Puff Daddy to become the face of the company and chief promoter – for 50 per cent of profits. Puff transformed Cîroc from a no-name non-entity to a major player in the vodka space by doing what he does best: sprinkling stardust all over it. Through adverts, product placement, name-drops in rap songs, appearances in rap videos, sponsorship deals of Hip-Hop-themed events and much more, he made Cîroc not only a luxury must-have product but a household name.

In 2011, Puff (alongside a carefully selected, cool, intergenerational and interracial cast, including Frank Vincent, Eva Pigford, Michael K. Williams, Aaron Paul, Dania Ramirez, Chrissy Teigen and Jesse Williams) starred in a glossy Cîroc mini-movie advert set in Vegas, to the sound of Frank Sinatra's 'Luck Be A Lady'. The advert was classic Puff Daddy: super-stylish, polished, opulent and dripping with the good life. Above all, it was effective: it helped synonymise Cîroc with great times.

Asked by *Adweek*'s Christopher Heine about working with large multinationals as opposed to brands he created, Puff Daddy said:

I am actually used to dealing with these big public companies. It's like a family, and that's the way it's been with Diageo. But it's

give-and-take. You learn, and you teach. At the end of the day, you
hold hands, and it's about the bottom line. Every campaign, we get
closer to finding our true voice. [Cîroc] is like a really talented
protégé. We are very good at what we do, but every day we get
better.[8]

'Very good at what we do' was an understatement. Within the
first six months of the deal, Puff had helped increase the sales of
Cîroc tenfold to 400,000 crates – and that was not even near its
peak.

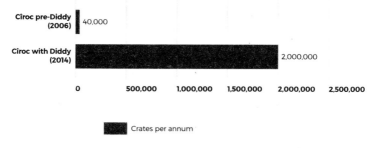

Figure 19: Cîroc: the Puff Daddy effect. Source: *Adweek*[9]

Following the huge success with Cîroc, Puff and Diageo
teamed up again to purchase DeLeón Tequila. Puff's other projects
have included acquiring AQUAhydrate: a 'great tasting high-
performance water specially formulated for people with an active
lifestyle' with the actor Mark Wahlberg and the billionaire Ronald
Burkle. In 2013, he entered the Wild West of online, linear
media and film with the establishment of Revolt TV and Revolt
Film. He also owned Justin's, a (now defunct) restaurant chain
named after his son.

Puff Daddy tapped into his CDD at a time when Hip-Hop
was still viewed as a political hot potato and in the aftermath of
the murder of his friend and marquee artist, the Notorious BIG.
According to his former bodyguard, Gene Deal, when Puff saw

Suge and Tupac at the 1996 Soul Train Awards at the height of their beef, he ran away. In a 2021 interview with VladTV, Deal recounted twenty-six-year-old Puff Daddy's reasoning: 'Gene, I got 126 employees and these people depend on me for their livelihood . . . if these white folks thought or would think I had anything to do with any gun play, they would not fuck with me. I'm a businessman. I'm about making money.'[10]

And make money he did. Sean 'Puff Daddy' Combs, the son of a single mother and a drug dealer (who was murdered when Puff was two), is today a human multinational conglomerate worth an estimated $740m – most of which was earned from his CDD enterprises.

Needle Scratch: The Sun Don't Shine For Ever

'The sun don't shine forever', the opening bars on Puff Daddy's 1997 hit 'Victory', is a prophecy that appears to be becoming true in real time. It looks like the dark clouds of decline are beginning to surround Puff Daddy's empire. He faces existential legal issues on all fronts: corporate, criminal and civil.

Cassie

As I type these very words news has just broken that Puff Daddy has been sued by his ex-girlfriend, the singer Cassie Ventura. The allegations are as serious as it gets. They include rape, sexual exploitation, sex-trafficking, serious assault and coercion into intercourse.[11]

UPDATE: In what can only be described as 'lightning speed', less than 24 hours after Cassie's lawsuit was filed (which, in what may be a legal first, contains a trigger warning on the cover), news has just broken that Puff Daddy has settled the suit for a reported $30m.[12]

Keefe D

Potentially adding to Puff Daddy's legal concerns is the surprising September 2023 arrest of Duane 'Keefe D' Davis, a former 'shot caller' (i.e. leader) of the Southside Crips. Keefe D also happens to be the uncle of Orlando 'Baby Lane' Anderson – the man who Tupac attacked at the MGM Grand following a 1996 Mike Tyson fight, and he also happens to be the man widely believed to be Tupac's killer.

In a bid to gain immunity from a drug charge that could have landed him a life sentence, Keefe D confessed to not only being the driver of the car that pulled the drive-by shooting on Tupac and Suge Knight (who happens to be a childhood friend of Keefe D) but also the person who handed the gun to his nephew, Orlando.

When questioned by police in 2009, he made a 'queen for a day' statement, also known as a 'proffer agreement' (which is a written agreement between a federal prosecutor and an individual under criminal investigation, which permits these individuals to tell the prosecutors about their knowledge of crimes, with the supposed assurance that their words will not be used against them in any later proceedings). He did not know that these discussions were being recorded and claimed, in critical detail, that Tupac's murder was committed for a $1m payday at the behest of Puff Daddy, who at the time was in a serious feud with Suge Knight and Tupac.

Keefe D has spent much of the last decade reiterating Puff Daddy's involvement to anyone who will interview him or listen to him, even though he never received the money as, according to him, Eric 'Von Zip' Martin, the late, highly respected New York gangster and associate of Puff Daddy who introduced the pair, never passed the money on. Puff Daddy has consistenly denied any involvement in the murder of Tupac Shakur.[13] When radio host Charlamagne Tha God attempted to ask about Keefe D's assertions in a 2016 interview on the Breakfast Club, before the question even landed Puff Daddy responded rather dismissively and nonchalantly: 'We don't even talk about things that are nonsense. We don't entertain nonsense, my brother. So we're not even going to go there, with all due respect. But I appreciate you as a journalist asking. Thank you.'[14]

Diageo

Much of Puff Daddy's modern woes seem to start in May 2023 when news emerged that his 15-year super-lucrative relationship with Diageo, distributor of Cîroc (his main CDD earner), had soured to the point of termination. The reason for the termination: racism allegation. According to the *Financial Times*:

'A drinks company owned by Sean Combs, known as Diddy, has sued Diageo for alleged racial discrimination, arguing the global conglomerate has not adequately invested in brands associated with the rapper.

In court documents filed in New York state court in Manhattan, the musician's company Combs Wines and Spirits said: "Diageo has treated Mr Combs and his brands worse than others because he is black."

The DeLeón tequila brand co-owned by the two groups, and Diageo's Cîroc vodka brand in which it collaborates with Combs, have been "typecast" and treated as "black brands" that should be targeted to "urban" consumers, according to the legal suit.'[15]

Also according to the *Financial Times*, Diageo alleged Combs had threatened them with racism allegations to force the company 'to accede to several outrageous and extra-contractual demands, including for supposed billions of dollars of damages.' Diageo said that Puff Daddy had failed to fulfil his duty as a 50 per cent owner, alleging he had only invested $1,000, while Diageo put in more than $100m. The company said the rapper earned almost $1bn through their partnership.'[16]

The battle lines between new money and old money have been drawn. Time will tell who will win. What is not in doubt is that the concept of 'happily ever after' exists only in fairy tales. In business, like in life and in literature, all things must come to an end. Every sentence has a full stop. Sometimes, however, what looks like a full stop may actually be a comma. Time will tell whether the current woes of the man who told us he 'can't stop, won't stop' are indeed a temporary pause, the beginning of another exemplary chapter in business rebounding or The End.

Rap Snacks

Puff Daddy, Rihanna and Dr. Dre demonstrated the power of leveraging personal clout permeating from visibility in Hip-Hop to diversify into different areas. James Lindsay, a former marketing manager for fast-moving consumer goods, did the opposite.

Lindsay is a unique, little-known yet critically important figure in the business of Hip-Hop. Unlike most other examples of Hip-Hop-related CDD, he was not a rapper or a rap executive. He was not even in Hip-Hop when he recognised the potential embedded within the culture to diversify his own career. Lindsay was not a Hip-Hop insider attempting to diversify outwards, he was an outsider attempting to move inwards. In the process, he helped demonstrate the case for the diversification of the culture into different and unrelated arenas. In short, he helped demonstrate the CDD of Hip-Hop itself.

The calmly spoken Philadelphia native was the first in his family to go to college and, perhaps most critically, the first in his family to start a business. His first job was with a Black beauty- and health-product manufacturer and retailer called Johnson Products (makers of Ultra Sheen Hair Grease, amongst other products). Lindsay worked directly for Mr Johnson, the owner of the company. The experience shaped his life:

> It gave me confidence to believe that I could really do this myself. Seeing someone who looked like me start a multi-million-dollar company and be successful at it – and find out how he did it, was probably the biggest inspiration of my career. I got that entrepreneurial bug from him.

After leaving Johnson Products, Lindsay went to work for Warner Lambert, producers of a range of products including Listerine, chewing gum brands, razors, pharmaceuticals and more. While visiting retailers, he noticed that there was a lack of products in the snack industry that engaged with Hip-Hop. Right there, he saw a gap in the market and decided to fill it.

> I was just noting that there was nothing out there that spoke to the culture, that was really fun. Something that someone that looks like me and is in the culture can relate to. This was twenty-six years ago [from time of interview, i.e. 1995] – but I just knew that Hip-Hop was going to dictate what we eat, how we clothe ourselves, how we drink, products – everything. I just had that foresight. One morning I just woke up and Rap Snacks just came to me.

Lindsay contacted a manufacturing facility called Nibble With Gibble's Inc. He spoke to the president of the company, a 'sixty-five-year-old white gentlemen who didn't know anything about Hip-Hop' called Bob Funer, and told him that he wanted to start his own chips company. Funer asked him what flavour, and he responded, 'BBQ and raunch' as his research showed that 'BBQ was the number-one selling [potato chip] item in the inner city', and raunch was something he could experiment with. He laid out his idea to Funer in some detail. The following day, he went to see Funer, who informed him what he needed to do business with him.

It was no easy task: he had to find the money to manufacture and buy a minimum of 800 cases of his own prototype product: Rap Snacks. Lindsay got the money together and Nibble With Gibble's produced the sample. All 800 cases sold out within two hours. Lindsay handed in his notice immediately and never looked back.

Rap Snacks started with 'MC Potato' on the packaging – literally a rapping potato. At the turn of the century, Lindsay approached the Vice President of Marketing for Universal Music with a pitch:

> You guys are spending all this money on stickers; poster boards and you're getting no return – they rip them down. You can spend that same money putting rappers on the Rap Snacks bag, they'll become collectibles. On the back of the bag, we can put information of any new music or anything else the fan wants to find out. So [Universal] actually paid me money to put their artists on my [Rap Snack] bags.

Today, Rap Snacks are available in over a dozen flavours – each one linked to the personality and style of the rapper on the cover and an inspirational segment from the rapper on the back. Cardi B has two flavours: Cheddar BBQ and Jerk BBQ, the Notorious BIG has Jalapeño Honey and Cookout BBQ sauce. Perhaps the most befitting flavour belongs to renowned hothead Lil Boosie: 'Louisiana Heat' cheese puffs in a fiery red packet complete with Boosie staring menacingly at the consumer. Lindsay's 1994 epiphany now sells millions of bags of chips and culture across the world annually.

Rap Snacks has also diversified into noodles, cereals . . . and community empowerment-driven banking.

CDD: Honourable (and not so honourable) mentions

Instances of rap stars and executives becoming (or attempting to and failing to become) moguls by exploiting their CDD is understandably vast, given the lucrative and hypercompetitive nature of Hip-Hop and the figures within it. Before our final case study, here's a roundup of some of the more eyebrow-raising schemes:

- Akon leveraged his clout as a musician to attain a $1bn credit line from a Chinese-state backed entity to help roll out solar-powered electricity in several African states. In 2018, he announced the building of Akon City, a 'futuristic city' in Senegal based on the fictional technologically advanced Wakanda (from the *Black Panther* Marvel comics and movies). A December 2022 visit to Akon City by the BBC found goats grazing the grass and no signs of a 'futuristic city' in development[17]

- In 2013, Nas and Anthony Saleh (a rap fan and investing prodigy who would become Nas's manager and business partner at the age of twenty-three and also helped guide the careers of Lady Gaga and Nicki Minaj) launched QueensBridge Venture Partners, an investment vehicle that invests in 'technology companies in highly competitive and visible markets'. Reports suggest that they have struck gold with investments in Robinhood, Coinbase and Ring, later acquired by Amazon

- Ja Rule famously/infamously invested in Fyre Festival, a super-clout-upon-clout-based idea to develop a luxury festival on a remote island complete with influencers, celebrities, musicians and private jets. It all ended in misery, infamy, penitentiary (for one of his partners, but thankfully not Ja himself) and multiple documentaries

- Krept & Konan opened up Crepes & Cones, a restaurant 'offering a mix of savoury soul food with creative desserts & cocktails'. Krept also established Nala's Baby, a child skincare range

- In 2003, Russell Simmons entered the financial services business with RushCard (UniRush), a prepaid Visa debit card aimed at people who may struggle to attain conventional banking services. The business was sold for $147m to Green Dot, a rival company, in 2017

- From turning into a reggae star, a gospel singer, acquiring and then relaunching Death Row (as an 'NFT label'), Snoop Dogg does basically whatever he pleases

THE (FRESH) PRINCE WHO BECAME A KING

By the turn of the century, Will Smith could easily have been a 'remember him?' He could have been a long-faded old-school rapper who popped up principally in Hip-Hop trivia: 'Who was the first rapper to win a Grammy?' He could have become a mainstay of the 'I Love the 1980s' rap concerts or a cast member on *Love & Hip-Hop*. He could have been punching in early, working through lunch and leaving late at his 9–5 job – hoping to earn a few extra dollars in overtime pay or get promoted. Alternatively, Will Smith could have remained one half of DJ Jazzy Jeff and the Fresh Prince, as well as the lead actor *of The Fresh Prince of Bel-Air*, and still been one of the most accomplished and memorable rappers ever.

However, due to his meticulously cultivated and managed career and brand, his willingness to take creative and business risks, his perpetual movement with the times and his mastery of the business as well as his ability to bounce back from mistakes (such as *Wild Wild West*), perhaps the foremost case of CDD in Hip-Hop would have to be the 'fresh' West Philadelphian prince of rap who became a Hollywood king.

From the modest (by comparison) beginnings of 'Girls Ain't Nothing But Trouble' (DJ Jazzy Jeff and the Fresh Prince's 1986 debut single), Will Smith leveraged the clout he accrued as an irresistibly charming pop-rapper to become one of the most bankable actors in Hollywood. Over the course of the last three decades, Smith has been the star power behind over thirty blockbuster films generating roughly $7bn, towering over the estimated $150m generated from the direct sales of his music (solo and duo).His production company, Overbrook Entertainment (named after the West Philadelphia area he originates from), has become a major force in film and TV.

To measure the fruits of Will Smith's CDD exclusively in financial terms would be a blockbuster-worthy error, for its societal impact may be of greater importance. From vaudeville to minstrelsy to the first major hit movie (D. W. Griffith's *The Birth of a Nation*), Hollywood long served as the propaganda arm of white supremacy. It long worked to reaffirm the very worst of vicious stereotypes about Black people and maintain the status quo.

In the roles he played, money he generated, power he accrued, jobs he created and how he used his considerable influence, Will Smith – as an actor and as an executive – has played a crucial role in the ongoing transformation of how Black people are treated, rewarded and portrayed by Hollywood. Critically, he has helped Black people win back control of their image.

When he started out in the mid-1980s, the 'sensible' money would have bet against Will Smith achieving even 5 per cent of what he has achieved – thus far. Today, he is a highly profitable fountain of soft power with all of the chops to acquire the ultimate hard power of the state: the US presidency. Will Smith is an all-American dessert, a truly delicious treat. The memories he has brought to the world through his music, movies and moments are all things that make the world feel good. Just keep his wife's name out of your mouth.

Hip-Hop-inspired Tips on Diversification

The ultimate goal of diversification of many of Hip-Hop's mogul was ownership.

When the music stops, the pauper is the person who doesn't own a throne to sit on or a castle to sit in. To be owner is to be king.

Conclusion

THEY CAME, THEY SAW, THEY CAPITALISED

A DJ KOOL HERC PARTY:
'Back To School Jam'

Address: 1520 Sedgwick Avenue

Date: August 11, 1973

Time: 9:00pm–4:00am

Admission: .25c for ladies, .50c for fellas

Given by: DJ Kool Herc

Special guests: Coco, Cindy C, Klark K, Timmy T

Source: BBC[1]

With the benefit of hindsight, the (replica) invitation to Chris 'Kool Herc' Campbell's 'Back To School Jam' above was an invitation to witness the beginnings of a highly influential global industry, one that would wield enormous amounts of power (both hard and soft), help demarginalise a beleaguered population and generate countless billions.

Like practically all of the other estimated 1,300 genres of music, rap was supposed to be a flash and fall, at best a post-disco infatuation that should have fizzled out by the early 1980s. It was not supposed to be a culture that would become a haven for a new generation of unique thinkers, philosophers, and poets . . . as well as pimps, pushers, pornographers and, of course, profit-seeking business visionaries.

History places two turntables and a microphone at the genesis of Hip-Hop. But this recollection of events misses one key element: economic deprivation. Economic deprivation rooted in the enslavement of Africans in America. It was this deprivation that drove much of the creativity in rap. From the artform to the culture to the industry and its business practices, rap music's proponents achieved everything they have by embracing everything they didn't have. Hip-Hop and the business practices that have facilitated its dominance make up a true *Made in America* story, one that is reshaping the world in its image – one mic and one mind at a time.

There is one final business lesson that Hip-Hop has to offer, and it may be the most important lesson of all.

Some call it 'internalising your externalities' or 'sowing good omen'; others call it 'corporate social responsibility'. In rap, it is just referred to as 'giving back to where you came from' (in some situations, it is also loosely described as 'checking in').

Giving back is not solely about altruism. The most dangerous person in society, as Malcolm X taught, is the person with nothing to lose. It follows that there is no one at greater risk of catastrophe than the person who has it all but is surrounded by people with nothing. The Notorious BIG, Nipsey Hussle, XXXTentacion, Tupac Shakur and, sadly, many other successful figures in Hip-Hop lost their lives at the hands of such figures: people with nothing to lose.

Rap moguls, especially those who emerged from hardship, have taken a range of steps to help alleviate poverty, suffering and insecurity in the environments they came from. These include providing educational opportunities (despite being a culture consisting mainly of school dropouts), food for the poor, electricity for Africans (thanks to Akon's Lighting Africa project . . . complete with a credit line from the Chinese state), jobs (as well as presidential pardons) for ex-felons, and justice- and police-reform initiatives.

Most importantly, Hip-Hop gave a voice to the truly voiceless. From the United States to the United Kingdom, Russia to Rwanda, Nigeria to the Netherlands, Black and other marginalised people around the world would be significantly more marginalised without Hip-Hop.

To whom much is given, much should be given back. In the words of the late great DMX: 'Give to the needy.'

Congratulations. You've now completed your Hip-Hop MBA. You are ready for the world.

If you follow the lessons in this book, play your cards right and prove unbelievably lucky, you're either billionaire-bound or en route to exemplary disaster. Either way, you've bullet-proofed your resumé, developed an inflated sense of self and thrown your graduation cap in the air. Without further ado, go forth and conquer, accumulate and create opportunity – like a true rap mogul.

ACKNOWLEDGEMENTS

I always wanted to contribute a verse to – somehow, someway – leave my little mark on Hip-Hop. Lord knows I tried but for the life of me I just cannot rap, so *The Hip-Hop MBA* will have to be my sixteen bars. From the bottom of my heart, I thank every single rapper, DJ, producer, engineer and, of course, entrepreneur who helped bring the culture to life. And kept it alive.

My greatest thanks goes to the rappers who have time and again nourished my mind, fuelled my pen and helped me conquer that vicious tyrant known as the blank page: O'Shea 'Ice Cube' Jackson Sr, Phonte Coleman, Nasir 'Nas' Jones, Christopher 'Biggie Smalls' Wallace, Tupac Amaru Shakur, Dead Prez, Talib Kweli Greene, Fatimah Nyeema 'Noname' Warner, Felipe Andres 'Immortal Technique' Coronel, Raymond Lawrence 'Boots' Riley, Darren 'Klashnekoff' Kandler, Shawn 'Jay-Z' Carter, Patrick Earl 'Project Pat' Houston, Keinan 'K'naan' Abdi Warsame, Alexander 'Skinnyman' Holland, Wasalu 'Lupe Fiasco' Muhammad Jaco, Brad 'Scarface' Jordan and, of course, the Queen of Hip-Hop literature and political thought, Lisa 'Sister Souljah' Williamson.

Thank you so much to everyone who shared their time and knowledge with me, notably: Wendy Day, Bryan Turner, Dan Charnas, Bill Adler, Dwayne 'Megaman' Vincent, Ed Young, Wallace E. J. Collins III, Clover Hope, Heather Joy Thompson, Kim Osorio and James Lindsay.

Huge appreciation to my compadres and consiglieres: Deji Bakare, Sheyi Teluwo, Chris Frimpong (I revisited this the night of the AFCON final: you, Pervell, Prince, Ansu, Ronald and Mohammed should consider yourselves remarkably lucky to be on here), Jaye Harewood, Christian Cobblah, Yomi Adegoke, Mohammed Kamara, Lanre

Adebola, Ronald King, Prince Kwakye, Femi Cole, Mustafa Akindele, Pervell Jecty, Jermaine Atie, Yemisi Adegoke, Salman Ahmed, David Tullett, Peter Gabriels, Jerome Danvers, Ansu Bai-Marrow, Symeon Brown, Sharmaine Lovegrove, Reni Eddo Lodge, Dane Baptiste, Jill Achineku, Elijah Lawal, David Prest, Rukaiya Russell, Cebo Luthuli, Jasmine Dotiwala, Hugh Muir, Simon Albury (happy eightieth birthday), Elizabeth Pears, Georgia Tobo, Tarita Mullings and Victor Abbey. Thanks for coming to my rescue, repair, radicalisation (in a good way) and subsequent de-loonification time and again. Thanks for all your help and guidance.

Thanks to everyone who worked on this book.

Huge thanks to the family: Anne Abbey, Tokunbo Abbey, Dennis Ejihritobo, Paul and Esohe Ejihritobo, Alero Abbey, Eyitemi Abbey, Vivienne Abbey and Stefano Brusa, Odun and Funmi Babalola, Faith Abbey, Segun and Funmi Abbey, Victor Abbey, Tosan and Tolu Bewaji. Nathanial, Nicole and Khalil Abbey. Jason and Janine Babalola. Oreofe and Eriife Bewaji. Jemine and Phillipe, Temi, Lotunda, Sikama and Sola Makany, Oscar, Kunbi and Genesis Falodun, Beverly Falodun. Georgia and Jason Ejihritobo. Stella and Frank Ajilore. Ernest and Ingrid Mcintyre. John and Ruth Edwards. Richard Edwards, Laura Chamberlain, Ellie and Alex Edwards, Eyabo Macauley, Deji, Mel, Eliora, Elijah and the Bakare family. Sheyi, Felicia, mummy and the Teluwo family, Chris Frimpong and Tarita Mullings and family. Ronke and Nolitha Olusanya. Anna, Bruno and Joshua Edenogie and family. May the Lord watch over us all.

Immense appreciation to everyone who has worked with or attended Uppity: The Intellectual Playground.

Kate and Naomi*, my girls, my gang. Thanks for your encouragement, patience, enthusiasm, love, warmth and hot scones. I'll make good soon enough.

Thank God, without whom nothing is possible.

On to the next one . . .

Nels
London, 2024

---

* This is your obligatory shoutout, Nay-Nay.

NOTES

INTRODUCTION: THE RISE OF THE NOBODIES

1   Marcy Projects: the public housing project where he grew up. From a Reebok advertising campaign for the 'S. Carter' shoe line, launched in 2003.

2   In a joint interview with Jay-Z. See: 'Warren Buffett and Jay-Z On The Power of Luck', Forbes YouTube channel, 22 September, 2010. https://youtu.be/OF4JCmqF6ec?t=96

3   Vagins, Deborah J. and Jesselyn McCrudy. 'Cracks in the System: 20 Years of the Unjust Federal Crack Cocaine Law'. ACLU, 26 October 2006. https://www.aclu.org/documents/cracks-system-20-years-unjust-federal-crack-cocaine-law. If you're wondering about the disparity, it's worth examining the social demographics of users and dealers of both drugs and assessing who tends to get the easier ride from the US justice system.

4   'Billboard Explains: How R&B/Hip-Hop Became the Biggest Genre in the U.S', *Billboard* YouTube Channel, 8 November 2021. https://www.billboard.com/music/music-news/billboard-explains-rb-hip-hop-biggest-genre-9613422/

5   Lynch, Mark. 'Foreign Policy: Jay-Z Schools Us in U.S. Hegemony', NPR, 14 July 2009. https://www.npr.org/templates/story/story.php?storyId=106588112&t=1646913344625

6   Gartner Finance Glossary.

7   Ganapati, Priya. 'June 4, 1977: VHS Comes to America', Wired.com, 4 June 2010. https://www.wired.com/2010/06/0604vhs-ces/

8   Quach, Georgina. 'Inside the Grid: 10 years of Instagram being the music industry's best friend', *Loud and Quiet*, 15 January 2021. https://www.loudandquiet.com/short/inside-the-grid/

CHAPTER 1: MARKET RESEARCH

1   Twin, Alexandra. 'How to do Market Research, Types, and Example', Investopedia.com, 14 April 2023. https://www.investopedia.com/terms/m/market-research.asp.

2   'What is an Internship?', Southern Connecticut State University. https://
    insidesouthernct.edu/internships/what-is-an-internship/what-is-an-internship.

3   'Andre Harrell Reveals Why He Fired Sean Combs', Wall Street Journal
    YouTube Channel, 19 September 2014. https://www.youtube.com/watch?
    v=vkyKkHfqzbE.

4   She labelled it a confidence- and financial acumen-building exercise. Bate,
    Ellie. 'Cardi B Told Mariah Carey Why "Nobody Could Shame Her" For
    Working As A Stripper', BuzzFeed News, 24 February 2021. https://www.
    buzzfeednews.com/article/eleanorbate/cardi-b-mariah-carey-interview-
    stripper; 'Cardi B explains why she "drugged and robbed" men', BBC
    News, 27 March 2019. https://www.bbc.co.uk/news/entertainment-arts-
    47718477.

5   Kelly, Kate. 'The Short Tenure and Abrupt Ouster of Banking's Sole Black
    C.E.O.', New York Times, 3 October 2020. https://www.nytimes.
    com/2020/10/03/business/tidjane-thiam-credit-suisse.html.

6   A dean's list is an academic award, or distinction, used to recognise the
    highest-level scholarship demonstrated by students in a college or
    university.

7   The Death Row Chronicles, BET. First broadcast 2018.

8   Street problems are issues arising from semi-legal to illegal activity in the
    urban aspects of the informal sector of the economy. Abbreviation BNBG:
    big negro, big gun.

CHAPTER 2: BUSINESS DEVELOPMENT

1   Pollack, Scott. 'What, Exactly, Is Business Development', Forbes, 21 March
    2012. https://www.forbes.com/sites/scottpollack/2012/03/21/what-exactly-is-
    business-development/.

2   'Pillow Talk' was originally written for Al Green, now known as the
    Reverend Al Green, but he refused it on moral grounds.

3   Levy was an inspiration for the character Hesh Rabkin, a former record
    executive who also happened to be a New Jersey mob boss's business
    adviser, in the HBO television series The Sopranos.

4   Blogpost by anonymous author. 'Music Legends – Sylvia Robinson', BIMM
    University blog, 4 March 2019. https://blog.bimm.co.uk/music-legends-
    sylvia-robinson.

CHAPTER 3: RAISING CAPITAL

1   Abhyanker, Raj. '8 Ways to Help Get Startup Business Funding',
    AmericanExpress.com, 6 October 2022. https://www.americanexpress.com/
    en-us/business/trends-and-insights/articles/startup-funding-8-best-ways-to-
    raise-capital/.

2   Ganti, Akhilesh. 'Angel Investor Definition and How it Works',
        Investopedia.com, 29 September 2023. https://www.investopedia.com/
        terms/a/angelinvestor.asp.

3   'Kurtis Blow on Being 1st Rapper Signed to Major Lavel, 1st Rap Single
        to Go Gold' DJ Vlad YouTube channel, 7 August 2016. https://www.
        youtube.com/watch?v=zRCvjFpfpwo

4   'Warren Buffett and Jay-Z On The Power of Luck', Forbes YouTube
        channel, 22 September, 2010. https://m.youtube.com/watch?v=04JCmqF6ee.

5   Millennial readers are likely to recognise the sound of this record as the
        Mariah Carey and ODB classic 'Fantasy', whereas Gen Z readers will
        probably recognise the sound as the summer 2022 hit 'Big Energy' by
        Latto and Mariah Carey.

6   Charnas, Dan. *The Big Pay Back: The History of the Business of Hip-Hop*. New
        York: Berkley, 2010.

7   Aswad, Jem. 'Reservoir Acquires Iconic Tommy Boy Music, Ground-
        breaking Hip-Hop Label, for $100 Million', *Variety*, 4 June 2021. https://
        variety.com/2021/music/news/reservoir-acquires-tommy-boy-1234988666/.

8   Slotnik, Daniel E. 'Matt Dike, Hit-Making Founder of Hip-Hop Label,
        Dies at 56', *New York Times*, 20 March 2018. https://www.nytimes.
        com/2018/03/20/obituaries/matt-dike-hit-making-founder-of-hip-hop-label-
        dies-at-56.html.

9   Delicious Pizza in Los Angeles is an offshoot of Delicious Vinyl.

10   'Freeway Ricky: Most Rappers Get Initially Funded by Drug Dealers (Part
        17)', DJ Vlad YouTube channel, 25 July 2021. https://www.youtube.com/
        watch?v=g_nP4yfbgDA.

11   Dry-snitching is when authorities are inadvertently or accidentally alerted
        to entrepreneurial activity that falls outside the realm of the law.

12   SOLAR Records was the recording home of acts such as Absolute,
        Babyface, Calloway, Collage, The Deele, Midnight Star, Shalamar and The
        Whispers.

13   *Harris v. Interscope Records* (California Court of Appeal, 9 June 2004). https://
        www.anylaw.com/case/harris-v-interscope-records/california-court-of-appeal/
        06-09-2004/CKO6R2YBTlTomsSB6y9g.

14   'Big Meech interview', uploaded by smurk252 to YouTube, 4 September
        2010. https://www.youtube.com/watch?v=0WcGV1X-tV8.

15   For the uninitiated, this is a reference to a scene where the *nouveau riche*
        protagonist, Tony Montana (a rough-around-the-edges Cuban immigrant
        drug baron on the up in Miami), fresh from murdering his boss and
        mentor and taking his all-American blonde wife (with her husband's blood
        still quite literally on his hands), looks out onto the Miami skyline and sees
        a blimp with an electronic ticker reading: 'THE WORLD IS YOURS'.

16   Associated Press. 'Jacob the Jeweler Jailed', CBSNews, 24 June 2008.
        https://www.cbsnews.com/news/jacob-the-jeweler-jailed/.

17 Day, Julia and Owen Gibson. 'Cameron raps Radio 1 DJ for violent lyrics', *Guardian*, 8 June 2006. https://www.theguardian.com/politics/2006/jun/08/uk.conservatives.

18 Broder, John. 'Quayle Calls for Pulling Rap Album Tied to Murder Case', *Los Angeles Times*, 23 September 1992. https://www.latimes.com/archives/la-xpm-1992-09-23-mn-1144-story.html.

19 'Sky News Australia barred for week by YouTube over Covid misinformation', BBC News, 1 August 2021. https://www.bbc.com/news/world-australia-58045787.

20 Pleat, Zachary and Brennan Suen. 'When O'Reilly Urged People to Boycott An Advertiser That Featured "A Man Who Degrades Women"', Mediamatters, 5 April 2017. https://www.mediamatters.org/fox-nation/when-oreilly-urged-people-boycott-advertiser-featured-man-who-degrades-women.

21 Coscarelli, Joe. 'Most People Who Watch Bill O'Reilly Are Rapidly Approaching Death', *New York Magazine*, 29 May 2014. https://nymag.com/intelligencer/2014/05/most-people-who-watch-bill-oreilly-are-over-70.html.

22 Reuters, 'PepsiCo Pulls Ad By Rap Musician', *The New York Times*, 29 August, 2022. https://www.nytimes.com/2002/08/29/business/pepsico-pulls-ad-by-rap-musician.html.

23 Reuters, 'Bill O'Reilly settled $32m sexual harassment claim before signing Fox News deal – report', *Guardian*, 21 October 2017. https://www.theguardian.com/media/2017/oct/21/bill-oreilly-32m-harassment-claim-fox-news-deal.

24 Mlynar, Phillip. 'The Oral History of Rawkins Records', 18 April 2014. https://upnorthtrips.com/past/83155484303/the-oral-history-of-rawkins-records-via-myspace.

25 Mlynar, Phillip. 'The Oral History of Rawkins Records'.

CHAPTER 4: MARKET ENTRY

1 'Market Entry' – definition in BDC.ca business terms glossary. https://www.bdc.ca/en/articles-tools/entrepreneur-toolkit/templates-business-guides/glossary/market-entry.

2 'What is a Product Life Cycle? (Definition, Stages and Examples). TWI.com. https://www.twi-global.com/technical-knowledge/faqs/what-is-a-product-life-cycle.

3 'Episode 180 Master P', *Drink Champs* (Podcast), 18 October 2019. https://drinkchamps.com/episodes/episode-180-w-master-p-drinkchamps/.

4 The full title was 'How To Rob (An Industry Nigga)'.

5 O'Connor, Roisin. '50 Cent and Ja Rule: A beef history', *Independent*, 7 November 2018. https://www.independent.co.uk/arts-entertainment/music/features/50-cent-ja-rule-beef-history-timeline-what-cause-rap-instagram-latest-a8621631.html.

6   Coincidentally, as 50 Cent was trashing Murder Inc. on the airwaves and on wax, Murder Inc.'s offices were raided by federal agents under the suspicion of being a money-laundering front for Kenneth 'Supreme' McGriff. A subsequent trial cleared them.

7   This was, of course, not without risk itself. Dr. Dre is known for signing artists and placing them on the shelf. But the leverage and unorthodox approach to business that 50 Cent had built up meant he just could not be ignored. The key lessons here are to look far and wide when searching for appropriate partners. And to pick partners that enhance the likelihood of successful market entry and introduction. Dr. Dre is the closest thing Hip-Hop has to a god: everyone bows before him. Eminem is the best-selling rapper ever. Interscope is the strongest entity in music. By picking them as his partners, 50 Cent's presence and prowess in the market was always likely to be earthshakingly successful.

8   Callas, Brad. 'Jim Jones Didn't Sign Drake Because He Didn't Know What to Do With Actor "In a Wheelchair" on "Disney Channel"', Complex, 28 February 2022. https://www.complex.com/music/jim-jones-didnt-sign-drake-because-actor-in-a-wheelchair-on-disney-channel.

9   Ju, Shirley. '"If Drake Goes Independent, the Music Business Is Done," Says United Masters' Steve Stoute', Variety, 18 July 2020. https://variety.com/2020/music/news/drake-independent-music-industry-business-steve-stoute-russ-1234710345/.

10 See: 'When Suge Knight Left Vanilla Ice "Very Scared"', ABC News YouTube Channel, 30 January, 2015. https://www.youtube.com/watch?v=p5b3_aS-Wy8; and 'Vanilla Ice Wrote "No Parts" of "Ice Baby" claims Co-Writer': https://allhiphop.com/news/vanilla-ice-wrote-no-parts-of-ice-ice-baby-claims-co-writer/.

CHAPTER 5: REPUTATION AND BRAND

1   Merriam Webster definition.

2   Stoute, Steve. *The Tanning of America: How Hip-Hop Created a Culture That Rewrote the Rules of the New Economy.* London: Penguin, 2011.

3   'Kid (Kid 'n Play) on Starting Failed Label with Steve Stoute, Who's Worth $55M Today (Part 2)', DJ Vlad YouTube Channel, 2 February 2021. https://www.youtube.com/watch?v=B-qYCXFQZRg.

4   Hiatt, Brian. 'Record Executive Says "Puffy" Combs Aimed To Kill Him', MTV News, 21 May 1999. https://www.mtv.com/news/514342/record-executive-says-puffy-combs-aimed-to-kill-him/.

5   Fleischer, Adam. 'Can You Believe Def Jam Passed Up On Signing Nas Over 20 Years Ago?', MTV News, 15 April 2014. https://www.mtv.com/news/1726220/def-jam-passed-up-signing-nas/.

6   Aswad, Jem. 'UnitedMasters Announces $50 Million Series B Investment Led by Apple', *Variety*, 31 March 2021. https://variety.com/2021/music/news/unitedmasters-investment-apple-1234941281/.

7   *Unjust Justice: The James Rosemond Story.* Podcast. Criminal Minded Media. First released March 2022. https://podcasts.apple.com/us/podcast/unjust-justice-the-james-rosemond-story/id1610807742.

8   Ani, Ivie. 'Jimmy Henchman Gets 2 Life Sentences for Murder of 50 Cent Affiliate Lodi Mack', Okayplayer, November 2018. https://www.okayplayer.com/news/jimmy-henchman-gets-2-life-sentences-murder-50-cent-affiliate-lodi-mack.html.

9   Unfortunately, it was sold to Martin Shkreli, a man who has widely and credibly been described as a 'scumbag'.

10   'N.O.R.E. on How Lyor Cohen Motivated Him to Make a Hit', Radiodotcom YouTube Channel, 24 March 2016. https://www.youtube.com/watch?v=RMp7y7z9H1M.

11   'Lance "Un" Rivera Breaks Silence on The Incident with Jay-Z where He Got Stabbed (Part 31)', DJ Vlad TV YouTube Channel, 20 May 2023. https://www.youtube.com/watch?v=jzfS4dDGQk0.

12   'Screw Rick Ross', The Smoking Gun, 21 July 2008. http://www.thesmokinggun.com/documents/crime/screw-rick-ross.

13   Watkins, Grouchy Greg. 'Exclusive: Rick Ross Denies Ex-Correctional Officer Claims', Allhiphop.com, 14 July 2008. https://allhiphop.com/news/exclusive-rick-ross-denies-ex-correctional-officer-claims/.

14   Flilter, Emily. 'She Spent 16 Years as Morgan Stanley's Diversity Chief. Now She's Suing.' https://www.nytimes.com/2020/06/16/business/morgan-stanley-discrimination-lawsuit.html.

15   'RUN DMC adidas: All You Need To Know About the Partnership', Sneakerbreaker.com. https://sneakerbreaker.com/run-dmc-adidas-all-you-need-to-know-about-the-partnership/.

16   Lieber, Chavie. 'How Tommy Hilfiger Thrived on Hip Hop (Without Being Accused of Cultural Appropriation)', *Business of Fashion*, 9 September 2019. https://www.businessoffashion.com/articles/fashion-week/how-tommy-hilfiger-thrived-on-hip-hop-without-being-accused-of-cultural-appropriation/.

17   Bayley, Matthew. 'So Solid Crew – man shot dead', *Daily Mail*, 13 April 2012. https://www.dailymail.co.uk/news/article-177646/So-Solid-Crew--man-shot-dead.html.

18   Weiner, Jonah. 'Dear Superstar: Method Man', Blender, November 2003. https://web.archive.org/web/20090224023412/http://www.blender.com/guide/articles.aspx?id=512.

19   Mohamed, Theron. 'Gap surges 42% after striking 10-year deal with Kanye West and Yeezy', Business Insider, 26 June 2020. https://markets.businessinsider.com/news/stocks/gap-stock-surges-10-year-apparel-deal-kanye-west-yeezy-2020-6.

NOTES

CHAPTER 6: RISK AND REWARD

1   Moyer, Justin Wm. 'Over half of dead hip-hop artists were murdered, study finds', *Washington Post*, 25 March 2015. https://www.washingtonpost.com/news/morning-mix/wp/2015/03/25/over-half-of-dead-hip-hop-artists-were-murdered-study-finds/.

2   Coleman II, C. Vernon, Kemet High and Joey Ech. 'The Current Status of Every Murdered Rapper's Case', XXLmag.com, 6 November 2022. https://www.xxlmag.com/current-status-murdered-rappers-cases/.

3   Coleman II at al., 'The Current Status of Every Murdered Rapper's Case', 2022.

4   Sisario, Ben. 'Wrongful-Death Lawsuit Over Rapper Is Dismissed', *New York Times*, 19 April 2010. https://www.nytimes.com/2010/04/20/us/20big.html. It should be noted that the lawsuit was ultimately dismissed: Martin, Dan. 'Notorious BIG death lawsuit dismissed', *Guardian*, 19 April 2010. https://www.theguardian.com/music/2010/apr/19/notorious-big-lawsuit-los-angeles.

5   Compounding the tragedy, in Detective Greg Kading's 2016 documentary *Murder Rap*, it is alleged that the person most thought to have murdered the Notorious BIG is rumoured to have been paid $15,000.

6   Jackson, Curtis. *Hustle Harder, Hustle Smarter.* New York: Amistad, 2020.

7   *Shark Tank* is the American version of the British TV show *Dragon's Den* . . . which itself happens to be the British version of the Japanese show *Tigers of Money.*

8   This is a highly lucrative yet often not recognised or remunerated concept known as 'cultural capital'.

9   Charnas, Dan. *The Big Pay Back: The History of the Business of Hip-Hop.* New York: Berkley, 2010.

10 Runcie, Dan. 'How 50 Cent's Vitaminwater Deal Influenced Hip-Hop', Trapital, 28 March 2022. https://trapital.co/2022/03/28/how-50-cents-vitaminwater-deal-influenced-hip-hop.

11 Heller, Jerry. *Ruthless: A Memoir.* New York: Simon and Schuster, 2006.

12 Heller, *Ruthless.*

13 Diaz, Angel and Jason Duaine Hahn. 'And You Know This, Mannnnn: An Oral History of *Friday*', Complex.com. https://www.complex.com/covers/oral-history-of-friday-20th-anniversary/.

CHAPTER 7: NEGOTIATION

1   'The Gangster Chronicles Episode 118: Record Company Pimps w/ Alonzo Williams (7-2021)', Digital Soapbox Network YouTube Channel, 8 December 2021. https://www.youtube.com/watch?v=gVuIK5ButrQ.

2   'Interlude: No Limits'. Solange, *Seat At The Table.*

3   Strauss, Neil. 'The Secret Power in Big Rap; Bryan Turner Makes Rap
      Records but Escapes the Criticism', *New York Times*, 3 September 1998.
      https://www.nytimes.com/1998/09/03/arts/secret-power-big-rap-bryan-
      turner-makes-rap-records-but-escapes-criticism.html.
4   Roman, Monica. 'Dimension grabs "Hook"', *Variety*, 12 January 1998.
      https://variety.com/1998/film/news/dimension-grabs-hook-1117435805/amp.
5   See Chapter 17: Finance and Legal for a detailed analysis of the deal.
6   Armour, TJ. 'The humiliating way Birdman was forced to apologize to
      industry veteran Wendy Day', rollingout.com. 23 November 2014. https://
      rollingout.com/2014/11/23/humilating-way-birdman-forced-apologize-
      industry-veteran-wendy-day/.
7   Another great place to learn to negotiate is African marketplaces.
      Everything is open to flawless and aggressive negotiation.

CHAPTER 8: PROMOTION

1   'Nipsey Hussle Lays a Smack Down Outside BET Awards', TMZ, 24 June
      2018. https://www.tmz.com/2018/06/24/nipsey-hussle-slaps-guy-bet-awards-
      parking-dispute/.
2   It became cheaper to produce the product, but the savings were not passed
      on to the consumer.
3   Rys, Dan. 'Nipsey Hussle Reportedly Makes $100,000 in One Night by
      Charging $100 for New Mixtape', *XXL*, 8 October 2013. https://www.
      xxlmag.com/nipsey-hussle-reportedly-makes-100000-in-one-night-by-
      charging-100-for-new-mixtape/.
4   Dot, B. 'Nipsey Hussle on Releasing $100 album', Rap Radar, 4 October
      2013. https://rapradar.com/2013/10/04/nipsey-hussle-on-releasing-100-
      album/.
5   There's an entire book on the subject: Keller, Ed and Jon Berry, *The
      Influentials: One American in Ten Tells the Other Nine How to Vote, Where to
      Eat, and What to Buy.* New York: Free Press, 2003.
6   https://twitter.com/i/status/1334912965762555910.
7   Maheshwari, Sapna. 'Kanye West and Gap Strike 10-Year Deal for "Yeezy
      Gap" Apparel Line', *New York Times*, 26 June 2020. https://www.nytimes.
      com/2020/06/26/business/kanye-west-yeezy-gap.html.

CHAPTER 9: VISION AND MISSION

1   Kantabutra, Sooksan. 'Vision effects: a critical gap in educational leadership
      research', *International Journal of Educational Management*, Vol. 24, No. 5
      (2010), pp. 376–390.
2   A low-income housing estate in New Orleans, famed for producing a slew
      of Southern rappers.

3   Groth, Aimee. 'Entrepreneurs don't have a special gene for risk – they
     come from families with money', Quartz, 17 July 2015. https://qz.com/
     455109/entrepreneurs-dont-have-a-special-gene-for-risk-they-come-from-
     families-with-money/.
4   'Juvenile: Tiny Desk Concert', NPR Music YouTube Channel, 30 June
     2023. https://youtu.be/kes2P4IC2bQ?t=12105.

CHAPTER 10: LEADERSHIP AND CORPORATE MANAGEMENT

1   When asked by *XXL* magazine why he left with Jay-Z, Memphis Bleek
     responded 'Brooklyn', the borough they both come from. It should be
     noted that Jay-Z discovered Memphis Bleek as a fifteen-year-old.

CHAPTER 11: PEOPLE MANAGEMENT

1   'Romney: Corporations are people too', CNN YouTube Channel, 12 August
     2011. https://www.youtube.com/watch?v=FxUsRedO4UY.
2   It is not unusual for a leading female rapper to be the only woman in her
     own crew – which would make any other woman in the group a de facto
     token woman.
3   These producers and musicians included Deric 'D-Dot' Angelettie (who a
     young Kanye West was once a ghost-producer for), Nashiem Myrick, Sean
     C & LV, Stevie J, Chucky Thompson, Mario Winans, Carlos '6 July' Broady,
     Younglord, and others.
4   Jennings, Angel. 'Diddy Rants on YouTube to Recruit New Assistant, *New
     York Times*, 30 July 2007. https://www.nytimes.com/2007/07/30/business/
     media/30Puff Daddy.html.
5   Papadatou, Aphrodite. 'Poor Management Costs UK Business £84 Billion a
     Year', HR Review, 19 June 2019. https://www.hrreview.co.uk/hr-news/
     strategy-news/poor-management-costs-uk-business-84-billion-a-year/116817.
6   Donner, Francesca. 'The true cost of a bad manager', Quatrz, 12 April
     2022. https://qz.com/work/2133725/the-true-cost-of-bad-managers/.
7   Allah, Sha Be. 'The Source Magazine Remembers "Baby Chris" Lightly
     Nine Years Later', The Source, 30 August 2021. https://thesource.com/
     2021/08/30/the-source-magazine-remembers-baby-chris-lighty-nine-years-
     later/.
8   http://mediaplayer.sourceforge.net/unitedcamps.com/vio-code/assets/CHRIS_
     LIGHTY_BIO.pdf.
9   Buckingham, Marcus. 'What Great Managers Do', *Harvard Business Review*,
     March 2005. https://hbr.org/2005/03/what-great-managers-do.
10   Charnas, Dan. *The Big Pay Back: The History of the Business of Hip-Hop*. New
     York: Berkley, 2010.

11   Witt, Stephen. 'Tekashi 69: The Rise and Fall of a Hip-Hop Supervillain',
      Rolling Stone, 16 January 2019. https://www.rollingstone.com/music/music-
      features/tekashi-69-rise-and-fall-feature-777971/.
12   Tekashi's own words.
13   Radio sensation Charlamagne Tha God warned Tekashi that inviting people
      to his genitals is a form of disrespect that necessitates that one either be
      ready to die or ready to kill. He left out the third option: ready to suck.
14   Hip-Hop's highly influential and agenda-setting premier morning radio
      show presented by Charlamagne Tha God, DJ Envy and Angela Yee.
15   'Mogul: The Life & Death of Chris Lighty Episode 2', Loud Speakers
      Network YouTube Channel, 5 July 2017. https://youtu.be/rnDmQ4y3DjE.
16   Racher, Dave. 'On Trial for Helping Off-Duty Cop Under Attack, Officer
      Passed Service Revolver to Defendant', *Philadelphia Inquirer*, 11 June 1994.
      http://articles.philly.com/1994-06-11/news/25834730_1_drug-charges-police-
      officer-service-revolver.
17   O'Callaghan, Quinn, 'The Unbearable Realness of Beanie Sigel', *Philadelphia
      Magazine*, 12 November 2015. https://www.phillymag.com/things-
      to-do/2015/11/12/beanie-sigel-what-went-wrong/.
18   'Beanie Sigel Reflects on Jay-Z Fall Out: "I've never been crushed like that
      ever in my life"', RevoltTV, 31 July 2021. https://www.revolt.tv/drink-
      champs/2021/7/31/22601785/beanie-sigel-on-jay-z-fall-out.

CHAPTER 12: DIVERSITY

1   'The D.O.C. Contrasts Working Under Suge Knight At Death Row To
      Actual Prison', UPROXX Video YouTube Channel, 5 June 2022. https://
      www.youtube.com/watch?v=d8m2cTr_dw8.
2   Wazir, Burham. 'Mutha knows best', *Guardian*, 5 August 2001. https://
      www.theguardian.com/theobserver/2001/aug/05/features.review27.
3   In 1984, the rap group UTFO scored a popular record with 'Roxanne
      Roxanne', a record about their competing love advances towards a lady
      called Roxanne being rejected. Legendary producer Marley Marl came up
      with an innovative idea to record a response record to 'Roxanne Roxanne'
      from a female perspective. He recruited thirteen-year-old Shanté Gooden to
      freestyle a response record to UTFO (over the original 'Roxanne Roxanne'
      instrumental) – in the process Gooden became 'Roxanne Shanté'. The razor-
      sharp freestyle was delivered with more advanced skill than the original
      record and eventually proved more popular too. UTFO decided to hire a
      female rapper to respond to the response. They hired Elease Jack and then
      Adelaida Martinez to perform as 'The Real Roxanne' to do the deed on a
      self-titled record, which also proved popular. This set off an extensive back
      and forth between Roxanne Shanté and The Real Roxanne that came to be
      known as the Roxanne Wars.

4   A studio-gangster is someone who is as hard as nails in the recording booth but a softie civilian in real life.

5   ChasinDatPaper, 'Detroit Rapper Danny Brown Reveals Why 50 Cent Refused To Sign Him To G-Unit "50 Didn't Sign Me Because I Wore Skinny Jeans'', PaperChaserDotCom, 22 February 2011. https://www.paperchaserdotcom.com/m/blogpost?id=3320403%3ABlogPost%3A73493.

6   Trust, Gary. 'The Weeknds's "Blinding Lights" Is the New No. 1 Billboard Hot 100 Song of All Time', *Billboard*, 23 November 2021. https://www.billboard.com/music/chart-beat/the-weeknd-blinding-lights-all-time-hot-100-1235001770/.

7   https://twitter.com/LilNasX/status/1145428812404068352?ref_src =twsrc%5Etfw%7Ctwcamp%5Etweetembed%7Ctwterm%5E1145428 812404068352%7Ctwgr%5E%7Ctwcon%5Es1_&ref_url=https%3A% 2F%2Fmashable.com%2Farticle%2Flil-nas-x-comes-out-pride-month.

CHAPTER 13: INNOVATION

1   Halperin, Shirley. 'How Adam Levine Took Control of His Career After Manager's Tragic Death', *Variety*, 27 November 2018. https://variety.com/2018/music/features/adam-levine-maroon-5-jordan-feldstein-12030 36920/.

2   Schumpeter, Joseph A., Redvers Opie (trans.). *The Theory of Economic Development: An Inquiry into Profits, Capital, Credit, Interest, and the Business Cycle.* Cambridge: Harvard University Press, 1934.

3   Nicolay and Phonte had never met in real life or spoken over the phone prior to or during the recording of *Connected*. It was an album recorded by two complete strangers over MSN Messenger – an enormous triumph of creative innovation.

4   Gee, Andre. 'From Drake to J. Cole, Little Brother's Influence On Rap Is Undeniable', UPROXX, 24 May 2019. https://uproxx.com/music/little-brother-drake-j-cole-rap-influence/#:~:text=He's%20not%20lying.,part%20 influenced%20by%20Little%20Brother.

5   'The Breakfast Club Classic – Kanye West Interview 2013', Breakfast Club Power 105.1 FM YouTube Channel, 23 November 2016. https://www.youtube.com/watch?v=zOHhaMvk-XM.

6   Guardian Music. 'Kanye West claims to be $53m in debt, and asks Mark Zuckerberg for help', 15 February 2016. https://www.theguardian.com/music/2016/feb/15/kanye-west-53m-debt-mark-zuckerberg-larry-page-martin-shkreli.

CHAPTER 14: COMPETITION

1   Marshall, Elizabeth Dilts. 'Exclusive: Goldman revamps employee reviews, opening door to greater job cuts', Reuters, 29 July 2020. https://www. reuters.com/article/us-world-work-goldman-sachs-exclusive-idUSKCN24S266.

2   Not listed here is monopsony – a unique type of competition in which all providers sell their services and goods to a single client.

3   Wayne. 'Nicki Minaj entry in Time 100 2016', *Time*, April 2016. https:// time.com/4298230/nicki-minaj-2016-time-100/.

4   Grady, Constance. 'The charismatic hustle of Cardi B', Vox, 11 February 2019. https://www.vox.com/culture/2018/1/26/16936414/cardi-b-grammys-bodak-yellow-charismatic-hustle.

5   The editors. 'Cardi B and Nicki Minaj Get Into Epic Brawl at the Harper's Bazaar ICONS Party', *Cosmopolitan*, 8 September 2018. https://www. cosmopolitan.com/entertainment/a23034552/cardi-b-and-nikki-minaj-get-into-epic-brawl-at-harpers-bazaar-icons-party/.

6   https://www.instagram.com/p/Bnc5gMAhCbD/?utm_source=ig_embed_loading.

7   https://twitter.com/i/status/1439933970582544386.

8   Ani, Ivie. 'Cardi B's Team Releases Statement Denying Nicki Minaj's Payola Claimes', Okayplayer, 11 September 2018. https://www.okayplayer. com/music/nicki-minaj-cardi-b-payola.html.

9   https://twitter.com/nickiminaj/status/1095036984332939264.

10   In 2015, Cash Money sued Jay-Z and his Tidal streaming service for 'tortuous interference with contract, unfair competition, and conversion, at least $50 million and injunction' for streaming *FWA* (*Free Weezy Tape*) on Tidal without their consent. The following year, it emerged that Cash Money didn't actually follow through with the lawsuit. See: Diep, Eric. 'Birdman Never Followed Through With His $50 Million Lawsuit Against Tidal and Jay-Z', Complex, 2 April 2016. https://www.complex.com/ music/2016/04/birdman-50-million-lawsuit-tidal-jay-z.

11   'Bubbles and bling', *The Economist*, 8 May 2006. https://www.economist. com/news/2006/05/08/bubbles-and-bling.

12   'How Elliot Wilson Co-Created ego trip, Built XXL, and Conquered Digital Hip Hop Media: Blueprint Season 1 Episode 16', Complex YouTube Channel, 6 November 2017. https://www.youtube.com/watch?v =GXok_quunTA.

13   He made this allegation in a March 2003 interview with . . . *XXL*, then under new editorship.

14   The person who leaked 'Foolish Pride' to *The Source*, a former friend of Eminem, took his own life. See: Eustice, Kyle. 'Benzino says person who sold him controversial "racist" Eminem tapes committed suicide', HipHopDx.com, 20 October 2021. https://hiphopdx.com/news/id.65313/ title.benzino-says-person-who-sold-him-controversial-racist-eminem-tapes-committed-suicide.

15   Ogunnaike, Lola. 'War of the Words at Hip-Hop Magazines', *New York Times*, 29 January 2003. https://www.nytimes.com/2003/01/29/arts/war-of-the-words-at-hip-hop-magazines.html.

16   Holmes II, Emory. 'Hip-Hop Goes Prime Time With Source Music Awards', *Los Angeles Times*, 20 August 1999. https://www.latimes.com/archives/la-xpm-1999-aug-20-ca-1854-story.html; *'The Source* Files for Bankruptcy', *Billboard*, 1 May 2007. https://www.billboard.com/music/music-news/the-source-files-for-bankruptcy-1324128/.

17   'Why 50 Cent Dissed Chamillionaire', Max Volume Music YouTube Channel, 7 January 2022. https://www.youtube.com/watch?v=mKpe9djnHbs.

CHAPTER 16: UNDERVALUED ASSETS AND CUSTOMERS

1   Vaughn, Mikeisha. 'What the Apple Bottoms Reemergence Means for Black Women', Essence, 4 November 2020. https://www.essence.com/fashion/nelly-hints-at-apple-bottom-return/.

2   Desloge, Rick. 'Vokal co-founder goes from zero to $25 million revenue in 8 years', *St. Louis Business Journal*, 26 June 2005. https://www.bizjournals.com/stlouis/stories/2005/06/27/story8.html.

CHAPTER 17: FINANCE AND LEGAL

1   'The Opie & Anthony Show: MC Hammer In-Studio (06/12/09)', O&A, R&F, TESD and Scorch Archive YouTube Channel, 1 June 2013. https://www.youtube.com/watch?v=yq8bG-MDOEM.

2   'Welcome to Death Row 2001 Documentary', Platinum Underground Records YouTube Channel, 5 February 2022. https://www.youtube.com/watch?v=45vonQJqMH0&t=419s.

3   'Fat Joe Lost Millions & Went to Jail After Being Robbed by an Accountant', Earn Your Leisure YouTube Channel, 13 March 2021. https://www.youtube.com/watch?v=J17aOEtgDqA.

4   'Young G's – Puff Daddy Feat. Jay-Z & Notorious B.I.G.', Sam YouTube Channel, 23 July 2011. https://www.youtube.com/watch?v=Ka--C2cDaXY.

5   Lifted from the title of Dele Ogun's 2009 book, *The Law, The Lawyers and the Lawless*.

6   David E. Kenner entry in Top Attorneys of North America. https://whoswhopr.com/2019/10/top-attorney-david-e-kenner/.

7   Heller, *Ruthless*.

8   'Welcome to Death Row 2001 Documentary', 5 February 2022.

9   'Welcome to Death Row 2001 Documentary', 5 February 2022.

10   Philips, Chuck. 'Tupac Shakur's Mom Sues Label for Recordings', *Los Angeles Times*, 19 April 1997. https://www.latimes.com/archives/la-xpm-1997-04-19-fi-50352-story.html.

11   Meghann-Cuniff. 'Seeking Retrial, Tory Lanez Hires Snoop Dogg and Suge Knight's Defense Lawyer', *Los Angeles Magazine*, 11 January 2023. https://www.lamag.com/citythinkblog/seeking-retrial-tory-lanez-hires-snoop-dogg-and-suge-knights-defense-lawyer/.

12   Lybrand, Holmes. 'Ex-Fugees rapper Pras Michel found guilty in scheme to help China influence US government', *CNN Politics*, 26 April 2023. https://edition.cnn.com/2023/04/26/politics/pras-michel-trial-verdict/index.html.

CHAPTER 18: DIVERSIFICATION

1   'The Studio Interview with Nipsey Hussle', Mass Appeal YouTube Channel, 26 March 2018. https://youtube.com/watch?v=lPHuZLM72U4.

2   Mangum, Aja. 'Rihanna: Beauty Chameleon', *The Cut*, 3 June 2009. https://www.thecut.com/2009/06/rihannas_beauty_evolution.html.

3   'Rihanna and LVMH Make a Deal and, Possibly, History', *New York Times*, 17 January 2019. https://www.nytimes.com/2019/01/17/fashion/rihanna-fashion-brand-lvmh.html; Berg, Madeline. 'Fenty's Fortune: Rihanna Is Now Officially A Billionaire', *Forbes*, 4 April 2021. https://www.forbes.com/sites/maddieberg/2021/08/04/fentys-fortune-rihanna-is-now-officially-a-billionaire/.

4   Berg, 'Fenty's Fortune: Rihanna Is Now Officially A Billionaire'.

5   Paulson, Sarah. 'Meet Rihanna, the Shy Gal', *Interview Magazine*, 10 June 2019. https://www.interviewmagazine.com/music/meet-rihanna-the-shy-gal.

6   'Forbes rich list: Which celebrities earned the most over the past year?', *BBC News*, 13 June 2017. https://www.bbc.co.uk/news/entertainment-arts-40248415.

7   Dealbook. 'Jay-Z Cashes in With Rocawear Deal', *The New York Times*. 6 March 2007. https://dealbook.nytimes.com/2007/03/06/jay-z-cashes-in-with-200-million-rocawear-deal/.

8   Heine, Christopher. 'Sean "Diddy" Combs Is Rebranding Ciroc for the Millenial Mindset', *AdWeek*, 17 November 2014. https://www.adweek.com/brand-marketing/sean-diddy-combs-rebranding-ciroc-millennial-mindset-161454/.

9   Heine, 'Sean "Diddy" Combs Is Rebranding Ciroc for the Millenial Mindset'.

10   'Gene Deal Says Puffy Ran After They Ran Into 2Pac at Soul Train Awards (Part 14)', DJ Vlad YouTube Channel, 11 August 2021. https://www.youtube.com/watch?v=-eQuI8RXJvI; 'Gene Deal: Puffy Said He Didn't Care if 2Pac & Biggie Died or Suge Went to Jail (Part 16)', DJ Vlad YouTube Channel, 13 August 2021. https://youtu.be/oJG06kvT5Ms?t=785.

11 'Casandra Ventura v. Sean Combs', United States District Court, Southern District of New York, Civil Case No.: 23-cv-10098. https://storage. courtlistener.com/recap/gov.uscourts.nysd.610475/gov.uscourts. nysd.610475.1.0.pdf.

12 Guardian staff and agencies. 'Sean "Diddy" Combs and singer Cassie settle abuse lawsuit one day after filing', *Guardian*, 18 November 2023. https:// www.theguardian.com/music/2023/nov/17/sean-diddy-combs-cassie-settle-abuse-lawsuit.

13 'Episode 4: Suge & Puff'. 'Collect Call with Suge Knight' Breakbeat Media YouTube Channel, 23 November 2023. https://youtube.com/ watch?v=EeYrNuTTunk?t=4525.

14 'Puff Daddy Interview at The Breakfast Club Power 105.1'. Breakfast Club Power 105.1 FM YouTube Channel, 1 April 2016. https://youtube.com/ watch?v=BsA7wpWgFZQ?t=20805.

15 Raval, Anjli and Madeline Speed. 'Diddy-owned drinks company sues Diageo alleging racial discrimination', *Financial Times*, 31 May 2023. https://www.ft.com/content/f346f7c8-429b-468f-8a00-a6f5c71585c8.

16 Raval, Anjli and Madeline Speed. 'Diageo parts ways with Diddy following social discrimination claim', *Financial Times*, 27 June 2023. https://www. ft.com/content/ba601d4d-ff2a-4765-ab35-510acca58ea3.

17 Griffin, Jonathan. 'Akon's Wakanda, grazing goats and a crumbling crypto dream', BBC N.ews, 24 December 2022. https://www.bbc.co.uk/news/ world-africa-63988368.

CONCLUSION: THEY CAME, THEY SAW, THEY CAPITALISED

1 Laurence, Rebecca. 'Hip-hop 50: The party that started hip-hop', BBC News, 11 August 2023. https://www.bbc.com/culture/article/20130809-the-party-where-hip-hop-was-born.

IDEAS—A SECRET WEAPON FOR BUSINESS

We all need creative ideas for solving challenging problems, innovating, and reconciling dilemmas. IDEAS sets forth what every executive should know about contributing to collaborative environments, thinking like a designer, and leading teams.

This book suggests a distinctive framework for collaboration informed by design thinking. Collaboration under the umbrella of such a process can be optimally effective in triggering inspiration, leading to fresh ideas that are highly responsive to stakeholders. Collaborative design thinking cannot be reduced to an algorithm; unlike math and science problems, there is no single, right answer. Nor are there formulaic or simplistic approaches, which may limit creative possibilities to solving problems or conceiving the right questions. This book will therefore:

- Render accessible the solution-oriented abilities that we all possess by providing practical tools for thinking imaginatively and critically.
- Demonstrate that elements of design thinking can be cherry-picked, weighted, and combined—depending on the project and its context—to yield a unique process for each problem.
- Focus on the collaborative approach necessary to elicit the best ideas from all stakeholders.

Rich with case studies and practical insights, this concise, ideas-oriented guide will unlock a new route to innovation for executives, managers, administrators, board members, and especially, aspiring leaders in many types of businesses.

Andrew Pressman, FAIA, an architect, Professor Emeritus and former Director of the Architecture Program at the University of New Mexico, and Adjunct Professor at the University of Maryland, leads his own award-winning design firm. He has written numerous critically acclaimed books and articles, and he holds a master's degree from the Harvard University Graduate School of Design.

IDEAS—A SECRET WEAPON FOR BUSINESS

THINK AND COLLABORATE LIKE A DESIGNER

ANDREW PRESSMAN

Routledge
Taylor & Francis Group

NEW YORK AND LONDON

Cover designed by: Andrew Pressman

First published 2025
by Routledge
605 Third Avenue, New York, NY 10158

and by Routledge
4 Park Square, Milton Park, Abingdon, Oxon, OX14 4RN

Routledge is an imprint of the Taylor & Francis Group, an informa business

Library of Congress Cataloging-in-Publication Data
Names: Pressman, Andy, author.
Title: IDEAS-a secret weapon for business : think and collaborate like a designer / Andrew Pressman.
Description: New York, NY : Routledge, 2025. | Includes bibliographical references and index.
Identifiers: LCCN 2024031122 (print) | LCCN 2024031123 (ebook) | ISBN 9781032542928 (hardback) | ISBN 9781032542829 (paperback) | ISBN 9781003416142 (ebook)
Subjects: LCSH: Creative ability in business. | Problem solving. | Creative thinking.
Classification: LCC HD53 .P74 2025 (print) | LCC HD53 (ebook) | DDC 153.4/3—dc23/eng/20240723
LC record available at https://lccn.loc.gov/2024031122
LC ebook record available at https://lccn.loc.gov/2024031123

ISBN: 9781032542928 (hbk)
ISBN: 9781032542829 (pbk)
ISBN: 9781003416142 (ebk)

DOI: 10.4324/9781003416142

Typeset in Helvetica
by Apex CoVantage, LLC

Dedicated to Lisa, Daniel, and Samantha.
I cannot imagine being
part of a better collaborative design-thinking team.

CONTENTS

EXCERPTS FROM THE TEXT

If you can go beyond overt conscious wants and delve into what really drives, excites, and motivates a person, group, or company, then you can begin to propose solutions that are enlightening, wonderful, and cost-effective.

—MADLEN SIMON

Stepping back and always asking yourself what's the big idea—what is the organizing principle to what you're doing—is a key part of design thinking.

—JAY WICKERSHAM

The mature design thinker is always ready to try something else, is not afraid of information, and is not afraid that he or she would not have another idea.

—VICTORIA BEACH

FOREWORD

"An idea is salvation by imagination."

—*Frank Lloyd Wright*[1]

This quotation from the storied architect could not be more fitting for *IDEAS—a Secret Weapon for Business*, not just because the author, Andrew Pressman, is also an architect, but because the book itself is just such an idea, reflecting opportunity for the reader to obtain economic salvation by utilizing the concrete and well-described technique of imaginative design conceptualization to solve "problems."

"Problems" is in quotation marks, as the design technique is applicable to choosing the path forward out of any uncertainty, from the critical ("How do we raise the capital to launch this business?"), to the less critical ("How can we reduce the error rate in our production line?"), to the mundane ("What should the pitch be for this upcoming sales presentation to prospect X?"). In other words, imagining every question as a problem to be solved lays that question open to the rapier of *IDEAS*, making it truly a weapon in the cause of advancement. It is noteworthy that the collaborative design thinking process can be a secret weapon for any kind of organization, not just businesses.

Importantly, while that description might lead the reader to conclude this book is only for managers, and maybe top managers at that, it is not so. A key principle of design thinking, as Mr. Pressman emphasizes, is that this weapon's most effective use occurs when the person faces the "problem," conceives the question, and then proceeds by associating others to obtain input from those well-chosen individuals, who ideally have a good mix of talents and perspectives.

Those associated individuals may well include subordinates and outsiders, and, possibly even superiors. The added value of this book is that it also provides guidance for being a good participant in the design process when led by others. It thus seems wise to complete this Foreword with another quotation, this time from a storied businessman, Sam Walton, the Walmart founder:

"Our best ideas come from clerks and stockboys."[2]

Morris A. Nunes, Esq.

Waleska, Georgia

May 2024

NOTES

1 www.azquotes.com/quotes/topics/power-of-ideas.html
2 Ibid.

PREFACE

Why is an architect—from a profession that is notoriously bad at business—writing a book about generating innovative ideas for a business audience? Because architects are great at design and collaboration! Architects typically question—and collaboratively transcend—a list of requirements for a building given to them by clients in order to create something more meaningful than simply solving the functional problem at hand. Why shouldn't other professionals take advantage of the mindset that this idea-rich process represents? It is tempting to suggest that many challenges in business—and in many types of organizations—may be expressed as design problems and effectively managed as such. Solutions to even the most mundane problems can benefit from an infusion of purposeful creativity—derived from the seemingly mystical arts of design thinking and collaboration within a talented team.

IDEAS—a Secret Weapon for Business—with its unique dual focus on collaboration and design thinking—will unravel the mystery and provide valuable guidance to excel at collaborating, innovating, and solving problems. Indeed, the part that seems to be consistently missing from the literature is *how* team members can perform successfully and work as a collaborative entity—for the good of the project.

So, what exactly is collaborative design thinking, and how is it distinct and different from other problem-solving approaches in developing and operationalizing powerful ideas? Will the reader be able to understand the process sufficiently to apply it to help solve problems or work on projects more creatively? If so, how? *IDEAS—a Secret Weapon for Business* dives into the process itself, explicitly defining collaborative design thinking and then presenting various design strategies to cultivate it, which may ultimately provide breakthrough ideas. This, in turn, delineates a way of thinking that might prove quite valuable for those who are not design professionals.

Interpreting the process of collaborative design thinking and *customizing* it so that it will be personally relevant and useful is not easy, but let us stipulate from the outset that the effort is worth it! The best process is inherently dynamic, changing in response to the nature of the situation and the individuals involved. A project leader can adjust the collaborative design thinking approach to the required matrix of specialties, personalities, tasks, and circumstances—and determine how and when collaboration occurs—to yield the best possible outcome. Here is where the art of collaborative design thinking is manifest. Moreover, because collaborative design thinking is a process, the ideas are scalable so as to address a full spectrum of ventures large and small—from the most vexing to the everyday.

IDEAS is more than a simple guidebook; it challenges the status quo—and the reader—to think critically about both collaboration and design thinking in order to apply a unique form of problem solving from inception to completion. It is suggested that truly effective collaborative design thinking is a means to reassert leadership in business.

IDEAS supports the notion that collaborative design thinking must be taken seriously as a generalizable and multidimensional process with rigorous discipline in contrast to casual teamwork. For example, taking time to reflect systematically and critically on the process may be essential to its successful outcome: Viewing intrinsic tension, discord, or opposing viewpoints as constructive on the path to a solution, instead of as simply annoying, can serve as a relevant, even liberating insight. "Teamwork" has become ubiquitous and is used as a buzzword to connote anything from a very casual group encounter or one-time work session to participating on a committee. Collaborative design thinking, on the other hand, requires a studied commitment to a sequenced, multilayered process with discrete magnitude and direction.

The following three vignette abstracts, among many other stories that are elaborated and woven throughout the book, demonstrate how collaborative design thinking can help to create order out of complexity, reconcile conflicts, integrate many variables, and consider constraints as the fuel that motivates great solutions. It is hoped that some of the lessons from the stories recounted herein will be applicable to readers' unique circumstances and will inspire more widespread use of effective collaboration and design thinking.

- A great example of how collaborative design thinking supports government is the way former New Hampshire congressman Richard N. Swett, a Democrat, started work on H.R. 1, which became the Congressional Accountability Act (1995) that he coauthored. The law was part of the Republican Party agenda in the Contract with America. The act requires members of Congress to abide by the same laws it passes for the rest of the country. Swett began the process with an open-ended brainstorming session by his committee members that later coalesced into the landmark legislation. While the approach at first seemed to invite chaos, it helped bring all the pieces sought together in a meaningful way.

- Another example is the way Meredith Kauffman, a PhD involved in consumer products, led teams that devised improvements to denture adhesive dispensers. One solution for partial dentures, which use a very viscous, experimental adhesive, was to rethink the original tube design and develop a novel applicator similar to a clicking pen and for which each click provided a metered dose. It is easier on an arthritic hand and would not require a squeezing force.

- Still another breakthrough outcome of collaborative design thinking came from James Barker, former President of Clemson University. Barker helped to disrupt a thought loop that the team was stuck in by diagramming the university's relationship to the region's automobile industry as overlapping circles. Ultimately, the team saw that there was no existing overlap and that the connection needed to be made. The result: six new buildings on the campus forming the International Center for Automotive Research, and $220 million invested by South Carolina's private corporations.

IDEAS—a Secret Weapon for Business is for leaders who want to grow their collaborative leadership skills and elicit the best work from partners and collaborators. And it is for team members who seek insights to better job performance, innovative project outcomes, and an appreciation for both the leader's role and their own. Executives, managers, administrators, board members, and those who aspire to those positions in many types of organizations will benefit from this book.

Cooperation is a natural social characteristic in animal and primate realms.[1] However, among humans, there are variables that interfere with that tendency, such as politics, personality, money, power, and ambition. Charles Darwin[2] was prophetic when he said, "In the long history of humankind, those who learned to collaborate and improvise most effectively have prevailed." Learning to collaborate effectively, create fresh ideas, and design innovative solutions to problems will ensure that an organization constantly evolves to maintain a competitive advantage. May this book help you to do just that.

Andrew Pressman, FAIA

Washington, D.C.

May 2024

NOTES

1 Martin A. Nowak, "Why We Help," *Scientific American* 307, no. 1 (July 2012): 36–39.
2 Charles Darwin, accessed February 5, 2024, www.goodreads.com/author/quotes/12793.Charles_Darwin

ACKNOWLEDGMENTS

First and foremost, I want to thank Francesca Ford, Publisher, Architecture, for referring me to Meredith Norwich, Senior Editor, Business and Management. This opportunity opens up a new audience for my mandate to promote a special brand of collaborative design thinking to the business community.

I am grateful to Meredith Norwich for recognizing the value and potential of this endeavor and for her support and professionalism throughout the publication process.

Sincere appreciation and special thanks to the Routledge production team, especially Alison Macfarlane and Bethany Nelson.

I am deeply indebted to Maury Nunes for writing a powerful and articulate Foreword and for providing many constructive ideas and edits throughout the manuscript.

I would like to acknowledge Peter Pressman for superior editorial acumen and incisive critiques.

The following individuals (in alphabetical order) graciously gave their time to be interviewed and contributed wonderful insights that significantly enrich this volume: James Barker, Victoria Beach, Gabrielle Bullock, Mark Childs, Charles Heuer, Mark Johnson, Meredith Kauffman, Bon Ku, Scott Phillips,

Diego Ruzzarin, Roger Schwabacher, Mady Simon, Richard Swett, Michael Tardif, and Jay Wickersham.

And, of course, much gratitude and love to Lisa, Samantha, and Daniel for providing sage advice and inspiration, as always.

All figures are by Andrew Pressman unless otherwise noted.

1

COLLABORATIVE DESIGN THINKING OVERVIEW

Collaborative design thinking is a team approach to problem solving that is based upon the process of design. This is a methodology that becomes extremely powerful as it intersects with another distinct skill set—collaboration. The fusion of these two discrete sets of

DOI: 10.4324/9781003416142-1

skills and patterns will be explored and operationalized for an array of professional landscapes.

The collaborative design thinking process is framed, clarified, placed in perspective, and thoroughly analyzed in the forthcoming chapters. Importantly, the book sets forth a dynamic template for the process, which can itself be "designed" or customized as a function of a particular challenge. Here, the book begins to unravel some of the vagueness typically associated with design thinking by clearly examining the process as a whole; identifying and analyzing all the various building blocks or components of design thinking; and determining which components can best be applied and prioritized for a given field and specific situation, culminating in a comprehensive master plan that has been driven and shaped by design thinking.

It will be shown that the elements of the design thinking process can be cherry-picked, refined, weighted, and combined into various hybrids, depending on the problem and its context, to yield a unique process for each problem. Running through a series of elements could be considered completion of a customized loop, which will produce new information and effective ideas—and may either crystallize a solution to a problem or suggest new questions for yet another loop of inquiry, which will yield more synthetic insight and build on previous ideas.

Various tools and strategies that can nurture curiosity, exploration, and discovery and advance the collaborative design thinking process to arrive at the optimal solutions will also be described. Insights will be offered to help support an open mind in order to further optimize potential as a collaborative design thinker.

DEFINING COLLABORATION AND DESIGN THINKING

Collaboration

John Cleese of Monty Python fame captured the essence of a collaborative process in the following vignette.

The really good idea is always traceable back quite a long way, often to a not very good idea which sparked off another idea that was only slightly better, which somebody else misunderstood in such a way that they then said something which was really rather interesting.[1]

It is implicit in this funny account that knowledge is freely exchanged, can be misinterpreted, but somehow becomes synergistic. The serious and sometimes accidental business of generating a good idea is enjoyable for a skilled yet diverse team.

Collaboration is a collective intellectual function that can be a force multiplier in an effort to reach an intended objective. In a general sense, collaboration represents a device for leveraging resources. Collaboration requires efficient communication channels between all levels, dimensions, and distances for those striving toward an objective. Collaboration requires a well-defined process, rigorous discipline, and critical reflection throughout time.

There is a spectrum of collaborative activities and styles—even without being informed by design thinking. Collaboration can range from a casual comment in the midst of a phone conversation, to the result of a napkin sketch that triggers new ideas, or during a work session that includes well-choreographed brainstorming toward creation of various alternative solutions to vexing problems.

Critiquing each other's work is a form of simple collaboration. Everyone benefits from bouncing ideas off someone else; talking to just one other person can clarify a proposition, or perhaps suggest an alternative path of investigation, or even modify a good idea to make it better—that's the most basic form of collaboration. Even if the other person says nothing, the simple act of talking out loud can spark an idea, or similarly, an individual's comments can elicit a new idea or approach from someone else (as in the John Cleese quote just presented).

Another example of collaboration in action is a songwriting session with Adele, the British soul singer, and Paul Epworth, a songwriter and producer. This is a universal experience and could just as well be a brainstorming session in any number of disciplines. Mr. Epworth describes it as follows.

> A good musical collaboration is like a Jackson Pollock of musical paint, where everyone's throwing ideas at a canvas and some of them stick and some of them don't, and the final picture you end up with is a combination. She'd come forth with an idea, and I'd say, "How about this," and it develops and hybridizes on its own into something.[2]

Incorporation of critical comments (one of the building blocks of design thinking described in Chapter 2) almost always translates to an opportunity to make the work even more potent. Change does not have to be viewed as compromise; rather, it is something that can potentially make a project more responsive to a client requirement, an aesthetic priority, a technical issue, a unique circumstance, and so on.

Conversations and critiques can serve to question the status quo, the preconceptions, and the automatic responses to what may appear to be typical problems. Conversations and critiques, then, can be considered a fundamental type of genuinely sustainable collaboration. This assertion may sound self-evident, but in today's digital world, even basic communication seems often reduced to acronyms, icons, and memes. Real exchange, discourse, and enlightenment—the synergy of conversation—seems increasingly absent. We may be more immediately efficient, but in the long term, the solutions we develop often seem to fall short. Getting into the anatomy of routine informal collaboration, we need look no further than presenting a project in process to colleagues, who would constructively critique the work—perhaps outside of the office context and away from the constraints of a business environment. There is great benefit to this type of external, collaborative review. Fresh eyes, unimpeded by explicit or implicit agendas, can be focused on quality and introduce new perspectives. The greater exposure there is to diversity in points of view, the more possibilities become evident. Benefits also accrue to the reviewers. Experience in evaluating the work of others will augment one's fund of knowledge, improve collaborative and interpersonal skills, and will also contribute to more objective and effective self-criticism.

Attitude is important. Everyone on a team has an obligation to strive for the group's success. Roger Goldstein, FAIA,[3] Principal at Goody Clancy, believes that attitude has more to do with building rapport than anything else. He says, "Being respectful of peoples' contributions, even if you disagree or think some ideas are not worthwhile, helps on the trust dimension" and inevitably will reinforce the habit of vocal contribution.

Scott Simpson, FAIA,[4] Principal and Senior Director at the Cambridge office of KlingStubbins, elaborates on attitude:

> Collaboration is an attitude more than a process. Participants assume that each member of the team has something valuable to offer, and that by using many brains synergistically rather than working in "silos," overall outcomes will be dramatically improved. In a collaborative effort, it is understood that different points of view add richness and depth to the project, but this means that ego must take a back seat.

I hasten to qualify Simpson's point; opposing viewpoints may also slow progress and create an impasse. This is where a team leader must intervene and keep the effort moving ahead. There is a delicate balance between promoting discussion of conflicting ideas that may lead to innovation and knowing when to advance the work.

Design Thinking

There is no general agreement on a precise definition of design thinking; there are variations across disciplinary cultures, and different meanings depending on its context.[5] The design process is dynamic and can be complicated, messy, and nuanced as a function of specific realm and application. Moreover, there are additional layers of mystery associated with creativity itself, hence the challenge inherent in efforts to define it.

Notwithstanding the daunting qualifications noted earlier, it is imperative to develop a general sense of design thinking—a view from 35,000 feet—in order to set the stage for an explicit delineation of the specific components of the design thinking process. First, here are some general thoughts. Design thinking is:

- A process that results in a plan of action to improve a situation.

- A skill that incorporates situational awareness and empathy into idea generation.

- A tool that invokes analytical as well as creative thought to solve problems that consider context, stakeholder requirements and preferences, logistical issues, and cost.

- A mindset in which ideas are triggered from diverse, even discrepant sources, and then built upon to inform progressively better solutions to challenges.

- A series of actions and an accumulation of provisional inputs that are structured by a loop in which problems are defined, research and analysis are conducted, and ideas are proposed and then subjected to critical feedback and modification, which in turn leads to repeating parts of the loop to further refine the ideas.

Personally, I would characterize design thinking as a fundamentally creative process that is driven by specific problems and individuals yet transcends conventional or obvious solutions. While there is no magic formula, I would assert that the components of design thinking can be studied, systematically characterized, and rationally wedded to a process that yields effective and innovative solutions. Moreover, while a great outcome isn't always possible, design thinking can help to identify an optimal one. Focusing and beginning to operationalize, it includes the following building blocks:

- ***Information gathering***. Thoroughly research the context and stakeholders to arrive at a deep understanding of all relevant issues, conflicts, and constraints surrounding the problem. Examine historical perspectives and a range of precedents that might be applicable to the problem. Conduct effective interviews, perform a mini-ethnography, and consult with key knowledgeable people to accelerate understanding. All of these data may provide a richer background that informs the design investigation and may trigger ideas.

- **Problem analysis and definition**. Rigorous analysis is necessary to ensure identification of the most salient problem, which may be masked because of an immediate acceptance of the problem at face value. Question the status quo; question initial assumptions and reframe the problem. Analysis is also a meaningful prerequisite for brainstorming; it results in a clear, orderly, and fine-grained view of the problem from multiple perspectives.

- **Idea generation**. Brainstorming and visioning sessions to create as many ideas—good and bad, both conventional and unconventional (and even silly)—as possible, informed by the information gathered to date together with the problem analysis. Consider and combine various influences to create innovative diagrammatic concepts or outlines of ideas.

- **Synthesis through modeling**. Take the best ideas to a higher degree of resolution and detail, resulting in several alternative prototypes, models, or draft solutions. These vehicles not only serve as good simulations of proposed preliminary solutions but, most importantly, can and should facilitate manipulation, experimentation, and even play. In all cases, regardless of success or failure, learning and discovery are paramount.

- **Critical evaluation**. With this essential step of testing the model, there is an opportunity to make the solution or project better; to validate (or not) concepts and solutions relative to the problem definition by subjecting them to critical appraisal from stakeholders, colleagues, and objective outsiders. Feedback from stakeholders is especially valuable to make meaningful revisions. Embrace constructive criticism from whatever source, make changes without diluting a strong idea, and test again.

Solutions should pass through the aforementioned loop of components as many times as appropriate to the problem (see Figure 1.1). In other words, get feedback, evaluate the outcomes, adjust the components, and repeat the loop with new data. Then implement. The clichés apply: nothing succeeds like a try, and nothing succeeds like a response to the most recent failure.

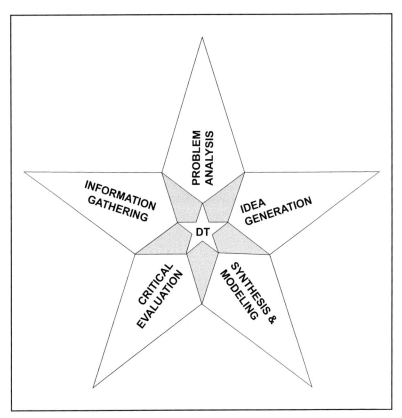

Figure 1.1 The fundamental building blocks of design thinking (DT) that together form a "loop." This diagram is intended to underscore the nonlinear nature of DT, and how the blocks may be interconnected and overlapped.

How Is Design Thinking Distinct and Different From Other Problem-Solving Approaches?

Design thinking is *not* an algorithm; unlike math and science problems, there is no single, right answer; there are multiple solutions, some perhaps more optimal than others. Indeed, design thinking—especially learning about problems through analyzing context and stakeholders—is closely aligned with social science thinking. Likewise, journalistic approaches to gathering information[6] — a very important first step — is integral to design thinking. Peter Merholz makes the point that design thinking can be a great complement to other disciplinary ways of approaching problems, bringing a diversity of perspectives to bear to solve complex problems.[7]

The process of design thinking may be disruptive in a most constructive fashion. When a potential solution is evaluated, it may actually lead to a change in the initial question, or even to a significant modification or rejection of the original hypothesis. The term "disruptive technologies" is attributed to Clayton M. Christensen and Joseph Bower, who used it in their 1995 *Harvard Business Review* article, "Disruptive Technologies: Catching the Wave." Since then, the term has evolved to include any innovation that disrupts conventional models. Disruption, then, is one element that fundamentally distinguishes design thinking from straight hypothesis testing or conventional research.

CUSTOMIZING THE PROCESS

A prescriptive how-to "step-by-step" approach to design thinking, while useful in some situations, may be flawed by oversimplifying or by positing rigid algorithms. These pitfalls may discourage or suppress innovation, unique personal perspectives, and nuances. So before jumping into the work, consider the degree to which each of the building blocks summarized in the previous section (and detailed in the next chapter) are applicable.

The building blocks are dynamic and can be cherry-picked, modified, prioritized, and choreographed into various hybrids and amalgamations (see Figures 1.2, 1.3, and 1.4). Take cues from the specific circumstances of the problem — the stakeholders, context, and the nature of the problem itself — to yield a unique design thinking method for each situation. A fresh gestalt arises with each and every project, which is one reason that design thinking is so fascinating and exciting. *The process can be just as creative and unique as the outcome.* Keep your eyes open and free your imagination in response to the challenge at hand.

A design thinking master plan for a particular problem can be developed as a general guide or template. Certainly, there will be variations in focus, content, and sequence of steps as a function of personal and project idiosyncrasies, and some steps may even be skipped or combined. For example, the information gathering and problem analysis blocks may be merged, condensed, or omitted entirely when there is already a reasonable familiarity with the problem, its background, and surrounding issues (see Figure 1.2).

Another scenario could imply that idea generation and synthesis through modeling blocks should be intertwined. If the deliverable is a written proposal

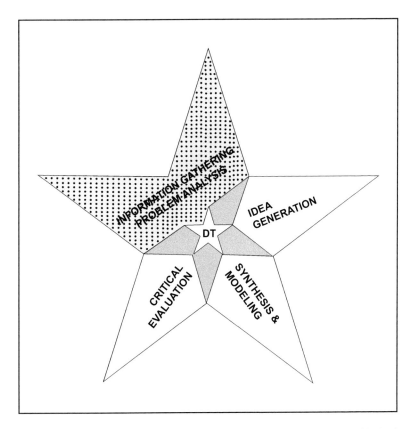

Figure 1.2 The information gathering and problem analysis blocks (gray with dots) may be merged, condensed, or omitted entirely when there is a reasonable familiarity with aspects of the problem, its background, and surrounding issues.

or business plan, for example, writing a draft and producing a final document (prototype) are all part of the same, continuous effort. It makes no sense to have an artificial boundary, especially when individual work habits are so variable (see Figure 1.3).

Expanding the idea generation block to include representative stakeholders by conducting a special workshop or "charrette" (see the next paragraph) is a potential opportunity to advance the work (see Figure 1.4). As an

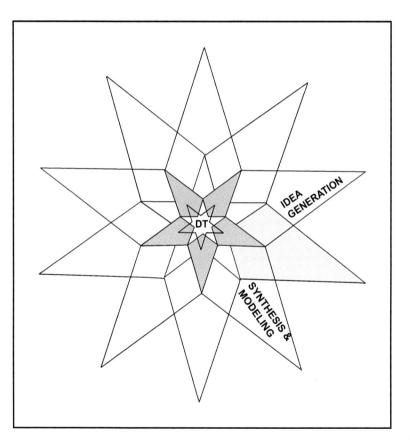

Figure 1.3 Depending on the specific challenge and individual work habits, some building blocks may be intertwined as part of a continuous effort; for example, idea generation and synthesis and modeling (light gray).

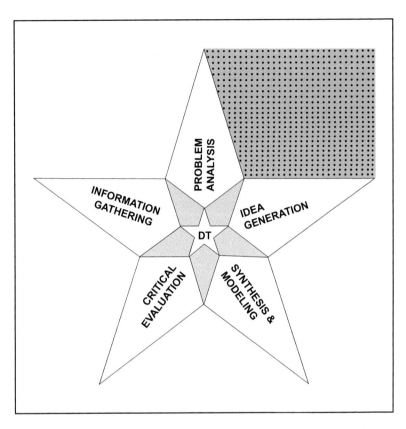

Figure 1.4 Expanding blocks, such as problem analysis and idea generation, to include representative stakeholders (gray with dots) may be an opportunity to enrich the process as a function of the unique problem circumstances.

added benefit, this strategy may also *incorporate* the information gathering and problem analysis blocks by diving into the "design" work at the start. It launches ideation as a means to fully grasp all the issues and salient factors; to elicit more information and develop detailed, relevant questions; and to test preliminary ideas and an overarching vision for the solution—and to receive immediate feedback on which to base further investigations.

Charrette is a term used to describe a process technique to jump-start creative design thinking, usually at the beginning of a project, and involves a total immersion in brainstorming investigations in a very compressed, uninterrupted time frame. This strategy can be extremely effective, even inspiring, in identifying key issues and as a starting point for meaningful in-depth discussions with stakeholders. (See Sidebar 3.1, "Workshop and Reflection at Each Milestone," for details on charrettes.)

A slightly different way of imagining the design thinking process is described by Tim Brown, former Chair of IDEO, an innovation and design firm in Palo Alto, California. He says: "The design process is best described metaphorically as a system of spaces rather than a predefined series of orderly steps." Brown tags the spaces as follows: (1) *inspiration*—for the circumstances (i.e., problems, opportunities) that motivate the search for solutions; (2) *ideation*—for the process of generating, developing, and testing ideas that may lead to solutions; and (3) *implementation*—for the charting of a path to market (or to wherever or however the solution is manifest).[8] Just as with the iterative loops described earlier, as work evolves, it passes through the first two "spaces" multiple times.

In contrast to a rigid formula for design thinking, creating a diagrammatic framework (as exemplified in Figures 1.2, 1.3, and 1.4) for engaging a specific problem provides guidance while promoting flexibility—and suggests an optimal, customized design thinking process—based upon unique individual and problem circumstances.

Sidebar 1.1 Implementing a Strategic Technology Plan

Design thinking has been recognized as an important means to innovate in the context of developing new products and technologies. But design thinking can also be applied to other business-related challenges such as devising entrepreneurial practice models, expanding professional services, operations, and even setting fees or pricing plans.

One of the things I so enjoy about my work is that whatever the particular challenge or business problem is, I always take a design approach to developing a solution. One of the most important aspects of that approach is that it enables me to maintain a focus on the "big picture," or overall vision, even as I'm grappling with the weedy details. When talking to other business owners and entrepreneurs, a common refrain is feeling overwhelmed by all the logistical/management details that have to be attended to, and that can suck the life out of your dream. I certainly have my bad days like everyone else but having a vision and a high tolerance for ambiguity (which is the same as having a high tolerance for risk) are enormously helpful to me. It puts the tedious details of running a business into a larger context and gives those activities meaning.

—Michael Tardif

Michael Tardif has over 20 years of experience applying information technologies to the design, construction, operation, and maintenance of buildings. He currently leads Building Informatics Group based in North Bethesda, Maryland.

Strategic Plan as Jigsaw Puzzle

Michael had been asked to develop a strategic technology plan to implement Building Information Modeling software in a construction company—complete with itemized tasks and schedule milestones—and then "drive" implementation of the plan. After studying business operations for three months, he realized that rolling out a strategic plan—executing a linear sequence of steps—would fail, because it would be so highly invasive and disruptive to existing business operations. Instead, Michael proposed a vision (or design concept)—a set of measurable goals for the company to achieve—and then set out to achieve those goals opportunistically, in a nonlinear fashion, without working out the specifics of execution in advance.

To accomplish this daunting undertaking, Michael invented a brilliant metaphor: *strategic plan as jigsaw puzzle*. Michael sought opportunities

Figure 1.5 Strategic plan as jigsaw puzzle. Insert pieces as appropriate, in nonlinear fashion, to complete the vision.

on different projects to implement portions of the strategic plan; in other words (invoking the metaphor), putting puzzle pieces into place wherever he could. The process was messy and nonlinear. Michael and the staff had to synthesize information as it became available and make adjustments to the "design solution" while maintaining the vision. But the vision always remained clear, and the "complete picture" of the strategic plan emerged over time. This was fundamentally a design thinking process.

When the process began, Michael knew conceptually what the end result should look like but didn't quite know how they would get there. If they had waited to have all the detailed elements in place before starting, they would have never started. And they would have failed, because the details would have been wrong and would have diverted attention from the overall vision they were trying to achieve.

The puzzle metaphor proved more useful than Michael could have dared to hope for. Conversations about the strategic plan revolved around the question, "What piece of the puzzle is that?" Most importantly, at any point in time, no one cared that the picture was incomplete; staff understood that they were moving toward a complete picture and understood how they were getting there. Michael could have called the strategic planning a design process instead of a jigsaw puzzle, but that metaphor would have been lost on anyone other than architects.

Eureka Moments and Intuitive Leaps

Michael frequently has Eureka moments in the course of solving problems. In the previous example, the Eureka moment was finding the right metaphor—jigsaw puzzle—that others could understand and rally around. That metaphor broke the logjam both for Michael and the company and enabled them to move forward successfully.

Eureka moments don't just happen. All one can do is create the circumstances (via imagination and awareness) that will enable them to occur. It requires a willful, temporary suspension of disbelief and—as Michael Graves once famously said—a high tolerance for ambiguity. Design constraints exist only in the physical world; they don't exist in the mind. So, one or more constraints can be held at bay while others are pondered (i.e., look at one piece of the puzzle). Doing this allows analysis of a problem from multiple angles. Eventually, a view of the problem comes into focus that suggests one or more potentially viable solutions. Prospective solutions can be tested against the constraints until the best solution is identified and operationalized.

According to Michael's analysis of design thinking, the most important factors to consider when addressing a full spectrum of problems include the following.

- Recognizing that every problem has a solution—not a perfect solution, but an optimum solution (there are always tradeoffs).

- Recognizing that all of the information needed to solve any problem is not available when you start working on the problem.

- Recognizing that you have to begin developing solutions before you have all the information you need to arrive at an optimum solution.

- Recognizing that your process may lead to one or more dead ends, which may require you to rethink your original assumptions.

RATIONALE FOR COLLABORATING

The ability to work effectively in teams has become increasingly important because of the generally increasing complexity of projects requiring expertise from a variety of specialties and demands from clients for better results. Soaring consumerism has set the bar for products and services higher than ever before, and negotiating an ever more complex regulatory landscape only adds to the need for collaborative work, early and often!

It could be argued that the final outcome—the product of collaborative design work—is actually superior to initiatives that may involve only a solo practitioner or single principal, regardless of that agent's talent or experience. Michael Schrage[9] takes it one step further: "Collaboration does not curtail the [manager's] overarching vision. Collaboration becomes a medium that makes the vision possible." It would seem that there could be no better time for seizing the opportunity to reestablish and operationalize the notion of team practice and collaboration.

The following list underscores the urgency and need for multidisciplinary collaboration.

- ***Competitive advantage achieved through strategic collaborations***. The caveats, of course, are that everyone must embrace their respective roles and work together well.

- ***The requirement for environmental sensitivity***. The conventional wisdom is that multidisciplinary collaboration must occur at project inception—and conception—if sustainable or environmentally sensitive outcomes are to be successful.

- **Unstable and recessionary economic trends**. Especially during these times, clients require the assurance of an optimal cost-effective and efficient process with reliable quality in outcomes.

- **Innovations in technology**. Many state-of-the-art practices, which are increasingly required by clients, are inherently collaborative.

- **Globalization**. Culturally, environmentally, and economically sensitive design is at a premium. Collaboration provides a means to deliver appropriate services internationally.

- **Contractual and liability issues**. In some cases, these concerns have heretofore impeded the best possible collaborative environment for multidisciplinary participants and are starting to be addressed by sophisticated clients and firms who are advocating risk-sharing and risk-allocation provisions in alliancing contracts, and by the participants themselves.

Why Is There Resistance to Collaboration?

There are many forces that collectively and progressively have tended to encourage working in isolation and that must be unlearned or overcome in order to be successful at collaborating. Here are some examples of those forces; acknowledging and recognizing them may help to actively surmount the problems.

- Many people abhor working in teams because, for a variety of reasons, team members do not equally share the burden of work. A great deal of resentment can build up if one or two people feel they are unfairly carrying the workload of others.

- Many academic programs still implicitly celebrate a subculture in which graduates spend their careers working as heroic, solitary, and palpably elitist individuals. This attitude has been represented and perpetuated by the Howard Roark character in Ayn Rand's *The Fountainhead*,[10]

"Norman won't collaborate."

Figure 1.6 Notwithstanding this image of the heroic, solitary designer, cooperation is a natural social characteristic in animal and primate realms. We must cultivate this innate tendency to work successfully in multidisciplinary creative teams.

Source: Robert Weber/The New Yorker Collection/www.cartoonbank.com.

which remains a best-selling novel even today. Roark jarringly summarized the point: "No great work is ever done collectively, by a majority decision. Every creative job is achieved under the guidance of a single individual thought."

- Avoiding the stigma of failure has contributed to defensive, noncollaborative, risk-averse, and, ironically, low-energy behavior.

- Decision-making by a single individual is faster—not necessarily better—than in a collaborative context.

- The importance of establishing a professional reputation based on one's own body of work—either in academia or the profession—is considered necessary for career advancement in many cases. University faculty, for example, do not become tenured professors unless they can demonstrate national and international renown based on their own individual portfolio of scholarly and creative work. As professors are role models, this situation certainly has an influence on their students.

- In terms of professional recognition, awards and publications typically celebrate individuals, not teams. The attention that is associated with this publicity helps to market services and acquire commissions or new clients.

When Not to Collaborate

All projects typically require a certain amount of collaboration with consultants or others on all but the smallest-scale projects. However, the great caution, of course, in the realm of collaboration is that the work is indeed amenable to a team approach and that an individual could not better or more efficiently execute it. It must be recognized that some challenges (or parts of some challenges) are, in fact, best met by a single, good performer—or well-seasoned professional. Moreover, collaboration can consume lots of time and resources. Therefore, in the master plan of executing a project, *there will be an amalgamation of teamwork and individual work in some ideal proportions* as designated by the leader. And, it is important to underscore that good leadership augments collaboration; a leader may provide special motivation, coordination, and the overall management that assures effective and efficient collaboration.

NOTES

1 Michael Schrage, *No More Teams: Mastering the Dynamics of Creative Collaboration* (New York: Currency/Doubleday, 1995), 33.
2 James C. McKinley Jr., "Hot Tracks, the Collaborative Method," *The New York Times*, February 9, 2012.
3 Roger Goldstein, personal communication with the author, November 3, 2008.
4 Scott Simpson, personal communication with the author, October 24, 2008.

5 Ulla Johansson-Sköldberg, Jill Woodilla, and Mehaves Çetinkaya, "Design Thinking: Past, Present and Possible Futures," *Creativity and Innovation Management* 22, no. 2 (2013): 121.

6 Peter Merholz, "Why Design Thinking Won't Save You," *Harvard Business Review Blog Network*, October 9, 2009.

7 Ibid.

8 Tim Brown, "Design Thinking," *Harvard Business Review* 86, no. 6 (June 2008): 88–89.

9 Michael Schrage, *No More Teams: Mastering the Dynamics of Creative Collaboration* (New York: Currency/Doubleday, 1995), 46.

10 Ayn Rand, *The Fountainhead* (New York: The Bobbs-Merrill Company, 1943).

2

BUILDING BLOCKS OF DESIGN THINKING

INFORMATION GATHERING

Design thinking begins with an immersion in the unique circumstances of the problem. It is a process of discovery in which clues to the solution may become evident as the issues are explored fully and deeply from multiple perspectives.

DOI: 10.4324/9781003416142-2

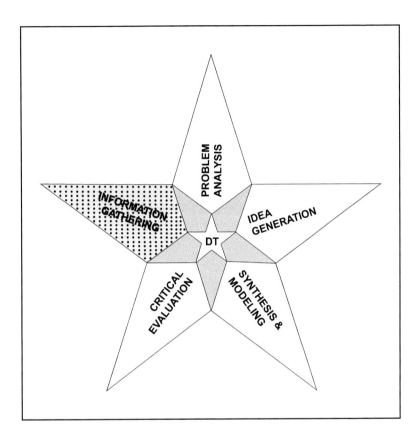

Empathy

Borrowing from anthropology, conducting an abbreviated and customized form of qualitative research—ethnography—or what Clifford Geertz described as "thick description,"[1] is a way to become immersed in a problem and go beyond a superficial understanding. In an increasingly high-tech and sterile world, spending time with, effectively observing, and interacting with stakeholders in their natural surroundings can reveal much about the relevant issues, illuminate motivations, provide insight about underlying positions, and generate ideas about solutions. Conducting an effective focused interview is a fabulous tool for this type of information gathering and is a very valuable and surprisingly undervalued component of the design thinking process.

An alternative or adjunct to the interview is to enlist an expert who can provide a briefing on the issues and thus accelerate understanding of the problem. However, there is really no substitute for a firsthand participant-observation perspective, which can facilitate "an emotional connection to a problem, and with that connection comes insight."[2] Madlen Simon, a professor at the University of Maryland who teaches a course on design thinking, neatly underscores this point:

> We often don't know the people who matter in our interactions. That's valuable in order to acquire knowledge that is relevant and important. Therefore, it is great to have a toolkit of skills for learning how to better understand people. People always have to be involved. The concept of immersing yourself in another person's environment and situation—asking probing questions at a minimum—is essential.[3]

Because stakeholders often have difficulty in articulating needs and problems, there is an opportunity to be a creative diagnostician in the design thinking process. Moreover, if you simply accept a problem at face value, you can only deliver a solution to that problem. If, however, you can go beyond overt conscious wants and delve into what really drives, excites, and motivates a person, group, or company, then you can begin to propose solutions that are enlightening, wonderful, and cost-effective. *The universe starts to open up once you get inside the minds of people or groups*.[4] One of the great attributes of design thinking is this ability to transcend the pragmatic and do more than merely solve a *given* problem.

Sidebar 2.1 Visioning, Listening, and Diagramming at a University

Design thinking can prepare you to accomplish a great deal more than you realize—be open to what those possibilities might be.
—James Barker

James Barker, former President of Clemson University, transformed the university by launching major economic development initiatives, raising more than $1 billion in private funding, and leading Clemson through a period of deep funding cuts, resulting in a financially healthier institution today than it was before the recession.

Design thinking—particularly *visioning, listening, and diagramming*—had prepared Jim Barker to serve as President of the university in so many ways that it gave him a certain confidence about what he might be able to achieve. The following accounts illustrate how Jim successfully applied these key components of design thinking to his nearly 14-year-long tenure as President, and how they can be generalizable to many types of problems.

Visioning

Design thinking enables you to see things that aren't there—as President, Jim claims that visioning was absolutely essential. And then it behooves you to effectively communicate what those visions are, why they are valuable, and why dollars, energy, and time should be invested in those things that do not yet exist. The notion of vision is very important because it provided the campus community with something to critique and rally around, or occasionally advise that the vision—or part of it—was a bad idea.

Jim's vision was that in ten years Clemson ought to be a top-20 public university in the *U.S. News* ranking. They were 74th at the time. The Board asked Jim and his team to produce metrics. They submitted a report card every quarter, which helped to make it possible to demonstrate that objectives were being met.

During the financial crisis of 2008, Clemson was losing some valuable internships that they prided themselves on having for many of their students. The sponsoring companies were cutting their budgets, so internships were one of the first things to go. How could Jim solve this? In Jim's words:

I was walking to my office thinking how big an operation the university is. I was looking at a budget that was a billion dollars. I needed a big vision about what's possible with this place and its corresponding budget. We are, in many ways, similar to a small city; we are multifaceted. For example, not only do we teach construction science but we build buildings; not only do we teach about energy and sustainability but we have an energy plant here. Why don't we create internships on campus as opposed to relying on those companies that go up and down? We could create 500 of those internships! We are a complex organization with resources for teaching and offering internships that students can take advantage of. We gave that assignment to our career center and they met the 500 goal.[5]

Jim offers two axioms in support of visioning:

- **The vision requires time to ferment.** "The length of time varies for me. In between sessions, issues keep arising. They stay in my mind, and every now and then there will be a little more insight added to the vision to make it better."

- **An awareness of history and context is critical.** "I had been thinking of Clemson as my alma mater, which made a big difference because I knew I could effect change if I could make the case that I knew about the University's traditions. If you know about tradition, then you can say, 'I understand all that, now let's make some changes.' If you don't know about tradition, then you're always suspect that you don't really understand the place."

Listening

Jim had to deal with some tremendous challenges due to the 2008 financial crisis in addition to the problem with internships previously noted. Jim credits his excellent CFO, who urged him to take some dramatic steps to address those challenges. The most difficult intervention was to reduce the salary of everybody on campus by 2.5% to 3%, including the coaches. Unfortunately, when that process begins, the state mandates that the directive be applied to everyone, including employees who were below $15,000 in total salary. Even though they were required to follow those guidelines, Jim suggested creating a fund to help their colleagues. He made the first donation and said, "If enough of us contribute, we might be able to help those with the greatest need through this difficult time."

It was almost counterintuitive for Jim to say that he was cutting salaries, and, at the same time, asking that part of each employee's salary (above a certain level) be given to something else that is noble. Jim said,

> Design thinking has taught me to know when it is time for patience and when it is time for urgency. I knew this was a time for urgency. So we acted quickly, and recovered relatively quickly as a result of that initiative.[6]

The financial crisis example has to do with listening. Jim admonishes,

> We don't listen as well as we should. We want to talk; explain what we have in mind as opposed to the other side of it. I have found that if I could *focus on what someone was saying, and what they were saying between the lines, and what they meant by what they said, not just the words they were using, I could derive great insight*. For example, I could see in the voice and eyes of our CFO that he was not panicked but very concerned. I picked up on that nuance not just by what he was saying, but by what I think he was feeling. That helped me to understand the sense of urgency and how we should begin to address this tremendous challenge. Of course, nobody knew at the time how big it was. The skill that design thinkers have about listening was a tremendous help to me.[7]

Diagramming

Jim draws diagrams very frequently. He prefers to meet only in rooms that have white boards and magic markers. He typically sketches and diagrams as he attempts to work his way through issues, which also serves to illustrate his thoughts to others on the administrative team (Figure 2.1).

Figure 2.1 Translating information into diagrams that are analytically illuminating can inspire creativity, lead to a deeper understanding of problems, and help to think about possibilities for solutions.

Jim asserts that he does his best thinking with a pencil in his hand, making marks on a piece of paper. Sketching or doodling is a precursor to focusing on a problem, then as a means to reaching a solution. Simultaneously thinking and doodling is a great way to start problem solving. A doodle or mark of any kind—*writing included*—is a symbol of what's going on in one's head.

Jim is giving a talk next month, and in preparation, he is jotting key words and phrases by hand on paper: a column of ideas that are contrasted with another column of ideas. Then he tries to connect them. The result is a *hybrid between a sentence and a diagram*. And then he includes some diagrams at the bottom of the page. So he ends up with a series of words, phrases, and diagrams that essentially become the preliminary outline for his talk.

Here is an example of how diagramming can be so effective in helping to clarify a problem and solution. Jim was involved in a new initiative called the Clemson University International Center for Automotive Research. It was going to be another campus, in the heart of the region's automobile production, which included BMW, Michelin, and some others, about 40 miles from Clemson. Jim and his team were examining how best to define this project. Jim kept diagramming it as two circles where the academy and business community overlap. The more Jim reflected on the idea, the more he talked to people while showing the diagram. He finally concluded that the two circles do not, in fact, overlap, and that they had to build the connection. They needed to create a bridge between the two circles, and to determine what that bridge is going to look like.

That simple diagram freed the team to stop searching for something that didn't exist and redirected their focus. It gave them an energy boost; what should this new creation look like? From there, they were able to build this bridge, the International Center for Automotive Research, which is now thriving. There are six buildings on the campus, with $220 million invested by private corporations in the state. It was very rewarding to see how that thought—as depicted in the diagram— was translated to physical reality.

Jim fervently believes that design thinking can prepare you to accomplish a great deal more than you realize—be open to what those possibilities might be.

As noted, a principal tool of engagement is the interview. The following are some tips to facilitate a great interview.

■ **_Do your homework_**. Preparation is critical. Take some time before an initial meeting to form some specific hypotheses about the issues, hopes, and dreams. Utilize these notions to shape initial questioning to either confirm or reject your ideas. In addition, have questions in the event the conversation starts to fade. Learn something about the interviewee or the interviewee's perspectives that will jump-start the conversation and put the interviewee sufficiently at ease to open up and set a relaxed tone.

- **Establish rapport**. Share your own story and listen to their story. Be yourself; get personal—share your vision of the problem; you should neither affect some wooden formality nor be excessively casual and familiar. Cultivate a respectful alliance. The stakeholder's perception that at some level he or she is cared for or taken seriously will likely enhance participation and the quality and depth of information offered, and ensure wishes voiced. Acknowledge and appreciate the stakeholders' unique perspectives, especially if they differ from your own. *Put yourself in the interviewee's shoes*. At this early stage, maintaining an open mind and a low-profile ego will enhance truly reciprocal communication and promote rapport. In other words, model the behavior you want others to emulate.

- **Listen actively and carefully**. Empathy will help you to figure out the interests and motivations of the stakeholders. Active listening means fully understanding and actually processing all that is being said by focusing complete attention on the speaker and testing and amplifying what they communicate. Discover the value of what is being said between the lines, then check it out with follow-up questioning. Test any new hypotheses by simply asking if they make sense. Paraphrase responses to your questions to invite clarification, correction, and additional detail. Repeat key words or phrases, again to invite clarification and elaboration.

- **Formulate thoughtful, probing questions**. From the initial questioning, confirmation of hypotheses allows you the luxury of eliciting valuable details, or conversely, rejection of expectations should immediately set up questions designed to discover new facts that will in turn support alternative ideas. Be genuinely curious, and remember that the goal is to keep learning even if you believe the responses to a given question may not at all illuminate what you're exploring. Dig deeply after a response. For example, ask: Why did you do that? How did it work out for you? How do you feel? What did you expect? Be curious and care, but be careful not to be confrontational, as that may impede forthright responses.

- **Observe sensitively and with focus**. This applies especially when you have the opportunity to engage an interviewee in the environment in which the problem or challenge is situated. A firsthand experience can be very revealing and contribute to a deep understanding, particularly to an outsider who can be objective (see the context analysis in the next section for more information). Note body language, mannerisms, facial expressions, emotional state, and even taste in clothing. Consider the details of the surrounding environment: what do furnishings, artifacts on the desk, and photos or images on the wall say about the person or the problem? Is the person organized or messy? Respond sympathetically, even if you don't necessarily agree; convey that what is being said is important to you.

- **Maintain a sense of humor**. This can be a terrific strategy to successfully establish rapport and engage stakeholders. Steve Martin's[8] observation of Carl Reiner as a film director is a great model: "He had an entrenched sense of glee; he used humor as a gentle way of speaking difficult truths; and he could be effortlessly frank."

- **And, avoid the following**: (1) the temptation to interrupt, as you could miss an important comment or nuance; (2) questions that result in yes or no responses; (3) leading questions that consciously or unconsciously elicit the response you want to hear—try not to manipulate the interviewee; and (4) writing or referring to notes or an iPad screen. Writing while someone is taking the time to talk with you may be experienced as distancing or rude, so take notes privately; reflect and record impressions after the interview. Likewise, reading questions can disrupt the flow of the conversation. Prepare questions, as previously noted, but as a way of imprinting background information rather than for explicit reading. On the other hand, note taking (with the interviewee's okay) can be perceived as a compliment, showing that you value the input. It's a judgment call depending on the circumstances.

Ask questions about what people want—and what they don't want. Review the problems-issues and elicit suggestions for improving or detailing them; probe to discover the unstated problems.

Sidebar 2.2 Conversation as a Model for Effective Interviews

> Recognizing that the interviewee paused for a moment, and the way they paused; or changed affect or emotion—the nonverbal expressions need to be acknowledged and investigated to get to the important insight.
>
> —Scott Phillips

Interviews provide a means to deeply understand an issue, a problem, or even a proposed solution. Gaining insights, or learning anything valuable from an interview for that matter, requires great skill and a plan. Scott Phillips regards interviews, which are a crucial tool for his business SearchLite, as a special kind of design problem. SearchLite is a market discovery and validation platform—the company helps inventors, entrepreneurs, and growth companies to discover which markets to address first, and which key factors will influence their ultimate market success. Their service includes an "iterative process that integrates key findings from phone interviews, secondary research, and on-line engagement." The process description that follows, which focuses on the interview, is generalizable to many situations that require insights from interviewing.

Scott's customers are usually technology transfer offices at universities. Anytime a professor invents something that may have commercial value, it must be disclosed to the university's tech transfer department. The faculty inventor(s) then work with this department to explore the commercial potential of the invention, either by licensing it or building a company around it.

Before the university allocates funds for provisional patenting, patenting, or prototyping, which are expensive, they want to know if anyone really cares about the invention and, if so, why and how much. The professor is married to the idea and has been working on it with a grant for the last 20 years, but they don't know how to get it out of the building, or talk to anyone in the real world to see who cares.

Enter Scott's company. For every client or invention, they interview 15 to 20 people, do secondary research, and report back on its commercial viability: there is either a product/market fit or there isn't. The intention is to render—very quickly—an objective opinion based on the voice of the market. This is accomplished primarily through phone interviews; they are listening for the problems—not selling the solution.

Design thinking is applied in the way that interviews are conducted. Whereas others might conduct a structured interview using an interview guide, SearchLite has a 30-minute dinner conversation with people. The interviewers are trained on the art of listening specifically for, or digging deep into, tasks that the interviewee is trying to accomplish, professionally or personally, and why. They listen for an outcome, a metric, and a direction. For example, they are listening for: "I wish my dishwasher could clean two times better in one-third of the time." However, the interviewee will not usually quantify that initially, so the skill is to continue asking probing questions such as, "Could you say more about that?" "What did you mean by that?" or "What quality level, and how fast?"

Scott's interview method to probe deeply for best understandings is derived from Steve Blank, who was a forefather of the lean startup movement. The idea is to know when to let a conversation wander a little bit, when to focus it, when to probe more deeply, and when to move on.

Another point is to be alert for (and avoid) confirmation bias. For example, if you invented something and you are conducting the interviews, you are undoubtedly listening for everything that you believe is an endorsement of your solution. It is difficult to *listen objectively* without recognizing your own mental or behavioral biases. In SearchLite's case, the interviewers are trained to not have an opinion going into any solution that they are evaluating.

SearchLite always has two people on every interview; one conducting it and one taking notes. Both hear and interpret what was said, with the moderator focusing on talking to the interviewee. Without the appropriate follow-up questions as a function of listening well, there would be a much more superficial set of takeaways from the same 30-minute phone call.

The raw ingredient of their deliverable is conducting great phone interviews that have deep insights. They don't necessarily cover a scripted list of 20 questions in a structured format because they will miss the "aha" moment or the insight. Their job is to do 15 of those interviews with relevant people and look for trends and common key takeaways.

Active listening is a noteworthy skill. Scott references Stephen Covey's *The 7 Habits of Highly Effective People* (Franklin Covey Co., 1998) in which listening with the intent to understand instead of only listening with the intent to respond is underscored. For example, recognizing that the interviewee paused for a moment, and the way they paused; or changed affect or emotion—the nonverbal expressions need to be acknowledged and investigated to get to the important insight.

In sum, the best insights from interviews require the art and skill to find the right person to talk to, knowing how to conduct a 30-minute conversation, knowing what to listen for, and how to synthesize that across multiple interviews.

But there is more. Part of the process occurs in parallel to the primary phone interviews. SearchLite has researchers who examine what transpired in the interviews—what is not clear or what needs validation. So their challenge is uncovering secondary research and background to add clarity to material that is muddled from the interviews. This allows them to accelerate the process. Subsequent interview questions are modified as a function of what is learned in secondary research. Likewise, the secondary research challenges are modified when something new is learned in an interview.

The interviews evolve. The 15th interview will be very different from the first in two ways. One is that the person they are talking with in the 15th interview is spot-on. The reason they are spot-on as a subject matter expert is because at the end of every interview the interviewers inquire about other people with whom they should be talking. The first three people they talk to are not the right people, but they are close enough that they know someone who is better suited to talk about the subject. Several more interviews later, they have more referrals from the last group of experts, and eventually they will be talking to the person who is at ground zero for the topic. The other thing that is different is that they are five weeks smarter about asking the right questions. The best interviews, therefore, are always at the last moments of the last few interviews.

The information from the beginning interviews is not at all discounted because it is a process of validation, i.e., how frequently a point is made. The last person really places the information or insights in context.

It's hard to discern patterns if the interviews are all different. However, that underscores the importance of another skill set necessary for good interviews: synthesizing the key findings. A symptom of a bad interview occurs when the interviewer does not review notes for a few days after the interview and didn't have a second person taking notes. It becomes stale and it is easy to forget the most impactful insights. Even though there may be copious notes, it still behooves the good interviewer to write down what they just heard—those insights and impressions—immediately following the interview when it is still fresh.

After every interview, all the notes are culled into one document with the top five takeaways highlighted at the beginning. Once a week, the team brainstorms on the three or four interviews from the past week, then compares all the insights from prior weeks. They are placed in three categories: critical, very important, and important—everything else is background or simply not relevant. So every week they force themselves to have only three insights in each of those categories, which is somewhat arbitrary, but it forces synthesis. At the end of the consultation, they want to tell the client that they need to address *three* insights.

Scott equates the reexamination of the interview questions with the iterative process of design thinking. When they check in with the client every week, they summarize what has been learned, and the client can say they know enough about that issue so they can proceed to another one. In that sense it's iterative. Each week the client can direct them to iterate deeper on this topic or pivot to a new one, based on the findings of the previous interviews (Figure 2.2).

Figure 2.2 Developing new interview questions that probe more deeply or pivot to a different issue based on findings from previous interviews is very much analogous to the iterative process of design thinking.

It is critical to acknowledge an interviewee's time. With permission of the client, SearchLite provides a summary of key findings to each person who speaks with them as a courtesy (in lieu of an honorarium). They generally limit the interview to 30 minutes. And, as a final note, they are sure to end the interview cordially and ask if the interviewee would mind a follow-up; the usual response is that they will either make more time or respond to further questions via email.

Much tangential information is bound to result from responses to questions and conversations with stakeholders. Use some open-ended questions but give gentle direction to help keep focus on the issue at hand (i.e., "I'd like to hear more about that, but I was particularly intrigued by what you started to say about . . ."). Try to avoid preoccupation with irrelevant factors, however colorful they may be. Keep the big picture in clear focus. And remain alert to valuable bits of information that may spontaneously emerge as something unexpected, which could be a clue to a possible solution.

So, embrace and celebrate the unforeseen! You may find that an interviewee is a bit quirky, illogical, or even somewhat crazy. This is not necessarily a bad thing because a very diverse range of people can trigger some of the most creative and innovative ideas.

Empower the stakeholders to meaningfully contribute to the solution. During interviews, keep in mind that it may be helpful to identify and formally recognize select stakeholders as collaborators who could enrich an idea generation workshop or brainstorming session later in the process. Professor Simon weighs in on interviewing with this astute comment.

What you're really looking for in addition to the facts is the emotions. If you can put up sensitive antennae and listen for emotional shifts in the conversation, you can begin to know when you've touched on something that the person you're interviewing feels deeply about. And if you can make a connection with their emotions, chances are you can design something that's going to please them in a meaningful way. That's one of the places where great solutions to problems come from: creating things that people feel emotionally connected to.[9]

Additional Benefits of Empathic Skills

Madlen Simon offers a distinctive application of design thinking:

> Design thinking has enhanced my travel experiences. Now that I'm armed with empathy skills, I find that I'm much more able to reach out to people; to start conversations and learn a lot more about the place I'm visiting, rather than just walking around by myself. I'm really trying to see places through other people's eyes—that's an incredible way to enrich the travel experience.

It is interesting to note that the same empathic skills used for interviewing can cross over to other endeavors. For example, Mark Johnson, as marketing manager for a building product manufacturer, stated, "I learned quickly that the coaching and mentoring skills needed for success were based largely on listening, watching, and focusing on individual motivations."[10]

Precedents

Invoking ideas from the past—analyzing, understanding, and interpreting them—can inspire design solutions in the present and for the future. The underlying principles revealed in an analysis of a relevant precedent—a previous solution to a similar problem that could be used as an example— may have significant value in the discovery or ideation phase of design thinking.

However, since every (design) problem is unique, blindly copying solutions from the past is fraught with risk and superficiality. Emerson famously claimed: "The imitator dooms himself to hopeless mediocrity."[11] If there is no critical thinking, it is all too easy to extract the wrong lessons, especially if the context and specific circumstances surrounding the problem are not fully considered. So, use the great idea, but tweak and purposefully apply it; *build on it and make it better.*

There is benefit to searching for, and becoming informed about, similar problems and their solutions—even if the solutions are mundane. It assists in getting up to speed with "cookbook" solutions, which can then jump-start thinking in creative ways in relation to a different set of conditions. This knowledge base can save time by obviating the need to reinvent the wheel. Moreover, diving deeply into the issues surrounding a similar challenge can help to illuminate all facets of the present problem.

Another perspective involves applying precedents from apparently unrelated areas to solve a problem. Examining alternative ideas that may seem far afield and exploring how those insights might be incorporated in a solution to the current problem could yield a potentially exciting and fresh "design" response. (See Chapter 5, the "Design Approaches to Health Care Delivery and Treatment" section, for an example.) Architects do this all the time: for example, recalling the way a roof structure was configured or the way materials or natural light were manipulated on a building visited while traveling and documented in a journal can help to generate a creative concept for a new project.

Peter Rowe, in his seminal book on design thinking, underscores the point that analogies to ideas in other realms can serve a designer's purpose and become part of a repertoire of ideas that can be mined for different projects in the future.[12] For example, overlapping fish scales were the inspiration for the design of body armor that has typically conflicting characteristics of being both protective and flexible.[13] This is a brilliant engineering solution arising from a precedent from nature. Imitate! And apply the idea in a new way.

Context

Context includes all the relevant influences shaping a problem, from environmental variables (physical constraints) to social, cultural, and historical factors (stakeholder requirements and preferences). The systematic investigation of all of these conditions contributes to a solid foundation for design thinking—and connects the problem to the specific setting, conditions, and constraints. While collecting these data may at first seem tedious and unimaginative, it can be an avenue, or, indeed, the point of departure for an exciting resolution.

Context is important because of its contribution to making a problem unique and circumstance-specific. The best solutions are informed by the context, and they are certainly not developed in isolation. Appreciating the context helps to develop perspective and its underpinnings, anticipate challenges on the path to solutions, and create more effective and sensitive design responses. Without contextual knowledge, assumptions about possible solutions could be way off base. *A good idea in one context may not be good at all in another.*

One strategy for fully evoking and understanding context is to be a detective: observe. Every situation possesses a unique mosaic of attributes and external forces that must be identified, integrated, and interpreted. Begin with listing and describing them, and then record observations both objectively and impressionistically. Define what it is about the context that drives the possibilities and challenges of the solution.

If applicable, determine the social factors that may influence the project. Identify and then solicit opinions from stakeholders and influential people who may only be tangentially connected with the issue at hand. Ask about pressing problems and political exigencies; ask what might be done to maximize community support if appropriate. Sensitivity to all this potential input will help to promote the ultimate success of a project or solution to a problem, as stakeholders will feel somewhat invested knowing their feedback has been acknowledged.

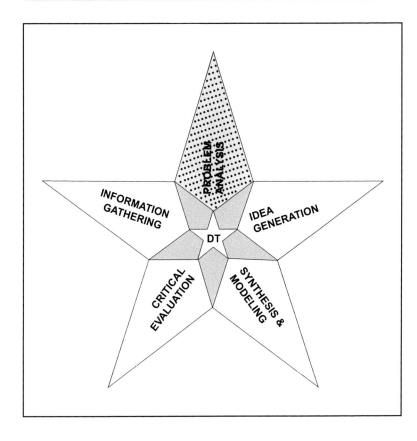

This may seem counterintuitive, but defining the right problem may actually be a creative act. Even if a problem is not fully articulated, it may be useful to forge ahead and work through the design thinking loop with incomplete data as a means to further delineate and amplify the issues. This is another great attribute of design thinking. Other conventional problem-solving techniques suggest that there must be a clear problem formulation before taking action to solve it. With design thinking, however, continuing dialogues, diagnoses, and reframing of the problem throughout the process ensure an optimal solution.

Sidebar 2.3 Questioning the Problem

Design thinking in a legal context is as much about problem definition as problem solving.

—Charles R. Heuer

Chuck is a Principal in The Heuer Law Group based in Charlottesville, Virginia, and in Cambridge, Massachusetts, and is a mediator/arbitrator for the American Arbitration Association.

According to Chuck, lawyers occasionally employ a methodology that is too rigid. For example, when a client wants to litigate, a typical response is: prepare complaint > determine the parties involved > imagine every legal wrong > proceed with all of them. The cost for that approach is great; the relative return is de minimis. Lawyers don't usually discriminate; clients may spend $50 to protect against a $5 problem.

Another scenario is that after the realization that a good outcome is unlikely, a decision is made to terminate after there is a substantial investment in legal services. Critical thinking and discrimination should occur at the beginning, not after funds are spent; otherwise, the outcome could be an elegant solution to the wrong problem.

Chuck believes that many attorneys don't think about other, perhaps more fruitful approaches. Instead of following the usual or expected protocol (invoking the fairly rigid methodology just noted), Chuck encourages stepping back from the situation and thinking deeply about the context and circumstances. He maintains that, "Design thinking in a legal context is as much about problem definition as problem solving." Therefore, identifying alternate problems that may in fact be more relevant to the situation should be a priority.

When a client presents a problem, an immediate initial response should be, "Is that really the problem? Is there something else that we can solve that will make it go away?" Chuck implores us to *question the problem in order to find the most appropriate solution.* Reflect on what is being said by the client. Try a different angle; evaluate it; then proceed, or not. The most powerful solutions ignore the noise, avoid the confusion, and are not corrupted by doubts and misunderstandings.

In other words, do not accept the problem at face value; challenge it. The problem might turn out to be the actual problem as initially presented, but in any case, the problem as stated should not be considered a given. Focus on trying to ascertain a global understanding of the situation to find the right problem. For example, in architecture, the answer may not necessarily be a new building; instead, it might be renovating existing space to be more efficient, or scheduling the use of spaces differently, and so on.

Ask probing questions to find the real problem. Be naturally skeptical; take in everything with a grain of salt. Keep your mind open to look for something seemingly unrelated to the problem for inspiration. Look for connections. For example, Chuck cites a litigation case in which a woman fell going down steps and mentioned (during a deposition) to the lawyer for the defendant that her daughter was getting married. The lawyer picked up on this seemingly unrelated fact, and a video was discovered of the woman who fell on the steps dancing at the wedding *after* the incident, providing sufficient evidence that she was not injured as she had claimed.

Chuck has a fascinating take on the iteration component of design thinking: *dialogue as iteration*. The dialogue is part of the iterative loop: conversing back and forth several times as a means to get to the core issues. You can become wiser and improve the case with greater understanding with each successive loop.

Establishing a productive dialogue with an adversary is crucial. Figure out the underlying interest in a certain position. One way to do that is to explain your concerns related to a position with the expectation that the other party will then open up. Model the behavior to jump-start the dialogue (or, follow the cliché and give some to get some).

Never accept problems at face value—always challenge them to either affirm their validity or recast them after further investigation. While we want to be very sensitive to what stakeholders—clients or consumers or patients—tell us, we must be cautious about accepting their highly biased reports, and also their conclusions about what it all means and what they think is the best response. The real problem may be masked for a variety of reasons; it is easy to be misled by a less serious problem or a symptom. Take time to periodically review and reflect on all the information gathered from interviews and conversations with stakeholders, all aspects of the context, precedent searches, and any other relevant sources. A main objective is to develop a deep, objective, and evidence-based understanding of the issues, constraints, challenges, and possibilities surrounding the problem along with its root causes.

Defining the right problem requires asking the right questions. *If the problem is framed too narrowly, it could limit an effective solution, much less an innovative one*. For example, in the 1960s, IBM was seeking the answer to a key question: "If a more reliable, cheaper, and faster process for photocopying were available, how many more copies would people make in a given year?" The problem was framed too narrowly as "copies from originals," rather than considering a potentially much larger market that included "copies of copies of copies." There was a big missed opportunity that might have been anticipated if the right questions had been asked.[14] Avoiding the status quo and business as usual—even in asking initial questions about the problem—is an important part of the design thinking mindset.

Analyze, organize, visualize, and quantify the information collected in a way that helps to clearly articulate the essence of the problem, or at least have a working definition of the problem as it evolves. Consider the following tasks as a prerequisite to idea generation:

■ Document specific and frequently expressed points or noteworthy comments from interviews with stakeholders, emphasizing different sides of the problem or illuminating some aspect of the problem.

■ Identify areas for further research to complement the interviews.

- Develop lists, diagrams, and images highlighting key context observations; graphics can render lots of complex material in a way that is far more readily understood and interpreted.

- Formulate new questions related to the validity of the initial problem statement.

- Note any novel or unexpected patterns, relationships, or insights that may be evident.

- Eliminate the mass of extraneous material (carefully).

- Uncover the fundamental causes of the problem.

- Collapse a seemingly overwhelming problem into smaller, more manageable components (but keep the big picture in mind).

- Filter the relevant information into two categories for complex problems—general and specific. This will facilitate initial idea generation by not overloading that phase of the process with too much information at one time.

- Set forth the scope of the problem, including constraints, concerns, and challenges; also include the ultimate objectives, hopes, and dreams (and their rationale). This could be considered the design criteria on which proposed solutions are evaluated.

Analysis is essential to set the stage for the most meaningful idea generation session. Effective brainstorming can begin with a multidimensional and coherent understanding of the problem and its context from different points of view.

IDEA GENERATION

Your conscience shouts, "Here's what you should do," while your intuition whispers, "Here's what you could do." Listen to that voice that tells you what you could do. Nothing will define your character more than that.
—Steven Spielberg[15]

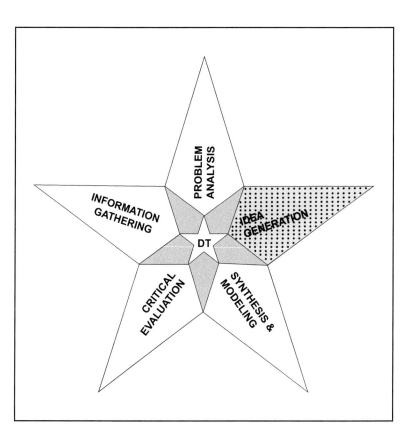

Now that much information about the problem, stakeholders, and context has been elicited, researched, and analyzed—and all that knowledge internalized—the real fun begins. One thing to keep in mind is that objectively and narrowly responding to this input—while absolutely necessary—will take you only so far. It is time for getting loose; allowing an infusion of imagination, epiphany, innovation, and creativity; interpreting information and *merging it with your own creativity* into a meaningful solution.

There are likely to be conflicting perspectives and hopes for certain outcomes as a function of the priorities of multiple stakeholders in any given problem. It behooves the design thinker to be as objective and responsive as possible to those priorities with one caveat: the personal traits, background, experience, intuition, and unique vision of you, the designer, should be acknowledged. It is important to be open to the ideas of others while at the same time committing to one's own ideals and impulses. This sounds like an inherent contradiction. Is it more courageous to listen and respond only to stakeholders, or to stubbornly stand behind some personalized ideal solution? Perhaps it is the tension between the practical and the ideal that motivates innovation and keeps creativity tied to the solution of mundane but often significant challenges.

Brainstorming

Brainstorming has been successfully deployed in some form for many years across numerous professions, industries, and businesses. Building on the ideas of Alex Osborn, who first outlined the principles of brainstorming in 1939,[16] the following are a few of the basics that are essential to design thinking:

- **Do not initially criticize or judge ideas**. Evaluation should occur *after* the session and not while brainstorming is in process; otherwise, you risk becoming frozen, and kernels of potentially novel ideas will not have a chance to be developed. Work hard to mitigate the natural tendency that we all have to constantly evaluate.

- **Generate unfettered, wild, and crazy ideas**. In addition to generating the usual array of standard, expected, or obvious solutions, this strategy has a greater probability of leading to a solution that is innovative and creative. Here is where the now clichéd colorful Post-its, index cards, sketches, and diagrams—filled with ideas—take center stage.

- **Try to develop as many ideas as possible**. The more ideas that are on the table—flawed or not—the better the chance to trigger something special and excellent. Perfection is not the goal; at this stage, sheer quantity is. Experiment. Do not wait for the lightning bolt of inspiration to strike.

- **Combine and build upon ideas**. Synthesizing or improving upon preliminary ideas that have been proposed should be part of the natural progression of a brainstorming session. Subdivide the ideas, then organize, prioritize, or categorize them as a way to focus on a particular aspect of the problem (for example, attach Post-its under "big picture" and "specifics" headings, or place ideas into different information baskets). Coalesce the best elements from many ideas into a completely new idea. Mark Johnson affirms the clear benefits of this element of design thinking: "We found each experiment to reinvent our [building product] business process often led to another innovative idea."[17]

At regular intervals, or after a brainstorming session, *reflect* and take stock: summarize important points, ideas, features, etc. Compare those to the overarching objectives that were outlined in the problem definition to ensure that the process is proceeding on the right track.

An outstanding example of brainstorming was documented by ABC News *Nightline* anchor Ted Koppel and correspondent Jack Smith,[18] who visited the design and innovation firm IDEO in Palo Alto. IDEO was asked by ABC to

Figure 2.3 Example of a quintessential brainstorming session. This photograph captures the energy, excitement, and dynamic engagement inherent in a successful collaborative effort.

Source: GaudiLab/shutterstock.com.

redesign a shopping cart in just five days to demonstrate what IDEO termed a "deep dive"—a form of design collaboration involving "a process of enlightened trial and error."

There was no hierarchy among team members—no titles, and no assigned positions except for the leader. (The project leader was selected because of his ability with groups, not because of seniority.) The team was described as "eclectic and diverse." Initially, the team split into smaller groups to conduct interviews and a bit of research to find out what the people who use, make, and repair shopping carts think. These people were viewed as experts who could enable the entire team to learn as much as possible about the issues as quickly as possible. They also wanted to ensure that all stakeholders' points of view were represented. The smaller groups reconvened to share everything they learned.

On the next day, brainstorming began. Ideas in the form of quick sketches and notes written on Post-its were placed on the walls. The team narrowed down the hundreds of ideas by voting. Criteria for selection: an idea must be both "cool and able to be built in a day." Time constraints moved the leader to become autocratic and suggest: (1) ending the brainstorming process; and (2) deciding "what things will be worked on."

Teams were subdivided to focus on one of the following areas: shopping, safety, checkout, and finding what you're looking for in the store. Each team built a prototype reflecting their area of focus. Then, the final step, a coalescing of design ideas; the best elements from each prototype were combined into a new, completely redesigned shopping cart.

IDEO has mantras posted on the walls of their studio. They are worth sharing because they are basically an update of Osborn's principles (previously summarized) with the addition of these: (1) one conversation at a time; and (2) stay focused.

Design Thinking Attitude

The importance of approaching the ideation phase of design thinking with the right attitude cannot be emphasized enough. Do not underestimate the value of having fun as an integral part of idea generation. It helps to diffuse tension and stress, making it easier to loosen up and unlock creativity, and examine problems in many different ways. If the work is viewed as play, then it is easier to brainstorm: free associate, turn ideas upside down and sideways, generate ideas quickly without caring about failure or criticism, and simply keep the work flowing. Learn to overcome inhibitions acquired through years of adulthood! Be mindful to do the following:

- **Embrace ambiguity**. There are bound to be many unknowns. New information may be brought to bear after work is initiated. Expect feedback from preliminary ideas to inform further development. In the search for that "Eureka!" moment of a great design solution, we must often follow unclear instincts, fuzzy clues, or paths that seem to hold no promise. Yet, it is through this ambiguous terrain that we come to find our best solutions.[19]

- **Have confidence in design thinking and your own instincts**. Be aware that there will always be a certain amount of insecurity or anxiety in the beginning of a project in which the outcome is unknown; assume that, with perseverance, there will be a successful result. Understand that initial ideas—especially those that are new or innovative—are especially delicate.

Alternative Solutions

An optimal solution is more realistic than seeking one that is perfect. There is a common misperception that perfection should be the overarching goal. Indeed, there is no single, right answer or perfect solution to most problems; there are shades of gray—alternatives, with varying tradeoffs. Usually, one of those alternatives is the most promising. The optimal solution successfully addresses the highest-priority objectives and/or satisfies most of the constraints and stakeholder wishes—in addition to providing the "goose bump factor" (see the description later in this chapter).

An outcome of idea generation should be several very different alternative schemes that address the issues outlined in the problem definition and its analysis. If one idea is rejected for whatever reason, then there are ten other very good ones to propose. If there is an obsession with creating the single perfect solution, you are more likely to end up frozen, with the inability to imagine any other viable potential solutions.

Sidebar 2.4 Alternatives and the Big Idea

Thomas Jefferson was unique among US Presidents, as he was both a lawyer and an architect (and mastered other disciplines as well). Did he apply his design skills to write the Declaration of Independence, or as President? Perhaps we'll never know, but in any case there are lawyers today who believe that design thinking greatly facilitates the way they confront situations in their legal practices.

The following narrative describes how attorneys—and others—can apply design thinking in remarkably fresh and unique ways. Design thinking spurs creative thought by essentially forcing deeper thinking by developing alternative solutions, and then involving the client in discussing their respective pros and cons. Another invaluable aspect of design thinking is never losing sight of the need to maintain a certain integrity to the "big idea" when developing projects or solutions.

> The power of visual thinking is immense.
>
> The notion of alternatives is an extremely valuable part of design thinking.
>
> Stepping back and always asking yourself what's the big idea—what is the organizing principle to what you're doing—is a key part of design thinking.
>
> —Jay Wickersham

Jay Wickersham is Principal of the Cambridge, Massachusetts, law firm Noble, Wickersham & Heart LLP. Jay holds both law and architecture degrees from Harvard.

Design training has been helpful to Jay in three ways. One is the synthesizing of different kinds of information from a whole host of different sources. Design thinking is very powerful in training you to *keep looking more broadly; to keep looking beyond the borders of what one might think is the problem.* Draw in information and knowledge from all kinds of different sources. In that sense, design training is quite the opposite of legal training. In legal training, you are trained to screen things out, to keep narrowing down, and to make a decision that turns on one or two key legal points, so you can dismiss everything else as irrelevant.

In contrast, design thinking stipulates that you look as broadly as possible, and then find ways to integrate the information you've gathered. Related to that point, in architecture you come to *respect the perspective and expertise of others*. Architects have a unique responsibility to coordinate vast amounts of multidisciplinary input: on any project of modest scale, architects might have from 10 to 30 or more consultants in other disciplines, any one of whom knows more about their part of the project than the architect does.

And the same is true when it comes to the contractor. Any one of those subcontractors and suppliers know more about their particular piece of the building than the architect. So the architect's challenge is to extract that expertise, weigh it, and figure out how to coordinate that particular piece of information with all the other pieces of information.

Here is an example of how Jay operationalizes that from his law practice. The practice's attorneys do a lot of work in ownership transitions, helping architects reorganize their firms, and help the next generation to come forward and take on responsibility and, ultimately, ownership. The legal part of that absolutely has to go along with the financial side. So, whenever they work on succession planning, there is always a very close partnership with the accountants. Jay is very aware that accountants have the expertise in the finances of the firm as well as tax implications. Jay's job is to understand; to be able to ask the right questions. Very often, Jay realizes that he has become the translator—he explains to his clients what the accountants are saying. He puts it in simple English. His role is to gather, synthesize, and then translate that information, and he does this on a regular basis.

Another valuable skill from design thinking is the ability to think and communicate graphically and visually. This is not at all about incredibly elaborate three-dimensional modeling or rendering, but, rather, very simple kinds of diagrams. One of the things Jay believes is invaluable is, whenever possible, to translate legal information to some graphic form—i.e., charts or diagrams. This is a way to harness and present complex information to a nontechnical audience in a simple, straightforward way. The power of visual thinking is immense and has the potential to help everybody. Jay is a huge fan of Edward Tufte, who has authored numerous books (such as *Envisioning Information*, *Beautiful Evidence*, and *Visual Explanations*) on graphically presenting information. (I would add that diagramming is not only helpful to the audience or reader, but also to the design thinker as a tool to conceive of potential solutions.)

A second extremely valuable part of design thinking that Jay has learned is the notion of alternatives. Do not fall in love with your idea! You need to generate five more! Jay is always trying to give his clients alternatives, whether it's figuring out how to resolve a dispute, structuring contracts on a complicated international project, or thinking about an ownership transition. List the pros and cons of each of the alternatives or approaches. Jay, of course, has a sense of which he thinks is favorable, but this should also be a discussion with the client.

If there are several options, the final solution, scheme, or alternative usually borrows elements from each one. Jay states that, in his law firm, they don't pretend to have the "right" answer. Whenever possible, they present alternative approaches as a way of eliciting the discussion (Figure 2.4), which usually results in an answer that will be probably better than any of the alternatives. And it will get people on board to support it.

Jay believes that if you give people the sense of different options, they don't feel like they're being railroaded into doing just one thing. They are much more receptive to having an open conversation about the pros and cons. If you feel strongly about one option, it is often easier to

Figure 2.4 Whenever possible, present alternatives (together with their respective pros and cons) as a means to elicit discussion and to arrive at an even better solution.

convince somebody if you've been able to show why one approach is not as strong as another.

Here is the third way that design thinking is so important to Jay: *how the process is iterative*. This is central to design thinking. The process starts at the conceptual level—and this applies to the alternatives as well—but keeps narrowing in. When Jay is putting together contracts or some legal agreement, he'll make the analogy that they don't want to jump into construction documents before they've done the concept design—and the client is asking him to move right into construction documents! The concept design must be completed first, then fleshed out in the next phase, and then they can move into the actual agreement.

There's a real risk, particularly when someone has an expertise (i.e., a lawyer), that a client assumes you're going to move directly into the final product. In design thinking, you start conceptually and then flesh it out, develop greater detail, and then as you move into a larger scale, you are forced to tackle a whole new set of issues. Note that always, through all iterations and scales, you must try to maintain a kind of integrity to the design or big idea. That's a wonderful model for a process and end result. Jay keeps that in mind when developing a legal structure for any kind of situation.

In terms of resolving disputes, a classic mediation technique is to find the places where there is agreement; start in the areas of agreement and, if there are disagreements, table them. Once the agreed-to areas are established, that constitutes a basis for people to work together. This is a great strategy for formulating the "design" of a solution or a project.

With a design, there are times when you know there are certain parts that are just not working. Leave that part of it alone for a while, and develop the parts that are working, then come back to the problem areas. For example, Jay's wife, who is a writer, was working on a book and had a lot of fantastic material, but she knew that the overall structure wasn't really developed. She needed some organizing thread. She finally came up with an idea that she thought might be effective, but wasn't sure. Jay opined that she should use it, almost arbitrarily, as an organizing device or parti. At the very least, it would help her to gain control over the material and wrestle with how the project could be organized. If it works—great. If not, abandon it, but know that it has been a useful exercise.

Jay thinks that the idea of stepping back and always asking yourself what is the big idea, what is the organizing principle to what you're doing—is a key part of design thinking.

Baby Steps

If at first things seem overwhelming, just chip away one bit at a time. If appropriate, temporarily eliminate minor details so attention can be focused on major elements only. This strategy is similar to computational thinking, which is defined in part as "using abstraction and decomposition when attacking a large complex task or designing a large complex system. It is separation of concerns."[20]

Typically, at project or problem inception, there are so many variables to consider that it is practically impossible—or too daunting—to work with all of them at once. One strategy is to take baby steps in order to break down the problem into manageable pieces—let some of the constraints float for a while and work on other constraints. Go back and forth. One investigation informs the other. Another strategy is to consider the analogy to a jigsaw puzzle, where you work on one piece at a time as a means to arrive at the complete picture (as exemplified by Michael Tardif in Sidebar 1.1). Moving back and forth between pieces here as well, while they are still being developed, can be very effective.

Brainstorming Tips

The following are some strategies to facilitate idea generation. Some will be more worthwhile than others as a function of the specific problem—and your personal style and proclivities. In any case, the leader should review these tips, in addition to underscoring the importance of courtesy and respect, at the start of a brainstorming session as a reminder to all.

- **Withhold judgment**. If you are constantly evaluating ideas, then some potentially great solutions may be missed. Fight against the natural inclination to erase or delete; archive the work—you may want to revisit an idea after some time and further explorations, to see it in a new light.

- **Focus the brainstorming sessions**. They can be dedicated to working on an aspect of the problem, the design of the process itself for solving the problem, or the big picture. If there is a lack of focus, team members should prompt the leader, "Are we off track? Are we in the weeds?"

- **Engage in trial, error, and refinement**. This old dictum is a fine strategy for stimulating creativity. Sometimes you just need an arbitrary starting point from which to jump in, with the caveat that, for the most part, design decisions should be accountable. So, take action; doing so provides a basis for further exploration and, eventually, evaluation.

- **Become immersed in the circumstances of the problem**. Ideas will emerge and become evident the deeper you go and the more fully the issues are understood.

- **Do something different; take a risk**. Commit to the idea of discovery and innovation within the circumstances of the problem. Try changing the way you work to foster creativity. There is little growth or learning without risk.

- **Bad ideas and failure are essential**. Bad ideas are great because they often trigger exceptional ideas. The bad idea must be appreciated; that is, all ideas need to be considered (as noted previously), nurtured, then rejected, accepted, or built upon—not immediately crushed. Acknowledge unsuccessful work as a valuable part of design thinking, and as an opportunity to learn and to discover valuable information, and as motivation to innovate. The IDEO mantra, now a cliché—"Fail often to succeed sooner"[21]—is particularly salient. Failure is so important on the road to innovation and success that a new museum—the Museum of Failure—recently opened in Sweden. It showcases high-profile failures such as the Bic for Her pen, Harley-Davidson perfume, and Colgate Beef Lasagna. According to Dr. Samuel West, an organizational psychologist and the museum's curator,

  > The purpose of the museum is to show that innovation requires failure; if you are afraid of failure, then we can't innovate . . . if you're creating something new, you're going to fail. Don't be ashamed of it. Let's learn from these failures instead of ignoring them.[22]

- **View constraints as opportunities rather than as limitations**. With a bit of creativity, problems can be transformed into unique assets. For example, in a renovation there is an existing structural column in the middle of an important space that seemingly disrupts the space. Instead of a costly removal, consider making it an integral part of the larger three-dimensional composition by adding another (nonstructural) matching column to create a gateway, or delineate a circulation path, or create a support core. Keep an open mind to new possibilities. Constraints are great because they force you to get more creative to arrive at a worthy solution. Remember to recognize the genuine opportunities as well.

- **Take the time to play "what if."** Develop a series of questions about what might be possible. Then consider the consequences, but do not worry about the answers right away. "If I do X, then Y or Z happens," or, "If I do X, then I have to address Y set of problems." Be wary of the trap wherein it becomes so enjoyable to pose the questions that you don't get around to speculating about the answers. Here is a great snippet illustrating the what-if game from architect Don Metz:

  > As always, the process consists of questions built upon questions: What if? If this goes here, will this fit there? What is the appropriate hierarchy between this sequence of rooms? What are the sight lines and sources of light inside the house? What are the views from inside to outside—and from outside to inside? If I arrange the bedrooms at opposite ends of the house instead of above or below, how would that alter the client's expectations of interior zoning? Are there ways to profitably impose or disrupt a rhythm of elements (windows, doors, posts, beams, corners, casework, stairs), expand a space, or condense it down? Can I gain a sense of openness by letting a wall stop short of a ceiling—and still retain a sense of privacy? Some ideas begin to suggest others, some lead nowhere. As I prove and disprove each thesis, the search will lead to something that may work. Or not.[23]

  The questions Metz poses to himself become the primary means to stimulate creative responses.

- **Be passionate**. Look for some special element in the problem that has a personal connection on some dimension, which can activate something in your own soul and move you to express that in a way that substantively contributes to a potential solution.

- **Assume your solution will be implemented**. This kind of mindset will help to realize a self-fulfilling prophecy, and will ensure your personal investment, which is so important in design thinking. Create your own brand of virtual reality by imagining yourself as each type of stakeholder and how they would specifically experience the solution or project. In this fashion, visualize your design solution and see it come to life, complete with all its benefits and problems.

- **Use words to facilitate idea generation**. Words that are intentionally vague allow for flexibility in interpretation, thus helping to spark new ideas. For example, what images come to mind when you reflect on words such as cluster, leverage, promote, layer, screen, and intersect? Another way to use words is to create a narrative vision of what a proposed solution might be like. Design the story surrounding the problem and solution—imagine different scenarios including events, mixes of people, and times.

- **Work in multiple scales simultaneously**. Take a step back; zoom out and zoom in. This can be beneficial because it ensures that you always keep the big picture in mind while not sacrificing attention to detail.

Typical Mistakes in Brainstorming

Following are some typical pitfalls to be recognized and avoided. In accordance with the cliché, these are easy to say, not so easy to do. But being aware of them can help with design thinking.

- **Responding to criticism is regarded as compromising design intent**. With a different attitude, revising a proposed solution can also be viewed as a chance to do more brainstorming, and make the solution or project even better.

- **An initial idea that is perceived as excellent should be carried through, completely intact, to the final outcome**. Related to an obsession with finding the perfect solution, infatuation with an idea should not get in the way of larger goals or the big picture. Openness to alternatives (perhaps equally infatuating but very different) is a hallmark of experience. That said, here is a caveat: in some rare cases, a great, substantive initial idea may be worth fighting for.

- **The tail wagging the dog**. No single aspect or feature of a solution should be considered precious. Do not let an impressive detail dominate all decision-making.

- **Brainstorming resulted in lots of great ideas; let's use them all**. In general, when too many things are happening simultaneously, there is no one strong point of view. Do not dilute a good, solid concept with a constellation of clever gestures. Albert Einstein said, "Any intelligent fool can make things bigger and more complex. It takes a touch of genius—and a lot of courage—to move in the opposite direction."

- **Working on tasks that do not thoughtfully advance the work**. Time is one of the most important resources we have. Mismanaging time by working on tasks that are interesting but only tangentially related to the problem is a common occurrence. Constantly monitor what you are doing to ensure that you don't get mired in inconsequential activities.

- **Keep revising a bad idea to make it work**. If it appears that too much revision is required, it may make sense to abandon the idea and start on a fresh alternative.

The Goose Bump Factor

One feature that distinguishes design thinking is striving to integrate some sort of magical element, a critical intangible that separates a competent solution from a great one. Not all problems are amenable to this, but always look for opportunities to transcend solving the practical problem. Honor the problem, but also create something beyond the immediate utility of the solution; perhaps something that the stakeholders might never have imagined. Reach for the greatest potential within the constraints, hopefully eliciting an emotional response. This represents design thinking at its best.

All the "dos and don'ts" in the preceding discussion may seem self-evident and may in fact be natural and automatic for some, but it is metaphorically worth rediscovering the wheel on occasion as we engage in what appear to be more challenging problems as society becomes increasingly complex and also full of constraints—economic, regulatory, and ideological. The reality is that it is more difficult to be creative and effective these days, so design thinking may well be more relevant than ever.

SYNTHESIS THROUGH MODELING

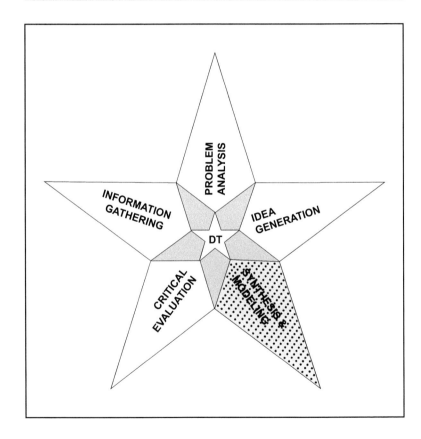

If I can make it there
I'll make it anywhere.

— Theme from *New York, New York*, composed
by John Kander with lyrics
by Fred Ebb, 1977.[24]

The operative words in the quote are *make it*. Take the best ideas from brain-storming sessions to a higher degree of resolution and detail by building a model or prototyping the solution. A model or prototype is not necessarily an object; it is some sort of solution or "deliverable." For example, it could be anything from a strategy, an app, a story, or an experience, to a business model that functions as a demonstration—an "operational prototype"—of the idea.

This phase of design thinking involves narrowing down all the ideas from brainstorming to those that are the most promising (*convergent* thinking). Revisit the problem definition and apply the design criteria set forth therein to help select and focus on the most suitable—and inspiring—ideas. This certainly involves a shift in mindset from idea generation, which, in contrast, could be characterized as *divergent* thinking.

There are two significant goals of creating a model. The first is using the act of creating the model as a tool to develop an idea into a coherent solution. Making things—whether it be a physical, three-dimensional model or a narrative description of a strategy—is crucial to innovation (and, in many circumstances, funding). "You can think about how you might do something, but cogitating will only get you so far. Sometimes it takes building a prototype to have that Eureka moment,"[25] says Martin Culpepper, a professor of mechanical engineering at MIT. For example, build a crude study model out of cardboard: rip it apart, change something, rebuild it. *Experiment. Play. Explore.* There are similar analogies in working with other media, such as writing, drawing, or digital. You can cut and paste words and sentences as easily as you can cut and paste a piece of cardboard.

Do not underestimate the power of serendipity when building a prototype. Creative work is frequently manifest by varying, shifting, and merging elements of the model, whether they are words, sentences, parts of an outline, pieces of cardboard, tracing paper overlays of thick marker diagrams, spreadsheets, photos, or digital layers. Be curious—see where the modeling takes you. Whatever tool you use to construct the model—drawing, writing, model building—should help you to think conceptually (see Chapter 4, the "Diagramming, Reflecting, and Presenting" section). This is an exciting part of design thinking because you don't really know the outcome, and there are so many great possibilities.

The prototype should facilitate a "conversation" between the design thinker and the project. Build quickly and keep the dialogue flowing. "Ambiguity and abstraction are particularly important at the early stages of conceptualization because they provide the opportunity for the recall and creative association of ideas from memory."[26] Moreover, do not take time to strive for perfection; the first few iterations are "drafts," that is, they will likely be developed and improved upon.

The second objective in building a model is to get feedback through testing and critical evaluation. The model, therefore, should be a very close embodiment of a proposed (draft) solution in order to elicit the most constructive comments and critique. (See the next section, "Critical Evaluation.")

Always keep the following axioms in mind during the "synthesis through modeling" phase:

- Consider stakeholders' perspectives at every step of prototype development.

- Pursue several alternatives concurrently for critical evaluation by others.

- Responses to early prototypes may provide new information and insights that could alter the direction of subsequent prototype development.

- No matter how brilliant an idea appears on paper, a (functioning) prototype is what becomes a persuasive alternative.

CRITICAL EVALUATION

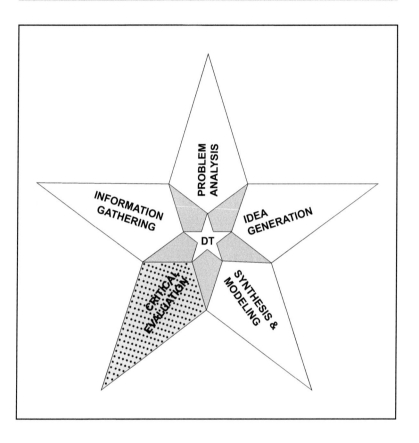

Having frequent conversations about the work—exposing it to criticism—with people of *diverse backgrounds and experiences* can serve to amplify or refine ideas, eliminate ideas, or suggest new ideas. I would underscore the importance of seeking challenges from individuals with varied perspectives and skill sets (particularly those whose points of view are not aligned with yours)— harnessing and synthesizing their ideas in synergistic fashion can help us all do better in whatever tasks we undertake. Indeed, valid criticism should be considered an opportunity to learn, and to improve the work. Dialogues and criticism are therefore among the most essential tools to arrive at the best possible solutions.

Why is feedback so important? Madlen Simon elaborates:

> Conversations and critiques help design thinkers to personally reflect on the process. When you have to articulate an idea and respond to criticism you are forced to think through more aspects of an issue, and ideas tend to become more concrete. On the other hand, if you keep something locked inside your head without having a dialogue, the reflection phase is neglected as you charge forward, with potential loss of opportunities and insights.[27]

Critical feedback can also help to shed light on the various viewpoints of complicated issues thereby ensuring that all aspects of a problem are considered.

Note an important caveat here. All this is not to say that you should always be unconditionally deferential and subservient to criticism. There are times when comments may be frankly absurd, off the mark, or just plain wrong, and you have to recognize that someone else may have an agenda that might not be in your project's best interests. So attend carefully to critical challenges, extract the best of it, and build on it, but readily acknowledge and dismiss what is clearly off base or irrelevant.

External Criticism

This last component of the iterative loop is so influential in shaping the final outcome. Embrace pragmatic and appropriate feedback on models or prototypes, be it from stakeholders, peers, experts or specialists, and anyone else who might be even tangentially relevant to the work. Integrating feedback in real time—as it becomes available—into the loop is a unique attribute of design thinking.

Change or adjustment in response to criticism should be seen not as compromise, but as something that makes a project more sensitive and responsive to some special issue that may not have been illuminated if not for the additional attention. Another response to criticism is to think of the project as a completely different assignment, which demonstrates that there are many ways to approach a problem. I actually look forward to constructive criticism because the work usually gets better.

An added benefit of responding to constructive suggestions from stakeholders, especially if it represents a genuine and substantive contribution, is that the stakeholder will be that much more invested in the project. Be sure to reference an idea the stakeholder proposed, squiggled on the back of a napkin, or showed as a precedent from another similar problem. Point out how, for example, the squiggle triggered an idea, was translated into some aspect of the solution, or was influential in making a design decision.

It is not always easy to accept and respond to criticism, but there are several truisms that are important to keep in mind in order to derive the most from feedback. The most obvious and important one is to avoid the natural propensity for being defensive. Try to understand precisely what the critic is asserting. If there is any ambiguity, form a hypothesis about what is being said and try to restate the critic's comments. In this way, clarification is more likely (the critic may elaborate in valuable fashion), and you demonstrate your efforts at understanding. But more dialogue—to reiterate this valuable point—can spark a new idea or initiate a line of inquiry not previously imagined that could benefit the work. The cliché that tensions can lead to creativity, or that conflicting views tend to stimulate more and deeper thinking, is certainly true as long as participating individuals are healthy and secure enough to be receptive to competing or dissenting ideas.

The Art of Self-Criticism

Cultivate the habit of self-criticism, which can be a powerful component of design thinking. Self-criticism can efficiently inspire new ideas, infuse projects or solutions with special meaning, and help formulate cogent arguments in support of convictions and aspirations. Used properly as a design tool, says Christopher Mead, former Dean and Professor of Art History and Architecture at the University of New Mexico, self-criticism can serve to test the strength of initial ideas against the problem definition, mission, or mandate. Once the value of those ideas has been proven, continue to test to ensure their coherent development by editing out missteps or flaws.[28] When critically reflecting about a solution, ensure that every decision, move, or idea relates to the bigger concept in some way.

Be your own devil's advocate. Pose tough questions about potential solutions and their consequences.[29] This simulation of creative tension can be a catalyst for thinking about other, very different groundbreaking alternatives as well as an effective strategy to help recognize shortcomings.

Mead succinctly summarizes the value of criticism in relation to design thinking: "Criticism can make us see familiar things from new perspectives, shake us out of our shopworn habits, and provoke us into thinking about problems we might otherwise overlook."[30] I would add that critical evaluation helps to make solutions optimally responsive to stakeholders and context, cost-effective, and artful. Seek as much feedback as possible; it will enrich your work.

NOTES

1   Clifford Geertz, *The Interpretations of Cultures* (New York: Basic Books, 1973), 5–6, 9–10.
2   Alice Waugh, "Constraints and Viewpoints," *Spectrum*, Winter 2017, 11.
3   Madlen Simon, interview by the author, College Park, MD, May 6, 2016.
4   Ibid.
5   James Barker, interview by the author, March 22, 2016.
6   Ibid.
7   Ibid.
8   Steve Martin, *Born Standing Up: A Comic's Life* (New York: Scribner, 2007), 192.
9   Ibid.
10 Mark Robert Johnson, interview by the author, Washington, DC, July 21, 2016.
11 Ralph Waldo Emerson, "Address Before the Senior Class," *Harvard Divinity School*, 1838 (accessed March 13, 2024, www.harvardsquarelibrary.org/biographies/emersons-divinity-school-address/).
12 Peter G. Rowe, *Design Thinking* (Cambridge, MA: MIT Press, 1987).
13 Ashley Browning, Christine Ortiz, and Mary C. Boyce, "Mechanics of Composite Elasmoid Fish Scale Assemblies and Their Bioinspired Analogues," *Journal of the Mechanical Behavior of Biomedical Materials* 19 (March 2013): 75–86.

14 Paul J. H. Schoemaker and Steven Krupp, "The Power of Asking Pivotal Questions," *MIT Sloan Management Review* 56, no. 2 (Winter 2015): 39–47.

15 Steven Spielberg, speaking at Harvard's commencement, May 26, 2016.

16 Alex F. Osborn, *Applied Imagination: Principles and Procedures of Creative Thinking* (New York: Charles Scribner's Sons, 2011 [first printing 1953]), 297–301.

17 Mark Robert Johnson, interview by the author, Washington, DC, July 21, 2016.

18 ABC News, "The Deep Dive: One Company's Secret Weapon for Innovation," *Nightline*, July 13, 1999.

19 Clark Kellogg, "Focus on the Future: Learning from Studio," *Design Intelligence Knowledge Reports*, January 2006, 9.

20 Jeannette M. Wing, "Computational Thinking," *Communications of the ACM* 49, no. 3 (March 2006): 33.

21 Tom Kelley with Jonathan Littman, *The Art of Innovation: Lessons in Creativity from IDEO, America's Leading Design Firm* (New York: Currency/Doubleday, 2001), 232.

22 Christine Hauser and Christina Anderson, "At This Museum, Failures Are Welcome," *The New York Times*, April 21, 2017, www.nytimes.com/2017/04/25/arts/museum-of-failure.html

23 Don Metz, *Confessions of a Country Architect* (Piermont, NH: Bunker Hill Publishing, 2007), 101.

24 Theme from "New York, New York," from NEW YORK, NEW YORK. Words by Fred Ebb, music by John Kander, © 1977. (Renewed) United Artists Corporation. All rights controlled and administered by EMI Unart Catalog Inc. (Publishing) and Alfred Music (Print). All rights reserved. Used by Permission. Reprinted by permission of Hal Leonard LLC.

25 Quoted from Elizabeth Thomson, "In Praise of Building: MIT's Maker Czar Celebrates Hands-On Learning," *MIT Spectrum* (Spring 2015): 10.

26 Richard Nordhaus, "Drawing on the Computer," in *Professional Practice 101* (New York: Wiley, 1997), 258.

27 Madlen Simon, interview by the author, College Park, MD, May 6, 2016.

28 Christopher Mead, paraphrased by the author in "It's Not Personal, It's Business: Peer Review and Self-Criticism Are Crucial Tools That Elevate the Quality of Preliminary Designs," *Architectural Record* 187, no. 9 (September 1999): 28.

29 For more information and related research, see Paul J. H. Schoemaker and Steven Krupp, "The Power of Asking Pivotal Questions," *MIT Sloan Management Review* 56, no. 2 (Winter 2015): 39–47.

30 Christopher Mead, "Critical Thinking in Architectural Design," in *Architectural Design Portable Handbook* (New York: McGraw-Hill, 2001), 42–44.

3

MODELS OF COLLABORATIVE DESIGN THINKING

*I*t's 2:00 pm sharp, and the project team is already assembled, ready to go. The owner, architect, consultants, and construction manager are all there—each a senior member of the team who is authorized to make decisions on the spot if needed. Everyone arrives on time. Cell phones are turned off, without a reminder, and there's hot

DOI: 10.4324/9781003416142-3

coffee and water on a side table so that no one has to leave the room. On a large whiteboard, the delivery date of the project is written in big, red letters: "February 28." Just below is a simple agenda with five bullet points outlining the key decisions that will be made during the course of the meeting. Off to one side is the "dinner box"—anyone who's available for a bite at the end of the day will check the box, and reservations will be booked before the meeting is over.

The agenda is quickly reviewed as the session begins, and then the team gets right to work. Item one: the contractor is having trouble fabricating the compound curvature for a wood stair rail and wants to know what alternatives might be considered. Ideas are tossed back and forth freely among all the participants, covering aesthetics, materials, code requirements, cost, and schedule implications. After due consideration, the team decides to switch from wood to aluminum, which can be fabricated off site. Decision made. The team works the agenda until all five issues are covered. The meeting ends at 2:57 p.m., with three minutes to spare. The time, place, and agenda for the next meeting are noted, and everyone leaves the room knowing what has to happen next to keep the project on track. By 9:00 a.m. the next morning, meeting notes have been issued via email so that those who were not present know what to do. That night, five of the seven attendees make it for dinner, covering lots of napkins with sketches . . .

The essence of a traditional collaborative landscape is painted in broad strokes in the preceding text. Scott Simpson[1] illustrates an ideal scene applicable to many different types of projects and problems that we can all emulate.

TRADITIONAL COLLABORATIVE BASICS

There are a number of common elements in successful collaborations across disciplines. Here are a few axioms in which a traditional mode of collaborative performance can be cultivated and sustained.

■ **Overarching noble theme and agenda that motivates every single team member**. Provide a vision—a set of shared aspirations—together with specific goals that everyone buys into. Take full advantage of the great intrinsic motivation and passion inherent in a meaningful and challenging project to create a range of alternatives and an optimal solution. An example of a general overarching vision is sustainability. It should not be too difficult to get everyone on board with that—in fact, that vision may help to attract the best talent to your firm. Focus on the (design) idea for a specific project. Here is where individual agendas could intersect or align with the collective agenda of developing innovative solutions. It cannot be underscored enough that intrinsic motivation is a key to a successful collaborative effort from all team members. Leaders should spotlight this because it is even more important than social skills. In sum, creatively and cleverly framed design challenges, proffered at every phase of a project, are intrinsically motivating and lead to higher productivity and quality.

- **Seek diversity in team composition**. This applies to experiences, background, culture, worldview, area of expertise, talents, skills—and ideas. The more diverse—and the greater the potential for creative tension—the more likely there will be innovative ideas and solutions to challenging problems. In other words, celebrate differences to promote design excellence. Collaborators who know each other well want to work together, but that can tend to produce mediocre results and narrow-minded groupthink. One way to prevent this from happening is by selecting new team members with fresh perspectives. Obviously, assemble the best and brightest talents as the highest priority to yield the best ideas and results. The softer skills of working together are of lesser importance, albeit valuable.

- **Only collaborate strategically—not on every task**. Not all tasks are amenable to collaborative work. In fact, within a given project, the best outcomes result when the project leader knows when to assign tasks to a team and when to assign tasks to an individual. In general, *individual* preparation prior to engaging in *collaborative* work can optimize productivity and outcomes. Indeed, excellent preparation is as important as spontaneity during a collaborative session.

- **Provide effective leadership**. The leader must ensure that there are not too many good ideas on the table, and that compromise does not dilute a strong idea. The leader should present ideas to be elaborated upon, almost like giving an "assist" in basketball, so that another talented player can take the idea, build on it, and slam-dunk it—or make it better. The leader must ensure that each collaborator feels that their individual contribution has been meaningful to the progress of the collective work so that they can legitimately claim investment in and ownership of the design ideas. See the section "Leading Projects" in Chapter 4.

- **Be mindful of the soft skills; learn them and practice them**. With the promulgation of powerful new software tools for remote collaboration, understanding collaborative behavior is just as important as understanding the technology. Even though these psychological and communication skills are not as valuable as genuine expertise, they can greatly facilitate working together. See more on soft skills in the next subsection.

- **Have fun to innovate and create**. Derive satisfaction from and promote a sense of fun—and humor (while still taking the work seriously)—in interactions with others. If the interactions are fun, there is a greater likelihood of project success, that is, a deeper understanding of stakeholder issues and a better environment in which to cultivate innovative ideas. The gratification of working on a successful collaborative effort is incomparable.

- **Promote innovation and risk taking to get the best work**. No idea should be deemed too precious to hold on to like grim death. Conversely, every idea should be taken seriously and thought of as a potential contribution to be built upon. Don't judge (at least don't make judgments too quickly). Treat new ideas with particular attention and sensitivity; do not let them be crushed; discussion of conflicting ideas should be promoted. Acknowledge unsuccessful work as a valuable part of the collaborative process and as an opportunity to learn. The IDEO mantra, now a cliché, "Fail often to succeed sooner,"[2] is particularly salient.

- **Take time to critically reflect on the collaborative process, both during the project and after**. Analogous to the morbidity and mortality (M & M) conference in medicine, this is a means of retrospectively and critically analyzing every detail of a failure or bad outcome so as to heighten awareness of pitfalls and increase the probability of better outcomes in the future. Reflect on and process the criticisms and dialogue of the collaborative sessions. What was successful? What didn't work? What would you do differently on the next project? What was good that you should build upon in the future? Become mindful of your own role in the process; evaluate your participation in the team effort—was it substantive, tangential, constructive, too much, too little? Were you an active listener? Did you acknowledge criticism or dismiss it? Perhaps it is the creative tension between practical exigencies and ideals that motivates innovation and keeps creativity tied to the solution of (sometimes) mundane but significant problems.

- **Every team and every project is different**. Design the collaborative process accordingly; there is no formula. All team members must buy into the specific process of the project as defined by the project leader.

- **Assume responsibility**. All design team members must take individual responsibility for their respective areas of expertise in the context of working for the good of the project.

A productive, collaborative work session requires talented people who are empowered to make decisions (on behalf of their firms or divisions on large projects) and who are unafraid to push disciplinary boundaries. Integrated concepts cannot evolve successfully without the participation of all relevant disciplines with the manager leading the way, eliciting ideas and comments.

Soft Skills

Building rapport, goodwill, and respect among all the players is also essential to the best collaborative sessions. How do you do that? "Transparency, openness, and a willingness to share information," states Jim Summers,[3] an associate in the Boston office of Burt Hill, "will enable the change of focus from individual to project." Their team members will spend a significant amount of time together to understand a clear scope of responsibilities, design objectives, degree of risk, and bottom line; this "fleshing out" is part of the discovery process, involving multidisciplinary consultants and resulting in a contract that supports a unique workflow. Summers is amazed at "the soft skills you need to work through that process and come to an agreement," *and this is before the project itself even starts*.

Some of the soft skills that can be sharpened to make you a better collaborator include establishing rapport and respect, active listening, speaking, writing, drawing, negotiating, and using humor, all toward enhancing truly reciprocal communication between all collaborators. These collaborative abilities are best developed through experiences, and through actively reflecting on them. Here is some elaboration on the benefits of employing those collaborative skills.

Rapport

If there is such a thing as the standard condition for engaging people, it is rapport. To have rapport with another, be yourself; you should neither affect some wooden formality you may believe is "professional" nor be excessively casual and familiar. In the case of collaborating with a client (or stakeholder, as noted in Chapter 2), the client's perception that he or she is being *cared for* will likely enhance participation, the quality of information offered, and wishes voiced.

Respect

Respect everyone else on the team; presumably, they are on the team because they have a certain level of expertise. Respect the project and client. Try to resist the natural inclination to judge people. This is especially true for collaborators. Rather, focus on the project and the design work to realize the great vision and to implement the concepts.

Active Listening

Try to appreciate your collaborator's unique perspectives. Focusing on what a collaborator says, how they say it, and why they say it sets the stage for interpreting ideas and incorporating them into the project. If an idea represents a genuine contribution, acknowledge and celebrate it, and the collaborator will be that much more invested in the project.

Speaking and Writing

Team members can't advocate for the value of the project, much less their good ideas, if they can't communicate effectively. Avoid jargon and pseudo-academic gobbledygook. Instead, use a style that is "clean, straightforward, focused, vigorous, serious but not solemn, friendly but not flippant."[4] Honestly share expertise, knowledge, ideas, and criticisms. In other words, promote genuinely reciprocal communication.

Drawing or diagramming (see Chapter 4). Those who can draw simple diagrams or use a diagramming app (just about anyone can with a bit of practice) have a huge advantage in working collaboratively because they can use the universal language of drawing as a means to create, communicate, and even play—with others. Drawing is effective in communicating ideas across cultures and diverse stakeholders. Fully develop and exploit this skill that uniquely distinguishes a collaborative design thinker in brainstorming sessions and one-on-one.

Negotiating

Collaborators can creatively apply negotiating strategies to numerous situations beyond contracts, such as promoting a particular feature or idea for a project. For example, in the classic text *Getting to Yes: Negotiating Agreement Without Giving In,*[5] the authors describe a method they term "principled negotiation." This method includes four basic tenets: separate people from the problem, focus on interests as opposed to positions, invent options for mutual gain, and insist on objective criteria. Further, they suggest recasting personal attacks as attacks on the problem itself.

Humor

Infusing conversations and meetings with humor might just be one of the most important strategies in successfully engaging collaborators—and in establishing rapport. Humor can also help to diffuse frank criticism or comments without having them appear as a personal attack.

There is consensus that there is nothing better than face-to-face sessions to foster collaboration and meaningful relationships. This is particularly true at the start of a project, when even one such meeting will pave the way for sub-sequent videoconferences. Socializing can also help a group to coalesce into a team. However, it must be stated that social ties can potentially also lead to maladaptive relationships and disruption of a chain of command.

Counterintuitive Truths About Collaborative Design Thinking

The following 12 statements are intended to trigger reflection about collaborative experiences. They represent collective wisdom, are somewhat counter-intuitive, and, in some cases, may even be provocative.

1. ***Do not automatically trust your fellow team members***. Develop rapport and respect instead. It is unrealistic to trust team members with whom you have had little contact. Trust is not a necessary prerequisite for effective collaboration; respect is. Professional judgment and exper-tise are very important in establishing common language, rapport, and respect. Having a beer, sharing a meal, giving a gift, or experiencing a good time does not define the notion of "trust." These events do not and should not engender trust. Trust is cultivated over many years through shared adversity as well as smooth sailing.

2. ***Intentional narcissism is important for effective teamwork***. Do not check your ego at the door. Do not insist that others check their egos at the door. Confidence and even a bit of arrogance are helpful to innovate and to transcend mediocrity. Sometimes those with great ideas are motivated to invoke a measure of theatrics to awaken a stagnant team. But, at the same time, others' valuable contributions or roles must be acknowledged. In any case, individuals must always be acknowledged for their contributions to the team effort and to advancing the project. There is nothing wrong with a healthy ego that is responsible for pushing the envelope.

3. ***Work independently to collaborate better***. Collaborators must take individual responsibility for their own area of expertise—or role on the project—as a prerequisite to creating a synergistic, collective work prod-uct above and beyond individual contributions. There is an "I" in collab-oration. That's how much of the work gets accomplished. Moreover, a

colleague can be stoked up and inspired by another's clever work—or another's vacuous work, which leads to the next statement.

4. **Bad ideas are essential**. Bad ideas are great because they often trigger exceptional ideas from others. So the bad idea must be appreciated; that is, all ideas need to be considered, nurtured, then rejected, accepted, or built upon—not immediately crushed—as an integral part of the collaborative process. The secondary benefit of not automatically casting off the bad idea is to save face for the collaborator who proposed it, bolstering his or her ego, and enabling fruitful participation in the future.

5. **Teamwork can dilute powerful ideas**. This is especially true without strong leadership. Never underestimate the power of the majority to slow and even suffocate the creative individual or the iconoclast. The leader is charged with mitigating peer pressure or emergent norms that may reflect apathy on the part of the team.

6. **Effective teamwork is significant independent of technology and tools**. All too often, technology is nothing more than distraction. Preoccupation with technical hardware or software inevitably narrows a design thinker's frame of reference, may result in blind spots or myopia, and may remove one from the real world of textures, subtleties, nuances, and constantly changing patterns.

7. **The best leadership is plastic, not necessarily transparent**. To lead well, design an approach to elicit the best work from each collaborator as a function of their personality, the task at hand, and the project circumstances. Leaders should tailor their interventions to specific collective and individual styles.

8. **Personality can be misleading in selecting an optimal collaborative team**. Time and again, the more seductive personality is chosen over the more creative or effective professional. Do not select the more facilitative personalities; rather, recruit individuals whose background and skills best complement the team and support the project at hand. Playing nice is important but overrated. Team chemistry can be an elusive but critical variable.

9. **Excellent work can be achieved as much by an individual as by a collaborative effort**. The cliché argument "What is better: the auteur or the team" is a meaningless academic exercise. It just depends on both the individuals involved and the project challenges. Approach and method should be adjusted to the context. The leader must be prepared to improvise.

10. **A great team could be characterized as one big unhappy dysfunctional family**. You don't have to like the other team members to have a great team and produce great results. Project and personal agendas— intrinsic motivations—transcend this. Tension between team members can be seen as constructive—as the gasoline that fuels innovation and excellent work.

11. **Avoid compromise that undermines the big ideas**. Compromise may help to streamline the process but can dilute strong concepts.

12. **Collaborate with your fiercest competition**. Add great strength, networks of consultants and clients, knowledge, and insight to a particular project. In other words, keep friends close, enemies closer.

MANAGED COLLABORATIVE FRAMEWORKS

In general terms, managed collaboration is a proposal for an inclusive process that informs and enriches a project—that optimizes contributions from the participants in synergistic fashion. It is an aggressive method (adjusted subtly for the specifics of each project), capable of guiding deployment of all team members and stakeholders at various integration points. These nodes of integration promote both efficiency and quality among consultant teams on a large project, or when an internal team meets on a small project. In both cases, the manager designs a process of inquiry for the project along with an optimal set of team members (Figure 3.1).

The trajectory of a managed collaborative process can be viewed as a rapid evolution through time marked by a series of inputs from consultant teams that represent the involved specialties. At each input from a specialty, the manager faces an integrative challenge: to wed the specialist's work gracefully with the

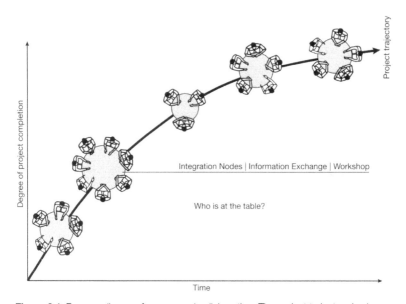

Figure 3.1 Process diagram for managed collaboration. The project trajectory is characterized by a series of inputs from consultant teams that are managed and led by the project manager. Selective team members and consultants are deployed at various integration points depending on project circumstances. Workshops can be an inspiring way to advance the project at integration nodes.

work on a project to date in a manner consistent with, and complementary to, the overall concept.

In this manner, specialized and talented teams working independently provide highly focused, substantive, and innovative pieces of the whole. Joining, tweaking, and refining the sequentially contributed pieces from each team in a manner consistent with the overarching mission or concept becomes the responsibility of the team leader who manages the collaborative process. Any managed process is intended to enhance efficiency and lower costs by controlling or manipulating as many variables as possible in a manner that accelerates pace and minimizes redundancy and waste.

It is perhaps counterintuitive, but personality and politics are thus minimized, and creativity and efficiency are optimized, since there is in effect a reduction of competing noise from "too many cooks." Rather than an entire orchestra of contributors, a project leader or manager is freed to critically appraise, distill, and assemble the independently developed components.

This managed process (see Figure 3.1) is a model of professional collaboration that places the team leader in a more authoritative and also more creative position (in contrast to a traditional collaborative mode). Ideas, not ideology or personality, become the focus. Individual specialty teams collaborate actively among themselves but not across teams—except during integration points. Again, intervening variables, potential obstructions, or delays in the idea generation phase are minimized, with personality and politics less prominent since the evolution of the project through time is shepherded by a single individual. In the absence of noise or frank interference arising inevitably from competing voices or ideas from each specialty team, the team leader is given a greater opportunity to see more clearly and precisely how specialty inputs may fit with or reinforce the main ideas.

Sidebar 3.1 Workshop and Reflection at Each Milestone

A workshop or *charrette* is an inspiring way to advance and manage the project at integration nodes (or at those points of significant information exchange). A workshop is deployed at certain times during a project as a means to collaborate more vigorously and deeply. At each workshop, the design becomes more resolved and integrated, problems are addressed, and work is coordinated. The workshop is a vehicle to engage in in-depth discussions with all consultants, the client, and other stakeholders as appropriate.

Arranging the initial workshop at project inception is hugely beneficial. The workshop allows the team leader to:

■ Provide an ideal time to jump-start design thinking.

■ Facilitate getting to know the collaborators to assess their professional expertise and social skills, including their ability to work with others on the team.

- Enable the team to fully grasp all the available information about the project, including programmatic, contextual, and budget factors, in order to get the best possible input from all present and to develop more detailed questions.

- Elicit critical feedback on preliminary ideas and the overarching vision for the project.

- Describe the workshop process with proposals for specific roles and tasks, project expectations, and leadership, decision-making, and communication protocol.

Several additional salient observations with regard to leading workshops include the following. It almost goes without saying that the leader should not be condescending, arrogant, or egotistical because the quieter members will be even more reluctant to participate. At regular intervals during the session, take stock and summarize important points, ideas, features, etc., and compare those to the overarching objectives for the project. The leader can be the session facilitator but also the session designer, ensuring appropriate engagement and accomplishment in accordance with the distinctive role of each collaborator, and of course, the agenda.

Notwithstanding the inherent excitement of such a session in kicking off a project, one secondary benefit is the camaraderie among collaborators in creating something special together. It should be noted that sessions may be more productive if team members prepare before a session—but not too much—so that they are not overly scripted and can be free to wing it in response to input from other collaborators.

Structuring this workshop process for each integration node is, in itself, another design problem for the team leader. Collaboration across specialty teams occurs at the integration nodes, which must be specifically defined for the project at hand to best utilize the consultants and tools in the context of the project circumstances.

Only relevant stakeholders should participate as collaborators in these unique, highly focused sessions in which there is an intensive, total immersion in a compressed, uninterrupted, and dedicated time frame focused on a review of work to date, design analysis, and integration at the appropriate level of detail. It not only affirms that the project is progressing in accordance with initial ideas (i.e., functionality, aesthetic and social purpose, cost issues, sustainability goals, and so on), but it provides a roadmap for advancing the project to the next increment of resolution and integration. These workshops provide extraordinary opportunities to expose the project to a high-level critical analysis and reflection by all collaborators.

Insightful criticism can be folded into the design process at each workshop so that projects can become better—and more innovative. This is one of the most important aspects of the workshop component of this collaborative process. The workshop held during an integration node is not just about coordination or details. It is an opportunity to consider proposed solutions thoughtfully and collectively: the big picture and vision, and how they are developing for the project.

The team leader provides guidance for next steps, including responses to the critical assessments and experimenting or innovating to advance the proposals (which may also serve to inspire the team). After processing the initial vision, concept, early ideas, and subsequent direction after every workshop, the consultants or other team members should be free to infuse their work with their own interpretation of that information and guidance. The leadership should ensure that this happens so that the consultants are truly invested in the project. Moreover, a workshop also has a benefit of mitigating against feelings of isolation by team members and promoting feelings of investment in the project and contributing to design decisions.

After a couple of these workshops have been completed—once there has been some success in working together—a social gathering might be propitious. It can serve to nurture relationships and set the tone for energetically completing the project.

In sum, the workshop deployed at integration nodes is an exciting, inspiring, and effective brainstorming strategy to identify key issues, resolve problems, critically reflect on the design, and advance the project. The team leader designs each workshop with a focus on some aspect of the project to elicit high-quality and immediate feedback on which to base further investigation and inquiry.

It is intriguing to explore the application of a managed style of collaborative process to any professional endeavor. This approach already exists in medicine to a degree, with its specialty or consultation focus in responsive service to the internal medicine or surgical attending physician. Within architecture, there are the routine instances of consultation by structural, mechanical, and civil engineers. And, in some businesses, there are internal divisions such as sales, finance, and HR, and external consultants including IT, legal, and insurance agents. The leap in the present conception lies with the understanding or assumption that the team leader serves as a relatively freewheeling evaluator and integrator of ideas provided by the component specialty teams. The team leader arrives at an idea for the project in the project's earliest phase (consistent with idea generation component of design thinking), but thereafter serves primarily to assure that the specialty teams produce work consistent with that idea. Collaboration involves a focus on ideas, on the marriage of the work of specialty teams to a dynamic integrative process, which occurs periodically at nodes of integration and finally at the "executive" level of the team leader. Competing personalities and personal agendas, then, are necessarily of less prominence.

Team members will have to accept specific direction about where they can contribute, and live with a team leader who will be assertive and even autocratic. Collaboration in this managed collaborative conception is directed by a prominent exercise of leadership. The empowered leader deploys the collaborators at exactly the right time and place to minimize redundancy, noise, and clashing personalities—versus the traditional model of collaboration, in which collaborators are bound by mutual obligations and personal relationships. It may well be a challenge for team members and consultants to accept and participate in a managed system as characterized here; expectations for personal and professional behavior will inevitably favor those who are more comfortable functioning independently and without the traditional crosstalk and continual interaction with some proximate matrix of colleagues. In fact, arguably, the "virtual" office in which principals work in relative isolation and electronically transmit their work to some central integrative point is the optimal framework for a managed approach to collaboration.

How does the team leader deal with many voices trying to contribute at the same time or in random fashion, as in a brainstorming or charrette session? The answer is that the leader designs and diagrams when and how team members participate. In contrast to the constant ebb and flow of discussion and feedback, much of which can be of little consequence, the leader can schedule creative and problem-solving sessions in which focus and yield are maximized.

In a strictly managed framework, then, the team leader would be empowered to break down silos to support a project most efficiently. This model of collaboration works when specialties are guided as if by an orchestra conductor. The leader does not allow the collaborative activity to happen naturally; the leader makes it happen as a function of what is important at that specific point in the project, and for advancing the project. This approach is optimally cost- and time-effective. The team leader becomes a designer and manager of the process—as much as he or she may be manager of the project.

The team leader clearly defines the process of working together, which is different for each unique project (as a function of scale, budget, stakeholders, etc.). For example, creative tracks can be identified, each of which has a specialty leader. A diagram of when the tracks cross (and how long [time] and how thick [scope] they are) serves to illustrate integration nodes and the extent of a given specialty's input relative to the whole project. But for every project, project goals and more global agendas of team members are up front and center. Collaborative activity can best be framed as a design problem; list the variables. Consultants have varying degrees of immersion; the team leader must limit or increase participation as a function of project and design requirements. Identify when to apply focused team effort— anywhere from a large inclusive team to a small deep dive. Scale the team to the specific task.

Client, Consultant, and Stakeholder Involvement

In a managed practice, the team's relationship with the consultants is *not* reciprocal. Alas, there is little time and money to entertain their input on all of the issues (unless you want to cut profit). There is great respect for their expertise, but not necessarily for their input in other areas. As the team leader, imagine how you would discuss the project with consultants; elicit their feedback related to their area of expertise and how that will influence the project. Moreover, the team leader must facilitate the consultants' dialogue with each other when relevant for the project.

Some consultants (i.e., a lawyer, accountant, structural engineer, etc.) may have their own liability concerns that might be reflected in input that is too conservative. In that case, the leader should encourage them to present options with associated risks so that the internal team could assess their risk tolerance, and whether added insurance can moderate the risk.

This discussion is not at all meant to suggest that "silos" of expertise be promoted. There is overlap in expertise, which must be incorporated into initial thinking about the project and development of concepts for truly integrated solutions.

Orchestrating active client collaboration together with an array of consultants and team members from project inception is essential for creating innovative solutions. Incorporating ongoing dialogue with all stakeholders at critical points during the design thinking process and translating and integrating these data into the project is the only way the outcome can ultimately be considered successful.

The project leader is the team member who has the responsibility to take an intuitive leap to synthesize the data from other team members in a special way that drives the project toward excellence. The stage is set for a critical thought process whereby key information serves as the focus, and irrelevant information is ignored. One of the project leader's tasks is to educate the client about great design or great solutions and show them exciting possibilities that they couldn't imagine—possibilities that are, of course, based on the client's input. That is why the client is *not* an equal collaborator, even though they are a critically important part of the collaborative effort. Actively listening to the client is an absolute requirement. Translating, filtering, and inferring what the client says—not necessarily explicitly doing what the client says—is also an absolute requirement. Clients and other stakeholders can trigger ideas and inform the project design, but, alas, they are not the collaborative design thinkers. Stakeholder participation should be carefully limited and choreographed to provide value to the design thinking process depending on the sophistication and expertise of each stakeholder.

Don't waste time pursuing poor proposed solutions or design ideas; this can be a big liability if the collaborative process is not managed well. On the other hand, stakeholders are essential in informing the development of the design, especially the parameters and the goals.

How collaborators participate in a project depends on the project circumstances and the consultants involved. As one of the first steps at project inception, the project leader has to design the process including the nature and frequency of interactions with consultants and other team members, taking into consideration his or her own knowledge and capabilities. For example, the manager could have a conversation with a specific consultant to inform the development of a concept based on the consultant's specific expertise. There might not be a reason to meet with *every* consultant at *every* phase of the project.

Consultants or other team members should not be regarded as mere technicians to execute a concept or squiggle by the project leader in a silo, but as collaborators from the start who participate in a dialogue at strategic points in the process to innovate, integrate, inform, and iterate.

The concept of managed practice addresses a project leader's primal fear of losing control—or, more important, of diluting his or her great ideas—in a collaborative model of practice. In this model, however, they are thrust into a transcendent and very creative role; that is, directing, integrating, driving, and harvesting ideas in support of the concept—and ensuring its integrity.

Precedents for Managed Collaboration

Collaborative practice has played a significant role in many professions and industries, and examples of this framework can yield fresh insights into its prospective benefits.

A dramatic illustration of managed collaboration comes from recent aviation history. The Airbus Industries A380 airliner is a breathtaking achievement in aircraft design and construction. In 1999, the European aircraft manufacturer Airbus initiated the A380 project to manufacture the world's first truly double-decker airliner with a theoretical high-density passenger seating capacity of more than 800. Airbus adopted what is considered a revolutionary decentralized manufacturing process. The centers that manufactured various parts were arrayed across Europe, and the final assembly was completed at Toulouse, France, under the watchful eyes of a handful of project managers who possessed *absolute authority*. State-of-the-art composites that reduced the overall weight of the aircraft were used to optimize the strength-to-weight ratio, which in turn revolutionized fuel economy and range. Although the A380 has been eclipsed by the most recent generation of twin engine wide-bodied aircraft, Airbus, with its increasingly refined model of managed collaboration, continues to lead the world in the quality and quantity of superb passenger aircraft.

Other seminal examples of managed collaboration include the Skunk Works founded in 1943 and the Manhattan Project founded in 1941, in which conflicts were notorious, with *many more physicists than team builders*. In each instance, the huge talents and huge egos were minimized, integrated, and melded into a synergy by a handful of strong leaders who identified a clear task and timetable and made certain the project adhered to and achieved the goals. In the case of the Manhattan Project, J. Robert Oppenheimer was endowed with autocratic power by the project leader, General Leslie Groves.

Groves was an experienced manager who had overseen the construction of the Pentagon; he was described as pushy and overbearing, but his organizational and managerial acumen drove the Manhattan Project ahead of similar German and Russian efforts.

At Lockheed's Skunk Works, which closed in 1990, Kelly Johnson worked for more than four decades as the organizing genius, design authority, and aggressive manager. He designed and/or contributed to the development of more than 40 revolutionary aircraft. The first of his "Fourteen Rules of Management" was: "The Skunk Works manager must be delegated practically complete control of his program in all aspects."[6]

Also consider the Apollo Project (1961–1972). While 400,000 people and 20,000 firms and universities were wrapped up in the effort, only a handful—arguably, three or four administrators and managers—are credited with shaping and directing the entire program and its historic result. The essence of managed collaboration is networking or connecting actors with others in some algorithmic matrix that supports focused productivity quickly and effectively, while providing a single authoritative vision that creates common ground among what may be a diverse set of stakeholders and the creative products of their effort.

There is a synergy in collaboration that is nothing short of a powerful force multiplier. The common denominator among the examples presented here, revealed by temporal analysis of the planning and design processes, is sequential integration of the work of discrete and talented teams facilitated and directed by, at most, only a few individuals.

INTEGRATED COLLABORATIVE MODELS

This section examines an approach to collaboration that integrates aspects of traditional and managed models by applying a model from the realm of government and political science. The discussion will explore the notions of a *traditional* "confederation" and the more *managed* "federation" in which individual member components (i.e., the states) operate separately from, yet are integrally part of, a (federal) whole under some executive leadership.

In other words, a confederation is a means of unifying an alliance that consolidates authority from other autonomous (or semiautonomous) bodies in support of common action. In contrast, in a federation, the component states are in some sense sovereign, but far greater powers and control reside with the central leadership (representing the managed side of collaborative practice).

The character and degree of central leadership and influence of the federation differ from case to case. Cases differ essentially in terms of how much control rests with the leader. Moreover, there is a dynamic give-and-take between the executive leadership and the component "states." Each state has its own resources, initiatives, and leadership that are to some degree aligned with, and supportive of, the overarching priorities and goals of the federal whole.

Strictly federal (managed) leadership assures coordination and forward movement, which may arise even out of chaos and fragmentation. Greater executive or central power and authority pushes confederation toward the pole of "federation."

Confederation vs. Federation: Traditional vs. Managed Styles

In a metaphor for practice, the members of the confederation are specialty teams and consultants (which comprise the bulk of the resources and capacity for doing the work). The leadership function is assumed by the team leader. The tone is likely to be more traditionally cooperative and interactive. If the team leader invokes and applies aspects of a "managed" style consistent with "federation," the tone becomes more directive and even autocratic. In each instance, in order to optimize process and fit firm function to client and project requirements, the leader makes a considered determination about style of practice.

The Integrated Approach

In football parlance, with the integrated model, the more successful game manager or quarterback is able to "call an audible." After "reading" the defensive scheme arrayed in front of him and taking careful account of position on the field, weather and turf conditions, and his team's strengths and weaknesses, the quarterback may need to adjust or change a predesigned play. At the line of scrimmage, the quarterback must be willing to, and be capable of, throwing or running the ball downfield. This metaphor establishes a project leader as an "option quarterback" of sorts, able to adjust their leadership style and the way in which their team functions according to the specific realities and challenges of both personnel and the project.

The integrated model offers the possibility of hybridizing both the soft-and-gentle traditional style and the hard-and-fast managed style. The skilled leader would be enabled to blend the loosely organized, purely collaborative webs within and outside a firm with occasional directive, autocratic helmsmanship. On the other hand, a purely managed style of leadership is clearly a simpler approach; it is, in fact, almost algorithmic, and it favors application by leaders who are less comfortable with the "option quarterback" style.

Leadership Within an Integrated Approach

According to Fred Fiedler,[7] there is no ideal leader. In his typology, "task-oriented" and "relationship-oriented" leaders can be effective if their leadership orientation fits the situation. Extending this proposition in terms of "traditional" vs. "managed" approach to facilitating or leading a collaborative endeavor in practice, it is not a stretch to begin to develop the theoretical basis for an "integrated" style. Fiedler's theory allows for a well-resolved description of the elements of such a style:

- **Leader-member relations**, referring to the degree of mutual trust, respect, and confidence between the leader and the subordinates.

- **Task structure**, referring to the extent to which group tasks are clear and structured.

- **Leader position power**, referring to the power inherent in the leader's position itself.

When there is a good leader-member relationship and a clearly structured set of tasks, a "traditional" style may be optimal. With very high leader position power and a complex and widespread task structure, a "managed" style may be ideal. In the language I have been invoking, leader-situation match and mismatch would then dictate the optimal collaborative style. Since personality is relatively stable, Fiedler's model suggests that improving effectiveness requires modifying the situation to fit the leader. This he calls "job engineering" or "job restructuring."

Strictly task-oriented or managed leadership would be appropriate to leading teams responding to a disaster requiring an immediate and multilevel response, such as an earthquake or flu pandemic. In an uncertain space, leader-member relations are typically and necessarily one-dimensional and minimalist, and the task is highly complex and fluid. The successful leader usually has a strong and even charismatic or therapeutic presence, but does not know subordinates personally. The task-oriented leader who gets things accomplished usually emerges as the most effective. If the leader is "traditionally" considerate (relationship-oriented), critical time may be wasted while disaster-associated events escalate.

The traditional (relationship-oriented) style may be optimal in an environment where the situation is more benign and well-delineated. Clearly, there is some self-selection in the movement of leaders with their unique styles toward firms with practices that may best match that style, but it is certainly not always the case. Recognition of very specific flavors of collaborative leadership—or design of relationships—is an important step in a conscious effort to engineer them in support of more effective and efficient practice. Whether we alter our styles of leadership to promote a superior fit with firm personnel and projects, or recruit leaders whose personalities better match the situational reality, we at least recognize the significance of the spectrum of professional collaboration.

Sidebar 3.2 Strategies for Collaborative Design on Large Projects

Roger Schwabacher, AIA, is a Design Principal with HOK in Washington, D.C. In his essay that follows,[8] Schwabacher discusses large-scale collaborative projects, but the underlying ideas are so universal that the strategies can apply equally to projects of just about any scale—and any type of project. His projects include the King Abdullah Petroleum

Studies and Research Center (KAPSARC), a 220-building campus in Riyadh, Saudi Arabia; and the LEED Gold certified NOAA Center for Weather and Climate Prediction in College Park, Maryland, USA.

The first thing to understand about the process of collaboration on large, complicated projects at HOK is that the design teams have become huge. Team leaders need to inspire not only the creativity of a group of architects, but also to harness diverse opinions from a broad spectrum of individuals such as the landscape architect; interior, sustainable, lighting, and graphic designers; specification writer; structural, mechanical, electrical, plumbing, civil, geotechnical, blast, and fire protection engineers; curtain wall, thermal, maintenance, acoustic, IT, life safety, elevator, hardware, and security consultants; cost estimator; and commissioning agent, not to mention the often times large and diverse client teams. The key to collaborating with such a large group is to empower the group's leader, often the project designer or architect, to solicit opinions from this wide net and to choose the solutions that work best with the overarching design goals of the project. Without this strong leader, who can resolutely make decisions in the best interest of the project, the diversity of opinions will dilute the original design intent.

How then is this strong project leader fostering collaboration and not becoming a dictator? By empowering each individual on the team, giving them a clear understanding of project goals and providing timely dissemination of information from meetings and discussions.

It has been my experience that different strategies are needed to foster collaboration with what I have identified as three distinct groups: the client, the architectural design team, and the engineers and consultants.

Client

Collaboration sessions with the client, whether in face-to-face meetings, through video conferencing, or through an exchange of sketches, need to start with a clear understanding of their organization and how they work. A first, basic step is to make sure that the key decision-makers are involved in the discussions; often this requires wading through layers in the organization to get to the people who have the power to make decisions. Without identifying and including the key decision-makers in these meetings, design efforts can spiral without progress. Once the correct people are identified, a strategy to foster collaboration is to approach the design problems with the client's priorities in mind, which often are very different than the design team's point of view. By "speaking their language" and understanding their key points, the design solution becomes more layered and complex. Listening is a skill often overlooked; collaboration with this group frequently involves helping them to clearly articulate their ideas and translate them into the built form. Tools most often used include three-dimensional renderings, animations, physical samples, project tours, and key facts/numbers about the building—items accessible to people not directly involved in the design and construction industry. Skills needed include *patience* to deal with language barriers and any inexperience with design and construction, *understanding* of cultural differences, and *flexibility* to respond to issues as they arise. The end goal is to gain the client's trust; collaboration does not work if the client is suspicious of your motives or goals.

Architectural Design Team

The key to fostering collaboration within a design team is channeling the variety of strong design opinions into a unified goal. On large HOK projects, this team may include up to twenty design professionals including architects, interior designers, landscape architects, sustainable designers, graphic designers, lighting designers and specification writers. Each of these team members needs to be vested in the project; they are not working on someone else's design, but are creating new ideas and actively developing the design to make the overall project a success. The idea of a "master architect" who makes every decision does not exist in today's practice. With the invention of collaboration soft-ware (i.e., Building Information Modeling) and the trend towards increasingly complex buildings with greater levels of coordination between disciplines, delegation of responsibility and collabora-tion between team members is the only way to work with any efficiency.

I have found that design team collaboration works when the overall design intent is clear and designers feel free to add to the vision. It fails when information is guarded, and independent thought is not encouraged. Design leaders need to be open to discussion, available to the team, and have clarity of thought and enthusiasm for the project. Collaboration between peers is also based on trust and respect; while visions may be different, the overall goal of improving the work of the office must be shared.

The best innovations on a project, whether they are overarching themes or specific details, usually come about organically in the design process and most typically occur in group conversations. The key is to have open dialog between team members so these ideas can come to light and the right people present in these con-versations recognize when a magical idea is perfect for a project.

Practical tools to foster collaboration include informal meeting spaces in the studio and periodically scheduling pin-ups (reviews of proposed solutions) for a wider group of designers to give input and help the team clarify their ideas. Over the past few years I have coordinated a series of these in-house pin-ups, where we have tried to utilize the collective design talent in the office by focusing on an individual project around the end of schematic design. To make these sessions productive, I have learned the following lessons: first, the team presenting the project should not lecture; presen-tations should be kept short, and the majority of the time should be dedicated to interactive discussions. Second, keep the review group small; if more than ten people are in the room, side discussions will always form and the group focus gets lost. Finally, a wide variety of viewpoints makes for the most interesting discussions: young and old, disciplines ranging from landscape to graphics, technical architects, and conceptual designers.

Engineers and Consultants

When architects collaborate with engineers and the wide variety of consultants, a clear agenda is needed for each meeting or else the conversation can get mired in minutia. Collaboration between these groups does not depend on each party understanding every intricacy of the design; instead, it depends on distilling down the important areas where the disciplines overlap. I have found that the level of experience of the participants of these collaboration sessions is a key factor; experience brings respect for the other's field and the knowledge of how to focus on the pertinent and to have the foresight to know where problems might evolve.

Successful collaboration with consultants is also dependent on timing—early enough so that an integrated solution is feasible, but not so early as to stifle a completely open design process. The structural options for a building may inform the major concept, such as when we designed a perforated, mass-wall mosque in the middle of the desert out of load bearing cast-in-place concrete; or the civil and plumbing engineers may be integral to the story, such as when we designed a five-story-tall rain-fed waterfall transferring water from a building's roof to a bio-retention area on the site. Essential to this collaboration are leadership, clear direction, and someone making sure that each specialized team member understands how they fit into the design. Only then can the team members channel the vast number of design options into a solution that is both efficient and graceful.

COLLABORATIVE PRECEDENTS TO EMULATE

The Film Industry

There is a strong analogy between making movies and teamwork; collaborative effort is necessary for success. The idea of assembling a team of experts by forming ad hoc alliances appropriate for a specific project (i.e., a movie)—whether considered networked, virtual, or merely an assemblage of talent in a discrete entity—can be a powerful strategy to deliver a project. Only the best people work on the project, which the project manager—or director—selects and leads.

In film, as in many other endeavors, there are schedule and budget constraints in addition to the challenge of managing talent. Extending the analogy, a film's technical crews, i.e., sound, costumes, and lighting, have their own crews, similar to consultants who have their own staff. People who frequently don't know each other often have to become immediate coworkers—and collaborators.

One of the greatest directors of all time, Ingmar Bergman, represents the essence of a collaborative approach in filmmaking. He wrote the script—sometimes outlined only with ideas—and planned the production process, which served as the creative foundation for the subsequent collaboration with the actors in production. An article in the *Harvard Business Review*[9] explains Bergman's objective: "Bergman wants to capture the fresh, creative urge that occurs in acting of the highest caliber, which is characterized by a spontaneity that cannot be practiced in advance"—or independently. So, Bergman set forth the concept and vision for the film and enabled the other team members to build on his ideas and make them better, or to use them as a point of departure. This could just as well be a description of an ideal collaborative approach to solving a complex problem or designing a project.

Director Arthur Penn is profiled in the same article.[10] Similar to Bergman, his collaboration with actors was paramount.

> He needed them to behave in ways that were spontaneous, authentic, original, and imaginative; to take risks by trying things they perhaps had

never tried before; to be open to his suggestions and ideas; and to develop new ideas of their own and work with them. He was constantly open to the moment, not only abandoning his own preconceived ideas about how a line or scene should be played, but also actively helping actors shed their own preconceptions as well.

In this way, Penn was able to promote innovation and create a work of art.

The final point with regard to a director's approach to collaboration is in his or her relationship to the technical crews such as sound and lighting. There are some directors who choose to delegate oversight in this realm to heads of the respective crews. The global analogy to project development is to delegate responsibility to consultants who lead their respective teams in their own deep dives.

Crew Resource Management

Crew resource management (CRM) evolved from a workshop sponsored by the National Aeronautics and Space Administration in 1979. The workshop focused on human error in air crashes, and the research concluded that most of the failures were in the realms of interpersonal communications, leadership, and decision-making; in other words, the crew's inability to collaborate effectively. The notion of CRM training was subsequently developed to improve flight crew performance, and it is defined as the effective utilization of all available resources—equipment and people—to achieve safe, efficient flight operations. The overarching objective of CRM is successful teamwork as a function of both technical proficiency and interpersonal dynamics. CRM training has been embraced by the aviation industry worldwide and has been adapted to other settings as well, including fire services, health care (operating and emergency rooms), and industries such as nuclear power plants and offshore oil operations.

So, what are the basic elements of CRM[11] that are relevant to collaboration in other disciplines? Assertiveness and advocacy are important behaviors. The key take-home message from CRM is for collaborators to advocate clearly and assertively—yet respectfully—for suggestions, ideas, concerns, and a

Figure 3.2 Pictured here is the cockpit crew for a modern passenger aircraft. Crew resource management (CRM), widely embraced by the aviation industry, is relevant to collaboration in general. If one member of a team sees a clear advantage in a position or course of action, then it is incumbent on that individual to advance that option persuasively.

Source: Skycolors/shutterstock.com.

course of action. It is important to speak up for a position, especially if you feel passionately about it, or disagree with someone else's position. Be willing to ask probing questions about a course of action, for example, and express opinions forcefully and gracefully (i.e., without being threatening) if necessary for the good of the project. As a final step, ensure that everyone understands the perspective and is onboard.

When ideas, schemes, or proposals are being evaluated, team members are sometimes reluctant to call attention to a frankly bad idea because they don't want to embarrass or undermine another team member, or because the team member may be too intimidating. Notwithstanding previously described strategies for constructive criticism and communication, the message must be conveyed. As part of the culture of collaboration, there should be a tacit understanding among all collaborators that assertive inquiry is an important part of the process and ostensibly benefits the work.

The essence of CRM, then, interpreted for collaboration in other disciplines, is that if one member of a team sees a clear advantage in an alternative or different course of action, then it is incumbent on that individual to advance that option persuasively. Elite teams and great leaders have been practicing this well before the promulgation of CRM; sometimes it is valuable to recall strategies that have made great teams great.

Learning from the Orchestra

If architecture, according to Goethe, is frozen music, then collaboration is an orchestra playing a symphony. To orchestrate is to collaborate to maximum effect. The orchestra demonstrates—perhaps more than anything else—the benefit of strong and responsive leadership; leadership by enthusiasm, energy, and feeling as opposed to leadership by criticism or narcissism. What follows are some observations about an orchestra that may provide some insights into successful collaboration in business.

- **Don't underestimate the importance of the leader**. The conductor is the *single individual* who "establishes and maintains the rhythm, drives the emphasis, and controls the tone of the piece being played."[12] The project leader, likewise, is the one who, with input from stakeholders and the team, creates the concept and vision for a project, designs and directs the process, sets the ground rules, and inspires the collaborators. And collaborators must be mindful of and appreciate different leadership styles.

- **The best people play with passion and great skill**. Musicians—or project managers and their consultants—must be selected with that in mind as a prerequisite to joining the team and creating meaningful work.

- **Musicians understand their relationships to the whole yet are highly individualistic**. Individuality should be cultivated. Working well in a collaborative environment toward shared objectives and preserving individuality are

Figure 3.3 James Gaffigan leading the Juilliard Orchestra in Mahler's Symphony No. 4 at Alice Tully Hall on April 20, 2013. If architecture, according to Goethe, is frozen music, then collaboration is an orchestra playing a symphony.

Source: Photo by Hiroyuki Ito/Getty Images.

not mutually exclusive. Awareness of what other sections/consultants are doing is part of the collaborative design process.

■ ***Musicians have impeccable timing***. Knowing when to participate and to what extent is particularly salient for collaborators (or for directing the collaborators).

■ ***The conductor is the only one who sees the big picture***. The project leader, as well, is in this unique position; this is one reason why collaboration should not be a democracy.

■ ***The conductor knows the musicians***. The conductor knows their strengths and limitations and knows how to get their best effort. The project leader needs to be cognizant of his or her collaborators' unique abilities and must ensure that there is appropriate and ongoing critique and reciprocal communication to elicit innovative work.

- **_Fresh interpretations of the music are inspiring_**. So too is looking at typical solutions and precedents in innovative ways.

It behooves all of us to apply as much design thinking to shape a new collaborative model of practice—on each unique project—as we do to developing the solutions. It is the thoughtful assimilation of a suitable collaborative model (including the most appropriate tools and technology) in support of design excellence and a true service ethic that will define the best in practice. However, it is axiomatic that with all the emphasis on collaborative processes of one form or another, it is important to keep in mind that process must always lead to tangible outcomes. These include a successful project (however that may be defined), a satisfied client, and sufficient profit.

NOTES

1 Scott Simpson, personal communication with the author, October 27, 2008.
2 Tom Kelley with Jonathan Littman, *The Art of Innovation: Lessons in Creativity from IDEO, America's Leading Design Firm* (New York: Currency/Doubleday, 2001), 232.
3 Tom Kelley with Jonathan Littman, *The Art of Innovation: Lessons in Creativity from IDEO, America's Leading Design Firm* (New York: Currency/Doubleday, 2001), 232.
4 *Effective Business Strategies in Architecture*, 3rd ed. (London: Routledge, 2021), 266. See the entire essay (pp. 264–68) for practical advice on how to write well.
5 Roger Fisher and William Ury, *Getting to Yes: Negotiating Agreement without Giving In* (New York: Houghton Mifflin, 1981).
6 Lockheed Martin, "Kelly's 14 Rules," accessed March 11, 2024, www.lockheedmartin.com/content/dam/lockheed-martin/aero/photo/skunkworks/kellys-14-rules.pdf
7 Fred E. Fiedler, Martin M. Chemers, and Linda Mahar, *Improving Leadership Effectiveness: The Leader Match Concept* (New York: John Wiley & Sons, 1976).
8 Roger Schwabacher, "Strategies for Design Excellence on Large Projects," in *Designing Relationships: The Art of Collaboration in Architecture*, by Andrew Pressman (London: Routledge, 2014), 71–74.
9 Eileen Morley and Andrew Silver, "A Film Director's Approach to Managing Creativity," *Harvard Business Review* 55, no. 2 (March–April 1977): 64.
10 Morley and Silver, "A Film Director's Approach to Managing Creativity," 66.

11 James E. Driskell and Richard J. Adams, *Crew Resource Management: An Intro-ductory Handbook* (Washington, DC: U.S. Department of Transportation Federal Aviation Administration, 1992), 8–32.

12 Ten Things Entrepreneurs Can Learn from Musicians," accessed April 18, 2013, http://blog.crowdspring.com/2011/03/10-things-that-entrepreneurs-can-learn-from-musicians/

4

ADVANCING THE WORK

Leadership and firm culture, discussed in this chapter, are important aspects of fostering and advancing a collaborative design thinking mindset.

DOI: 10.4324/9781003416142-4

> We're talking about somebody's life here. We can't decide it in five min-
> utes. . ... We nine can't understand how you three are still so sure. Maybe
> you can tell us.
>
> —Henry Fonda as a juror (and leader) in *12 Angry Men*[1]

With just two brief quotes from this 1957 film classic, Henry Fonda's character
(a design thinking architect!) begins to emerge as the leader of a group of men
who are deciding a capital murder case. He is the lone dissenter initially but

Figure 4.1 Henry Fonda plays an architect in the film *12 Angry Men*, the story of a
jury deciding the fate of a man on trial for murder. Initially, his is the sole
vote against a conviction, but eventually—in a demonstration of great
leadership—he is able to persuade the other jurors to reexamine the evidence and acquit on the basis of reasonable doubt.

Source: Photo by United Artists/Courtesy of Getty Images.

eventually is able to persuade the other 11 jurors to revisit the evidence and acquit the suspect on the basis of reasonable doubt. His successful strategies for leading the group include encouraging equal and inclusive participation and taking time to deliberate slowly. He listens carefully and considers the varying agendas of the other jurors without judgment so he can understand their perspectives, proffer new ideas persuasively, and then influence the outcome.

While life-and-death decisions are not usually part of a project leader's daily routine, and collaborative teams are not normally as unruly as that jury was, design thinkers who are capable leaders hold great power. Appropriately applying that power to lead a collaborative team and direct efforts to integrate the work of all of the team members into a synergistic whole can result in innovative and creative projects and solutions.

How should the manager lead and mobilize the team to move the project forward, to complete the next steps to the highest degree of excellence? The conventional approach is framed by the question, "I know the right thing to do; now, how can I learn how to collaborate with people so I can get them to do what I want them to do?" A better question, however, for leading a high-powered, multidisciplinary team is, "I have some thoughts about what we should do, how can I effectively share my insights and what I care about with others while also authentically listening to their insights?" This suggests an attitude about leadership and collaboration, one that requires enough wisdom to know that someone else may have an even better idea.[2]

Skilled practitioners of the collaborative design approach have the ability to think critically and go beyond the status quo to form meaningful new ideas. This skill set can be developed and, in concert with expertise, gives them the ability to see the big picture, reframe questions to see different perspectives, create innovative solutions to problems, attend to detail, and manage complex relationships. Project managers who possess these skills, which are also characteristics of great leaders in many disciplines, can leverage these insights to lead effectively.

Exposing staff at all levels in the firm to clients and consultants as often as possible can be an effective approach to leading teams in addition to cultivating leadership from the ranks. This is a powerful way for staff to understand client and consultant perspectives, and why it may be that the principals are leading the project in a certain fashion. If staff hear it directly from the client, they are more likely to become truly invested in the project, which promotes collaboration. One of the goals of this strategy, then, is to develop, among all team members, the ability to listen intently to clients from the very start when they express what they need their project to do for them.[3] This is analogous to a clinical or therapeutic approach to leading a team.

Numerous surveys indicate that architects (in other words, design thinkers!) are highly respected in our culture. Maybe that aura together with the charismatic personality is what made Henry Fonda's juror so influential. Regardless, a distinctive and energetic personality style by itself could translate into enormous potential for reaching diverse groups including clients, community members, and other stakeholders who may not always be receptive. Inspired and dynamic leaders embrace change and challenge in general, listen well, articulate their vision, motivate, think critically and creatively, reflect, prioritize, and then act.

Leadership Basics

Collaborative design thinking requires great leadership in addition to someone who is ultimately responsible for making decisions.

Given knowledgeable and responsible problem solvers, the leader must free the team member to plug whatever creative talent they have into the collaborative process. You can't orchestrate the making of magic, but you must set the stage to let it happen. The leader is in essence a teacher and mentor who has the ability to push and pull, critique, improvise, and use significant amounts of intuition to advance the project.

What are the three most important tools for team leaders?

1. **Donuts and coffee**. In many different contexts, providing these tools will facilitate face-to-face sessions to build goodwill, rapport, respect, and an understanding of positions. Don't underestimate the power of the donut (or some healthy snack) in breaking down barriers of all types.

2. **Thick markers and tracing paper or diagramming apps**. Design thinkers have a huge advantage in leading and working collaboratively because they can use the language of diagramming to inspire, create, and communicate with others. Leverage this skill; use it as often as possible.

3. **Ongoing and frequent dialogue**. Dialogue, both collectively and individually in a range of media, is essential for engagement and inclusion, which leads to investment in the work. Effective dialogue means that a good leader listens well and continually motivates to advance the project.

In collaborative design thinking, the project manager assumes responsibility for leading the whole process within the context of the professional, corporate, and institutional framework, while responding in varied ways as a function of the project and the team. The leader's purview also encompasses engagement with the team at all levels and on a personal as well as a professional basis. The team leader on a project has the overarching vision and purpose, sets the tone, creates the concepts, understands the context, engages and directs the consultants and team members, and inspires them with the vision. What follows are some basic leadership tips that operationalize the mandates of leadership.

■ **Listen carefully to team members and have frequent one-on-one, face-to-face conversations**. This is how a genuine connection is established and sustained. This is by far the best way to communicate important information, and to direct the individual's talent to the work of the project. Take full advantage of media that promote an exchange of ideas. This exchange must be reciprocal so that the team member can express passion for the project and the ideas will flow. Arrange meetings between various select team members as needed for coordination and integration; then the larger team meetings may be more focused and effective.

■ **Provide explicit goals, expectations, and roles for both the team as a whole and each collaborator**. Then, as the project evolves, figure out how to grow the inspiration and confidence within each team member.

■ **Demonstrate how, and ensure, that individual team members feel that their input was helpful in advancing the project**. Indicate how their scribble on a Post-it, for example, contributed to the solution.

- **Be decent and responsible when giving critical feedback**. Be constructive and positive. Don't be judgmental, at least initially. Avoiding exclusively negative feedback—for example, by instead suggesting exploration of specific alternatives—can preserve self-confidence, and help to elicit a more creative contribution. Be mindful that all team members are in this together, including the leader.

- **Nurture the best in each diverse personality**. Reach out and connect with each individual as a unique and valued member of the team.

- **Be a resource for the team**. Serve the team rather than rule as a dictator. Provide support. Educate, encourage, facilitate strengths and mitigate weaknesses to the extent possible.

- **Be a consistent and reliable presence, a role model for the team**. Establish and demonstrate work habits, professionalism (i.e., engage team members with respect and appreciation), fairness, lead from the front (no task is too menial), and be authentic.

- **Be persistent in trying to inspire and develop innovative ideas**. Reframe ideas to allow collaborators to apply their own specialized expertise to the problem.

- **Allow others to lead at certain times, as circumstances and expertise suggest**.

- **Diagram team members' characteristics, especially their strengths, to assist in broadly suggesting roles most consistent with expertise and personal style**. Be cognizant of and then direct how collaborators can bring their unique, creative expertise and potential to bear on the project.

- **Obtain adequate authority**. Delegate it clearly when necessary or beneficial. (See Leslie Groves and Kelly Johnson for model examples of delegating authority in Chapter 3, the section "Precedents for Managed Collaboration.")

- **Be mindful of the timeline; offer interventions as appropriate to keep the project on track**—from nuanced suggestions to audacious proposals.

- **Genuinely care about those under your leadership**. Ensure that everyone has an opportunity to meaningfully contribute, learn, and grow.

Decision-Making

Ironically, successful collaboration almost always requires some degree of autocratic leadership. No ambiguity about it—the team leader must be empowered to make final decisions, while occasionally deferring to expert specialists. Openness to alternatives at every phase is implicit in this model. Nevertheless, a team leader or champion must be identified early on, and it must be agreed that final authority rests with that individual. Sarah Harkness,[4] one of the original partners with Walter Gropius of the Architects Collaborative, has quoted Gropius as proclaiming that

> [to] safeguard design coherence and impact, the right of making final decisions must be left exclusively to the one member who happens to be responsible for a specific job, even though his decision should run counter to the opinion of other members.

The point is that one way to avoid either endless, unproductive discussion or the cliché, "a camel is a horse designed by committee," is to have a leader who is empowered to make informed decisions after listening to, understanding, and appreciating the perspectives from all team members.

A hybrid approach to making decisions can be useful depending on the specific nature of what is being decided (and the time frame) during the course of a project. For example, the leader can defer to an expert, there can be discussion and consensus, or the leader can make an informed unilateral decision, as described earlier.

Ego Management

Orchestration of a collaborative design thinking work session usually involves a complex and subtle manipulation on the part of leadership so that the inevitably talented and distinctive personalities that make up a team may interact positively and productively. Management of healthy egos is a priority because it is not always realistic, possible, or even desirable to follow the conventional wisdom that egos must be checked at the door. Participants must believe they can do the impossible in order to *do* the impossible and innovate.

It behooves the leader to simultaneously encourage individual participation and "foster an environment where the team owns ideas, rather than each member owning his or her own," says Morris A. Nunes,[5] a Fairfax, Virginia, attorney who represents practices and privately held businesses. He underscores that the team should be coached, nurtured, and incentivized as a team. In other words, every collaborator works for the good of the project—and shares the rewards as well as the risks. Nunes claims that Ben Franklin's famous quote, "We must all hang together or we shall surely hang separately," should be a constant refrain.

Leadership With a Light Touch and Sharing Power

Some degree of hierarchy and authority is necessary even in the most democratic collaborative groups. There must be a distinct leader who keeps the team focused, is mindful of deadlines, and directs decision-making. Totally free-form approaches may waste precious energy, time, and money and, in the long run, may sow the seeds for further anarchistic impediments. However, there is certainly a light touch to leading teams at Gensler. Jordan Goldstein,[6] managing director of the Washington, D.C., office, describes their team leaders as "facilitators and conductors of the larger symphony, which includes the design team, client, contractor, consultants, and vendors." The leader is frequently the one who initiated the client relationship. He says that Gensler aims to have horizontal team structures in which every team member is contributing to decision-making so that it is not being delayed by levels of internal bureaucracy.

Leading by example—demonstrating how to be a good team member and team leader—is an important ingredient for success. Morris Nunes[7] succinctly underscores the message: "The overall tone must be set from the top and must be lived and embraced day to day as part of an organization's culture. When an organization's leaders are successful in inculcating that spirit, teamwork becomes second nature." As the leader, make sure you are visible so team members can observe how you behave collaboratively; for example, let others listen in on phone conversations and sit in on meetings to see how you communicate in action.

Inviting Dialogue and Alternative Views

Basic consideration and kindness preserve goodwill and self-esteem of the individuals on the team. A great leader should be able to reference one individual's valuable comments and how they may complement another's, and in this way stimulate collaboration. Self-conscious but genuine appreciation of the contributions of each team member bolsters confidence and is crucial to sustaining an effective and efficient process and outcome. A specific invitation to each team member to modify, challenge, and even offer starkly contrasting alternatives to the consensus goes a long way in supporting a team's capacity to drive an evolving synthesis of ideas.

Collaboration as Fun

Humor, shared meals, gatherings or retreats in places other than the office, and team workouts are all strategies for injecting some enjoyment and novelty into the work routines. The associated team building will also result in enhanced team cohesion, collective self-esteem, and efficiency in breaking down barriers to collaboration. Picture a group of 11 or 12 men and women on mountain bikes, peddling in smaller groups of 2 or 3. They are all brainstorming about a particularly challenging problem. Don't underestimate simply having fun as an integral part of the collaborative design thinking process; it may promote better understanding of each other's perspectives, diffuse tension and stress, make it easier to address conflicts, and in general promote an esprit de corps.

The Art of Working With Difficult Team Members

Take time to quietly discuss a problem one-on-one and face-to-face to get the individual on board as an ally. Examine the issue objectively and make an appeal for a *fair* analysis. Acknowledge the difficulties and inevitabilities of conflict among distinctive and talented personalities. Offer concrete examples of approaches to managing clashes. Relate similar situations that you personally encountered and managed with varying degrees of success or failure.

Revealing and freely recounting failures can be a very effective means of connecting with employees and colleagues and developing trust and respect.

View resolving conflicts as a design problem. Most problems are survivable, are negotiable, and may even constitute an opportunity. Relationships that endure a tough start-up may turn out to be the most gratifying and meaningful. One approach that has stood the test of time is to assume a self-effacing posture and ask for help, suggestions, or guidance based on the other person's legitimate experience and achievement. In other words, flip the script; diffuse the chip on the shoulder by making an antagonist into a helper. Incorporating suggestions, even at the expense of some of your own ideas, is likely to serve you well—and you may learn something too. Development of more genuine personal bonds is then facilitated, and with the passage of time, it will be easier to disagree without emotional or professional cost.

Reinterpreting antagonistic, even hostile, questions and comments to promote analysis can be a graceful tactic. Tension can be diffused and progress can be restored by yielding to, or acknowledging a critical or confrontational barb.

The Art of Being a Good Team Member

Let's review: effective team members tend to (1) be passionate about the work, and of course enjoy doing it and derive satisfaction from it; (2) know what they are doing, or at least possess a mastery of the basics (fundamental knowledge and skills) plus the ability and desire to learn; and (3) possess a warm and outgoing personality.

Everyone must make the collaborative design thinking process their own to some degree in order to perform their best and achieve magical results. There must be a cognizance of the unique issues involved in collaborating in any given case. Motivations at all levels and among all stakeholders are very important to understand. As a professional, you are obligated to care for other people. The first people you care for are the people sitting next to you. There is a brotherhood that is based on the principle of caring for other people—part of the definition of service professions. Idealism about saving the environment, for example, is the sort of noble intention that drives teams toward excellence. That kind of ambition—striving to do important things—can inspire and motivate every team member.

Some traditional conventions for participating on teams, in general, include the following:

- Recognize, first, that the project will benefit from a collaborative effort; and second, that you *want* to participate in such an effort.

- Each team member must be committed to the success of all of the other team members, especially when there are issues of coordination and overlap.

- Each team member must be committed to the success of the project. Be unpretentious and willing to respond positively to critical feedback for the good of the project.

- Be courageous. Don't hesitate to take a position and disagree (in genuinely courteous fashion) with other team members, the leader, and client in support of a good idea that will benefit the project.

- Temporarily assume a leadership role when circumstances suggest it; for example, your special expertise will be driving decisions and project direction.

- Don't be shy about developing and presenting new ideas for appraisal by collaborators.

- Don't confuse long hours and going through the motions with commitment.[8]

TEAM COMPOSITION AND SIZE

Getting the right team together is part of the design problem. Team size matters—and typically varies as a function of project scale, complexity, and phase, perhaps ramping up from preliminary phases to production, becoming smaller during implementation. While there is no magic number, in general the larger the team, the more time-intensive and difficult it is to manage communication, relationships, performance, and quality and coordination of the collective work product.

Mentoring is certainly more challenging with large teams, claims Roger Gold-stein,[9] as "younger staff feel like small cogs in a big machine, dissociated from the essence of the project." His firm mitigates the fragmentary nature of this situation by having each person take responsibility for consultant coordination related to their domain with oversight by the project manager.

Diversity across the board makes for the best teams. The best teams are composed of highly competent individuals with at least a modicum of inter-personal skills and a balanced mix of personalities, passions, experience, and expertise. At Gensler, team leaders staff their projects with a combination of junior and senior people from multiple disciplines, so there is a range of voices around the table. That, together with launching projects in a charrette or workshop fashion, amounts to a bit of "design combustion that focuses the team around a shared vision for success and innovation," asserts Jordan Goldstein.[10] After project direction is addressed, frequently there are "break-out sessions [by expertise] to do deep dives into more intricate issues." More-over, participation by everyone in the charrette activity itself contributes to motivating the team.

According to recent research reported in the *Harvard Business Review*,[11] a mix of those team members with different cognitive styles such as "creatives," detail-oriented people, and conformists can together promote creativity and innovation. The conformists facilitate cooperation, support the other mem-bers, and instill confidence in the work. Creatives may provide the great ideas but are complemented by the detail-oriented types who can ensure that the work gets implemented on time and on budget.

The project team is dynamic; members join and depart at various times as a function of evolving project circumstances, and the expertise and experi-ence of the member. New members can infuse the team with fresh ideas and mitigate the insular thinking that tends to prevail among team members who know each other well. How does the team leader optimize the contributions of both part-time and full-time team members?

■ ***Create a studio (or, as they say in the Navy, a ward room)***. The ward room is a shared space or room where team members can routinely, or as needed, get together face-to-face and work, share meals, or simply take stock informally. A common area is very desirable for optimizing high-quality interaction among those with diverse personalities, skill sets, and experiences. One caveat: sometimes, serendipitous collaboration can occur almost anywhere—virtually, in a coffee shop, at the water cooler, or while waiting for a plane, among other places. Always be open to thinking about and advancing the work no matter what the context.

- **Take time**. Time is an essential investment at project inception—and even before an agreement is signed—to optimize both schedule and resources: (1) clearly define the project and its scope, or at least have all the appropriate questions necessary to define the work; and (2) develop an outline or master plan of the process by which the project will be executed (designed) and delivered. Include all collaborators and their respective roles, when they should optimally be involved, and integration nodes in which individual and multidisciplinary teams should come together. And maintain control of the process throughout the life of the project.

- **Start the project with a workshop and include all stakeholders**. This will facilitate getting to know the collaborators personally and professionally as well as their ability to work with others on the team (see Sidebar 3.1). It is an opportunity to observe and assess professional expertise and social skills. Lay out as much information about the project as possible to get the best possible input from all present. Describe the workshop process (visually and verbally) to the team in the first meeting with proposals for specific roles and tasks, project expectations, and leadership, decision-making and communication protocol.

FIRM CULTURE TO FACILITATE INNOVATION

Cultivating an environment in which there is a swift and easy exchange of ideas is an important part of the collaborative design process in many companies, both large and small. What may not be so obvious are strategies to foster optimal functioning and creative thinking in such a team-oriented environment.

There is increasing recognition that a firm's cultural environment is a critical factor not only in producing the best possible work but also in attracting and retaining both new staff and clients. Many firms include sections on their websites dedicated to describing a distinctive office culture. Their intent is to demonstrate that the firm has a climate in which innovative work can be nurtured, so they can serve as a magnet for talented people, who are always in great demand.

By definition, collaborative design thinking involves some degree of innovation relative to a unique set of project circumstances. It follows, then, that creating the environment to facilitate an innovative subculture that promotes collaboration should likewise be a main objective.

A firm's culture, as succinctly characterized by Jean Valence,[12] "encompasses its history and accomplishments, its leaders' ambitions and goals, its definition of and criteria for excellence, its attitude about clients and staff, its traditions and lore, and its mood and energy." In other words, a firm's values describe its culture, and the subcultural components such as those promoting collaborative design thinking, innovation, continuing education, communication, justice, equity, diversity, and inclusion (JEDI) initiatives, and so on, impart a distinct personality.

Sidebar 4.1 JEDI Initiatives Can Benefit Collaborative Design Thinking

JEDI initiatives can be an integral part of a healthy workplace culture. The following example from a multinational architecture firm explains why and is drawn from a conversation with Gabrielle Bullock,[13] a Principal and Director of Global Diversity at Perkins & Will.

If architects focus on justice, equity, diversity, and inclusion in creating designs, managing firms, and producing the work, the resulting architecture is more likely to authentically benefit the communities that use our buildings. But more than that, in terms of practice management, a JEDI-infused culture will contribute to better design, improved business, and a richer work experience.

Many clients want to know how to navigate the design process through the JEDI lens, and exactly what that means, because our society and communities are more diverse than they ever have been, which requires customized design responses—not one algorithmic size fits all. Gabrielle states that there are two fundamental ways in which JEDI has changed the process:

- "You change through design by changing who designed it." Developing a more diverse design team as a goal brings more unique perspectives and enriches projects. There are natural tensions and discussions that invariably provoke the best ideas. So, recruitment, retention, and development of diverse team members becomes an imperative.

- The design process itself is reexamined. Focus on and engage the community in an authentic way to deeply understand their needs, wants, and desires. The design team can accomplish this only by examining the sociocultural disparities and inequities and the economic circumstances within the community. Then the team can effectively interpret those needs and translate them into an optimal design response.

The caveat to incorporating the JEDI lens as a basic part of the design process is that it cannot be added on: "You can't design and then say, 'Let's look at the project through the JEDI perspective'; it has to be fully integrated into the process from the very outset, otherwise the outcome will be superficial," says Gabrielle.

Destination Crenshaw is an example of collaborative design thinking with an embedded JEDI sensibility. This project, in the heart of the black community in South Los Angeles, is a 1.3-mile-long open-air museum, which was included on CNN's list of architectural projects set to shape the world in 2023. It was important to the community and the client that the design team represent this community—not just look like them, but understand them. So, there is a very diverse team—some members actually live in Crenshaw. The design team led by first and foremost actively listening to the community; the community members have been an ongoing part of the design process from project inception since 2017 to the present and are considered true design partners. The team has been taking design cues from what the community feels is the core of their culture—those elements that have made this community both robust and adaptable. The emerging ideas were creative triggers for the project, which became an architectural interpretation of the community's story.

Strategies That Support a Subculture of Collaborative Design Thinking

Here are a few strategies suggested by experts to encourage innovation and collaboration that might surprise you: Hire naïve misfits who argue with you; encourage failure; avoid letting client input limit your vision; and fully commit to risky ventures. This is an extreme approach to fostering innovation and collaboration in an otherwise relatively static office environment that was proposed by Robert I. Sutton.[14] Sutton argued that fresh perspectives derive from mavericks with wildly diverse backgrounds and no preconceptions who challenge the status quo, champion their own ideas, and illuminate the metaphorical darkness.

Sutton points out that ignoring client input, for example, may seem counterintuitive, but clients can't always imagine what's possible. Likewise, failure is critical to the design thinking process—assuming the team learns from the failure—because, typically, as previously alluded to, many bad ideas must be generated to produce a terrific one. Even the bad ideas can illuminate a problem and serve as a creative trigger to its solution.

A somewhat more tempered and time-proven model of Sutton's dogma is embodied in the culture of the United States Navy with respect to leadership at sea. The role of the executive officer, or second-in-command, is historically charged with such principles as support and delegation of authority. But also implicit is the responsibility of providing alternative, even self-consciously innovative, solutions to problems that may arise in battle or in other emergency situations. Distinctly opposite viewpoints from those of the commanding officer are often invited and seen as requisite components of tactical decision-making. The resulting complementary tension that exists between the commanding and executive officers is considered a positive force that enriches the culture because it demands that alternative strategies be considered. Perhaps a formalized notion of a second-in-command equivalent that would add some creative and energetic tension could be a beneficial addition to a company's culture, improving the underlying process and dynamic of their design teams' collaborative efforts.

The concept of a council of experts made up of seasoned and senior members of a company, as a resource that contributes to a learning environment through mentoring teams and individuals with new ideas, and applying best practices, can be a powerful cultural attribute. Moreover, tapping into a firm's internal expertise or "corporate knowledge" can assist teams in understanding the underlying issues of a particular project or problem in an accelerated manner. We may be rediscovering the wheel here, but experience often equates to wisdom.

Look Outside for Insight

Applying cross-disciplinary knowledge to help creatively solve problems—and broaden perspectives—is a time-honored strategy. The Seattle firm Olson Kundig[15] employs a visiting lecturer series, which, according to its website, is "inspired by the power of cross-fertilization—where individuals who excel in many different disciplines come and share with us what they do." They have had presentations by artists, craftspeople, environmentalists, and even an exotic dancer.

Reorganizing staff can fuel new approaches to engaging everyday problems. Roger Goldstein,[16] a Principal at Goody Clancy in Boston, explains that intentionally mixing teams from one project to the next is an integral part of his firm's culture. He says, "There's a lot of value in applying the things we learn in one realm to another completely different context." There is, however, a delicate balance in composing a team with experts in a particular area (that appeals to prospective clients) and those with little experience who come to the table with no preconceptions, contribute fresh ideas, and challenge basic assumptions. "Team composition that might lead to the most efficient design thinking process does not necessarily lead to the best project," explains Goldstein.

"One way for a majority of staff to have a degree of ownership in the design process," claims Michael Ryan,[17] Principal of Environmental Dynamics Inc. (EDI), Albuquerque, "is to sponsor a group charrette [workshop] for larger projects in which everyone gets to participate in the initial phase." Roger Goldstein similarly believes that charging a team to spend a few days developing a number of ideas that may or may not be workable is not only intriguing for pushing the design envelope but contributes to a culture of innovation.

Does everything have to be touchy-feely in collaborative design thinking? Are competition and collaboration within the same company culture mutually exclusive? Not according to IDEO founder David Kelly.[18] He describes its brainstorming process as "focused chaos." They don't get too attached to their first few ideas because they know they will change and improve. They may select a couple of alternatives to pursue (out of a half-dozen developed by competing teams) after a workshop, or cherry-pick ideas from multiple sources to create yet another alternative—all to ensure the final design has benefited from a series of explorations and perspectives. In this case, an internal competitive environment can indeed push outcomes to new heights. (See the description of IDEO's design of a shopping cart in Chapter 2.)

The physical environment of an office can reflect and influence its culture. Ryan asserts that something as simple as a big open space—no special offices, no closed doors, and no cubicles—promotes an atmosphere of shared experience, mutual respect, and casual (and nonhierarchical) exchange. For example, an impromptu gathering around someone's computer is common when they have discovered something of interest or "to kick ideas around." EDI, like IDEO, also places a premium on humor and playfulness—whether it's a nickname for a principal or their computers spewing quotes from cartoons when new email is detected—to relieve stress and encourage whacky thinking.

IDEO even had a wing of an old DC-3 airliner cantilevered over a meeting room.

If you're successful, you're in jeopardy of becoming complacent. So get out of your corner office, fail often, argue respectfully with coworkers, adopt a learning culture, don't accept anything at face value, and initiate collaborative design thinking.

DIAGRAMMING, REFLECTING, AND PRESENTING

This section describes various tools and strategies that can nurture curiosity, exploration, and discovery, advance the collaborative design thinking process, and promote means to arrive at optimal solutions. Explicitly outlining a problem and delineating proposed solutions in some readily accessible medium such as drawing and diagramming, working with spreadsheets, using a whiteboard, even photographing, can be a great strategy to effectively think about it. New ideas may become apparent as a function of simply *utilizing* the appropriate tool.

Diagramming

Converting information into forms that are analytically illuminating can be quite useful. It can also inspire creativity. Visual depiction of data invariably helps design thinkers—and stakeholders—to understand problems more precisely and to think about possibilities for their solutions. Rough sketches can facilitate efficient organization of material; to underscore (or suggest) hierarchy and relationships between elements of a problem, and make it easy to discern patterns. Grouping similar elements—or recombining the elements in new ways—can likewise be revealing. The ultimate goal of diagramming is to explore—think through the problem—and then to "capture an idea,"[19] and finally, to communicate the idea.

I would broadly define diagramming to include bubble diagrams, mind maps, flow charts, organizational structures, decision trees, concept maps, Venn diagrams, outlines or bulleted lists, and even blocks of text on Post-its (see Figures 4.2 and 4.3)—anything that visually depicts information. Post-its are especially easy to move and therefore are easy to play with and experiment (the ubiquitous Post-it Notes are a staple for good reason).

The bubbles in bubble diagrams are abstract graphic representations of some element and are easy to manipulate. Lines connecting bubbles can be quite meaningful in suggesting the relationship between those bubbles. For example, a solid heavy line with arrows on one or both ends could be a direct relationship, a dotted or light line can imply a secondary relationship, and so on. Varying shapes (i.e., circles, squares) and colors can highlight or differentiate elements and categories. Overlapping bubbles—as in a Venn diagram—can also reveal important relationships between elements (see Figure 4.2). One key to making effective diagrams is to annotate the bubbles or boxes profusely as a way to convey additional information that doesn't lend itself to a graphic, and that fully elaborates the content.

Everyone has the capability to draw quick and unrefined diagrams—just think about the proverbial napkin sketch. Some of the most creative work is done on the back of a napkin on an airplane, in a coffee shop, or in a bar. For example, the founders of Southwest Airlines famously sketched the diagram that contained the essence of the route plan that launched the airline—on a cocktail napkin in a bar in San Antonio! Without any expectations, doodling, as a precursor to diagramming, is one strategy that can jumpstart more meaningful sketching, and might even lead to a serendipitous breakthrough.

Everyone has a favorite pen or marker. A soft pencil, thick marker, or fountain pen on plain white bond paper, newsprint, brown butcher paper, yellow trace, or a whiteboard holds a raw sensual appeal. There is an inherent pleasure—a mélange of tactile, visual, and auditory stimuli that invite you to continue drawing. Moreover, a small sketchbook, compact notebook, or field journal that can fit in a pocket, backpack, or briefcase to physically record ideas is an incredible tool. Take full advantage of this great medium in thinking about the issues.

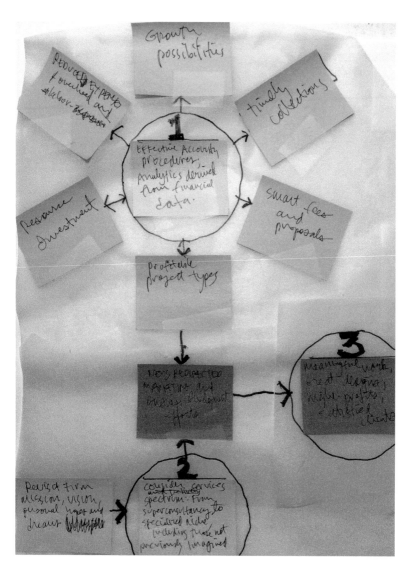

Figure 4.2 Evolution of a diagram: 1 of 2. The ubiquitous Post-its are ubiquitous for a reason: they are easy to use and manipulate. Here, thoughts are posted with a first attempt at organizing them.

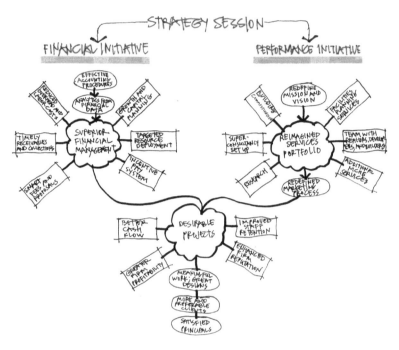

Figure 4.3 Evolution of a diagram: 2 of 2. Converting Post-its and building on them to arrive at a final diagram.

On the other hand, for those who are more comfortable in the digital realm, there are numerous apps for sketching, doodling, and creating diagrams. While drawings from these apps look great, I would caution that the end result should not be about how the diagram looks or how it is constructed, but that it is a helpful tool for exploration of ideas. "Technology is powerful, but sometimes it can make you less flexible, especially in the early stages of design,"[20] says Maria Yang, founder and director of MIT's Ideation Lab.

I would add that sketching is such a great tool because it is the most immediate brain-to-hand means of expression. It truly enhances creative thinking. In the immortal words of Donald Schön, drawing enables a "reflective conversation with the situation [you] are shaping."[21] Moreover, there is an ambiguity to the lines in rough freehand sketches, which is appropriate for conceptual thinking.

Framing the problem in visual terms is a basic strategy from the design thinking toolbox and presents a different way of examining ideas for possible solutions. Going through the exercise of laying out the components of a problem—visually depicting and ordering them—can facilitate a necessary familiarity with pragmatic issues and suggest possible relationships and connections, an emerging recipe, that heretofore was not considered or even imagined.

Reflecting

Perhaps one of the most overlooked yet readily available tools for modeling and promoting design thinking is *a dog*—especially for people who have a home office. This is an excellent suggestion from Michael Tardif.[22] A dog will ensure essential time for reflection, which will perhaps set the stage for that Eureka moment during a collaborative session. While working on a problem, after examining all the pertinent information and prior to making any substantive or key decisions, put it aside to let it incubate. Insist on a creative pause after an intensive work session, and take the dog for a walk. Talk to your dog, meet its curious and wide-eyed, head-tilted gaze. Consider alternate ideas and approaches. Present them to your unconditionally loyal and furry friend.

View the dog walk as an opportunity for the creative pause—to unwind and relax (see Figure 4.4). And be sure to leave your smartphone at home so there are no interruptions. "When stuck . . . step away, get some distance and then try again. Sleep on data since the mind continues to process information when resting."[23] Let the ideas percolate. Even if you don't have a dog, budget time for reflecting on all the information gathered to date, on failed attempts to solve the problem, and on the larger questions to see new perspectives.

If you are frozen and the work is not advancing, come back to the problem at a later time from a different viewpoint. Reflecting may put you in the right

Figure 4.4 A dog will ensure essential time for reflection—a creative pause to unwind and relax—to perhaps set the stage for that Eureka moment.

mindset. Isolate the issue; do more research, become more informed about it. Change the medium in which you are working (i.e., hand drawing, an app, writing, whiteboard, etc.). Alter your routine: work later, or start earlier. Vary your environment: go to a good coffee shop or library. Insights may strike you while taking a shower. Focus on a small idea rather than trying to find the big idea.

Do not underestimate the value of downtime, of dogtime. Ideas take time to grow. Sometimes working on an unrelated task and not thinking about the problem will yield insights later on. Acknowledge that not everything has to be considered billable time. Time for reflection is crucial for making sense of all the information, and for discovering meaningful insights. Time for man's best friend is crucial for a positive outlook on life as well as the problem at hand.

Presenting

Presenting prototypes, solutions, or alternative schemes to stakeholders is a key step in the collaborative design thinking process. Great work ends up on the cutting room floor if stakeholders do not perceive that it is great. It therefore behooves the design thinker to engage stakeholders in a discussion that includes the following: (1) a thorough understanding of the problem and surrounding issues; (2) a description of those who are impacted by the problem and its potential solution; and (3) an explanation of the solution and how it brilliantly addresses the problem.

Presumably, if the stakeholders have been part of the process, then there should be little mystery about how the solution was developed. If not, reveal some of the process of working through the problem since inception, and explain how ideas evolved and informed the final solution. Justify major decisions—clarify how they are accountable in some way (i.e., not arbitrary). Show initial prototypes that were used to test ideas and advance the work, which may also demonstrate how stakeholders' input was incorporated into the project.

According to Weld Coxe, who was a Founding Principal of one of the premier consultancies in management of professional service firms, *the objective of an effective presentation is to project a fresh idea and have it acted upon*. Salesmanship comes into play; "The techniques used," says Coxe, "will vary considerably according to the nature of the idea and the audience to be reached."[24] The logical conclusion to Weld's statement is to think about the presentation as a design problem. How would you tailor the presentation of your solution, and to whom, so that it would be optimally received?

Another useful perspective is to view the application of negotiating skills as a tool for productive conversations about the work. Excellent negotiating skills can be relevant to educating and selling stakeholders on design possibilities. Particularly noteworthy is the idea of "principled negotiation," proposed by Roger Fisher and William Ury in their classic book on negotiation, *Getting to Yes*, in which they recommend that issues be decided on their merits. An important caveat is to recognize that everyone theoretically ought to be on the same team, sharing the same goals. The "negotiation" should then be viewed as a mechanism for mutual understanding and enlightenment toward creating a better solution, not as something to win.[25]

Notes on Verbal Presentations

The following are some essential strategies for engaging in a constructive dialogue and effectively communicating with stakeholders.

- **Project confidence**. This is obviously easy to do when you know what you're talking about. Moreover, be passionate about the work, and be sure to express genuine, authentic enthusiasm. Convert any initial nervousness into excitement. Be animated and energetic. And enjoy the experience.

- **"Grab" the audience**. The overarching idea for the solution should be a natural hook. Be persuasive—build the entire presentation around this central focus, and support the hook with other relevant points. Being persuasive often simply amounts to illuminating a well-studied idea. Engaging the audience is just as important as grabbing the audience's attention: a conversation can be a great way to be inclusive and promote the work.

- **Speak clearly and without jargon**. Try not to patronize people by an exaggerated or simplified lecture; encourage questions and respond with a level of detail commensurate with the inquiry. Avoid acronyms that the audience might not know.

- **Ensure that the presentation is succinct**. Be aware that some people may have the attention span of a gnat. There will always be time to elaborate if there are follow-up questions. Take time to crystallize thoughts—*prepare* for the presentation.

- **Be mindful of the basics**. While speaking, vary cadence and volume to help keep everyone interested; avoid droning on and on in a monotone. It almost goes without saying how important it is to maintain eye contact with the audience. And move around—don't be shy about striding away from a desk or lectern—try to get up close and personal.

Notes on Graphic Presentations

Always think about how a proposed solution or project will be framed—both graphically and verbally—in ways that will be understandable and exciting to the stakeholders. Realize that a good solution can look bad by not paying enough attention to professional quality in its presentation.

- **First, do no harm**. With all the stunning graphic technology, templates, animation, and slick slideshow applications at our disposal, it is easy for the format to overshadow the content. So the basic rule is: never draw attention to the presentation mode; whatever medium is selected should support content, not distract from it.

- **Annotate drawings or diagrams**. Explanations complement the graphics and facilitate greater understanding. This point was mentioned earlier in this section, but it is so important, and frequently ignored, that it is worth underscoring.

- **Create a focus**. Just as the verbal presentation should have a hook, so too should each graphic element have a central focus. It makes it easier and more interesting to read, and indicates what is most important. The graphic focus could be larger, bolder, more colorful, or rendered with greater detail than its surroundings. Try to avoid using exclusively, equally weighted elements on a slide or graphic. This is the graphic analogy to avoid droning on in a monotone.

- **Be judicious with special graphic treatment**. For example, *a little bit* of color can have a big impact when applied in the right place at the right time. Color is terrific, but only if it enhances the message—its essence and uniqueness. Its use should not be arbitrary. You don't necessarily need to use a whole spectrum of colors—one or two might be most effective for any given presentation.

■ **Prepare a summary package**. There's nothing like a compelling takeaway of text and/or graphics to help sell a solution.

NOTES

1 Henry Fonda (Producer) and Sidney Lumet (Director), *12 Angry Men* (motion picture) (Beverly Hills, CA: Orion-Nova Productions, 1957).
2 Rob Sheehan, personal communication with the author, June 29, 2007.
3 William Rawn, personal communication with the author, June 20, 2007.
4 Sarah Harkness, quoted by the author in *Curing the Fountainheadache: How Architects and their Clients Communicate*, 2nd ed. (New York: Sterling Publishing Co., 2006), 59.
5 Morris A. Nunes, personal communication with the author, October 29, 2023.
6 Jordan Goldstein, personal communication with the author, November 4, 2008.
7 Morris A. Nunes, personal communication with the author, October 29, 2023.
8 Bill Parcells, quoted in *The New York Times Sports Magazine*, November 2006, 51.
9 Roger Goldstein, personal communication with the author, November 3, 2008.
10 Jordan Goldstein, personal communication with the author, November 4, 2008.
11 Ella Miron-Spektor, Miriam Erez, and Eitan Naveh, "Teamwork: To Drive Creativity Add Some Conformity," *Harvard Business Review* 90, no. 3 (March 2012): 30.
12 Jean R. Valence, *Architect's Essentials of Professional Development* (Hoboken, NJ: John Wiley & Sons, 2003), 13.
13 Gabrielle Bullock, personal communication with the author, February 9, 2023.
14 Robert I. Sutton, *Weird Ideas That Work: How to Build a Creative Company* (New York: Free Press, 2002).
15 Olson Kundig, "Culture," accessed March 13, 2024, https://olsonkundig.com/practice/#culture
16 Roger Goldstein, personal communication with the author, November 3, 2008.
17 Michael Ryan, personal communication with the author, October 12, 2007.
18 ABC News, "The Deep Dive: One Company's Secret Weapon for Innovation," *Nightline*, July 13, 1999.
19 Scott Berinato, "Visualizations That Really Work," *Harvard Business Review* (June 2016): 94–100.
20 Ken Shulman, "Maria Yang: The Prototype Moment," *Spectrum* (Winter 2017): 19–20.

21 Donald A. Schön, *The Reflective Practitioner: How Professionals Think in Action* (New York: Basic Books, 1983), 103.

22 Michael Tardif, personal communication with the author, May 5, 2016.

23 Paul J. H. Schoemaker and Steven Krupp, "The Power of Asking Pivotal Questions," *MIT Sloan Management Review* 56, no. 2 (Winter 2015): 39–47.

24 Weld Coxe, *Marketing Architectural and Engineering Services*, 2nd ed. (New York: Van Nostrand Reinhold, 1983).

25 Roger Fisher and William Ury, *Getting to Yes: Negotiating Agreement without Giving In*, 2nd ed. (New York: Penguin Books, 1991).

5

THE PROCESS IN ACTION

This chapter presents a series of vignettes that highlight how collaborative design thinking in corporate, institutional, and even political settings can help to solve problems or support work that is particularly challenging and fraught with constraints, and that requires creativity and innovation. It is hoped that some of the

DOI: 10.4324/9781003416142-5

lessons from these applications are generalizable to readers' unique situations, and will inspire more widespread use of collaborative design thinking across business and professional landscapes.

FAST-FAIL AND ITERATIVE

> Design thinking—primarily fast-fail and iterative—is provocative in the sense that it doesn't matter if we fail because we're going to get it wrong a bunch of times. But every time we get it wrong, the most important thing is to learn from the experience. That's where the iterative [process of repetition] part comes in. You get it wrong but you learn. And then you get it wrong again but you learn something new. In due course, you will get to a point where you have fewer mistakes, you have learned much, and you are willing to create something from this methodology.
>
> —Diego Ruzzarin

Diego Ruzzarin is a world-renowned food design expert and CEO of Foodlosofia, a company that creates profitable, scalable, and sustainable business models for the food and beverage industry.

Problems With Problem Solving in a Corporate Context

Diego says, "I'm a big fan of 'fast-fail and iterative.'" Why? Because coming from a corporate background, he learned that certain methodologies become more like an insurance policy and a burden than a guideline, booster, or motivator for project creativity. He believes that people tend to use conventional and ultimately unproductive methodologies and a good amount of time to justify their pay or to protect themselves from potential disasters.

Business as usual is often related to the democratization of ignorance. There are many people at the table for decision-making; everyone is polite, accommodating, and inclusive to a fault. So what happens most of the time is that the *least qualified, least committed* people sitting at the table are the ones who make the decisions on a default basis. This is so because everyone has tacitly adjusted their thinking to be inclusive and so that everyone agrees. In this sense of democratization, the risk is that *most of the innovative ideas may be lost*. Fear of failure and reluctance to take the time and effort to present unexpected or controversial material will likely be reflected in what may be, at best, just an adequate result.

An Example of Fast-Fail Iterative

The best solutions also arise from examining the whole problem, accounting for many variables—not just one, perhaps readily solved piece of the problem. Diego's frustration related to creativity and some companies is that people tend to promote fragmented solutions rather than considering the big picture. In the food industry, 90% of the effort to improve products is about flavor. But that is not the whole picture; there are many other variables that are more important than flavor. Nevertheless, research and development spending is so focused on flavor that they may lose the sense that the other significant variables exist.

Here is an example. Foodlosofia was hired by a major snack company to work on a specific cheese snack for which the market was shrinking; consumer acceptance was fading. The connection between the brand, product, and traditional consumer was very fragile. When Foodlosofia pushed them to innovate and create new products in this category, they would always play it safe and not want to move beyond the traditional products they sell.

Diego explained that doing concept design—creating new products and formulating new ideas—is not really expensive. If they do this now and fail, it is not important because it is just design—prototypes that can be modified. It will take a couple of months, but eventually they will get something right. The cost of developing the propositions is almost nothing compared with the potential for success. But if they play it safe and stay on this negative trend, it will inevitably be harmful to their market and business.

The snack company trusted Diego's judgment and said, "Okay, let's try it; you have six months to think differently and to innovate in a new direction." Foodlosofia took that liberty and, even though it was controversial, concluded that they could no longer sell an existing type of cheese snack to children as originally intended. Instead, the approach was to try to reposition them and to design a new collection of cheese snacks directed to adults—the adults who were originally in love with the brand 15 years before, but who are now older. They are in a different moment in their lives; they have different priorities, needs, and lifestyles. Their expectation from these cheese products is fundamentally different. So the company said, "It's a big bet, but let's try it."

Foodlosofia then created a new collection of products and tested them with consumers. They had excellent results from adults, who said,

> It's great to see these new products because when I go to the supermarket to look for my traditional cheese snacks, I see all this promotion for young people—they are trying to appeal to millennials. I can't relate to the story-telling and to the products anymore, but I used to love the experience. What happened? You lost me in translation.[1]

So Foodlosofia reintroduced the product that is now also relevant to adults. The adults immediately fell back in love with the story and brand, and they rediscovered why they used to love these products in the first place.

Diego has psychologists on his team who work with consumer research. The team learned from fast-fail at the beginning of the process. They talked to children to see why they were not connecting to these products anymore. Diego recalls one key response that epitomized learning from failing. Then the team asked the children why they don't eat these cheese snacks anymore—they used to love them, what happened? Are they not tasty anymore? Is the texture a problem? Is the packaging, graphics, or brand no longer appealing?

The children said no to all of those questions. They said that they take a break while at school in the morning. If they eat these cheese snacks, their fingers will be messy and they can't use their cell phones properly, so they'd rather not buy them. Such a simple, rational response, yet nobody took the time to *engage and empathize* with consumers, to listen to consumers, to the actual users who express that snacks are important to them but that, in this instance, they declare that cell phones are much more important today (Figure 5.1).

Figure 5.1 Why were children not connecting with the cheese snack products anymore? The response epitomized learning from failure.

It was critically important for Foodlosofia in this case to have a fast-fail attitude because they encountered myriad problems, barriers, consumers, and situations, and from *all* of these variables, they were able to determine how to recalibrate and make the market healthy again.

Dissecting the Process

Fast-fail begins with client input, which can vary tremendously and often cannot be predicted by established marketing algorithms. Here are examples of a wide range of client issues, preferences, and goals. How can new technology provide new products? Our market is fading—do we need to change the market or reposition the category? Do we need to create a new brand to position this product? Our brand is migrating to a new category—we used to do ice cream, now we want to do muffins—is that transition of value? Can you provide a concept and menu for a new restaurant for this type of food and customer type? Can you help us to create a unique olive oil product?

Normally this client input is accompanied by a great deal of data. Companies collect "big data," but they rarely know how to use it. So the first part of Foodlosofia's data analytic process is called "understand," which has two components: client-provided information, and research that the company undertakes. Diego has a team of what he calls "philosophers," who are spread around the world and form a network of people who are very critical in their mindset about the future of food. When Foodlosofia starts a project, they try to understand the context:

> What are we doing here? We are reinventing the future of ice cream. Let's think about ice cream. What is ice cream today? What does the data tell us? What do we believe are the trends happening around the world that would impact the future of ice cream?

Then the team comes together in an agreement—a mountain of intellectual capital that they all understand. From there, they jump to conclusions. Even if the outcome might be a disaster, they jump to conclusions:

> This is ice cream today. We believe ice cream in the next ten years is going to be about nature. We prototype this category for what ice cream would be like in the next five years: we say this is what ice cream will look like, these are the new technologies that are going to impact ice cream, these are the types of brands that are going to be big, and these are the new business models and distribution systems that are going to change the way the industry works in ice cream.[2]

Then they prototype that reality.

The client is part of *some* of these discussions, not all of them. Clients often have internal discussions where they underscore the sense that they know everything; because they have been doing things the same way for 30 years, out of fear, they assume things are not going to change. Foodlosofia keeps clients out of some of the conversations, and they take poetic license to explicitly advance important points that the client doesn't necessarily want to hear, and that ostensibly originate with the users of the product in question.

Foodlosofia engages in two types of prototyping: macro and micro. Macro prototyping is what they call scenario design. They provide a holistic simulation of the entire business environment because food design incorporates much more than the food itself. It includes the business model, regulatory requirements, distribution systems, branding, packaging, the product itself, and understanding the customers—their cultural development and lifestyle. Macro prototyping is, essentially, the context of a new category. Micro prototyping, on the other hand, dives into the specifics of the project, which normally happens on the third or fourth iteration of the process.

In macro prototyping, the first test is presenting to the client (not yet to consumers). For example, Foodlosofia sets forth what they think will happen to the ice cream category in the next five years. They ask if it makes sense: which elements from the future reality do they believe are real, and which of those do they want their business to embrace? Some of the responses are inevitable—simplicity of ingredients, transparency of origin and process, equality of players in the supply chain.

Then Foodlosofia asks if they believe the speculation that ice cream is going to be a heightened social category that will be related more to alcoholic drinks than to kids. There is also a stake in the ground saying that they want this to be the case; this is where they want to take the category. Some companies may still target children, but they believe there is an unexplored area that will grow: ice creams mixed with alcohol in the happy hour, and a salad with a scoop of rum ice cream. Foodlosofia believes this is the future in certain contexts.

Everyone now has a clear understanding of the idea. The team conducts more research and talks to consumers, potential clients, and those in the supply chain. They understand enough to launch into micro prototyping. What are the types of products that are needed? Are there safety and/or efficacy issues? Does the technology to manufacture them exist? What about the competition? Is production scalable? What are the marketing and financial projections? Do the packaging and brands exist? Can the types of flavors that are promised be developed? Is the texture what it should be? Then prototypes of the new products are developed—something that has color, aroma, flavor, and texture, and that can be put in your mouth to see how it melts. Something new is learned from this prototype, which may then be tested in focus groups. Finally, after production and distribution in commerce, post-market evaluation is conducted.

Refinements are made for a final round of prototyping: create a new brand, modify the packaging, change the price point. This final round includes 3 out of 15 products that are ready to go to the market. Five of the 15 products will go to the market in year two, two products in year four, and the balance in year five.

Foodlosofia creates their innovational roadmap so the company knows when to launch the new products. The vision of the category and the business is established, and changes related to the category are specified to arrive at their target level during the next five to ten years.

Diego has a "triple-headed mentality" that is floating above the iterative process to account for the other variables beyond just flavor. He has three types of professionals working on his team at all times. First, there are two types of designers: graphic (for branding, communication, and packaging) and food (for ingredients, texture, shelf life, and aroma). The second head on his team is about strategy. Does the idea translate to good business? Does the funding make sense? Is the pricing system right? Do people buy this product—is it affordable? The third head is the psychologist, who strives to be totally objective and is, at least in theory, impervious to foolish ideas and inaccurate statements. Both the design and business model can be great, but the psychologist can be "Dr. No" and say that it doesn't make any sense. And everyone needs to hear this reality check.

Diego cites an example. There was a recent presentation at an international conference about a chicken-flavored nail polish that Kentucky Fried Chicken (KFC) had just released. It's intriguing! It's funny, it's wow! People are aroused by the idea that fingers can taste just like KFC. It is likely that KFC doesn't have high margin on their products, so having one very distinct, very high-margin product seems like a good idea. A team psychologist might ask, "Does it make any sense? You can make it, you can make money, but do you need to make it? Does it help humanity to make progress in any fashion?" The design thinking construct applied in this example makes it crystal clear that genuine contribution is subservient to pure profit motives. And that is unacceptable.

Managers and account executives get trapped into fragmented realities when they say something like,

> I need to find inexpensive edible packaging with real nutritional value and real appeal, because if I refine this, it will be a panacea—a magical solution for some of the waste problems that plague the food industry. We are criticized because of wasting plastic. If I popularize this idea, then we don't have any more disposal issues.

Nothing could be further from the realities and scope of the food waste problem. A diverse team guided by design thinking principles would rapidly correct the simplistic assertions and misperceptions intrinsic to the overstated claims for a packaging initiative.

EMPATHY AS A MEANS TO INNOVATE IN A PHARMACEUTICAL COMPANY

> Empathy is the component of design thinking that helped us to develop a fresh mindset and a full appreciation for special needs that led to a new way of thinking.
>
> —Meredith Kauffman, PhD

This brief story demonstrates that empathy is one of the most important elements of design thinking. Empathy can be a key to transcending a given problem; it facilitates formulating questions that expand, illuminate, or otherwise open up the problem.

Developing meaningful empathy for stakeholders is a remarkable tool for problem definition and, ultimately, solution. A simple, commonsense idea that is surprisingly neglected is this: the better we can get to know the people who will be using the spaces, solutions, or, in this case, products that we design, the better problem solvers we can become, and the more significant the solution.

The design thinker on the team described next essentially assumed the role of stakeholder advocate, serving as a proxy for a typical product user. Armed with primary empathic data, he was then able to propose a wonderful, responsive, and economical solution that *the user could not have imagined*.

Meredith Kauffman, PhD, led research and development projects for a major consumer products company where she focused on using innovative science to design new products to help improve people's health and quality of life. The vignette that follows describes a snippet from one such project, highlighting the design thinking process in which defining the right problem to address (in this case, through empathy) is paramount to innovation.

Each brand in the company had a designated open office area called a hub, which accommodated about 20 people. It included specialists in marketing and packaging, research and development (R & D) scientists, and clinical research scientists. It was felt that innovation would be encouraged if people from different disciplines sat together. And indeed, there were two designers in the hub. One was a packaging engineer who was expert in the actual makeup of the package and who would follow a project from ideas to pro-duction, and hence was frequently away from the team visiting the factories. The other designer was embedded in the team full time and was intended to provide inspirational support for the brand.

The project in this case was denture adhesives. The core of the business was adhesives for full denture wearers (people who didn't possess any teeth), but the growth opportunity that was identified by the company was "partials"—for people who required adhesives for small sections that replaced one or two missing teeth. The biggest problem for these consumers was that their appli-ances didn't fit properly, and as a consequence, the appliance would wobble and put stress on their teeth. Food particles would lodge under them and cause irritation. That was the initial problem definition from a consumer-need perspective, and also what the team was focused on solving from R & D and marketing standpoints.

After about a month, during one of the team meetings, the designer walked in with a jury-rigged gardening glove, a simulation of what the consumers were going through. He said, "I've been listening to you talk about the consumers, and I've been thinking about their challenges. What you're missing is that you're not hearing them say, 'It's really hard to apply this!'" When they (accidentally) over-applied the adhesives, it was difficult to clean up; the adhesive was essentially a polymer mixed in oil, so consumers would end up with excess oil in their mouths.

The designer pointed out that the team was perhaps failing to address the right problem, which was over-applying the product. It was noted that the adhesives are very viscous products that are squeezed out of a tube. They are much more difficult for this consumer group to squeeze than toothpaste— and the designer wanted the team to understand that.

Back to the jury-rigged gardening glove. The designer had attached bits of hard plastic to the fingers on the glove to provide resistance so that it required more effort than usual when squeezing or doing any sort of motion to mimic an arthritic hand. This was intended to give the R & D team an empathic sense of the experience of the typical consumer. While using the glove, it was very hard to properly apply the new products that the team was trying to develop because they were all too thick.

One solution—for partials (using a very viscous, experimental product)—was to rethink the original tube design and develop a novel application device. It is similar to a pen clicking; a click would provide a metered dose, which was easier on the arthritic hand, and would not require a squeezing force (see Figure 5.2). With the glove on, it was much easier to click on the prototype device than it was to squeeze from a tube. Another solution—for full dentures—was an easier-to-open and easier-to-squeeze tube).

The caveat that is absolutely necessary to mention is that many different factors inform product development—not just consumer preference. Cost, for example, is critical to consider on every project. In this case, the redesign of the tube was also an opportunity to address the mandate for cost-cutting.

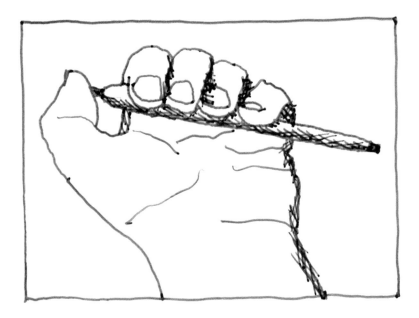

Figure 5.2 Empathy is so important in helping to discover the salient issues and to focus on the right problem, as exemplified in the development of this device, which provides a metered dose without requiring a squeezing force.

ENRICH SOLUTIONS AND MANAGEMENT THROUGH LISTENING AND INCLUSIVENESS

Design thinking can be a critical tool for addressing leadership challenges. The refrain is that design thinking promotes visualization of the big picture, reframing of perspectives, creation of innovative solutions to problems, attention to detail, and management and reconciliation of diverse and complex interests and relationships. Cultivating an attitude to authentically listen to insights from others as well successfully sharing one's own vision may not always be easy but can be very effective, as illustrated in the following vignette.

A good leader uses the design process as a model that promotes participation and thus improves and expands the politics of civic engagement . . .

The most creative and productive way [to apply design thinking] is to engage people—the [stakeholders]—in the process.[3]

—Richard Swett

Richard N. Swett was elected to the US Congress and served as the US Ambassador to Denmark. Dick underscores a fundamental aspect of design thinking that leads to successful resolution of problems or great projects that are rich in meaning: *be inclusive*. The magic occurs when the input is creatively interpreted, and all stakeholders feel heard and also see or are explicitly shown how their ideas influenced the outcome. The stakeholders are then more likely to be fully invested in that outcome, which is so important for success. This creative interpretation may reveal windows of opportunity not previously contemplated, and may thereby provide extraordinary solutions that are also responsive to stakeholder requirements and preferences.

A leader who applies design thinking is someone who has a vision, and understands where he or she is going to direct the process, but is not confined by the boundaries or preconceptions of what a solution could be. The design thinking method will allow—even encourage—everyone who is participating in formulating the solution to make their contributions, and the solution will then emerge. It could be a political, business, or some other organizational context where there is a need for leadership, but also where there is the likely benefit of participation. The end result is not clearly defined; rather, engagement with the whole process takes the team to a solution.

A caveat worth noting is that this type of leadership requires some assertiveness and presence; a design-by-committee environment can be frightening if the leader does not have the confidence to control the dialogue in that environment.

Dick Swett recommends working toward the best solution for *all* the stakeholders, perhaps promoting a shared vision of project objectives from the outset. If design thinking is utilized in its truest, purist sense, the end result can sometimes be a surprise. But as long as it is a better surprise than what everybody had in mind, then that's okay!

Dick Swett coauthored the Congressional Accountability Act, landmark legislation that was part of the Republican Party agenda in the Contract with America. The law requires Congress to abide by the same laws it passes for the rest of the country. I asked Dick how he was able to harness inclusive participation in order to get this landmark legislation passed.

The typical process in Congress involved first writing a bill, then seeking cosponsors, and finally the bill goes to the floor of the House of Representatives, where people try to pin amendments to it in order to change what they don't like. Dick suggested,

> Why don't we do this like we're designing a building: let's go around with a blank piece of paper to all the different groups that are interested in the accountability, and let's ask them to tell us how to design this, and we will interpret, integrate, and synthesize their different designs. We will come up with an amalgam of the best of what they have told us.[4]

Members are not all going to do this in the same room at the same time. The idea was so totally foreign to them that no one really understood what was going on—so much so that the American Enterprise Institute's Norm Ornstein at one point said,

> Wait a minute, you guys are letting everybody say what they think your legislation should be, and then you're going to come back to them with three different schemes to review, then they'll pick the one that they like the best?![5]

Dick responded, "That's exactly what we're going to do." Ornstein said that this is fascinating because no one has ever taken this approach in this body before.

It took three and a half years to complete the legislation; Dick and his coauthors had to warn everybody because they weren't moving the bill to the floor for a vote. Congressional members didn't want to be made accountable because they had this great House rules system where they could do whatever they pleased—their behavior never had to be connected to the laws that were passed for the rest of the country. Dick and others finally forced the vote; they won 97–3 in the Senate and something like 433–3 in the House. It passed by an overwhelming margin because everyone was participating, and yet Dick and his coauthors were still able to give this direction and to maintain a sense of control over what they were ultimately trying to achieve. It was an engaging exercise on all levels.

Part of the creativity lies in how Dick was able to *interpret the input in a way that was meaningful and effective*, while everyone felt as though they were heard and invested in its content (Figure 5.3).

Figure 5.3 It is important for stakeholders to appreciate how they have influenced the "design" solution. For example, point out something like: "This squiggle in the final design is the direct result of your comment on our initial draft."

Overhauling the Management Structure at the US Embassy, Denmark

In Copenhagen, morale at the embassy was "in the pits." When Dick first arrived as the US Ambassador, he couldn't understand why people were unhappy; after all, this was Denmark—a wonderful posting. There were 16 different agencies at the embassy at that time; all separate silos, and no one talked across those silos. There was a community of 250 Americans and foreign service nationals, all presumably working together, and yet there was little connection between them that would enable them to understand what their colleagues were doing, or to even identify their colleagues.

It was clear that this situation called for some kind of team-based management system. Dick wanted to create teams of people who would work together and use their creative connections not only to get to know each other, but also to come up with more imaginative and hopefully less expensive solutions to the myriad of problems they were facing.

It took a year to realize that no one wanted to embrace the team-based structure. Dick tried to promote the idea and taught critical path management among other project management skills and tools. But he finally figured out that the staff was stymied by the term "team." Team was anathema in this bureaucracy, meaning nobody gets credit and therefore nobody advances. Dick then understood how to approach this issue more effectively. He declared that each team would be made up of six to eight people, with only one from each agency. There would be agencies represented on every team, each of which was formed around projects such as issue campaigns and diplomatic dialogues. The embassy teams would be similar to the teams that form around projects in an architecture firm. Instead of using building materials, they used information as their building blocks. Instead of designing office structures, they designed information structures for scheduling and measuring results on complicated, interrelated diplomatic discussions.

The typical staff response was, "Why did you stick all these people on this team who know nothing about what I am doing?" Dick replied,

First, you sell them and yourself short because you'll serve on another team in the same capacity that they're serving on your team. That is, you're going to be an objective observer who is going to look at everything that is being done by that team—not through the eyes of the specialist, who thinks they know everything there is to know about that particular subject, but through the eyes of an observer from a distance who might see that there's a way to do something a little differently and a little bit better because they have a different perspective on the world. That doesn't take from your authority to give direction and vision to this team but you better listen to what these people have to say because their suggestions will make your decisions better.[6]

Implementing this new approach took time and training. Morale went way up. Everybody was enjoying work because they were being challenged, and they were discovering that they were able to find genuinely interesting solutions that were better than what they had previously.

It is important to empower teams by giving them the opportunity to authentically give voice to their desires. Architects are especially aware that their clients' level of sophistication varies. The less educated a client is about design, the more time is spent educating them to help them understand, for example, why spatial relationships are planned in a certain way. This analogy applies to most team situations. It is necessary to first understand the basic level of competency of the team, so the baseline from which they can start making choices can be established. The team should be given the opportunity to make decisions and then see those decisions actually being accepted and implemented into the program; this yields ownership or what amounts to "sweat equity" with respect to the program.

Many managers are reluctant because they don't understand how to empower a team yet remain at the helm; this is very much a learned skill that is shaped by design thinking.

Dick's observations demonstrate that to arrive at the best solution, design thinking does not have to be limited to a unilateral vision of a single individual; it requires skill to compromise in some ideal sense (or redesign to make the work better), and it develops a meaningful interactive—collaborative—relationship with stakeholders.

DESIGN APPROACHES TO HEALTH CARE DELIVERY AND TREATMENT

Peter Lloyd Jones, PhD, Associate Dean of Design in Medicine at Sidney Kimmel Medical College, Thomas Jefferson University, believes there is an emerging convergence between the medical and design fields: He claims, "If you train doctors to look at the world through the eyes of a designer, their clinical skills and empathy improve."[7] One of the vignettes below briefly discusses several design projects undertaken by medical students at Jefferson, under the direction of Dr. Bon Ku.

> We, and others, believe that design thinking can be a powerful tool in health care to improve care delivery, train future physicians, and improve the experience for both patients and providers.
> —Bon Ku, MD, MPP, Anuj Shah, and Paul Rosen, MD, MPH, MMM

There is a potentially strong correspondence between medicine, health, and design thinking. Medicine, particularly urban emergency medicine, is about making sense out of multivariate problems in a very compressed time period, and then designing, implementing, and evaluating short- and long-term solutions, again in a compressed time frame. Conceptually, this is a description that suggests design thinking can contribute to creative problem solving in this realm.

The *AMA Journal of Ethics* recently summarized the results of three studies that asserted that those providers who care for the underserved must possess the ability to recognize that the patient may have unexpressed needs, must have an appreciation of local epidemiological factors, knowledge of community resources, and a willingness to take on the role of the patient's advocate. Other necessary skills include the ability to communicate with patients who are from other cultures or speak other languages.[8]

Another example of the correspondence previously noted lies with the Urban Medicine Program of the University of Wisconsin School of Medicine and

Public Health. They have developed learning goals that could just as easily be applied to an urban design program in which design thinking is paramount:

- Promoting health equity and reducing health disparities.

- Accessing community resources.

- Enhancing cultural skills.

- Engaging with communities.

- Developing and implementing community-based public health projects, sustaining compassion, promoting wellness, and building resilience.

Bon Ku and others further operationalize this general correspondence and congruence. Ku is an emergency medicine physician and Associate Professor at the Sidney Kimmel Medical College at Thomas Jefferson University in Philadelphia, where he teaches design thinking to medical students and serves as director of the design program at the medical college. The program is the first in the United States to develop a design curriculum that includes all four years of medical school.

One of the reasons Dr. Ku started the design program for medical students is that he believes physicians lack the toolkit necessary to creatively problem-solve within the current landscape of health care delivery. Ku cites the emergency department where he works as a typical example of many problems in clinical settings today. "It's a very severe, overcrowded space. Patients are stressed, fearful, and anxious; providers are frustrated and stressed as well." Medical students in the design program are working on several projects (among others) to improve both the patient and provider experiences in the emergency department.

With the emergence of design thinking in health care environments, Ku no longer views problems as intractable but rather as opportunities to greatly improve health care delivery. Before this epiphany, states Ku, many providers, including himself, were skeptical: "We don't have the resources or support, so we're not going to even try to brainstorm or ideate about how to create and implement solutions."

The design process has allowed Ku's teams to have a safe space to brainstorm, and also the ability to rapidly prototype. Just having an invitation to think of crazy, out-of-the-box ideas to develop potential solutions—without considering, at least initially, if they are implementable—is liberating. They relish the chance to sit back with colleagues and students to use a clean whiteboard; to begin to solve the problems they are encountering today.

Recently, a team investigated how they might improve the outpatient services for the family medicine clinic at Jefferson. It's one of the busiest single-site clinics in the country, with over 80,000 patients per year. Ku's team initiated a design workshop with the clinic's providers to fully understand their challenges. One issue is the late patient who shows up 15 minutes after a scheduled appointment, and the resulting stress on the provider, who still has to see that patient—which causes the provider to be late for all the other patients throughout the rest of the day. Business as usual—a slip of paper with the scheduled follow-up appointment and a phone call reminder to the patient—is clearly ineffective.

The team thought about ways to assist patients to arrive on time for their appointments. They interviewed patients and providers, then prototyped and mocked up potential solutions. They used a storyboard technique to propose an app that would message patients at different times before their appointment, reminding them to show up on time. The team did not create anything brand new; there are existing platforms that accomplish the same thing. However, from the interviews with patients, they were able to ascertain that there are optimal times for reminder texts to be effective and to not be perceived as an annoyance. The team was successful in proposing a solution that could be immediately implemented in their family medicine clinic with a simple messaging app for the 90% of patients who had smartphones that could receive text messages.

Another recent project with medical students involved creating a journey map of how patients navigate the medical system when they get sick unexpectedly—i.e., when there is stomach pain or high fever for a few days, what does the route to treatment look like? Medical students conducted interviews with Philadelphians focusing on that question.

Profiles or personas of different patient types were extracted from the interviews. Here's an example. A single mother with two children has limited options for health care when she suddenly gets sick. As she is employed full time, she does not want to take a day off from work, and therefore frequently visited the emergency department during off hours.

One outcome of the team's work was the creation of an "ecosystem" app chronicling acute unscheduled care that described many different ways patients access health care. It was an exercise in understanding the "end user." Providers describe patients as noncompliant when they don't show up for their appointments. Providers develop treatment plans but don't often understand all the social determinants of their care, and therefore don't really understand the patient and don't specifically tailor their treatment plans. This is an obvious yet illuminating observation for medical students: not all patients are the same. Patient treatment plans should be "designed." Empathizing with the "end user"—a key component of design thinking—leads to better treatment plans for individual patients.

Currently in medical training, patients are labeled and blamed as noncompliant when they don't adhere to treatment plans prescribed by providers. A deeper understanding of patients, especially early on in medical school, may well help students to develop greater empathy, which will ultimately lead to better care.

Ku appreciates design thinking because there is a clear methodology that has traditionally worked in product design and service delivery. He believes design thinking can be an effective means for discussing improvements to patient care with colleagues and students. He emphatically states, "Design thinking *amplifies* the standard algorithms that we use."

A Design Approach to Treating Cancer

> The more scientists learn about cancer, the more diverse and vexing their opponent appears.
>
> —Jerome Groopman[9]

Amid star-laden fundraising galas and beautiful people events, we continually declare victories in the "war against cancer." But a hard look at morbidity and mortality data across this daunting landscape of pathology yields a somewhat different picture.

Despite the latest science and technology, despite efforts at early detection and aggressive multidimensional intervention, despite the authoritative what-to-eat/what-to-drink/how-to-exercise algorithms, despite all of this—notwithstanding some progress—the clinical reality is: human beings with cancer generally die at only slightly improved rates and with the same unavoidable outcomes today as they did decades ago. And significantly greater numbers of young adults are being diagnosed with various malignancies. So, the overarching question is, what do we need to do differently? Recent approaches suggest that *design thinking* with a dose of scientific creativity may help to provide some desperately needed answers.

Eradicating the spectrum of cancer presents an entire universe of complex problems. Traditional treatments include an array of chemo and immuno-therapies, surgery, radiation, nanodelivery systems, and genetic editing. The goal with these treatments is to destroy, remove, or attenuate cancer cells. While there are often impressive results, the treatments do not always result in long-term remission, and many interventions have significant side effects.

Elucidating a new treatment pathway for disease is the most basic challenge; the design problem in this case. Inspiration can come from just about anywhere, even from unrelated disciplines, which enables us to examine problems from a fresh perspective. It was parents, not researchers, who recognized that cannabidiol (CBD) was effective in treating rare pediatric seizure disorders that were unresponsive to mainstream therapies. Investigators, regulators, and physicians took their cue from parents and brought Epidiolex to market.

Reframing the question is another tactic in design thinking that facilitates new ways of examining a problem. Instead of, "Is there another, creative way of effectively destroying or removing cancer cells?" we might ask, *"What if* there is a different, perhaps better, means to achieve remission in a given case?" Articulating questions can be extremely valuable, whether or not they lead in

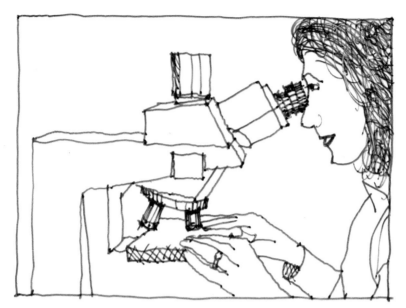

Figure 5.4 Reframing questions can shed light on possible new directions toward finding a solution. For example, instead of: "Is there another, creative way of destroying or removing cancer cells?" we might ask, "What if there is a different, perhaps better means to achieve remission in a given case?"

a fruitful direction. Posing the right questions is a component in the design thinking loop that can be weighted heavily in the process to provoke a creative response. And be mindful to pose questions that may be counterintuitive—or completely off the wall—to elicit the most potentially innovative responses (Figure 5.4).

Cultivating an optimistic and confident attitude, one that assumes success— that there is in fact the possibility of a new avenue toward a solution—is fundamental to design thinking and advancing the work.

One example of confident and innovative thinking involves a promising approach to *transform* the cancer cells, rather than destroy them. Dr. Jerome Groopman describes this exciting new research in his article in *The New*

Yorker, "The Transformation." The original idea was developed by an investigator in Shanghai, who was inspired by Confucius:

> If you use laws to direct the people, and punishments to control them, they will merely try to evade the punishments, and will have no sense of shame. But if by virtue you guide them, and by the rites you control them, there will be a sense of shame and of right.[10]

Herein lies the creative trigger for the big idea—*from an unexpected source in an unrelated domain*. Groopman quotes the investigator who developed a metaphor: "If cancer cells are considered elements with 'bad' social behavior in our body, 'educating' rather than killing these elements might represent a much better solution." Researchers are continuing to build on this new strategy of treating patients and controlling and normalizing the life cycle of some cancers without actually destroying cancer cells.

Obviously, specific and investigational treatment plans are far more complicated and individualized than suggested here, but the point is to demonstrate how bold new ideas can evolve from a different way of thinking.

DRAFT AS COMMUNICATION PROTOTYPE

Facing the blank piece of paper and being blocked is something many writers—novices and veterans alike—have experienced. Design thinking can facilitate inspiration, and help to unlock ideas and express them artfully in writing.

One of the best and most helpful analogies of writing to design thinking is to consider the draft (and subsequent versions) as prototype for testing and evaluation. Then the iterative loop is repeated, as critical feedback may trigger anything from a completely different tack to only minor modifications.

> Every time you test a draft (or prototype) you may actually change the question you're working on—and that's what makes it design thinking—as opposed to straight hypothesis testing or research.
>
> —Mark Childs

Mark Childs is former Interim Dean and Professor in the School of Architecture and Planning at the University of New Mexico, and the author of a half-dozen award-winning books.

Mark considers the iterative process of design thinking—or the repeating loop of tasks leading to prototyping—as fundamental to writing. In design thinking language, the draft is often the prototype for communication that gets evaluated. You write something and then test it in different ways at different phases—or drafts. For example, sending a preliminary draft to trusted advisors and also to *un*trusted advisors to provide feedback. Another way to test the prototype/draft is to review it carefully to ensure that it makes logical or emotional sense. Imagine an inverted cone with a spiral going up on the outside. The top is where the prototype is made, which goes down for testing, then repeating; making and testing, and so on. Every time you test a draft (or prototype), you may actually change the question you're working on—this is bi-directional communication, and that's what makes it design thinking, as opposed to straight hypothesis testing or research.

Mark believes that the aspect of design thinking that best applies to writing is crystallizing the central issue; determining what is really at stake. It's part of the process of starting down a path without necessarily knowing where it goes. There are branches along the way, and it is not clear which ones to select. So you go down some paths, and then you backtrack; then you go down some others.

Putting ideas and thoughts down in writing helps you to get to another place. You may start out with one kind of general approach, but the writing itself tells you that you're going somewhere else. It's almost like a point of departure for further exploration. Novelists talk about this effect in which the characters start writing the story. It's analogous to designing a building, in which you are truly listening to what the client wants, what the site "wants," what the constraints dictate from the budget, contractors, and city—all this is context. And once you start *playing* in that context, you have a much better idea of the real question or what the essence of the work should be. Mark reiterates that you don't necessarily know where this exploration will lead before you start. This is an example of one of the basic tenets and a recurring refrain of design thinking—comfort with ambiguity, which is progressively clarified and resolved.

Closure on an iterative process is ultimately a personal judgment. It's not as though you arrive at the right answer. Design thinking is not like a math problem or a scientific experiment when you know you it's complete. You could always add some other criteria, or refine or change the question a little bit, or try to do a little more. So how do you know whether you are finished? There really isn't an answer—it is a matter of judgment and experience.

You should always be looking for an "aha" moment or an intuitive leap. There's something that is gnawing at you, bugging you—completing a draft might just illuminate the issue. When you analyze it, you can immediately see that something is entirely backwards, i.e., let's put the conclusion at the beginning and try it that way. That's what you are looking for: *feedback from the work itself*.

Mark offers a piece of advice for beginning or inexperienced writers. Split your mind in two: for a while, just write while putting the editor part of your mind away. Many people are hesitant to put anything down because it's not perfect; but it has to go through the process a few times. Mark says,

> I have a few tricks to help silence my editor. If something comes up, I write a note in the margin and I know I'll get to it later. If I don't have the perfect word, I'll put it in brackets. If I know some thought must go there but I don't quite know what it is, I'll put stars there. The point is to just keep going.[11]

Once you have a draft, switch over to the editor mindset. Review the draft and all those marginal notes and tear them apart. Do they make logical sense? Do they make emotional sense? Can people follow the arguments? Is that the right word? Mark continues to reveal some of his personal process:

> A leap can occur after I've written all this, now that I know what the essential question is and what I should be writing about. A lot of the material then may just go to the side. I might completely re-outline.

Epiphany or intuition—"aha" moments—can occur with more experience because there may be pattern recognition, "you have prepared, and have confidence in the process that there will be a positive outcome, and you trust that the act of writing will get you there."[12]

Underscoring Mark's design thinking approach to writing, he emphasizes the theme that it is a circular iterative process, not a linear one. Mark often wants to do multiple drafts to compare, contrast, and find out what the issues really are.

After he feels somewhat comfortable with the draft, he then has a couple of people he trusts to review it—not just laugh at him when it's in a laughable form—they can look at it and be direct. He will redraft it and develop it further, and then unsympathetic readers can review it. If you don't have a sympathetic reader initially, Mark asserts, it could seriously undermine your confidence about the work.

Mark underscores the need to fully grasp both the content and context of any critique of the work, which includes who is doing the critiquing and their possible agendas. The specifics of the criticism may not be helpful or relevant, but it may point to broad issues to address. Pay attention to what critics are saying that may be problematic about the work, and try to determine the systemic issue. The problem may not be what they pointed to because they don't know as much as you do about the content (i.e., the earlier drafts with their deleted content, and future intentions). They are just pointing to a problem with the current version. So you need to take time to analyze and understand the specific nature of the criticism, and who the critic is. Is the critic representative of the target audience? Are they expert in a particular aspect of the topic?

There are many other ways to test the draft. Be sure to remember to keep the audience in mind from the beginning. What's the frame, what's the general purpose? And, near the end, what is the polish so people can read and understand what you wrote? Mark suggests evaluating it from the perspective of a child. Where would they get stuck, and is that okay? It shouldn't necessarily be changed but should prompt the question, "Am I being too pompous here?" or is there another problem?

Now, judgment comes into play: which one of those evaluations are you going to weigh, and how? That's where your inner voice ultimately rules. Know and interpret the context—the ground in which the work grows—to inform the direction of future drafts or iterations.

Take all criticism with a grain of salt: this is easier said than done. In litigation especially, hostility may be overt, and questions often move by data and focus on personal integrity, motives, and bias. Again, consider the source, and the evidence associated with the critique. One difficult moment is when someone with a very different agenda challenges your work. You must understand that they may have different goals, and then decide whether or not those are valid for the next iteration. Also, be cognizant that a draft is just a draft—it doesn't usually include everything else that's in your head, which is fine, because ultimately the thing has to live without you. The closer it comes to completion, the more it is just itself, and you can't be present to defend it on the basis of what you intended to do or what you thought about.

The ideation, brainstorming, or whimsy phase is also part of the writing process. Coming up with a whole bunch of ideas is very useful at the beginning when your internal editor (or client or others) says, "No, you can't." Whimsy is useful to jump-start another approach, and maybe take some approaches off the table.

One of the great attributes of design thinking is that multiple different tools can be used at multiple different iterations. For example, role-play people whose style you respect for their perspective on your work. You can pretend in your head that X is critiquing your work; what would they say about it? Model that person in your head. It won't be perfect because what you think they would say and what they would actually say are two different things; nevertheless, it's an exercise in developing a fresh voice, a set of goals, an approach, or an alternative way of evaluating. The tools you apply from design thinking are a function of the problem, your audience, the context, and who's paying for it.

Mark poses a question—and a reality check:

> How much are you doing the work for yourself versus how much are you doing work on behalf of others? There's always some degree of both, hopefully. If it's mostly about me, and my audience is me, then be aware that this is the potentially myopic stance that some artists take.

MANAGING GRIDLOCKED DEBATES

> In doing my job every day on behalf of Carmel, I have seen first-hand that design thinking can be transformative to gridlocked debates.[13]
>
> — Victoria Beach

Victoria Beach was a member of the Carmel City Council (California) where she served for four years, including a one-year stint as Vice Mayor. In the following story, she demonstrates how design thinking can be transformative in the management of gridlocked debates, and how it has helped her to resolve some wicked problems in the political arena.

An all-too-common reality in politics is an "us versus them" scenario in which stakeholders are entrenched in one position or another. One of Victoria's insights is that dealing with such a conflict should *not* be about persuading others to your point of view, which is frequently an exercise in futility. Rather, the strategy should be to apply design thinking to create or identify and then focus on a different path not previously imagined. In this way, *conflicts can become opportunities for progress*.

This approach requires a certain calm maturity, a realization that an initial position is not necessarily precious, and that there are multiple solutions to a problem. Nothing is so special or brilliant that it can't be built upon or changed for the good of a project or support of an issue. Unlike mathematics, where there is one right answer, in politics there may be a multiplicity of alternatives that can work. Design thinking can help to formulate an optimal one. So, table the argument for a moment and frame the problem in a different way.

Given the volatility of the current political climate, according to Victoria, "design thinking is not a luxury for society — it's a necessity."

Flanders Mansion: Creating an Option Not Previously Imagined

Carmel, California, is a small, picturesque village with a stunning beach and bluff shaded by cyprus trees. Behind the rows of quaint shops, there is a grid of small cottages, which are all sited within a forest of green. It is a visionary place, developed a hundred years ago as an artists' community and a home for academics.

Flanders Mansion, a vacant historic home within Carmel's largest park, had been at the heart of an impassioned controversy about its use for many years. It has been the focus of multiple lawsuits involving millions of dollars, environmental impact reviews, and even a referendum.

The issue: sell the mansion and make some money for the city (advocated by the City Council), or preserve it for public functions. But it's more complicated than that. Unfortunately, since the mansion is not located at the edge of the park, it can't be carved out as a discrete piece. If it were to be sold, a path to the building (complete with a fence to keep the public out) would be required for owners' access—but this would clearly disrupt the flow of the park. Many residents fought vigorously against this idea, dividing the peaceful little town; there was acrimony and vitriol, it was just awful.

Even though there was a referendum and a clear winner (approving the proposed sale), a strong minority was still protesting, "You just can't do that to the park." The City Council's position was if the courts require divestment because of the vote, no one on the Council was going to break the law.

An arduous state environmental impact review is required in California so that a municipality cannot carelessly divest itself of public parkland. In this case, wildlife migration routes were potentially at risk. If a sale were to take place, the new owners would be responsible for "scientific" compliance on an annual basis to protect native animals.

The referendum had *not* been based on projections about how much the city coffers would benefit from a sale. Realtors typically use a comparable to establish an asking price. There is no "comp" for a place like Flanders that accounted for its lizard and bat requirements, fencing and access issues, and the ongoing public dispute. Essentially, an owner would have to play the role of a park ranger or eco-biologist while living there, costing hundreds of dollars per year, not to mention the possibility of hostile residents protesting every time the owner used the driveway. In other words, this was not necessarily a slam-dunk for a multimillion-dollar sale.

At this point, Victoria examined the city's budget, which had a line item for care of parkland. The Flanders Mansion was a fraction below 1% of the total budget. So this was not some albatross around the neck of the city.

Also noteworthy is that this structure was placed on the historic register. This fact removed any option of demolition. Maintenance costs are not salient, since the unusual structure is made entirely of concrete. Not much has to be done to maintain it except for conducting periodic checks to ensure, for example, that the windows are not cracked and the bats are squeaking happily.

In summary, Faction A said, "You can't destroy or diminish the public park; there would be a major scar if a big piece were cut out of it. Selling it would interrupt the flow and enjoyment of the park." Faction B insisted, "We need money for our coffers; and we certainly can't have waste in the budget with the Mansion draining it every year. Who can argue with fiscal health?" This was intractable.

At a Council meeting, Victoria reviewed newly uncovered facts as a result of her research and consultations with experts, including maintenance people who had worked on the Mansion and prior park administrators. These facts, which had not been discussed before, included the relatively good health of the building, the lack of expense in maintaining it, and the comp issue and environmental requirements for a new owner in the event of a sale.

After ten minutes of presenting these facts, Victoria proposed a new solution: put the Flanders Mansion on the back-burner and think of it as a folly in the park. In other words, essentially *do nothing and stop talking about it* (simply talking about it costs the town a lot of money that could otherwise be spent more constructively). This option was never imagined because everyone was so entrenched in his or her own position.

In the political arena, people typically take sides on issues—similar to partisanship—that *must* be adhered to. But that's just a construct; sometimes the best solutions have no sides, no conflicts. Flanders Mansion is an example of applying design thinking to find a different, research-based solution to a problem that had pitted neighbors against neighbors for decades with millions of dollars wasted because no one was looking for a solution without conflict.

Victoria paraphrases one of her teachers in her analysis of this story.

> The mature design thinker is always ready to try something else, is not afraid of information, and is not afraid that he or she would not have another idea. Fear of not producing is common: the blank page; what am I going to say; maybe I can't solve this. If you are going in a direction that's not fruitful, or you don't know whether it's working and you have no way to

Figure 5.5 Empathic understanding is fundamental to design thinking. As the Flanders Mansion vignette illustrates, the focus of problem solving should not necessarily be about vigorous advocacy of a position, but rather the motives underlying the position in order to prompt a fresh solution.

test it, never be afraid to jettison it, critique it, or throw it to the side and try something else and then assess which option is best.[14]

When attempting to resolve a dispute, it is essential to be objective, to work at avoiding rigid investment in any one position. I realize this may be redundant, but it is an insight worth repeating. Victoria offers an example from architectural practice:

If you have two warring clients, a husband and wife, I always think we're going to find something that they both like if they talk to me in detail and explain the issues. If they help me research what's underlying the conflict, i.e., why don't you want to face south when you're doing the dishes and your spouse must face south, we will get to the placement of the sink that actually makes sense—if I can understand the thinking behind their motives. Analogous to the Mansion, the focus should not be what are we fighting about, rather, what are the underlying motives or structure underneath the positions? That will trigger some other way of thinking.

NOTES

1 Diego Ruzzarin, interview by the author, October 13, 2016.
2 Ibid.
3 Richard N. Swett and Colleen M. Thornton, *Leadership by Design* (Atlanta, GA: Greenway Communications, LLC, 2005), 248, 302.
4 Richard Swett, interview by the author, March 31, 2016.
5 Ibid.
6 Ibid.
7 Ben Schulman, "Biology by Design," *Architect* 106, no. 2 (2017): 61–62.
8 Brendan M. Reilly, Gordon Schiff, and Terrance Conway, "Primary Care for the Medically Underserved: Challenges and Opportunities," *Disease-A-Month* 44, no. 7 (1998): 320–46; Wendy Hobson, Roberto Avant-Mier, Susan Cochella, Nancy S. Kressin, Judith S. Long, Kathleen M. Mazor, Kevin E. O'Connor, Thomas E. M. H. N. Schacht, and Ronald A. Cohen, "Caring for the Underserved: Using Patient and Physician Focus Groups to Inform Curriculum Development," *Ambulatory Pediatrics* 5, no. 2 (2005): 90–95; and Robert Blankfield, Michele Goodwin, Carlos Jaen, and Kurt Stange, "Addressing the Unique Challenges of Inner-City Practice:

A Direct Observation Study of Inner-City, Rural, and Suburban Family Practices," *Journal of Urban Health* 79, no. 2 (2002): 173–85.

9 Jerome Groopman, "The Transformation: Is It Possible to Control Cancer without Killing It?" *The New Yorker*, September 15, 2014.

10 Ibid.

11 Mark Childs, interview by the author, April 7, 2016.

12 Ibid.

13 William Richards, "The Ethicist," *Architect*, February 2015, 37.

14 Victoria Beach, interview by the author, March 2, 2016.

INDEX

Note: Page numbers in *italic* indicate figures.